CompTIA® Advanced Security Practitioner (CASP) (Exam CAS-002)

D1522982

CompTIA® Advanced Security Practitioner (CASP) (Exam CAS-002)

Part Number: 093023
Course Edition: 1.1

Acknowledgements

PROJECT TEAM

Author	Media Designer	Content Editor
Jason Nufryk	Alex Tong	Michelle Farney

Notices

DISCLAIMER

TRADEMARK NOTICES

CompTIA® Advanced Security Practitioner (CASP) (Exam CAS-002)

About This Course

You have experience in the increasingly crucial field of information security, and now you're ready to take that experience to the next level. *CompTIA® Advanced Security Practitioner (CASP) (Exam CAS-002)* is the course you will need to take if your job responsibilities include securing complex enterprise environments. In this course, you will expand on your knowledge of information security to apply more advanced principles that will keep your organization safe from the many ways it can be threatened. Today's IT climate demands individuals with demonstrable skills, and the information and activities in this course can help you develop the skill set you need to confidently perform your duties as an advanced security professional.

This course can also benefit you if you intend to pass the CompTIA Advanced Security Practitioner (CAS-002) certification examination. What you learn and practice in this course can be a significant part of your preparation.

Course Description

Target Student

This course is designed for IT professionals who want to acquire the technical knowledge and skills needed to conceptualize, engineer, integrate, and implement secure solutions across complex enterprise environments. The target student should aspire to apply critical thinking and judgment across a broad spectrum of security disciplines to propose and implement sustainable security solutions that map to organizational strategies; translate business needs into security requirements; analyze risk impact; and respond to security incidents.

This course is also designed for students who are seeking the CompTIA Advanced Security Practitioner (CASP) certification and who want to prepare for Exam CAS-002. Students seeking CASP certification should have at least 10 years of experience in IT management, with at least 5 years of hands-on technical security experience.

Course Prerequisites

To be fit for this advanced course, you should have at least a foundational knowledge of information security. You can obtain this level of knowledge by taking the *CompTIA® Security+ (SY0-401)* course offered by Logical Operations. You may also demonstrate this level of knowledge by passing the Security+ (SY0-401) exam.

Although not required, we suggest that you either take the following Logical Operations courses or possess the equivalent knowledge in the areas of computer networking and computer maintenance:

- *CompTIA® Network+® (N10-005)* or *CompTIA® Network+® (N10-006)*
- *CompTIA® A+®: A Comprehensive Approach (Exams 220-801 and 220-802)*

Course Objectives

In this course, you will analyze and apply advanced security concepts, principles, and implementations that contribute to enterprise-level security.

You will:

- Manage risk in the enterprise.
- Integrate computing, communications, and business disciplines in the enterprise.
- Use research and analysis to secure the enterprise.
- Integrate advanced authentication and authorization techniques.
- Implement cryptographic techniques.
- Implement security controls for hosts.
- Implement security controls for storage.
- Analyze network security concepts, components, and architectures, and implement controls.
- Implement security controls for applications.
- Integrate hosts, storage, networks, and applications in a secure enterprise architecture.
- Conduct vulnerability assessments.
- Conduct incident and emergency responses.

The CHOICE Home Screen

Logon and access information for your CHOICE environment will be provided with your class experience. The CHOICE platform is your entry point to the CHOICE learning experience, of which this course manual is only one part.

On the CHOICE Home screen, you can access the CHOICE Course screens for your specific courses. Visit the CHOICE Course screen both during and after class to make use of the world of support and instructional resources that make up the CHOICE experience.

Each CHOICE Course screen will give you access to the following resources:

- **Classroom**: A link to your training provider's classroom environment.
- **eBook**: An interactive electronic version of the printed book for your course.
- **Files**: Any course files available to download.
- **Checklists**: Step-by-step procedures and general guidelines you can use as a reference during and after class.
- **LearnTOs**: Brief animated videos that enhance and extend the classroom learning experience.
- **Assessment**: A course assessment for your self-assessment of the course content.
- Social media resources that enable you to collaborate with others in the learning community using professional communications sites such as LinkedIn or microblogging tools such as Twitter.

Depending on the nature of your course and the components chosen by your learning provider, the CHOICE Course screen may also include access to elements such as:

- LogicalLABS, a virtual technical environment for your course.
- Various partner resources related to the courseware.
- Related certifications or credentials.
- A link to your training provider's website.
- Notices from the CHOICE administrator.
- Newsletters and other communications from your learning provider.
- Mentoring services.

Visit your CHOICE Home screen often to connect, communicate, and extend your learning experience!

How to Use This Book

As You Learn

This book is divided into lessons and topics, covering a subject or a set of related subjects. In most cases, lessons are arranged in order of increasing proficiency.

The results-oriented topics include relevant and supporting information you need to master the content. Each topic has various types of activities designed to enable you to solidify your understanding of the informational material presented in the course. Information is provided for reference and reflection to facilitate understanding and practice.

Data files for various activities as well as other supporting files for the course are available by download from the CHOICE Course screen. In addition to sample data for the course exercises, the course files may contain media components to enhance your learning and additional reference materials for use both during and after the course.

Checklists of procedures and guidelines can be used during class and as after-class references when you're back on the job and need to refresh your understanding.

At the back of the book, you will find a glossary of the definitions of the terms and concepts used throughout the course. You will also find an index to assist in locating information within the instructional components of the book.

As You Review

Any method of instruction is only as effective as the time and effort you, the student, are willing to invest in it. In addition, some of the information that you learn in class may not be important to you immediately, but it may become important later. For this reason, we encourage you to spend some time reviewing the content of the course after your time in the classroom.

As a Reference

The organization and layout of this book make it an easy-to-use resource for future reference. Taking advantage of the glossary, index, and table of contents, you can use this book as a first source of definitions, background information, and summaries.

Course Icons

Watch throughout the material for the following visual cues.

Icon	Description
	A **Note** provides additional information, guidance, or hints about a topic or task.
	A **Caution** note makes you aware of places where you need to be particularly careful with your actions, settings, or decisions so that you can be sure to get the desired results of an activity or task.
	LearnTO notes show you where an associated LearnTO is particularly relevant to the content. Access LearnTOs from your CHOICE Course screen.
	Checklists provide job aids you can use after class as a reference to perform skills back on the job. Access checklists from your CHOICE Course screen.
	Social notes remind you to check your CHOICE Course screen for opportunities to interact with the CHOICE community using social media.

1 | Managing Risk

Lesson Time: 2 hours

Lesson Objectives

In this lesson, you will:

- Identify the importance of risk management.

- Assess risk.

- Mitigate risk.

- Integrate documentation into risk management.

Lesson Introduction

As a security professional, you are familiar with the ways in which information is vulnerable to theft, destruction, alteration, and unavailability. But good security is not just a process of reacting to individual threats when they appear, or closing holes when they are discovered—it's a process of understanding how your information, by its very nature and the ways in which it is used, is at risk of being compromised. When you understand the risks you face from a foundational level, you can better prepare yourself to reduce or eliminate the chances of a security incident occurring and the impact it will have on your information.

TOPIC A

Identify the Importance of Risk Management

In our highly connected world, technology accelerates exponentially, granting newer and faster ways for human beings to work with information. With this rapid growth, it is inevitable that threats to our information advance just the same. The significance of security in modern information systems cannot be overstated.

The Importance of Risk Management in Information Security

To meet the ever-evolving needs of information security, a CompTIA® Advanced Security Practitioner (CASP) must be able to manage the risks that their information is exposed to. *Risk management* is typically defined as the cyclical process of identifying, assessing, analyzing, and responding to risks. This process is not meant to end; as long as information exists, it will need protecting. Therefore, risk management recurs indefinitely so that you may, at all times, keep your information as secure as possible. Without risk management, your security will be passive; and when you secure your information passively, it will be at the mercy of the quickly changing tides of technological advancement.

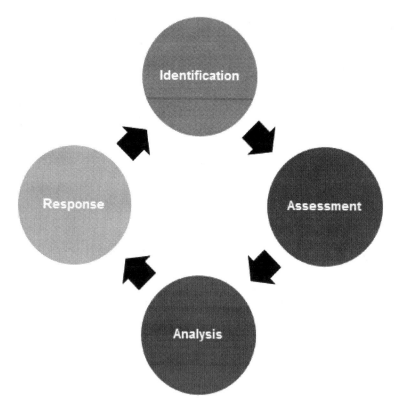

Figure 1–1: One way to represent the cycle of risk management.

Enterprise Risk Management

The comprehensive process of evaluating, measuring, and mitigating the many risks that pervade an organization is called *enterprise risk management (ERM)*. Information in today's computer landscape is found in interconnected systems across the world. These systems are typically run by enterprises of all functions and sizes, which store, transmit, and curate data in many different ways. Enterprises that run these systems typically do so on a 24/7 basis, leaving little room for error. The amount and complexity of resources that enterprises provide can be overwhelming, and certainly a challenge to those responsible for keeping everything safe and secure. This enterprise approach to resource availability and accessibility introduces numerous ways in which attackers can compromise the operations of a business, and just as many ways in which the enterprise's environment, employees, clients, and partners can unintentionally do likewise. In this reality, the ERM process becomes a vital part of any organization that strives to achieve its objectives.

Reasons to Implement ERM

The reasons that drive the adoption of ERM are numerous. The following are some examples:

* Keeping confidential customer information out of the hands of unauthorized parties.
* Keeping trade secrets out of the public sphere.
* Avoiding financial loss due to damaged resources.
* Avoiding legal trouble.
* Maintaining a positive public perception of the enterprise's brand/image.
* Ensuring the continuity of business operations to remain a contender in the marketplace.
* Establishing trust and liability in a business relationship.
* Meeting stakeholders' objectives.

Whatever the reasons may be, ERM is an increasingly important strategy in the business world, and an intricate part of any CASP's duties.

Risk Exposure

Risk exposure is the property that dictates how susceptible an organization is to loss. When quantified, risk exposure is usually defined as the product of the probability that an incident will occur and the expected impact or loss if it occurs.

An organization exposes itself to risk in every action it takes. These actions occur during the process of an organization conducting business, and it is the constant need for assessment of those risks that has given rise to the security industry as a whole. Without risk there would be no need for security, as there would be no consequences to poorly executed business processes. Since businesses are ever increasing their dependence on technology, an increasing amount of risks involve computer security professionals as the primary means to manage those risks.

Through ERM, an organization can keep its risk exposure low, but it can never really avoid it entirely. This is why it is so critical for security professionals to constantly be vigilant for the elements of risk—including threats, attacks, and vulnerabilities—that have the potential to cause harm to the enterprise's assets. Ignoring your organization's exposure to risk will limit its ability to survive in any industry.

Risk Analysis Methods

There are three main methods for analyzing risk to calculate for exposure.

Method	Description
Qualitative	*Qualitative analysis* methods use descriptions and words to measure the likelihood and impact of risk. For example, impact ratings can be severe, moderate, or low; and likelihood ratings can be likely, unlikely, or rare. Qualitative analysis is generally scenario-based. A weakness of qualitative risk analysis lies with its sometimes subjective and untestable methodology.

Method	Description
Quantitative	*Quantitative analysis* is based completely on numeric values. Data is analyzed using historic records, experiences, industry best practices and records, statistical theories, testing, and experiments. This methodology may be weak in situations where risk is not easily quantifiable.
Semi-quantitative	The *semi-quantitative analysis* method uses a description that is associated with a numeric value. It is neither fully qualitative nor quantitative. This methodology attempts to find a middle ground between the previous two risk analysis types.

 Note: To learn how to conduct a quantitative risk analysis, check out the LearnTO **Calculate Risk** presentation from the **LearnTO** tile on the CHOICE Course screen.

Risks Facing an Enterprise

As a CASP, you're likely to face risk in many different forms. Before you can even begin to mitigate risks, you need to know where they exist within your enterprise and identify how they can cause harm. The following table categorizes various types of risk that you may encounter in your enterprise.

Risk Type	Description
Legal	Every enterprise, no matter the industry, must comply with certain laws and regulations to stay within legal boundaries. Unethical business practices, unscrupulous employees, and negligent management can all place your enterprise in jeopardy. Even poor forensic practices can put your enterprise's ability to successfully prosecute attackers in court at risk.
Financial	Your organization likely has expected revenue and profit margins based on a number of calculations, and many different threats can cause your business to fail to meet monetary expectations. Financial risks may seriously affect your enterprise's survivability in a competitive marketplace.
Physical assets	Depending on your enterprise's size, you may have a great deal of valuable physical property stored in various company sites. Any physical product that your organization sells is your primary concern. Electronics like computers, industrial machinery, and office appliances are also at risk of being stolen or otherwise damaged. Both human threats and environmental factors may put your physical resources at risk.
Intellectual property	Organizations that create and own intellectual property, such as entertainment media, software, trade secrets, and product design, all risk these ideas and concepts being destroyed or used in unauthorized ways. Although intellectual property is typically not stolen in the same sense as physical theft, a threat may infringe on trademarks and copyrights that you have in place. A threat that destroys or alters your intellectual property may make it extremely difficult or even impossible to recover.
Infrastructure	An organization must depend on its structure to function at maximum efficiency. Whether physical or abstract, the frameworks that hold an organization together are vulnerable to a number of threats. This is particularly true of any infrastructure that supplies power or facilitates transportation. Infrastructure risk affects the business at its foundational level.

Risk Type	Description
Operations	Day-to-day operations are what keep your enterprise running and fulfilling not just its monetary expectations, but also its vision. Your organization is at risk of having its vision compromised if it cannot operate to the extent it needs to. Even if there are no immediate financial consequences, the enterprise risks losing its foothold in the marketplace, and its products or services may no longer be viable.
Reputation	The public's perception of an organization may greatly affect its success, and in some cases, may doom it to failure. Businesses often must maintain both great relationships with their customers and how society at large views them. Your organization's brand may be devalued if the public reacts negatively to scenarios such as theft of personal data, unethical business practices, and a decline in the quality of products and services.
Health	Whether it's your employees or the customers they work with, people are at risk of harm as a result of your operations. Although high-risk industries like law enforcement have obvious health concerns, even typical businesses can put their personnel and customers at risk by providing unsafe, untested products and services. Physical assets like industrial machinery and electrical equipment may pose significant health risks to employees who use them.

ACTIVITY 1–1
Identifying the Importance of Risk Management

Scenario

You are the new Chief Information Security Officer (CISO) at Develetech Industries, a manufacturer of home electronics located in the fictional city and state of Greene City, Richland (RL). You are now in charge of maintaining your company's security in the face of a wide variety of threats that target every dimension of your operations. Before you can dive into the diverse and complex world of cybersecurity, you need to develop your enterprise security strategies following the principle of risk management. When you can identify just how risk can negatively affect your enterprise, you'll be able to convince your employer, your team, and the rest of your employees of the importance of managing that risk.

---

1. Develetech, a relatively large electronics manufacturer, is looking to expand its business over the next couple of years. This may include everything from taking on new staff to establishing additional offices and warehouses. Why would these changes necessitate the development of an ERM strategy?

2. What are the specific types of risk that could affect Develetech as it expands its business?

3. You've identified a risk to the availability of your file servers at peak traffic hours. How would you prefer to calculate Develetech's risk exposure in this area? What are the strengths and weaknesses of the analysis you chose, and why do you think it's more beneficial than the others?

TOPIC B

Assess Risk

Now that you've identified the importance of risk management, you can begin the management process by assessing how risk will impact your organization. For an enterprise, there are many different elements of normal business operations that may affect its risk profile. Being able to identify how these elements are relevant to your enterprise's security will prevent you from missing crucial information when the time comes to mitigate risk.

Enterprise Security Architecture Frameworks

Enterprise security architecture (ESA) is a framework used to define the baseline, goals, and methods used to secure a business. When focused on risk, ESAs start with an assessment of the risk and quantify how internal and external threats and vulnerabilities manifest themselves to the organization; they then proceed to the mitigation of each specific threat, vulnerability, and risk. Beyond standard information security practices, ESAs are valuable for saving an organization time, money, and resources. This is possible because the cohesive design of an ESA framework is able to pull security practices together so that they work in complement with one another.

Once an organization successfully implements an ESA, they can generate a roadmap by evaluating which risks pose the most liability to the organization. Based on the liabilities, it may be possible to get further resources to mitigate those risks or it may demonstrate that the organization is adequately protecting itself from risk.

ESA Framework Assessment Process

Depending on how comprehensive the ESA framework is, there may be specific pre-defined steps the organization can follow to address the risk. The following is a list of assessment steps in an example ESA framework:

1. Develop a baseline assessment using internal resources and professional assessment software.
2. Conduct a thorough review of existing security policies.
3. Conduct an assessment of the physical and environmental elements of the enterprise.
4. Examine and assess the internal network for vulnerabilities.
5. Examine and assess external network connectivity and vulnerabilities.
6. Examine and assess wireless connectivity and security.
7. Examine and assess resource accessibility and policies that govern resource access.
8. Examine and assess all hosts, host configurations, and host documentation.
9. Examine and assess all infrastructure devices and connectivity.
10. Identify human factors such as resource use, resource access, and policies that surround use and access.
11. Examine and assess security awareness and training policies.

New Products and Technologies

Products, technologies, threats, and user behaviors are constantly changing within an organization, and with these changes come new risks. As new products and technologies are implemented, it is your job as a CASP to assess the risk to your organization and guide the implementation appropriately.

The following table gives the risk management strategies that are appropriate for each example of new risk.

Risk Example	Risk Management Strategy
New products	As new products are used by an organization, new vulnerabilities and threats are introduced—this increases risk. Depending on the prevalence of these products and the data they are associated with, the risks may be small or large. When evaluating new products, it is important to include the ERM process as well as consult with HR and legal counsel for any regulatory or employment law requirements regarding how the products are used. At the beginning of the risk management process, you should evaluate products first for vulnerabilities and then for threats which may target those vulnerabilities. After that, you can quantify the risks and liabilities those threats present to your organization.

From one product to another, the risks are often fairly static. For example, while two different web platforms may not have identical security features, they suffer from the same potential sorts of risks: SQL injection, cross-site scripting, cross-site request forgery, and so on. If new products interoperate with legacy products, this may put either or both at risk, as their security protocols may be incompatible. |
| New technologies | Similar to new products, new technologies must be evaluated for vulnerabilities and threats, but one technology might have markedly different risks from another. For example, mobile computing platforms like tablets and smartphones suffer from similar risks to traditional desktops, such as buffer overflows, yet have new risks, such as the ease of loss due to their small size and mobility. When implementing new technology, your organization should include HR and legal counsel to determine if any regulatory requirements exist.

In the ERM process, you may also draft certain policies that govern how new technology is deployed and used. For example, your policy might stipulate that all new technology be tested in a sandbox environment before being implemented live on the enterprise network. Like new products, new technologies that interoperate with older technologies may cause security issues. |
| New threats | Attackers are constantly inventing new attacks, and how organizations conduct business is always changing. This cycle of recurring change introduces new threats into an organization, and thus new risks. Even beyond human maliciousness, other factors may unintentionally threaten the security of an organization in the midst of a change.

For example, if an organization set up a new office in a coastal city, the prevalence of hurricanes may be a new threat the organization will need to analyze and develop a recovery plan for. Under a malicious threat, if a new weakness is found in an encryption protocol such as Secure Sockets Layer/Transport Layer Security (SSL/TLS), the organization will need to determine how to patch its systems or mitigate the threat in another way. You should always expect risk management to be a recurring process rather than a single static exercise performed periodically. |

Risk Example	Risk Management Strategy
User behaviors	Users often present the largest risk to an organization. Users have access to data, are usually not as technically savvy as systems administrators or security personnel, and are frequently targeted by attackers through the use of social engineering methods. In any well-rounded risk management program, security professionals must analyze the ways in which the organization does business both internally and externally with partners, outsourcers, and clients. By analyzing the business processes used, it is possible to find weaknesses which could be exploited by attackers.
	For example, if an organization relied on email as a means to submit work requests through a trouble ticket system, it may be possible for attackers to use Simple Mail Transfer Protocol (SMTP) spoofing to submit fraudulent work requests such as system modifications or actions that will expose sensitive data. The ability of attackers to manipulate a company's human element is one of the best ways to gain access to an organization that has invested heavily in technical controls, but not enough in employee training and awareness.

New and Changing Business Models

As the world adopts new technology, it effects new forms of doing business. The best example of this is comparing the pre-Internet era with the current one. Prior to the Internet, companies did most functions themselves. Things like payroll, administrative duties, product development, and communications were all integrated and managed by each organization. Today's interconnected world, however, offers rich opportunities for companies to partner with other organizations, outsource their operations, rely on cloud providers for support, and merge and demerge assets with other business entities. All of these business models and strategies have an impact on computer security and management of risk in the enterprise.

Partnership Model

A business partnership offers the partnering companies shared opportunities that either company might not have in its own. Partnership agreements are used to define the roles, responsibilities, and actions that each partner will take to make the partnership successful. Risk management is an important part of evaluating these agreements. Without this step, each of the partners may be exposing themselves to risks which could put both companies in jeopardy losing information or revenue, or by increasing liability past an acceptable limit. Similar to mergers and acquisitions, your security team should be brought in prior to the partnership being finalized.

The partnership agreement should define how the organizations will still secure their private data, to which sets of data each organization will have access to, and how that information should flow. Each organization, outside of the agreement, should conduct its own risk assessment of the processes proposed and what mitigating controls they should implement.

Example

An example of risk within a partnership is when two organizations decide to approach a common goal, such as when an operating system manufacturer works with hardware vendors. Think of the complexities of Google working alongside a smartphone manufacturer like Samsung when creating Android phones. Both organizations have agreed to partner to create a device with a blend of each other's software and hardware. The organizations must be linked together in some way to facilitate operations, yet each organization has other competing businesses that they must secure and keep separate.

Outsourcing Model

Outsourcing as a business practice can allow the organization to focus on core competencies while shifting high-cost, low-value, and non-core business processes to a service provider that can more efficiently run these processes. Risk management is a key component of outsourcing. Although the contracted organization is liable in part for the security risks of its operations, it is critical that organizations that decide to outsource evaluate and constantly audit the provider's actions. Audits should be performed to evaluate the provider's data handling, fulfillment of service-level agreement (SLA) criteria, and business conduct on behalf of the organization, Failing to perform recurring audits may lead to severe penalties against the parent organization. This is especially true when sensitive data is involved in the outsourcing arrangement or where legal regulations or compliance requirements are present.

A common pitfall in outsourcing arrangements is the depth to which an audit is conducted. In most cases, the outsourcing provider is contractually obligated to provide its yearly reports to clients, but those audits may not necessarily apply to all systems within the scope of the outsource provider's network. It is critical to understand the scope of all audit documents provided to your organization from any provider and evaluate nuances in the report such as the use of (or lack thereof) the phrases "all systems" or "in scope systems." It is also important that you never assume that security reports given by the system provider necessarily encompass everything that they should. The provider might conduct a technical penetration test that comes back clean, but this is no guarantee that a social engineering attack wouldn't compromise their systems.

Cloud Model

Cloud distribution models are an increasingly common business strategy for organizations looking to offload technical components like data backups, server hosting, and virtualization platforms to an easily accessible Internet-based resource.

Like typical outsourcing, cloud-based solutions require an enterprise to rely on a third party to host and maintain these components. However, the cloud model differs in that it offers automation of components and processes to more easily facilitate the enterprise's needs. An outsourcing provider might simply take on a system already in place to lighten the burden on the enterprise, but a cloud provider might give the enterprise an entirely new set of options and services that could greatly affect the enterprise's operations.

The cloud might provide an entirely new software suite, or even an entirely new platform, and the enterprise must incorporate these unfamiliar elements into its ERM processes. For example, the cloud service may provide always-online email functionality that raises security issues for sensitive correspondence. The auditing that the enterprise typically accepts from outsourcing providers may need to be reworked and targeted specifically for the cloud provider. Automating provides cloud resources provides a challenge to security administrators, as these resources may become more and more opaque to the client enterprise.

Mergers

Mergers occur when two organizations decide it is more profitable to operate under one banner rather than separately in a partnership. A merger provides an excellent time to conduct risk management activities since it gives both organizations a heightened sense of analysis and business management oversight to their operations. The two companies as a combined entity must consider influencers such as corporate culture, brands, business units, market opportunities, information consolidation, and numerous other components that drive ERM.

Mergers can also be dangerous as one organization may have more strict security controls than the other. When merging, differing technology platforms will need to be integrated, controls will need to be aligned between the two organizations, security reporting structures will need to be streamlined, sensitive data governance will need to be reviewed, and more; all of which can have significant impact to both organizations if done poorly. It is best to conduct risk assessments before a merger so that each organization is aware of the other organization's risk portfolio.

Example

As an example, a hosting company acquires a consulting company in another country. While the hosting company has many years of experience securing a network critical to its business, the consulting company has never had to secure its systems to the same degree. Most of its recurring security budget is spent on endpoint defense for the laptops being used in the field by its consulting personnel, and not on using advanced network intrusion detection systems, Internet gateway protection, host intrusion detection, or monitoring software. Once the merger is completed, the security team is brought in to integrate the systems. However, unbeknownst to both organizations, the consulting company's email systems had been breached many years prior to the merger. As a result, both organizations are now exposed to additional liability that could have been avoided had proper security activities taken place prior to the merger.

Demergers and Divestitures

When an organization splits its business into several entities, it may be restructuring to strengthen its brand awareness, or it may be responding to government intervention through anti-trust regulations. Whatever the reason, demergers and divestitures require the careful application of ERM, just as much as mergers do.

Like mergers, enterprise components like company culture, brands, and market opportunities all have their place in a demerger. When the company splits, each entity may take their own components with them—and in many cases, each entity may wish to still share some of the same ones. A proper risk assessment will take into account that any assets—especially those of a sensitive nature—must be reconsidered in light of this restructuring. If both entities retain access to the same sensitive data, but have diverging security policies, then this may introduce risk to one or both of the new entities.

Integration of Diverse Industries

Sometimes enterprises that operate in different industries will find it beneficial to integrate. There are various security concerns of integrating diverse industries which you can incorporate in your risk assessment.

Integration Element	Security Concern
Rules and policies	Crafting effective security rules and policies is all about fine-tuning them to your own specific needs as a business. A business that operates in a different industry will likewise customize their policies to fit their own needs. Therefore, integrating with a business that has policies that fail to meet your requirements, or outright contradict your rules, may pose a risk. Therefore, it's important to assess where these rules and policies are divergent.
Regulations	Different industries are susceptible to different government regulations. If your business integrates with another that fails to follow these regulations, yours could also be held liable if this impropriety is discovered. In other situations, simply integrating with enterprises in certain industries could require you to adopt these same regulations.

Integration Element	Security Concern
Geography	Certain industries may be more or less inclined to operate in specific geographic locations. For example, the transportation industry has a heavy presence in urban areas, and less so in rural locations. Your business may be unaccustomed to the increased security risks associated with congested, dense populations, so if you plan on integrating with a transportation business, you need to reassess your risk profile. Other geographic factors to take note of include: geopolitics, physical ease of access, strength of infrastructure (electricity, network cabling, etc.), climate, and natural disasters.

Third-Party Providers

When you assess risk in your own organization, you generally take into account the various ways in which a third party's lapse in judgment might impact your systems. But not every facet of the third party's operations might be open to you, and for good reason. They need to keep certain elements confidential, just as your organization does. So how do you assess risk in an environment you cannot completely and unrestrictedly survey?

One such approach is to assure that third parties have strong security training and awareness protocols in place within their organization. You, as a CASP, may have spent a good amount of time drafting a comprehensive policy for best security practices for employees, but your third party provider may not have a comparable policy for any number of reasons. So, you should share best practices with third parties so that they may better inform their employees. After all, the human element is often the biggest risk in any organization.

Likewise, depending on your arrangements with the third party, you may even extend or provision security controls to them to strengthen their systems. A risk assessment might uncover an area of the third party's operations that poses an unacceptable amount of risk to your enterprise, but providing them with proper equipment and protocols could help mitigate the risk.

Internal and External Influences

Many different types of events influence risk. Some of these influences are internal and some are external to the organization. You should assess how each influence aids or detracts from the risk management process.

Influence Type	Risk Assessment Relevance
Internal compliance	Internally, all the employees of an organization are stakeholders that are concerned with the safety and security of the organization. When senior management signs off on an ERM plan, everyone should be expected to assist with its implementation; that is, be in compliance with the plan. This is not always easy to do, as a great deal of training may be required and numerous policies and procedures may be put in place to ensure full compliance. When done properly, internal compliance assessments can identify controls which are not operating as intended and are not reducing the risk to acceptable levels. Since internal users bring a high degree of risk to an organization's network and systems, including them in your assessment of risk will produce more accurate results. After all, they are the ones who access and use those systems on a daily basis and can help identify areas where additional risk treatment is necessary.

Influence Type	Risk Assessment Relevance
External compliance	All businesses must comply with external regulatory entities. It is important that your organization follows all applicable laws, regulations, and standards. The federal government will, for example, enforce the Health Insurance Portability and Accountability Act (HIPAA) in organizations that work in the healthcare industry. Even standards that are not necessarily legally binding, like those enforced by the International Organization for Standardization (ISO), are ubiquitous in the enterprise landscape. While the goal of compliance regulations is to provide a minimum acceptable baseline for managing risks in a particular industry or organization, most regulations do not place requirements on the effectiveness of a control, but instead on whether or not the control is present. Without measuring a control and applying a baseline to the regulation, it is impossible to determine if the controls are effectively deployed within the enterprise. This is why simply being compliant will not necessarily produce an optimum risk assessment. Your organization may be compliant, but still may not as secure as it should be under the intent of the regulation or standard.
Internal client requirements	Internal clients are often stakeholders in ERM planning and implementation because they are direct users of corporate resources. Internal clients should be involved in risk assessment, as they are at the forefront of recognizing risks that impact the enterprise. If they are not, it will be impossible to secure their environments, which in turn will lead to client dissatisfaction and reduced customer business.
External client requirements	The involvement of external clients depends on their needs. External clients have a vested interest in the ongoing activities of the organization with which they conduct business. In that regard, they are another front-line resource for identifying the threats and vulnerabilities of the business. At the same time, external clients who are part of ERM planning for their trading partners might demand that the ERM plan include business continuity protocols so that their source of supply can continue in the event of a loss. They might also insist on measures that protect the confidentiality that they share with their trading partners. Because of this vested interest, external clients can provide insight on the ways to assess risk in an organization that has business relationships.
Audit findings	Audit findings influence risk by providing evidence that controls are adequate in reducing or eliminating risk. Where an auditor's results are below acceptable thresholds, the organization should assess the residual risk and determine if mitigation, transfer, or acceptance is the correct approach. In some cases, it is impossible to reduce risk further; for example, where the use of legacy systems is required as part of an established business function. In cases such as this, it may be necessary to change the business process or outsource the function entirely to avoid the risk. Likewise, it may be necessary to rethink your technology infrastructure.

Influence Type	Risk Assessment Relevance
Top-level management	Top-level management is one of the key stakeholders in the risk assessment process. Without proper risk assessment, they will be unable to make informed decisions about how to operate the business. When presenting both internal and external risk to executive management, quantitative analysis and accurate metrics are two of the key components that you must communicate effectively. When this is done, it will be easier for you to get buy-in from executive management for risk mitigation plans and the appropriate funding of security initiatives.
Competitors	An enterprise's competition is often what drives the business forward, and competitors will likewise be a factor in the ERM process. The risk a competing company poses to the success of your enterprise may influence certain operations and behaviors as a response to that competition. This can include developing new products, incorporating new technology, and expanding customer markets. All of these activities bring their own risk to the enterprise. If they're done primarily as a reaction to competition, then your risk assessment will need to account for both the actions taken and the reasons for those actions, so that your organization can decide whether the risk is truly worth having.

De-perimeterization

De-perimeterization is the process of shifting, reducing, or removing some of the enterprise's boundaries to facilitate interactions with the world outside of its domain. In information security, this implies that a de-perimeterized business will shift its focus from creating a secure perimeter to incorporating security in other ways. For example, you might place more emphasis on encrypting your sensitive data rather than attempting to regulate access to your network from the outside (for example, the Internet).

The impact of de-perimeterization on risk depends on the ways the perimeter changes. The following table lists some of those ways, and the risk considerations of each one.

Perimeter-Changing Concept	Risk Consideration
Telecommuting	Telecommuting employees may use a virtual private network (VPN) to tunnel into your network and access what they need, or they may simply use equipment and services that you provide to them. These remote employees expand your network or business's boundaries, and may bring increased risk with them. Any external connection could compromise your network as a whole if it is not properly secured on both ends. This includes VPN services and remote authentication technology. Additionally, employees may use their own computers and solutions for their jobs, but these will not necessarily be as tightly controlled as the devices and solutions that are in your reach.
Cloud	Cloud services can reduce strain on your business by offloading it to an Internet-based provider with distributed resources. However, this also reduces the amount of control you have over your environments that are hosted elsewhere. Reputable cloud providers will offer at least some security guarantee, but this may not be sufficient, depending on your risk appetite. Additionally, the cloud provider's security measures will be useless unless properly integrated with the security in your own enterprise.

Perimeter–Changing Concept	Risk Consideration
BYOD	*Bring your own device (BYOD)* is an emerging phenomenon in which employees use their personal mobile devices in the workplace. If your business tolerates this, you will need to recognize that work done while in the office may leave the office after close of business. This pushes your boundaries farther than you can totally manage. You may be able to enforce secure handling of sensitive data while an employee is in the office, but once they are outside, that data will be at risk. This is because many users do not make the effort to secure their own personal devices, or in some cases, their devices may be inherently insecure.
Outsourcing	Like relying on a cloud service, outsourcing business operations to another enterprise will shift your security domain to an environment that you may not necessarily have control over. The company you outsource to may have its own set of security policies and procedures, or it may not have any at all. If you are unable to enforce your expected level of security, the assets you outsource could place the rest of the enterprise in jeopardy, especially if those assets hold information or infrastructure vital to the enterprise's survival.

Risk Determinations

A significant part of risk assessment is determining just how certain risks can specifically impact the enterprise. Two influential factors in risk determination are the likelihood of threats and the magnitude of impact.

You can determine the likelihood of a threat bringing risk to your organization by using the following methods:

- Discovering the threat's motivation. What does an attacker stand to gain from conducting an attack?
- Discovering the source of the threat. Who is the threat? Is it an individual or a group? Where are they from, and what is their experience?
- Determine the threat's *annual rate of occurrence (ARO)*. How often does the threat successfully affect the enterprise?
- Conducting a trend analysis to identify emerging threats and threat vectors. How effective are these threat vectors and how have they been exploited before?

You can express a risk's magnitude of impact in two ways:

- A *single loss expectancy (SLE)* value represents the financial loss that is expected from a specific adverse event.
- An *annual loss expectancy (ALE)* value is calculated by multiplying an SLE by its ARO to determine the financial magnitude of a risk on an annual basis.

 Note: The ALE may be a moving target, as threats cannot necessarily be quantified as occurring annually, but rather on an individual basis.

 Note: Two additional risk determination factors, return on investment (ROI) and total cost of ownership (TCO), are described in a later lesson.

Guidelines for Assessing Risk

 Note: All Guidelines for this lesson are available as checklists from the **Checklist** tile on the CHOICE Course screen.

Use the following guidelines when assessing risk in the enterprise:

- Implement an ESA to more easily define your security expectations.
- Evaluate new products and technologies in light of their new functionality and architecture, as well as how they interoperate with older systems.
- Stay up-to-date on the latest threats.
- Assess user behaviors as a point of weakness, especially due to social engineering threats.
- Draft security agreements for partnerships that include data handling requirements.
- Conduct thorough audits of outsourced assets.
- Conduct thorough audits of cloud providers that host your assets.
- Assess risk before a merger occurs to look for any differences in security policy, procedures, or controls.
- Consider lost or continually shared assets in the event of a demerger or divestiture.
- Consider the rules and policies, regulations, and geographic issues associated with integrating with businesses in different industries.
- Consider how internal and external compliance, internal and external client requirements, and audit findings influence risk.
- Consider how practices like telecommunication and BYOD may impact your organization's network perimeter.
- Determine what a threat is, where it comes from, and what risk it poses to the enterprise.
- Calculate the SLE and ARO of a threat, then use the product of these two values to ascertain your ALE.

ACTIVITY 1-2
Assessing Risk

Scenario

Now that you're aware of the importance of risk management, you'll want to begin by assessing risk at Develetech to get a better picture of just how the business currently fares. You'll also gain an understanding of how the evolving nature of technology will affect Develetech in the future, and what sort of unique challenges this poses to your ERM strategy. Assessing risk on an organizational level will enable you to later address and mitigate those risks. Without an assessment, your knowledge of Develetech's security situation will be limited, as will your responses.

1. One of the possibilities involved in expanding Develetech is the adoption of new technology. Your CEO may decide to drop legacy products, or even drop certain vendors altogether and replace them. What are the important things to remember about assessing new products and technologies, along with threats that inevitably come with them?

2. Besides its in-house technology, Develetech may decide to change its core business strategy. Recently, the other officers at the company have been discussing the viability of moving to a cloud provider for most of the company's web hosting infrastructure. How would a move to the cloud impact your risk assessment?

3. You've identified compliance to be one of the biggest concerns for the expansion. How will both internal and external compliance factors influence your risk assessment?

TOPIC C

Mitigate Risk

After assessing how particular elements in your operations can bring risk to the enterprise, you're ready to actively respond to those risks. Mitigation is all about balancing your response capabilities with your tolerance for risk, and there are several different approaches that may work best for you. As a CASP, you'll choose the most appropriate mitigation strategy to keep your enterprise as safe from harm as is feasible.

Classes of Information

Some information is more or less critical than other types. In general, there are four classes of information that organizations use:

- **Public** information, which contains no risk to an organization if it was disclosed, but does present a risk if it is modified or not available.
- **Private** information, which contains some risk to an organization if competitors were to possess it, if it were modified, or was not available.
- **Restricted** information, which might be limited to a very small subset of the organization, primarily at the executive level, where unauthorized access to it might cause a serious disruption to the business.
- **Confidential** information, which would have significant impact to the business and its clients if it were disclosed. Client information like user names and passwords, personally identifiable information (PII), protected health information (PHI), and cardholder data (CHD) would be in this category.

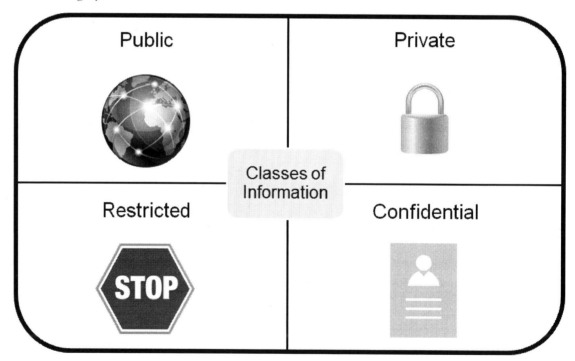

Figure 1-2: Classes of information.

Classification of Information Types into CIA Levels

Information can not only be classed by access levels, but it can also be thought of in terms of how a compromise of that information can threaten the three core security attributes of the *CIA triad (Confidentiality, Integrity, and Availability)*. When surveying information within an organization, it is important not to solely judge the type of information, but how that information is used throughout the business. Public information, if disrupted, wouldn't necessarily cause problems from a confidentiality perspective. However, availability may drop significantly, compromising a very crucial part of any enterprise's security focus. Ultimately, you should investigate how each information type in your organization fits into the larger three goals of security so that you may be better prepared to respond to risk.

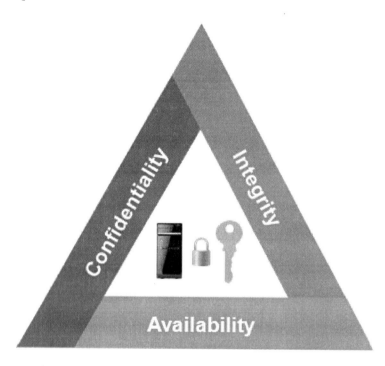

Figure 1-3: The CIA triad.

Example

Imagine a large outsourcing company which runs payroll applications for its clients. This outsourcing provider would have massive quantities of confidential information, including names, addresses, bank account and routing numbers, Social Security numbers, and tax return data. It may also have self-administered health plan data that would be classified under HIPAA as PHI, bringing a regulatory and compliance element to their operations as well. Now contrast that organization against a small company, where such data would be relative to the size of the company and there would be little to no required uptime to support it.

By comparing these two companies, you can see how organizational perspective and scope can increase or decrease the risks associated with different types of data. While penalties and liability associated with a confidentiality and integrity breach of the payroll records would impact either organization, the outsourcing provider has significantly more at stake. Not only would brand damage result from their exposure or loss, but they would lose immediate income through the refund component of their SLA. The smaller organization may be subjected to penalties for exposing the data or have some downstream impacts if the integrity were changed; however, there is very little liability at stake relative to the payroll provider.

Stakeholder Input for CIA Decisions

When making security-related decisions based around CIA, it's important to incorporate stakeholder input as part of the process. Together, stakeholders may offer a more complete perspective on dimensions of the business you may be unaware of. Even small, seemingly unimportant dimensions may cause damage if they escape your notice. Because they may have more experience in certain areas, stakeholders will also be able to communicate their unique security concerns to you for your consideration. Whether it's employees, customers, or investors, stakeholders will keep you fully informed about the many ways in which the principles of CIA affect your enterprise.

Technical Controls Based on CIA Requirements

Once a specific risk has been quantified, it is possible to determine the best approach to mitigating the specific risk. Risks can be mitigated based on the specific CIA attribute targeted, and the technology used to reduce the risk does not always cover all three attributes. Consider the following table, in which examples of technical controls are described in terms of how they do or do not uphold the CIA principles.

Technical Control	Upholds Confidentiality?	Upholds Integrity?	Upholds Availability?
User permissions for network share	Yes, by keeping unauthorized users from accessing shared data.	No	No
Load balancers for web servers	No	No	Yes, by routing traffic to hosts that are available and have capacity.
Message authentication codes (MACs) used in digital signatures	No	Yes, by comparing the expected message digest with the actual message digest upon output.	No

As you can see, no single technology in this list of examples addresses all three attributes. An organization has well-rounded security when it specifically upholds all three components of the CIA triad.

Application of Controls That Address CIA Requirements

There are several approaches you can use to address risks to confidentiality; for example, encryption and access control. In both cases, the goal is to limit the readability of data to only authorized parties. What you implement will depend on your needs as an organization; access control may be enough to keep unwanted users from accessing somewhat sensitive data, but in scenarios where data is much more sensitive, you may want to aim for encryption to achieve the strongest confidentiality assurances.

Controls to address risks to integrity primarily rely upon data validation and auditing. This includes the use of read-only data stores and strong authentication controls in applications using multiple factors. Auditing controls function by monitoring the integrity of the data as it exists in the system and as data is passed through input and output routines. Auditing is a useful policy for essentially all organizations, though it isn't as active in maintaining integrity as forms of validation like hashing are.

Most commonly, organizations implement redundancy measures to mitigate hardware failures, which have a serious impact on availability. By using failover techniques such as active-passive and active-active, it is possible to seamlessly failover to backup hardware. However, not all threats are caused by hardware failure. In some situations, the consumption of resources is responsible for the system becoming unavailable. An example of this would be a denial of service (DoS) attack which leverages a flaw in the software to consume resources past the intended limits of the system or architecture. Once started, a DoS attack can be very difficult to recover from. There are various flood control mechanisms that may prevent successful DoS attacks, such as load balancers.

 Note: For more information about DoS controls, visit **www.cisco.com/web/about/ security/intelligence/guide_ddos_defense.html**.

Aggregate CIA Score

Once information critical to the business has been classified by the risk associated with its CIA attributes, and stakeholder input and technical controls are considered in the context of the triad, it is possible to develop risk scores for the data. This is done subjectively and is based on a sliding scale of harm to the business, where:

*   The highest risks are rated at a **10**.
*   The lowest risks are rated at a **1**.
*   Data having no risk (for example, public data) is rated at a **0**.

The CIA attributes of information are compared to the threat that each attribute faces, then multiplied to produce a total. The totals for each attribute are added to produce the aggregate CIA score for that entire risk. Consider the following risk matrix. In this example,the threat of a DoS attack is being calculated on a network in terms of CIA. Although the analysis is subjective, you can still reliably and consistently quantify risk based on a sliding scale. This quantification is based on several factors, including how easy the attack is to perform, any controls that may already be in place to mitigate the attack, and the scope the attack is likely to cover.

CIA Attribute	Value of Information	Threat Value	Total Risk
Confidentiality	7	0	0
Integrity	3	0	0
Availability	8	10	80

The aggregate CIA score for a DoS condition is **80**. Using this score, you can compare it against other risks. Since enterprises have limited budgets and staff resources, not all risks may be able to be mitigated, so it is important to prioritize some responses over others. Compare the aforementioned DoS example with the database intrusion example in the following matrix.

CIA Attribute	Value of Information	Threat Value	Total Risk
Confidentiality	7	10	70
Integrity	3	5	15
Availability	8	5	40

The aggregate CIA score for the database intrusion condition is **125**. This is greater than the DoS attack, so you prioritize database intrusion over the DoS in the ERM process. In prioritizing, you are able to determine the minimum required security controls for each risk. This scenario dictates that you implement stricter requirements for intrusion protection than DoS attacks.

 Note: To learn more about how to calculate aggregate CIA scores for risks to the enterprise, check out the LearnTO **Calculate Aggregate CIA Scores** presentation from the **LearnTO** tile on the CHOICE Course screen.

Common Vulnerability Scoring System

Most vulnerabilities today are rated using the *Common Vulnerability Scoring System (CVSS)*. The CVSS is a risk management approach to quantifying vulnerability data and then taking into account the degree of risk to different types of systems or information. Since it is an open source formula for risk quantification, the CVSS is easily modified to fit a specific organization's needs. The CVSS is similar to the examples used previously, but is much more granular. The system consists of the three core metric groups and their associated sub-metrics: base metrics that qualify fundamental components of a vulnerability; temporal metrics that qualify components of a vulnerability that change over time; and environmental metrics that qualify components of a vulnerability that depend on specific contexts and implementations.

Base Metrics	Temporal Metrics	Environmental Metrics
Access vector	Exploitability	Collateral damage potential
Access complexity	Remediation level	Target distribution
Authentication	Report confidence	Confidentiality requirements
Confidentiality impact		Integrity requirements
Integrity impact		Availability requirements
Availability impact		

The strength of the CVSS is that it produces consistent results for the vulnerability's threat in the base and temporal metric groups, while allowing organizations to match those results with their specific computing environment.

Extreme Scenario Planning and Worst Case Scenarios

Planning for the worst is a necessity in any ERP strategy. Although extreme events are unlikely, they are often devastating enough to warrant some sort of plan of action. Some examples of extreme events include:

*   The total denial-of-service of your network and other systems.
*   The theft of encryption keys.
*   The theft, tampering, or destruction of trade secrets that keep your business competitive.
*   The theft, tampering, or destruction of financial data.
*   The theft, tampering, or destruction of national secrets.

To mitigate the risk of these worst case scenarios, consider the following strategies:

*   Gather intelligence to identify threats that can instigate extreme scenarios.
*   Identify the motivations of these threats.
*   Identify the skill level required to carry out these threats and the probability that the perpetrators will be able to successfully carry out an attack.
*   Identify what vectors these threats can take to instigate extreme scenarios.
*   Determine what assets in your organization are the most critical and susceptible to extreme scenarios.
*   Determine controls that will help prevent or mitigate an extreme scenario.
*   Identify what exactly you risk by failing to prevent an extreme event.

System-Specific Risk Analysis

To understand the risks to an enterprise, a security professional must be able to analyze the systems used within the enterprise, how those systems are used, and the threats to the enterprise's confidentiality, integrity, and availability. A number of different frameworks and processes have been established to assist this analysis. Although how you go about your analysis will differ with respect to what you're analyzing, the following are some common questions to ask when trying to quantify a risk:

- How is the attack performed?
- Can the attack be performed in the current network and are the assets accessible?
- Does the requirement for authentication diminish the possibility of attack?
- What is the impact to the confidentiality, integrity, and availability of the data?
- How exploitable is the flaw? Is it theoretical, or does a working exploit exist?
- Are there workarounds or patches available?
- How confident is the report of the vulnerability? Is it an established and tested approach?
- What is the damage to the organization?
- How many targets exist within the organization?
- What are the confidentiality, integrity, and availability requirements for the assets in question?
- How likely is the risk to manifest itself?
- What mitigating protections are already in place? How long will it take to put additional controls in place? Are those additional protections cost effective?

Examples

If, for example, your enterprise is a cloud provider with multiple sites worldwide, your analysis should focus on the chances of an attack succeeding, what an attack can compromise in terms of the data you host and its availability to your customers, and how exactly an attack can be performed. In this scenario, patches and software fixes may be irrelevant to stopping an attack, so you won't necessarily focus on that in your analysis. Likewise, you may be less concerned with the cost-effectiveness of any controls, since you have a considerable security budget.

If your organization is small and has primarily local customers, you'll want to approach your analysis differently. Cost-effectiveness becomes a significant factor in security controls, as your budget will likely be limited. Also, you may want to focus more on the damage an attack will do to your own systems, since you're unlikely to have the amount of redundancy that a large enterprise will. The point is, before you even begin your risk analysis, you should tailor it to your own situation to maximize its efficacy and dispense with irrelevant factors.

Risk Response Techniques

How an organization reduces or removes risk is based on the thresholds established for different risks and is entirely dependent on the risk appetite of the organization. The following table describes the four possible approaches to risk response.

Risk Response Technique	Description
Avoid	*Risk avoidance* means that risk has been completely eliminated (reduced to zero). This is generally achieved by terminating the process, activity, or application that is causing the risk. For example, if you do not need a chat program to facilitate collaboration among employees, you might simply block access to it from within your systems, thus eliminating the risk it brings. Total risk avoidance is virtually impossible in any enterprise, as it would necessitate that you remove many vital systems that your business requires to function.

Risk Response Technique	Description
Transfer	*Risk transference* moves the responsibility for managing risk to another organization, such as an insurance company or a outsourcing provider. This external organization takes over and maintains the risks associated with data and other resources. Examples include purchasing natural disaster insurance to cover servers and the data present on them, and relying on cloud providers to store and secure data. You should choose the transference approach if the risks become larger and more complicated that your enterprise can manage without impeding your operations.
Mitigate	*Risk mitigation* is the process of implementing controls and countermeasures to reduce the likelihood and impact of risk to an organization. Organizations will mitigate risk so that the potential harmful outcomes do not exceed the organization's risk appetite. For example, if you have a high-traffic network, you may reduce the risk the traffic poses to the network by implementing an intrusion prevention system (IPS).
Accept	*Risk acceptance* is a response in which an organization identifies and analyzes a risk, then determines that the risk is within the organization's appetite and no additional action is needed. The ERM plan that an organization develops and implements will outline its risk appetite, so any risks that are accepted are within the parameters of what the enterprise deems unworthy of further response. As previously stated, not all risks can be avoided; likewise, not all risks can be transferred or mitigated. In your organization, you must decide what level of risk is unlikely or harmless enough not to warrant extra effort and cost.

Risk Management Processes

There are several additional risk management processes that you can put into place to mitigate risk in your enterprise.

Process	Description
Exemptions	Some legacy systems may be exempt from risk management processes because they do not have certain functionalities that other, newer systems do. Replacing these systems with newer ones may raise your risk profile from both a financial and security perspective, so you must be mindful of what systems have exemptions and how those exemptions may no longer apply in the event of change.
Deterrence	It may be impractical or impossible to completely mitigate some risks. Deterrence is the process of influencing a threat's decision to exploit or not exploit these particular risks. You may convince a threat that carrying out a particular attack is not worth the cost, effort, or legal consequences. For example, a log in screen may warn unauthorized users that they face jail time if they log in under someone else's authorized credentials. If successful, this will keep vulnerable assets protected.
Identifying inherent risk	Inherent risk is the risk that an event will pose if no controls are put in place to mitigate it. Identifying an enterprise asset or activity's inherent risk will aid you in assessing which controls to put in place to mitigate the risk.

Process	Description
Identifying residual risk	Residual risk is the risk that remains even after controls are put into place. Identifying an enterprise asset or activity's residual risk will aid you in assessing the effectiveness of the controls you put in place to mitigate the risk.

Continuous Monitoring and Improvement

Risk is always changing within an enterprise due to new products, new technology, and new user behaviors. To address the constant flux of risk, organizations must continually evaluate their networks to ensure controls that they have implemented are operating as intended. A good example of this is the use of patch and vulnerability management software. Since new vulnerabilities are found regularly, and new patches are released for those vulnerabilities, organizations should expect to have a recurring process to update equipment. However, it is very time consuming to quantify the recurring change in an organization with a regular risk assessment approach.

In light of this reality, many organizations have adopted a process of *continuous monitoring and improvement* to detect changes in an environment and then quickly and efficiently address them. When risk is mitigated in this fashion, the business will be able to improve its operational processes and cut down on costly risk assessments. There are software tools that provide this functionality by alerting security staff of unanticipated resource access, invalid or expired software licenses, and mobile devices that attach from anywhere and at any time.

IT Governance

Information technology governance (IT governance) is a concept in which stakeholders ensure that those who govern IT resources in an enterprise are performing their duties in a way that fulfils the enterprise's strategies and objectives and creates value for the business. Other than evaluating IT management's performance, IT governance seeks to mitigate the risks that are associated with information technology resources.

As a CASP, you may not be directly in charge of guaranteeing good governance practices in your organization; however, an important element of good governance is proper risk management. The stakeholders that oversee IT governance will expect there to be a risk management framework in place that can both keep risk low and mitigate any growing risks. These principles will directly align with business objectives that mandate keeping the enterprise safe from threats and on good legal ground. To assuage the concerns of stakeholders, you should be prepared to communicate how your IT department measures, responds to, and mitigates risks.

IT Governance Frameworks

There are several existing frameworks of IT governance that businesses may adopt for easier integration. These frameworks can differ in terms of industry relevance, scope, and specific use cases. For example, the *Control Objectives for Information and Related Technology (COBIT)* framework is particularly popular for those enterprises that place a premium on risk management and mitigation.

Guidelines for Mitigating Risk

Use the following guidelines when mitigating risk in the enterprise:

- Categorize information into classes like public, private, restricted, and confidential.
- Classify information in terms of how it will impact your enterprise CIA.
- Incorporate stakeholder input for CIA-based decisions.
- Understand technical controls in terms of how they do or do not fulfill CIA.
- Create aggregate CIA scores to determine what threats to prioritize.

- Plan for worst case scenarios by gathering intelligence on threats and how they could impact your enterprise.
- Ask risk-related questions in the context of individual systems.
- Avoid, transfer, mitigate, or accept risk based on factors like cost, viability, resources, and necessity.
- Identify exemptions and inherent and residual risk in the enterprise.
- Use deterrence techniques where mitigation fails.
- Implement continuous monitoring to quickly detect changes to an environment.
- Communicate to relevant stakeholders how you measure, respond to, and mitigate risks.

ACTIVITY 1-3
Mitigating Risk

Scenario

Your team at Develetech has been busy assessing the various risks that could affect the company. Now it's time for you to analyze these results and respond appropriately. Choosing the right risk mitigation strategies is essential in meeting stakeholder expectations and keeping your systems secure at the same time.

1. Which classification denotes information that only certain personnel in an enterprise are authorized to access?

   ○ Private

   ○ Confidential

   ○ Restricted

   ○ Public

2. Develetech is interested in implementing routine backups of all customer databases. This will help uphold availability because you will be able to quickly and easily restore the backed up copy, and it will also help uphold integrity in case someone tampers with the database. What controls can you implement to round out your risk mitigation strategy and uphold the components of the CIA triad?

3. In choosing which risks to prioritize in your mitigation efforts, you use an aggregate CIA score to make a determination. How will you calculate this score, and how will you determine which risk to prioritize?

4. During their risk assessment, your team has identified a security flaw in an application your organization developed. To conduct a proper analysis of how this could bring risk to your enterprise, what are some of the questions you need to ask?

5. You've analyzed the application flaw and discovered that it could allow an unauthorized user to access the customer database that the app integrates with if the app uses poor input validation. If an attacker were to access the database this way, they could glean confidential customer information, making the impact to your business relatively high. However, you determine that your app's current input validation techniques account for all known exploits of this kind. How will you respond to this risk?

TOPIC D

Integrate Documentation into Risk Management

A less direct, but still important, part of risk management is developing documentation for future reference. Writing a policy and recording risk-related activity will move your ERM strategy from the conceptual to the concrete. This will provide the foundation on which to support your assessment and mitigation practices.

Policy Development

Policy development starts once an organization determines they need a formal information security policy. The driver for an information security policy varies by organization; it could be for compliance reasons, the increasing size of the organization necessitating a written security policy to replace informal guidelines, to meet contractual obligations, or in response to a breach. Regardless of the reasons for its development, ultimately the policy must be approved by the executive management, and in some cases, the board of directors, should the organization be large enough.

Once the organization has identified a need, there are several ways to begin crafting a policy. One of the easiest methods is to download one of the free policy templates available from security organizations such as the SANS Institute, then customize the policy to fit the organization. It is also common for organizations to bring in a security consulting company to aid them in policy development. Regardless of how you approach your company's policy, it is important to also compare and contrast the company's policy with those of other organizations; there may be topics or risks you did not previously consider which impact the elements of the policy.

Not all policies are created equal. It is best to use clear and concise language within the policy that is easy to understand. In other words, attempt to limit the legalese which pervades many policies. At the same time, it is important to understand that the information security policy of an organization is a legal document which you may provide to employees, customers, and in some cases, a court of law.

In conjunction with any legal or compliance regulations the organization may be under, it is important to include business leaders in the development of the policy. If a policy is too strict, it may impair workers' ability to conduct business, which in turn impairs the organization. A well-developed policy should address all the risks the business may face; it is a living document that should be updated regularly as the business, technology, environments, and risks in an enterprise change.

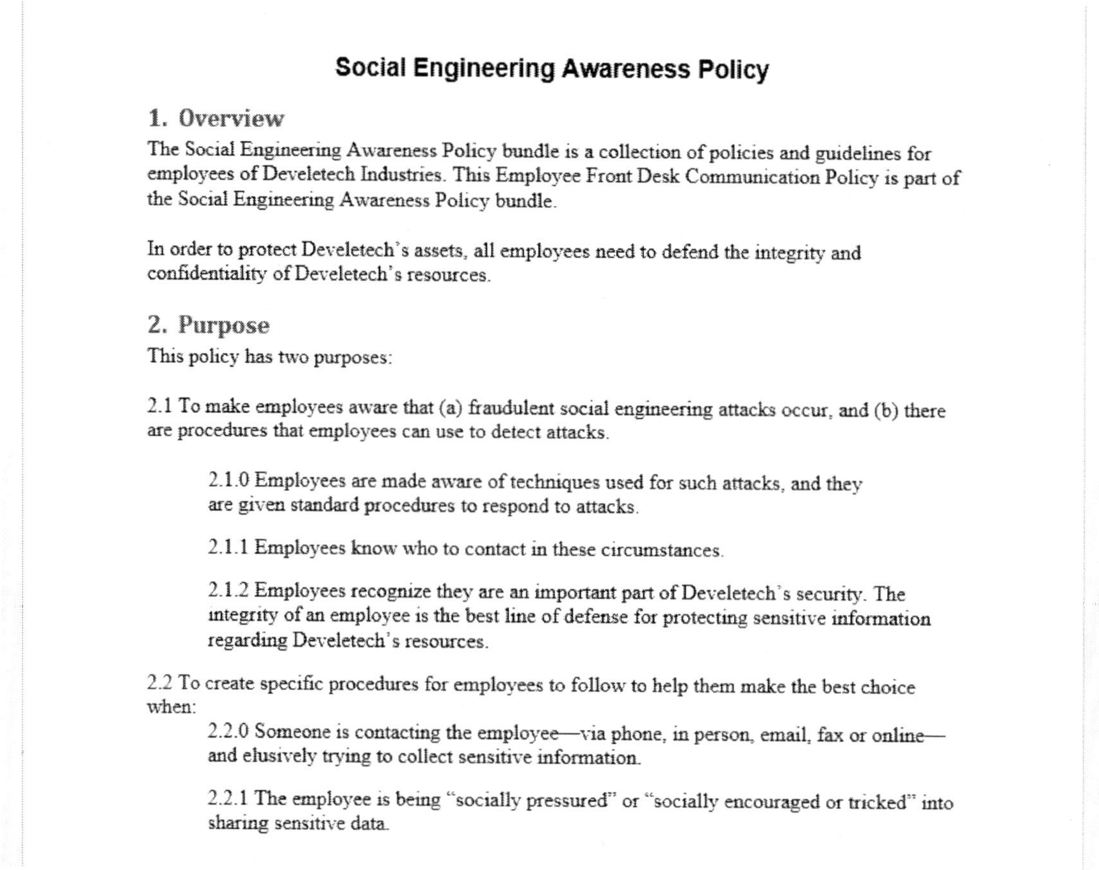

Social Engineering Awareness Policy

1. Overview

The Social Engineering Awareness Policy bundle is a collection of policies and guidelines for employees of Develetech Industries. This Employee Front Desk Communication Policy is part of the Social Engineering Awareness Policy bundle.

In order to protect Develetech's assets, all employees need to defend the integrity and confidentiality of Develetech's resources.

2. Purpose

This policy has two purposes:

2.1 To make employees aware that (a) fraudulent social engineering attacks occur, and (b) there are procedures that employees can use to detect attacks.

2.1.0 Employees are made aware of techniques used for such attacks, and they are given standard procedures to respond to attacks.

2.1.1 Employees know who to contact in these circumstances.

2.1.2 Employees recognize they are an important part of Develetech's security. The integrity of an employee is the best line of defense for protecting sensitive information regarding Develetech's resources.

2.2 To create specific procedures for employees to follow to help them make the best choice when:

2.2.0 Someone is contacting the employee—via phone, in person, email, fax or online— and elusively trying to collect sensitive information.

2.2.1 The employee is being "socially pressured" or "socially encouraged or tricked" into sharing sensitive data.

Figure 1-4: A security policy.

Process and Procedure Development

To support the policies your organization has developed, it is also important to create processes and procedures documents which very clearly explain how the organization implements different security functions. These are the how-to documents used by systems administrators and employees of the company that include the steps to implement and enforce the policies. They must be specific enough that any user who is expected to follow them can, regardless of their technical knowledge. If a predetermined level of technical prowess is required, then that should be explicitly stated. For example, a data handling procedure designed to be used by system administrators may make the assumption that the administrators are familiar with the platform they are supporting; however, a similar procedure designed for marketing and sales employees who have less technical familiarity may need more in-depth and explicit steps. In other words, you must understand your target audience and tailor the processes and procedures appropriately.

Process and procedure development is done in much the same way as policy development. Many standards organizations such as the National Institute of Standards and Technology (NIST) or the Center for Internet Security (CIS) have predefined procedures or standards documents that you can use as a starting point, then tailor them to fit your organization. Certain organizations will have specific types of standards they need to write to. Alternatively, you can bring in consultants to help define procedures or streamline business processes to make them compliant with particular policies. Irrespective of the approach, it is always a good idea to compare and contrast policies with other organizations to see how they are implementing the "how-to" of information security.

Just like the policies on which they are based, processes and procedures are living documents. If a policy changes in light of new business, technological, or environmental changes, then so too should processes and procedures. A policy that updates the enterprise's security posture in the face of new threats and risks is useless unless it is translated into practice through procedural documentation.

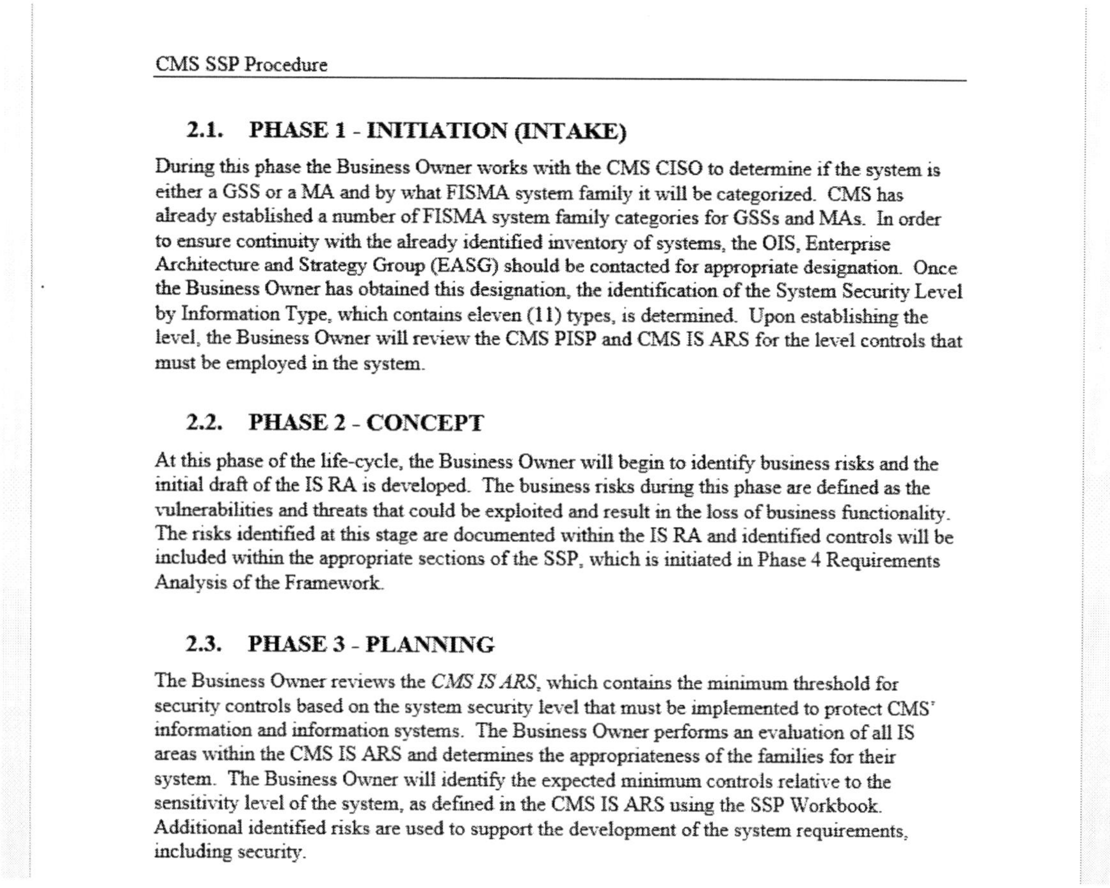

CMS SSP Procedure

2.1. PHASE 1 - INITIATION (INTAKE)

During this phase the Business Owner works with the CMS CISO to determine if the system is either a GSS or a MA and by what FISMA system family it will be categorized. CMS has already established a number of FISMA system family categories for GSSs and MAs. In order to ensure continuity with the already identified inventory of systems, the OIS, Enterprise Architecture and Strategy Group (EASG) should be contacted for appropriate designation. Once the Business Owner has obtained this designation, the identification of the System Security Level by Information Type, which contains eleven (11) types, is determined. Upon establishing the level, the Business Owner will review the CMS PISP and CMS IS ARS for the level controls that must be employed in the system.

2.2. PHASE 2 - CONCEPT

At this phase of the life-cycle, the Business Owner will begin to identify business risks and the initial draft of the IS RA is developed. The business risks during this phase are defined as the vulnerabilities and threats that could be exploited and result in the loss of business functionality. The risks identified at this stage are documented within the IS RA and identified controls will be included within the appropriate sections of the SSP, which is initiated in Phase 4 Requirements Analysis of the Framework.

2.3. PHASE 3 - PLANNING

The Business Owner reviews the *CMS IS ARS*, which contains the minimum threshold for security controls based on the system security level that must be implemented to protect CMS' information and information systems. The Business Owner performs an evaluation of all IS areas within the CMS IS ARS and determines the appropriateness of the families for their system. The Business Owner will identify the expected minimum controls relative to the sensitivity level of the system, as defined in the CMS IS ARS using the SSP Workbook. Additional identified risks are used to support the development of the system requirements, including security.

Figure 1–5: A process document.

Best Practices to Incorporate in Security Policies and Procedures

All information security policies and procedures contain topics specific to an organization and its requirements; however, there are several best practices that you should follow or at least be conscious of when you draft your documentation. Security documents that incorporate these ideas will help to reduce your overall risk. Therefore, you should support the development of policies and procedures that contain the best practices listed in the following table.

Best Practice	Description
Separation of duties	States that no one person should have too much power or responsibility. Duties and responsibilities should be divided among individuals to prevent ethical conflicts or abuse of powers. Duties such as authorization and approval, and design and development should not be held by the same individual, because it would be far too easy for that individual to defraud or otherwise harm an organization. For example, it would be easier for an employee to make sure that the organization only uses specific software that contains vulnerabilities if they are the only ones with that responsibility. In many typical IT departments, the roles like backup operator, restore operator, and auditor are assigned to different people.

Best Practice	Description
Job rotation	States that no one person stays in a vital job role for too long. Rotating individuals into and out of roles, such as the firewall administrator or access control specialist, helps an organization ensure that it is not tied too firmly to any one individual because vital institutional knowledge is spread among trusted employees. Job rotation also helps reduce the risk of individuals abusing their power and privileges, as well as preventing collusion between employees.
Mandatory vacation	A method of preventing fraud which provides you with an opportunity to review employees' activities. The typical mandatory vacation policy requires that employees take at least one vacation a year in a full-week increment so that they are away from work for at least five days in a row. During that time, your corporate audit and security teams have time to investigate and discover any discrepancies in employee activity. When employees understand the security focus of the mandatory vacation policy, the risk of fraudulent activities decreases.
Least privilege	Dictates that users and software should only have the minimal level of access that is necessary for them to perform the duties required of them. This level of minimal access includes facilities, computing hardware, software, and information. When a user or system is given access, that access should still be only at the level required to perform the necessary task. If you give a user or system access that exceeds what they require, then that is one more vector that can be used to compromise your organization.
Incident response	Defines monitoring, response, and reporting requirements for incidents that involve security breaches or suspected breaches. Generally, this set of policies requires a response to all incidents and suspected incidents within a defined time period and according to a reporting hierarchy that might depend on the severity of the incident. Security awareness and training play a role in incident response so that the personnel whose primary roles fall outside of information security know who and where to call for various levels of incidents, with a service desk or help desk being the first line in the reporting hierarchy. Without timely reporting to the right people, it will be much more difficult to mitigate the risk of a security breach causing harm to your enterprise.
Forensic tasks	Investigate from where a breach emanated, how a breach might have occurred, and who might be responsible for the breach. The forensic policy should include who is to be notified when forensics are required, under which conditions they are required, and how to contact individuals responsible for those duties. It is important to include legal counsel when formulating the forensics policy so that appropriate legal guidelines can be included as necessary.
Employment and termination procedures	Defines on-boarding and off-boarding procedures when employment both begins and concludes, respectively. Proper on-boarding involves acclimating new employees to the security practices that you expect them to follow. This ensures that there will be an expectation of liability in the arrangement. Likewise, when the employee leaves the organization, you should establish an off-boarding process. The terminated employee must agree to relinquish any access to company systems, data, and physical equipment. In some cases, terminating an employee may put your company secrets at risk of being leaked; to prepare for this, your policy should specify when you should enforce non-disclosure agreements (NDAs).

Best Practice	Description
Continuous monitoring	Outlines what mechanisms and tools are used to continuously monitor systems for changes that could increase risk to the enterprise. This practice also defines exactly what events and environments should be monitored based on a prior risk analysis. Some policies will include provisions for continuous improvement so that the enterprise can take a proactive role in addressing detected risks.
Training and awareness for users	Without comprehensive education, user-based attacks, such as social engineering, will be a major source of risk for an organization. In addition to teaching users about the inherent risks of using technology, it is important to also educate them on the policies and procedures required for them to operate safely within the organization's systems. Training should also take into account the types of access and roles that employees have. For example, you wouldn't train a salesperson on the risks of SQL injection attacks, but you would educate your website developers on this topic. Specific training mechanisms can range from subtle reminders through on-screen messaging at login, through paper-based pamphlets on employee desks or common areas, to training for specific elements of enterprise operations (devices, software, building security, etc.).
Auditing requirements and frequency	Defines the types of audits performed, who performs those audits, how frequently they are performed, and clearly delineates authority for remediating audit issues found in the process. Auditing policies typically include provisions for event triggers that are based on enterprise risk assessments. The audit policy should also define the auditing requirements for business partners and subcontractors, which should be included in all contracts with third parties who could have an impact on the overall security of the organization.

Legal Compliance and Advocacy

There are many different stakeholders in an organization—employees, customers, regulatory agencies, legal counsel, and management. As you develop your security policy, you should consider the expertise of the various stakeholders, as each will offer different skills and perspectives in the creation of a strong policy that supports legal compliance and advocacy.

- Human resources can help guide the policy development in accordance with established labor laws and privacy requirements.
- Consulting legal counsel during policy development will ensure the policy does not violate any laws and is in accordance with any regulatory requirements the organization may fall under.
- You may also consult regulatory agencies to help ensure that the policy meets any regulatory or compliance requirements needed.
- For your policy to be successful, you must include management's input and approval. Their involvement will also allow the policy to fit within the goals of the business.
- You may consult employees to help identify areas of the policy that may not fit into current business processes and identify where projects are needed to alter current business practices.
- Industry organizations, such as SANS, NIST, ISO, and other standards bodies, can help provide example policies or recommended best practices.

General Privacy Principles

Privacy is the expectation that non-public data is protected from threats to confidentiality and integrity. When an organization fails to protect data, it reflects poorly on the organization and can have a lasting impact on its image. This is referred to as *brand damage*. It is important to keep in mind that different places in the world define what needs to be kept private differently and organizations may have different definitions of how data is classified. When regulations are involved, there is not any flexibility in how data is defined; however, when no regulations apply then there is some latitude for organizations to leverage.

When drafting policies, you must be aware of what privacy expectations your clients have in working with the organization. *Personally identifiable information (PII)*, including full names, addresses, phone numbers, age, sex, and race, may or may not be considered sensitive information based on the context in which they are handled. Consider a website like LinkedIn that exists primarily as a social network for the business world. Full names and places of work are expected to be on pretty much everyone's profile, so a security breach that exposed those pieces of PII would not violate privacy policies, nor would it bring risk to the company. On the other hand, a dating website might discourage its users from associating their profiles with their real names and the companies they work for. If the site doesn't discourage this, then a breach that exposes this PII would put the site's reputation at risk and its users would worry about their privacy.

Regardless of how you define this information, you still have a responsibility to your customers, employees, and business partners to communicate how you plan to use their PII. Whether internal or public-facing, your privacy policy should be upfront, and you should even consider offering guidelines to your target audience on how they can help to ensure their own privacy.

 Note: The abbreviation PII is widely accepted in the United States, but the phrase it abbreviates has four common variants based on word forms for personal (or personally) and identifiable (identifying). These variants are not identical from a legal standpoint. Each term's definition can change depending on the jurisdiction and the reason the term is being used.

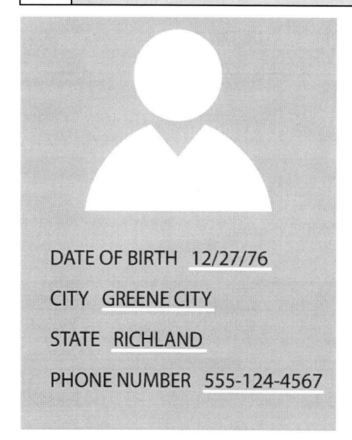

DATE OF BIRTH 12/27/76

CITY GREENE CITY

STATE RICHLAND

PHONE NUMBER 555-124-4567

Figure 1–6: PII.

Privacy Requirements

Every organization will have a specific privacy policy based on common business and legal requirements. The following table lists various privacy-related standards or laws that may be applicable to your enterprise.

Standard or Law	Description
SOX	The Sarbanes-Oxley Act (SOX) of 2002 dictates requirements for the storage and retention of documents relating to an organization's financial and business operations, including the type of documents to be stored and their retention periods. It is relevant for any publicly traded company with a market value of at least $75 million.
GLBA	The Gramm-Leach-Bliley Act (GLBA) of 1999 was primarily passed as a deregulation of banks, but also instituted requirements that help protect the privacy of an individual's financial information that is held by financial institutions and others, such as tax preparation companies. The privacy standards and rules created as part of GLBA safeguard private information and set penalties in the event of a violation. GLBA also requires a coherent risk management and information security process.
FISMA	The Federal Information Security Management Act (FISMA) of 2002 was passed to address the evolutionary nature of information systems security in the federal government. Some of the act's key provisions require federal organizations to: • Define the boundaries of the systems to be protected and then identify the types of information found within those systems. • Document system information and perform a risk assessment to identify areas requiring additional protection. • Protect systems using an identified set of controls and certify systems before use. An approval for operation is issued upon certification. • Continuously monitor systems for proper operation.
COSO	The Committee of Sponsoring Organizations of the Treadway Commission (COSO) provides guidance on a variety of governance-related topics including fraud, controls, finance, and ethics. COSO's ERM-integrated framework defines risk and related common terminology, lists key components of risk management strategies, and provides direction and criteria for enhancing risk management practices.
HIPAA	The Health Insurance Portability and Accountability Act (HIPAA) was enacted in 1996 to establish several rules and regulations regarding healthcare in the United States. With the rise of electronic medical records, HIPAA standards have been implemented to protect the privacy of patient medical information through restricted access to medical records and regulations for sharing medical records. Visit **www.hhs.gov** for more information on HIPAA regulations.

Business Continuity Planning

Business continuity planning (BCP) is the process of defining how an organization will maintain normal day-to-day business operations in the event of a business disruption or crisis. A viable business continuity plan should involve the identification of critical at-risk systems and components to ensure that such assets are protected. The BCP also ensures the survival of the organization itself by preserving key documents, establishing decision-making authority, communicating with internal and external stakeholders, and maintaining financial functions. The BCP should address infrastructure issues such as maintaining utilities service, utilizing high-availability or fault-tolerant systems that can withstand failure, and creating and maintaining data backups. The enterprise should review the BCP and test it on a regular basis. The plan must have executive support to be considered authoritative; the authorizing executive should personally sign the plan.

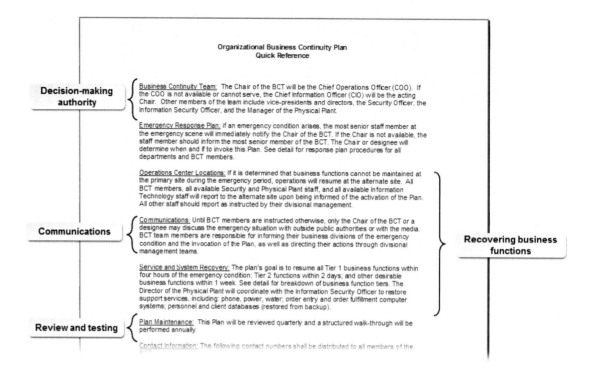

Figure 1-7: A BCP.

In enterprise risk management, the BCP will be your go-to documentation for keeping your organization financially and operationally afloat if risk becomes a reality. Beyond identifying key risks to critical systems and functions, BCPs often incorporate some form of risk mitigation strategies to prevent further damage to the organization. When an incident does occur, and you're able to mitigate the damage, you can update your BCP to reflect your success in addressing the problem. This will keep you better prepared for the next incident, and minimize the amount of disruption that will affect your business.

Business Documents that Support Security Initiatives

There are several common types of business documents a security professional should expect to encounter in their normal duties. Many of these focus on business partnerships and alliances; since all organizations do business with other entities, there are many types of common agreements used to govern those relationships. Some of these agreements specifically deal with security and risk management, whereas others may incorporate them secondarily or not at all.

Document	Description
Statement of applicability (SOA)	This document identifies the controls in place in an organization and explains their purpose. As SOAs identify why a particular control is being used, they are often directly influenced by the conclusions reached in a risk assessment. The SOA should reference the policies and procedures that will take advantage of the identified controls. It may be beneficial to not only explain why a certain control was included, but to also explain why certain controls were excluded.

Document	Description
Business impact analysis (BIA)	This document identifies present organizational risks and determines the impact to ongoing, business-critical operations and processes if such risks actually occur. BIAs contain vulnerability assessments and evaluations to determine risks and their impact. BIAs should include all phases of the business to ensure a strong business continuation strategy.
Interoperability agreement (IA)	This is the general term for any document that outlines a business partnership or collaboration in which all entities exchange some resources while working together.
Interconnection security agreement (ISA)	This type of agreement is geared toward the information systems of partnered entities to ensure that the use of inter-organizational technology meets a certain security standard of confidentiality, integrity, and availability. Because they focus heavily on security, ISAs are often written to be legally binding. ISAs can also support MOUs to increase their security viability. NIST provides a security guide for developing an interconnection plan, titled *Security Guide for Interconnecting Information Technology Systems Special Publication 800-47*.
Memorandum of understanding (MOU)	This type of agreement is usually not legally binding and typically does not involve the exchange of money. MOUs are less formal than traditional contracts, but still have a certain degree of significance to all parties involved. They are typically enacted as a way to express a desire for all parties to achieve the same goal in the agreed-upon manner. An MOU document might contain background information on each organization; the history of the relationship between the two organizations and circumstances that led to the partnership; and a general or specific timeline for collaborative business activities. Because they typically have no legal foundation, MOUs are not the most secure agreement for a partnership.
Service-level agreement (SLA)	This agreement clearly defines what services are to be provided to the client, and what support, if any, will be provided. Services may include everything from hardware and software to human resources. A strong SLA will outline basic service expectations for liability purposes. The document may include timeframes within which failures will be repaired or serviced; guarantees of uptime; or, in the case of a network provider, guarantees of data upload and download rates.
Operating-level agreement (OLA)	This agreement identifies and defines the working relationships between groups or divisions of an organization as they share responsibilities toward fulfilling one or more SLAs with their internal or external customers.
Non-disclosure agreement (NDA)	This is an agreement between entities stipulating that they will not share confidential information, knowledge, or materials with unauthorized third parties. NDAs also commonly state in which cases, if any, data may be used or processed by the receiving entity. For data acquired through public sources, an NDA is not enforceable.

Document	Description
Business partnership agreement (BPA)	This agreement defines how a partnership between business entities will be conducted, and what exactly is expected of each entity in terms of services, finances, and security. For security purposes, BPAs should describe exactly what the partners are willing to share with each other, and how any inter-organizational access will be handled.

Guidelines for Integrating Documentation into Risk Management

Use the following guidelines when integrating documentation into your ERM strategies:

- Download free policy templates to make crafting a policy easier.
- Consider hiring a consultant if your organization can't support internal development of policies.
- Use direct, concise language and dispense with legal jargon in policies.
- Include business leaders in policy development and make sure executive management approves of the policy before it is enforced.
- Support policies with clearly defined processes and procedures.
- Make processes and procedures easy to follow and tailor them toward your audience's technical aptitude.
- Compare and contrast policies, processes, and procedures with those of other organizations.
- Consider policies, processes, and procedures to be living documents, that is, subject to change as businesses and technology evolve.
- Incorporate best practices like job rotation, mandatory vacations, user training, and more, into your policies based on your specific enterprise requirements.
- Involve HR, legal counsel, management, and other entities in the policy development process to get unique perspectives.
- Ensure that policies have provisions for legal and regulatory compliance.
- Identify what PII that your organization handles is sensitive.
- Be upfront with your clients as to how their PII will be used and for what purpose.
- Advise your clients on best practices to maintain privacy.
- Draft a BCP to maintain day-to-day operations in the event of an incident.
- Define in the BCP what components are at risk and how they should be preserved.
- Review your BCP and test it on a regular basis.
- Identify the various business documents and agreements that are applicable to your enterprise needs.
- Use an agreement like an SLA in any partnership that requires strong security and legal and financial liability.

ACTIVITY 1-4
Integrating Documentation into Risk Management

Data File

C:\093023Data\Managing Risk\social_engineering_awareness_policy.docx

Before You Begin

You have a Windows Server® 2012 R2 computer to complete some of the activities in this course. The computer name is **Server##**, where **##** is your unique student number. The server is a domain controller for domain##.internal.

 Note: Microsoft® Windows® is the platform used to practice most of the security concepts presented in this course. There are also Windows-specific procedures included throughout the course to help you perform the guided activities. Be aware that there may be other methods for performing the tasks included in the activities.

 Note: Activities may vary slightly if the software vendor has issued digital updates. Your instructor will notify you of any changes.

The policy template you will work with in this activity is taken from the SANS Institute's website.

Scenario

Develetech has recently hired security consultants to assist in assessing the company's risk profile. During their assessment, the consultants identify the help desk employees as a large source of risk. On more than one occasion, unknown and unauthorized users have tricked these employees into divulging sensitive information and exposing their workstations and the network to malicious activity. For example, users have been sending the help desk emails enticing the employees to click on links to malicious websites. These sites execute scripts on the employees' computers that make their systems sluggish and unresponsive. Additionally, some malicious users have been contacting help desk employees through their private Facebook and AOL Instant Messenger accounts. The employees have been implicitly trusting anyone with knowledge of these accounts, giving away sensitive company information over unauthorized communication channels.

As Develetech's CISO, this is too much risk for you to tolerate. The existing strategy of reacting to security events as they happen is inadequate, so you want to stop the social engineering attacks from succeeding in the first place. You decide to draft a policy specifically concerning these types of attacks and the help desk employees who are their targets. Instead of starting from scratch, you'll use a template that has most of the guidelines you need already in place. You'll need to make some minor changes to improve the template before you publish it as official Develetech policy. With this policy in place, your help desk employees will be more educated about the threats they are vulnerable to in their position, and they will understand how exactly to respond to social engineering attempts and what the consequences will be if they fail to do so. This is an important step in managing risk for your enterprise.

---

1. View the SANS Institute's security policy templates.

   a) Log on to Windows Server 2012 R2 as **DOMAIN##\Administrator** with a password of *!Pass1234*

   b) On the desktop taskbar, select the **Internet Explorer** icon to open the browser.

    c) If necessary, in the **Internet Explorer 11** dialog box, select **Don't use recommended settings** and select **OK**.

    d) Navigate to **http://www.sans.org/security-resources/policies/**.

    e) Under the **Find the Policy Template You Need!** section, select **General**.

    f) Verify that there are several general security policy templates available.

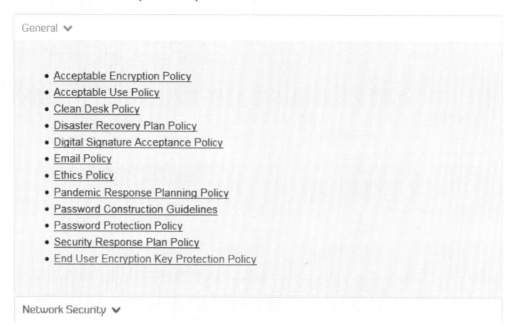

    g) Select any of the template links to see more information about the template.
There is a description of the template, as well as links to its PDF or DOC file.

    h) Select the **Back** button on your browser and select any of the other general security templates that interest you. Return to the categories page to view templates in other categories.

    i) When you're finished, close Internet Explorer®.

2. Open the social engineering policy template and set the company name to Develetech.

    a) Select the **File Explorer** icon and navigate to **C:\093023Data\Managing Risk**.

    b) Open **social_engineering_awareness_policy** in Word.

    c) On the ribbon, on the **HOME** tab, in the **Editing** group, select the **Find** drop-down arrow and select **Advanced Find**.

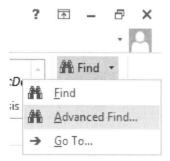

    d) In the **Find and Replace** dialog box, select the **Replace** tab.

    e) In the **Find what** text box, type **<Company Name>**

f) In the **Replace with** text box, type *Develetech Industries*

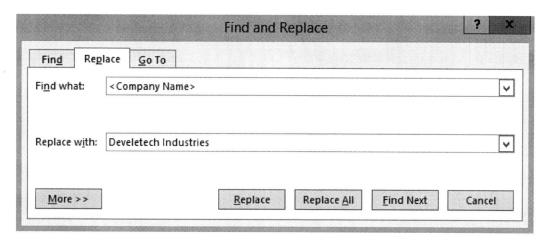

g) Select **Replace All**, then select **OK**.
h) Select **Close** to close the **Find and Replace** dialog box and confirm that the policy document refers to Develetech.

3. Review the overview and purpose of the policy and verify that it concerns protecting front desk/help desk employees from being tricked into leaking sensitive information to unauthorized parties.

4. Review the policy items and add more social engineering examples you've encountered.
   a) Scroll down to section 4 and review the policy items.
   b) After reviewing the policy items, place your cursor at the end of the 4.1.10 item and press **Enter**.
   c) Add a 4.1.11 item with the following text:

   4.1.11 The requester solicits the employee to click on links to unverified or irrelevant websites in email correspondence.

   d) Add a 4.1.12 item with the following text:

   4.1.12 The requester uses an unauthorized method of contacting the employee, such as through social media sites or non-sanctioned instant messaging applications.

5. Review the action items under 4.2 and change them according to your enterprise needs.
   a) After reviewing the action items, in item 4.2.1, change "30 days" to *one week*
   b) In item 4.2.4, change "the security personnel" to *any available Security Analyst*
   c) In item 4.2.5, change "the security personnel" to a *Security Analyst*

6. Add your revision to the revision history.
   a) Scroll down to the **Revision History** section and verify the table.
   b) In the **Date of Change** column, replace the date with today's date.
   c) In the **Responsible** column, replace **SANS Policy Team** with your name.

d) In the **Summary of Change** column, replace the text with *Created first draft of policy.*

8 Revision History

Date of Change	Responsible	Summary of Change
6/26/2014	Andrew Fiducia	Created first draft of policy.

e) Save the document to the desktop as **develetech_social-engineering-policy**.

 Note: If prompted to upgrade the document to the newest file format, select OK.

7. What are some of the other best security practices you can incorporate in a social engineering policy like this one?

8. Why is it important to maintain a revision history in policies like this one?

9. Close Word and Internet Explorer.

Summary

In this lesson, you identified why the ERM process is important, and went through the process by assessing and mitigating risk across a wide range of factors. You also reinforced your ERM strategy through documentation. The information you learned in this lesson will give you a foundation for understanding and applying security in your enterprise, which you will build upon in later lessons.

At your workplace, what security risks are there, and what risks do you envision for the future of your company?

What sort of documentation do you have in your company to support risk management? What other documentation should there be?

Note: Check your CHOICE Course screen for opportunities to interact with your classmates, peers, and the larger CHOICE online community about the topics covered in this course or other topics you are interested in. From the Course screen you can also access available resources for a more continuous learning experience.

2 | Integrating Computing, Communications, and Business Disciplines

Lesson Time: 2 hours, 15 minutes

Lesson Objectives

In this lesson, you will:

- Facilitate collaboration across business units.

- Secure communications and collaboration solutions.

- Implement security activities throughout the technology life cycle.

Lesson Introduction

Before delving into the more technical aspects of securing your enterprise, you need to make sure that your business operations are adequately protected. Two crucial factors of business are collaboration and communication; if these are impeded in any way, the business will suffer. This is why you must ensure that they operate smoothly and without drawing undue risk to the enterprise. Additionally, the business will keep its computing resources in a life cycle to maximize usefulness and minimize financial strain. Your task, as a CASP, is to integrate collaboration and communication in the enterprise so that they are not simply another attack surface for a malicious person to easily exploit.

TOPIC A

Facilitate Collaboration Across Business Units

Organizations typically design technology implementations to meet their functional requirements, and may treat security requirements as a secondary concern. To ensure that the organization achieves secure solutions, each discipline within the organization must be a part of the overall plan. As a CASP, you must convey the importance of security to all other job disciplines to identify, evaluate, and implement comprehensive security solutions throughout the entire organization. Understanding what others in the organization do on a daily basis will help you in interpreting security requirements and goals to communicate with stakeholders from other disciplines.

Communications with Stakeholders from Other Disciplines

The following table lists several important job disciplines, as well as how to communicate security issues to personnel of that discipline.

 Note: In smaller organizations, the lines may blur between each discipline.

Discipline	How to Communicate Security Issues
Sales staff	Sales staff not only generate revenue for the company, but they hold an inordinate amount of data, both on their computers and in their heads. You can communicate your security requirements by explaining that if they do not protect company data, they are putting their next sale at risk. For example, if the company has a breach, it loses consumer trust, and in turn the salesperson loses their sale. If a salesperson reveals sensitive information to the wrong person, they could also lose their sale to competitors from rival companies.
Programmer	Programmers develop and maintain an enterprise's applications. They are typically involved in the processes of building, testing, releasing, and monitoring their applications in a live environment. When communicating with programmers, it is important to work with them in the development stage of the code they are writing. It is much more palatable for a programmer to understand security needs from the beginning than to later be told that they did something wrong. When they know security issues upfront, they will likely implement security into their code instead of having to rewrite their code later to adapt to security.
Database administrator	The database administrator (DBA) oversees all aspects of a business database. This includes anything from initial database architecture design through implementation, administration, monitoring, tuning, backup, migration, and support. The DBA is also responsible for securing the integrity of information held in the database. DBAs need to be aware of the current security threat landscape and be given the tools to secure the company's data. When communicating to a DBA, it is important that you provide them with the proper up-to-date information that allows them to analyze and understand current database threats. DBAs should be fully aware of all database encryption and backup-related protocols that you implement in the organization, as well as access control policies.

Discipline	How to Communicate Security Issues
Network administrator	Network administrators are responsible for protecting the network's architecture, design (engineering), and implementation. Communicating with administrators and engineers should be based on how they are building the network, how they test the network for security vulnerabilities, and their plan of action to remediate any network risks. The networking threat landscape changes constantly, so make sure they are staying current. You can do this by sending them news articles on security, bringing in industry experts who can speak with them, or by making sure they attend industry-specific conferences or training.
Management	Management is responsible for the planning and overall strategy of the organization, as well as its profitability. When communicating with executive management, including the CEO, CIO, and COO, you need to sell your ideas and put them into a language they understand, which includes profitability and appearance. While profitability is straightforward, appearance refers to public perception and business reputation, such as keeping the company off of the front page of the newspaper for a breach or a compliance matter. When approaching the senior managers, relating to them on a business level will help them understand your security requirements.
Financial	Finance manages and monitors cash flow, accounts receivable and payable, and oversees all enterprise financial transactions. As applied to information security, finance has the ability to both assist in reducing cost and providing the budget for IT-related projects. Finance can be your best friend or your worst enemy, depending on how you communicate with them. When planning a new project, or to keep your security program moving forward, you need a budget. When communicating with finance, it is important to show what it can cost the organization not to be secure, as the finance team members tend to be risk-averse.
Human resources	Human resources (HR) plays a major role in the security of the organization. They are tasked not only with the hiring process and background checks, but also with ensuring that the employees understand and follow security policies and procedures. Once the security team finalizes policies, in many cases, HR educates and enforces those security policies across the organization. Regardless of the size of your organization or its security staff, you will not be able to accomplish effective compliance on your own; HR plays a significant role, including policy development, awareness, enforcement, and contingency planning.
Emergency response team	The emergency response team educates people about disaster preparedness for hazards that may impact their area and trains them in basic disaster response skills, such as fire safety, cybersecurity, team organization, and disaster medical operations. Response teams may be responsible for receiving, reviewing, and responding to computer security incident reports and activities. This discipline may be more familiar with security than others, but you still need to ensure clear communication of your requirements and goals. The response team should be closely included in the development of a business continuity plan (BCP) so that they can assist in incident recovery.

Discipline	How to Communicate Security Issues
Facilities manager	Facilities managers are responsible for the management of services and processes that support the essential business of an organization. They guarantee that an organization has the best working environment for its employees and their activities. When communicating with a facilities manager, you should inform them that having insecure facilities may lead to damaged or stolen property. If employees depend on these services in their day-to-day work, this might lower workplace morale and negatively affect the business as a whole.
Physical security manager	Physical security managers are responsible for protecting systems, buildings, and related supporting infrastructure against threats linked with their physical environment. Physical security staff needs to understand how the physical security precautions they take have an impact on the information security of the organization. To communicate effectively with physical security personnel, you should provide them with some examples as to how a physical breach can lead to an information security breach.

Collaboration Within Teams

Collaboration within the teams and disciplines that make up your organization is a must to effectively implement a new technology or security solution. As a CASP, you may be tasked with the collaboration effort in information security projects. Before you can determine how to develop comprehensive strategies within your organization, you'll want to know what will support or inhibit the collaboration you are trying to achieve. Knowledgeable and hard-working employees may nevertheless be unaccustomed to working in a team environment, which may impact their productivity and, consequently, the effectiveness of your security strategies.

A good way to make sure the process goes smoothly is to promote teamwork: make sure you take advantage of each the members' strengths, include all needed team members in the decision-making process, and communicate goals and progress accordingly. Be prepared to create a shared vision and effectively communicate that vision to build overall trust.

Security Processes and Controls

The types of processes and controls that you put in place depend on the level of protection that management and security your organization needs. Once that determination is made, you then need to be able to communicate to all staff, including senior management, the importance of those security processes and controls. After they acknowledge the need for a clear security process and controls, you need to provide objective guidance and impartial recommendations. Subjective and biased conclusions will likely be unconvincing and fruitless, so it's essential that you focus on backing up your claims with consensus-driven evidence and industry-accepted analysis.

For example, the International Organization for Standardization (ISO) and the International Electrotechnical Commission (IEC) are both widely recognized authorities in their domains. One of the most common process and control frameworks is the ISO/IEC 27001:2005 standard. ISO/IEC 27001:2005 requires that management:

* Systematically examine the organization's information security risks, taking account of the threats, vulnerabilities, and risks.
* Design and implement a coherent and comprehensive suite of information security controls and/or other forms of risk treatment (such as risk avoidance or risk transfer) to address those risks that are deemed unacceptable.
* Adopt an overarching management process to ensure that the information security controls continue to meet the organization's information security needs on an ongoing basis.

Security Control Groups and Categories

You can communicate the viability of security controls in a more effectual manner by breaking them down into two separate groupings of individual categories. The first security control grouping includes the procedural, technical, or physical categories. In this classification, the control category is based on what the control actually is, such as a policy, a security event monitor (hardware), or a physical door. The other way to categorize security controls is classification based on what the control does, such as detecting a threat, preventing an attack, or correcting a vulnerability. The common grouping for these categories are detective, preventative, and corrective security controls.

When management and other relevant staff understand what a security control is and how it functions, they will be able to recognize how this helps the organization.

IT Governance

Achieving IT governance goals depends heavily on the organization's ability to communicate and collaborate across its diverse business units. Almost all disciplines and departments have at least some stake in the enterprise's information technology operations, and they likewise are a component in your overall enterprise risk management (ERM) strategy. Each business unit can't fully meet the objectives outlined for them in the organization's strategy without at least some collaboration with other business units. In larger enterprises, networking administrators and database administrators must work together to ensure the confidentiality, integrity, and availability of data. Application developers and quality assurance professionals must collaborate to ensure that enterprise applications meets certain usability, authentication, and authorization standards.

Whatever the collaborative effort may be, it's important that each party establishes common ground upon which to build. When both parties realize what's in it for them, how their objectives and goals overlap, and how they can each work toward achieving these objectives and goals, IT governance becomes less of a daunting task for the security-minded professional.

Guidelines for Facilitating Collaboration Across Business Units

 Note: All Guidelines for this lesson are available as checklists from the **Checklist** tile on the CHOICE Course screen.

Use the following guidelines to facilitate collaboration across business units to achieve security goals:

- Learn about the day-to-day work of the many diverse disciplines that make up an enterprise.
- Convey the importance of security for each discipline.
- Target each discipline as its own audience, tailoring your security policies and plans to fit their understanding and concerns.
- Involve the relevant disciplines in policy and procedure development.
- Take advantage of team members' strengths.
- Include relevant team members in the decision-making process.
- Communicate goals and progress to all team members.
- Create and communicate a shared vision to the team.
- Provide objective guidance and impartial recommendations for security controls to management and key staff.
- Adopt widely recognized standards like ISO/IEC 27001:2005 for management's involvement in information security.
- Communicate security controls in terms of categories and groups that define what a control is and how it is used to secure the organization.
- Ensure that disparate IT departments work together and build common ground to achieve business goals and objectives.

ACTIVITY 2-1
Facilitating Collaboration Across Business Units

Scenario

Being a large company, Develetech has a diverse array of departments with many different people fulfilling many different roles. At the enterprise level, simply communicating your security requirements to a small subset of technically minded people won't be enough to guarantee widespread adoption. Instead, you'll need to make sure that *everyone* understands their role in keeping the organization secure. You must tailor this communication in certain ways, depending on your audience. This will ensure that there are no weak links in your enterprise.

1. Which of the following are key elements for successful collaboration within teams? (Select three.)

   ☐ Communicate goals to the team.

   ☐ Withhold progress reports unless asked.

   ☐ Play to each individual's strengths.

   ☐ Include all relevant team members in the decision making process.

2. You've already communicated your security expectations to the teams in the IT department. Now you must do the same for sales, finance, and human resources. How will you communicate the importance of security to these personnel that may not have the technical experience that your IT department has?

3. You plan on installing a demilitarized zone (DMZ) along Develetech's network perimeter to isolate a large chunk of the network from external traffic. This external traffic will only be able to access the servers you place inside the DMZ and not any outside it. How should you communicate the need for this security control to your CEO?

TOPIC B

Secure Communications and Collaboration Solutions

Business today is largely about real-time or near-real-time communication and collaboration. IT is largely focused on the delivery of this type of service to the business user—real-time chat, meeting, and phone capabilities for users located anywhere in the world are essential to the majority of businesses today. Due to the need for always-on communication across telephone, email, IM and other communication technologies, the security and availability of these systems are of paramount importance to most organizations.

Unified Collaboration

The concept of *unified communications (UC)*, or unified collaboration, is the integration of a large number of communication platforms that traverse disparate types of networking technologies. While some platforms traverse older technologies, such as phone or traditional data networks, UC is rapidly shifting its focus to Internet-based technologies. This shift from traditionally private technologies to Internet-based technologies requires additional security controls to ensure the continued confidentiality, integrity and availability of these critical communications as they cross the Internet. Security measures that worked on private networks may not be sufficient for protecting communications across the Internet.

Unified Collaboration Tools

Unified communications implementations are as diverse as the organizations that implement them. Every organization's UC deployment will reflect its own particular culture and technological needs. Furthermore, each of these choices will necessitate different types of security controls. The following table lists the various tools that are often associated with UC.

Communication/ Collaboration Tool	Security Considerations
Web conferencing	Web conferencing is a service that allows remote users to participate in a meeting held virtually using a web conferencing application over the Internet. Services like Skype® and Google Hangouts™ are popular examples of widely used and freely available web conferencing apps. Services like these are very useful and are quickly becoming a common component of many businesses. There are, however, a number of security controls that you should put in place to keep your business secure through web conferencing: • Draft the company policy to include guidelines for user access rights to conferencing. • Use Secure Sockets Layer/Transport Layer Security (SSL/TLS) transport encryption to keep the meeting confidential. • Install intrusion detection systems (IDSs) on your internal network to monitor for unauthorized activity. • Configure the web conferencing app's features appropriately, depending on the app used.

Communication/ Collaboration Tool	Security Considerations
Video conferencing	Video conferencing is a service that allows people in multiple locations to display video while participating in a meeting. Services like Skype and Google Hangouts also provide video features, which are typically used with webcams or dedicated video solutions. The security concerns and controls for general web conferencing apps mostly apply to video conferencing as well, but some organizations may wish to exercise additional caution if they do not want to reveal faces or locations.
Instant messaging	Instant messaging (IM) is a text-based communication method conducted in real time. IM apps like Microsoft® Lync® and Skype™ are useful for brief communications, and many organizations incorporate them as a supplement to email. IM clients are also useful for providing presence information to colleagues: where you are, what you're doing, and who you're working with. Because it is text-based and Internet-based, you should implement transport encryption for messages and harden the IM applications themselves. Depending on your security needs, you may need to draft policies that specifically forbid employees from communicating certain types of presence information, especially if where they are or what they're doing is confidential.
Desktop sharing	Desktop sharing is a communication tool that permits remote access and remote collaboration to a user's computer. There are two general types of desktop sharing: remote log-in and real-time collaboration. With remote log-in, a user can connect to their desktop even while physically away from their computer. Microsoft's Remote Desktop Protocol (RDP) is an example. With real-time collaboration, one user visually shares their desktop to present information to others in a virtual space. Web apps like Google Hangouts™ and iLinc™ provide this functionality. Because desktop sharing runs over network and Internet connections, you should consider choosing a service with strong authentication methods so no unauthorized users may gain entry to a computer. Additionally, services that incorporate transport encryption will keep data that traverses the sharing session confidential.
Remote assistance	Remote assistance is another remote access and collaboration tool that allows a user, typically a system administrator or support specialist, to temporarily control another user's computer remotely in order to provide help. Organizations use tools like Windows Remote Assistance (WRA) and other remote desktop software to support offsite employees with any computer-related issues they are having. Like desktop sharing, remote assistance requires strong authentication and confidentiality, but you should take extra care to make sure that remote assistance is generated by invitation only—from the end user to the authorized support specialist. Unsolicited invitations to remote assistance are a common social engineering tactic, and you don't want your users to assume that this is legitimate behavior.

Communication/ Collaboration Tool	Security Considerations
Email	Email is a communication method for exchanging digital messages, often used asynchronously (not in real-time). Whether by Internet or a domain-specific mail server, email is ubiquitous in businesses today. However, email is often insecure by default, and there are several ways you can secure its use: • Protecting email in transit by using secure encryption protocols like Pretty Good Privacy (PGP) and Secure/Multipurpose Internet Mail Extensions (S/MIME). • Harden any email servers used internally through proper authentication and IPS/IDS protection. • Implement antivirus and anti-malware software at employee workstations to protect them from downloading malicious attachments.
Telephony	Telephony is a communication method that delivers voice communications, often over phone lines. Internet-based telephony protocols, like Voice over IP (VoIP), transmit voice through digital networks. VoIP is often implemented in web conferencing software and requires much the same security considerations. Beyond confidentiality and authentication issues, VoIP can place a great deal of strain on your company's network, so you should be prepared to allocate enough bandwidth to the service to prevent network congestion and unavailability.
Collaboration sites	Collaboration sites are websites that offer a repository for posting information, managing knowledge, communicating with colleagues, and other collaboration types in a centralized virtual location. Cloud-based software like Microsoft® SharePoint® and social media sites like Yammer are examples of collaboration sites. Because they are web-based, sites that are exposed to the Internet, especially if they contain company-sensitive information, should use SSL/TLS encryption and strong authentication techniques. Collaboration sites will often have an access control hierarchy that you may use to delegate certain permissions. For example, following the principle of least privilege, you may disable the ability to delete pages by default, and enable the ability only for specific users.

 Note: To learn more about how to assign privileges to secure a collaboration site like SharePoint, check out the LearnTO **Implement Access Control in SharePoint 2013** presentation from the **LearnTO** tile on the CHOICE Course screen.

Mobile Device Management

Today's handheld devices are more powerful than the average laptop was a decade ago. This provides a huge amount of flexibility in communication and collaboration, but it also creates a large number of security concerns for the enterprise whose users store sensitive data on their smartphones and tablets.

While the threat posed by compromised, lost, or stolen mobile devices is significant, and many enterprises are struggling to minimize the risk, there are some basic practices that the enterprise can enforce to ensure that all mobile devices using corporate resources are secured.

Security Control	Description
Use device management systems	To help more easily and efficiently implement various mobile controls, you should set up a mobile device management system. The practice of managing mobile devices attached to a network is typically centralized through special-purpose servers that push updates and send administrative commands to those mobile devices.
Enable screen lock	The screen lock option on all mobile devices should be enabled with strict requirements on when the device will be locked. Once the device is locked, it can only be accessed by entering the code that the user has set up.
Require a strong password	The user who accesses a device should set up a strong password that they need to input once the device is turned on. Password requirements will be different for every organization and should be documented in the organization's security policy.
Configure device encryption	When possible, all mobile devices should be configured to use data encryption to protect company-specific data that may be stored and accessed on the device.
Require remote wipe/ sanitization/lockout	*Data wiping* is a method used to remove any sensitive data from a mobile device and permanently delete it. *Data sanitization* is the method used to repeatedly delete and overwrite any traces or bits of sensitive data that may remain on the device after data wiping has been done. *Lockout* is a method of restricting access to sensitive data on a device without deleting it from memory. However, a skilled attacker may be able to bypass a lockout and capture sensitive data, especially if it is unencrypted. Remote options are available, so you can perform these functions remotely in case the phone is lost or stolen. Wipe, sanitization, and lockout guidelines and requirements should be included in the security policies for companies that use mobile devices.
Enable global positioning system (GPS) tracking	GPS tracking service functionality is available on a number of mobile devices and can be added in most cases when required for business reasons. This feature is used as a security measure to protect mobile devices that may be lost or stolen.
Enforce access control	Like other computing platforms, you should regulate mobile devices in terms of who can access what. Implementing authentication and authorization when employees use mobile devices will uphold the principle of least privilege. This can encompass data shared on a network, or it can even extend to restricting access to the mobile hardware itself.
Enforce application control	Setting restrictions on what apps a user can access may prevent employees from unwittingly using insecure software on their mobile devices. Depending on your needs, you may whitelist a set of apps that you deem safe, while blocking the rest. Alternatively, you may draft a blacklist of apps you know to be off limits.

Security Control	Description
Use asset tracking and inventory control	Keeping track of the mobile devices that you provide your users is vital to establishing a certain security standard that the organization must abide. Take consistent inventory of any mobile devices provisioned to employees to ensure that every single one is accounted for. Likewise, there are many ways you can track devices in real time, such as through a Global Positioning System (GPS) or a Quick Response (QR) code.
Limit removable storage capabilities	Because removable storage like Secure Digital (SD) cards further detaches information from the user and device, your employees need to exercise caution. You should mandate that easily lost and often-shared removable storage components do not contain sensitive information, especially in plaintext. Major mobile operating systems limit the exposure certain apps and their internally stored data have to other apps and processes on a device, but removable storage is usually not afforded that same protection.
Implement *storage segmentation*	Mobile device proliferation goes hand-in-hand with the rise of cloud storage technologies, so be prepared to assess how best to manage data storage in your organization. Consider dividing data storage along certain lines (e.g., cloud vs. local) based on your security needs. When you segment the data storage in your network, you give yourself a greater level of access control over mobile devices and their users.
Disable unused features	Every feature has the potential to be another point of vulnerability in a mobile system, so it's good practice to disable any features that don't serve a purpose in your organization. For example, Google account syncing on a corporate-provisioned Android phone may be unnecessary.

 Note: For additional information, check out the LearnTO **Secure a Mobile Device** presentation from the **LearnTO** tile on the CHOICE Course screen.

Over-the-Air Technologies

One method of mobile device management is *over-the-air programming/provisioning (OTAP)*. OTAP technologies offer administrators the ability to wirelessly push software updates and configurations to mobile devices in a centralized, on-demand fashion. Every device included in an OTAP channel is forced to accept these changes, or the device may be removed from the channel. OTAP is particularly adept at streamlining enterprise mobile devices so that they conform to your specifications and policy requirements. Deployment is quick and doesn't require a physical connection. OTAP updates are typically deployed through Short Message Service (SMS) messages that interface with a device's unique subscriber identity module (SIM) card to activate certain configurations and download updates.

Figure 2-1: Pushing updates to mobile devices using OTAP.

OTAP Vulnerabilities

Although OTAP can be an excellent choice in streamlining your enterprise mobile devices for collaboration purposes, it carries with it some risk. Some SIM cards used today still communicate using Data Encryption Standard (DES), an insecure encryption algorithm that is breakable with modern computers. An attacker may be able to send an update over SMS and receive a rejection code that is signed with the DES encryption key. A brute force attack will crack the key relatively easily, and the attacker will now have free rein to sign malicious code updates with the key, causing devices in the OTAP channel to implicitly accept them.

Another vulnerability of OTAP lies on some SIM cards' reliance on outdated Java™ implementations. Some Java applets may be able to interface with other Java applets they're not supposed to and glean sensitive information. An attacker who is able to push OTAP updates could take advantage of this vulnerability to snoop on private communications. Before implementing OTAP in your enterprise, ensure that your provisioned devices use strong cryptography and updated versions of Java, if applicable.

BYOD Controls

Since mobile devices are now so integral to everyday life, it is inevitable that employees will bring their own to supplement the devices provided to them by their employers. As you know, this practice introduces a whole host of security issues and legal concerns into a corporate environment. Since an employee's personal property is out of the employer's control, it is difficult to account for every risk, threat, and vulnerability involved with these devices. Some companies have elected to outright ban BYOD to prevent such security incidents; however, for a number of reasons, this isn't always feasible.

The following table lists various controls you can implement to mitigate the security issues introduced by BYOD.

Security Control	Description
Corporate policies and acceptable use policies	One of the first things you should do to meet BYOD head on is to draft a corporate policy for how BYOD is treated in your organization. You might mandate that BYOD isn't tolerated at all, or you might include information on how your security team will respond to BYOD-related incidents.
	Likewise, you should draft an acceptable use policy that your employees need to be aware of and follow. You should clearly outline what types of devices are allowed and how they should or should not be used. This policy depends on explicit user acceptance to be effective, so be sure that everyone within your organization is compliant. Whatever policies you put in place, you need to also demonstrate to your employees that you are sensitive to the fact that it's their own personal device, and not company property.
On-boarding and off-boarding employees	New employees should be acclimated to the acceptable use policies as quickly as possible, as you won't necessarily know right away that they have brought their own device to use at work. Likewise, employees who are leaving the organization should be prevented from taking any sensitive data or access with them. This can be difficult without some prior control mechanism in place.
Decide on data ownership and support ownership	Although an employee's personal devices are their own property, the lines between ownership are often blurred when it comes to your company's data. You need to come up with a clear boundary that defines what the employee owns versus what the company owns. That way, an employee who is allowed to access and administrate company secrets on their personal device cannot claim ownership of said secrets.
	Another question to ask yourself is: who should offer support for BYODs? A company that provisions its own hardware and software should be able to provide help desk support, but what about the great variety of mobile devices that employees may bring into the office? Consider that, if you don't provide adequate support, any security vulnerabilities that exist in employees' personal devices may affect your network.
Patch management and antivirus management	Depending on the operating system and its software, some mobile devices can be easily patched. However, others may be more difficult to patch, which could leave them vulnerable. Consider implementing a patch management system to mitigate the threat of outdated hardware and software.
	Likewise, many mobile devices lack antivirus software. To protect your network from infection, you may want to encourage users to download antivirus apps onto their personal devices.

Security Control	Description
Consider architecture and infrastructure needs	As more and more devices are added to your corporate network, you may need to expand and update your infrastructure. Otherwise, your current office setup may be inadequate to serve a large number of mobile devices. If your network architecture isn't focused enough on wireless, that will need to change to accommodate BYOD. Keep in mind that wireless networking will likely introduce new challenges to your organization's security.
Forensics	As BYODs become more prevalent, so too will their relevance to the security investigations you conduct. This may present a challenge when you consider all of the different operating systems and hardware that you may need to perform forensics on. Your knowledge of forensic procedures and tools needs to be current, not just with a limited set of specifications, but encompassing a wide variety of devices.
Privacy	Employees may be concerned that their privacy is at risk by being exposed to the corporate network, especially if that network is shared by many people. You should reassure your employees by providing them with the tools and know-how to keep their private information and device usage secure.
Control for on-board camera, microphone, and video use	It's very easy to secretively take pictures, record video, or capture audio with mobile devices. For many organizations, this is already a concern. With personal devices in play, it becomes much more difficult to stop this from happening. You may need to re-evaluate the openness of certain rooms and systems to control for this threat.

Guidelines for Securing Communications and Collaboration Solutions

Use the following guidelines to secure communication and collaboration across your enterprise:

- Research unified communications and collaboration tools to see which solutions fit within your enterprise.
- Use transport encryption techniques like SSL/TLS in conferencing and telephony software.
- Ensure strong authentication to verify each participant in a meeting, recipient of a message, or initiator of a remote access session.
- Select apps and tools that are highly configurable and meet your security needs.
- Use encryption protocols like PGP and S/MIME in email communications.
- Allow end users to invite support technicians to remote assistance sessions, and not the other way around.
- Restrict employees from divulging presence information in IM programs, where applicable.
- Implement mobile device management controls like screen locking and password protection.
- Ensure the confidentiality of mobile device data by implementing data wiping/sanitization/lockout.
- Track and inventory all provision devices in your enterprise.
- Ensure provisioned mobile devices have strong encryption and update Java technology before deploying OTAP solutions.
- Write BYOD policies stipulating how devices should and should not be used in the enterprise environment.
- Clearly define ownership and support information for BYOD.
- Research the various devices that employees may bring in to your environment and how they may affect your confidentiality, integrity, and availability.

ACTIVITY 2-2
Securing Communications and Collaboration Solutions

Before You Begin

You will work with a partner in this activity. One of you will play the role of the helper, and the other will play the role of someone asking for help. You should also have some method of transmitting files to your partner, such as a Universal Serial Bus (USB) drive or an email address.

Scenario

You realize how important intra-organizational collaboration is to Develetech, and providing technical assistance is a huge part of that collaboration. Every day, users from many different departments request help in solving their computer problems. However, you know from previous experience that the help desk is a popular vector for social engineering attacks. You want your help desk staff to be able to help users remotely to increase collaboration and communication productivity, but remote access tools can also bring unwanted risk to the enterprise.

You've decided to use Microsoft's Remote Assistance service, which allows a remote helper to monitor and, in some cases, control someone else's desktop. This is bound to be a useful tool in your help desk's arsenal, as the help desk staff will more easily be able spot problems with a computer without having to physically be at the workstation or rely on verbal descriptions from a phone call. But, before you implement Remote Assistance, you will need to make sure it is hardened. You'll make sure that insecure legacy systems are blocked, that all connections are logged, and that remote helpers can only view and not control the other person's desktop. Perhaps most importantly, you'll ensure that all unsolicited help offers are denied; this will decrease the chances that a social engineer will be able to impersonate an authorized help desk staffer to trick an employee into revealing sensitive company information.

---

1. Install the **Remote Assistance** service.

   a) If the **Server Manager** window isn't displayed, select its icon on the desktop taskbar.

b) In the **Server Manager** window, in the **Configure this local server** section, select **Add roles and features**.

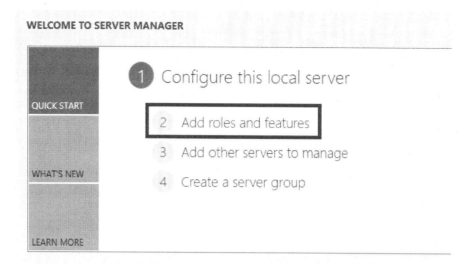

WELCOME TO SERVER MANAGER

QUICK START

WHAT'S NEW

LEARN MORE

1 Configure this local server

2 Add roles and features

3 Add other servers to manage

4 Create a server group

c) In the **Add Roles and Features Wizard**, on the **Before you begin** page, select **Next**.
d) On the **Select installation type** page, verify that the **Role-based or feature-based** radio button is selected and select **Next**.
e) On the **Select destination server** page, verify that your server is selected and select **Next**.
f) On the **Select server roles** page, select **Next**.
g) On the **Select features** page, check the **Remote Assistance** check box and select **Next**.
h) On the **Confirm installation selections** page, check the **Restart the destination server automatically if required** check box.
i) In the **Add Roles and Features Wizard** message box, select **Yes**. Select **Install**.
j) After the installation completes, select **Close**.

2. Configure security settings for Remote Assistance.

a) From the desktop taskbar, right-click the **Start** button and select **Command Prompt**.

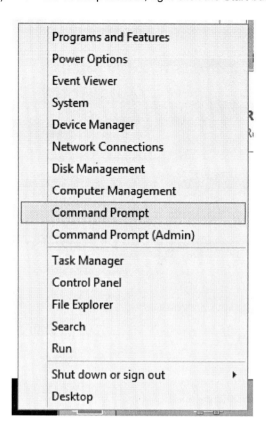

b) At the command prompt, enter *gpedit*
c) In the **Local Group Policy Editor** window, expand **Computer Configuration→Administrative Templates→System** and select **Remote Assistance**.
d) In the details pane, verify that none of the Remote Assistance policies are configured.

Setting	State	Comment
Allow only Windows Vista or later connections	Not configured	No
Turn on session logging	Not configured	No
Turn on bandwidth optimization	Not configured	No
Customize warning messages	Not configured	No
Configure Solicited Remote Assistance	Not configured	No
Configure Offer Remote Assistance	Not configured	No

e) Double-click **Allow only Windows Vista or later connections** to open its policy window.
f) Select the **Enabled** radio button to enable the policy, then select **OK**.
   This prevents users on Windows XP from using Remote Assistance. Microsoft no longer supports this operating system, and its implementation of Remote Assistance uses weak encryption protocols.
g) Double-click **Turn on session logging**. Select **Enabled**, then select **OK**.
   Windows will now keep a log of every Remote Assistance connection that is established.
h) Double-click **Customize warning messages** and select **Enabled**.
i) In the **Options** section, in the **Display warning message before connecting** text box, type *DO NOT accept a remote connection from an untrusted party. Refer to the Develetech Remote Access Policy for more information.*
j) Select **OK**.
k) Double-click **Configure Solicited Remote Assistance** and select **Enabled**.

l) In the **Options** section, select the first drop-down arrow and select **Allow helpers to only view the computer**.

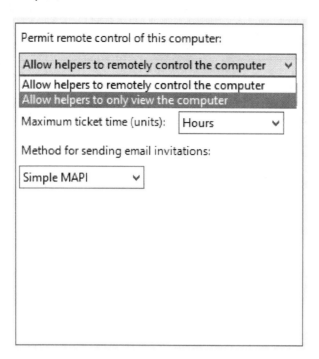

Remote helpers will not be able to take control of the computer.

m) From the **Maximum ticket time (units)** drop-down list and select **Minutes**.

n) Double-click in the **Maximum ticket time (value)** spin box, type **15** and select **OK**.
Any Remote Assistance invitations will only be valid for 15 minutes after creation, unless this time is extended by the person soliciting help.

o) Double-click **Configure Offer Remote Assistance** and select **Disabled**. Select **OK**.
This prevents the computer from accepting unsolicited help through Remote Assistance.

p) Verify that your policies are configured properly, then close the **Local Group Policy Editor** window.

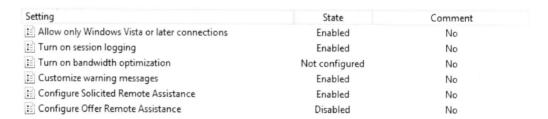

Setting	State	Comment
Allow only Windows Vista or later connections	Enabled	No
Turn on session logging	Enabled	No
Turn on bandwidth optimization	Not configured	No
Customize warning messages	Enabled	No
Configure Solicited Remote Assistance	Enabled	No
Configure Offer Remote Assistance	Disabled	No

3. **Partner soliciting help**: Invite your helper to a Remote Assistance session on your computer.

a) After the group policies have successfully updated, enter **msra** at the command prompt to open the **Windows Remote Assistance** wizard.

b) In the **Windows Remote Assistance** wizard, select **Invite someone you trust to help you**.

c) On the **How do you want to invite your trusted helper?** page, select **Save this invitation as a file**.

d) Save the file to your desktop as **Server##_invitation** where **##** is your server number.

e) Verify that a **Windows Remote Assistance** window is waiting for an incoming connection and displays a unique session password. You will provide this password to your helper later.

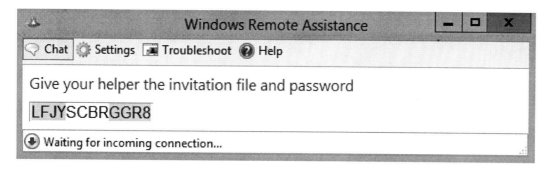

f) Send your invitation file to your partner.

4. **Partner providing help**: Accept your partner's Remote Assistance invitation.
   a) If necessary, open a command prompt and enter *msra*
   b) In the **Windows Remote Assistance** wizard, select **Help someone who has invited you**.
   c) On the **Choose a way to connect to the other person's computer** page, select **Use an invitation file**.
   d) Browse to where your partner's invitation file is located and open it.
   e) In the **Remote Assistance** dialog box, in the **Enter password** text box, enter your partner's session password.

5. **Partner soliciting help**: Accept and the Remote Assistance connection.
   a) Verify that a message box appears on your screen with the custom warning you defined earlier.

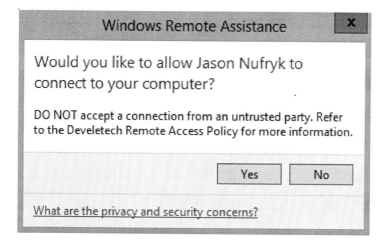

   b) Select **Yes** to accept the incoming connection.

6. **Partner providing help**: Test the Remote Assistance connection.
   a) Verify that you can see your partner's desktop in the **Windows Remote Assistance** window.
   b) From the toolbar in the top-left of the window, select **Request control**.

    c) Verify that a message box appears stating that you are not allowed to take control of the remote computer.

 Control of the remote computer is not allowed

Settings on the computer of the person you are trying to help are preventing you from taking control.

    d) Select **OK**.

7. **Partner soliciting help**: View the log of your Remote Assistance session.
   a) From the desktop taskbar, select the **File Explorer** icon.
   b) Browse to **This PC→Documents→Remote Assistance Logs**.
   c) Open the log file in WordPad.
      The log file is in XML format and has recorded various information about the Remote Assistance session, including:
      - The date and time the invitation was created.
      - The date and time the invitation was used to open a session.
      - The incoming connection's IP address.
      - The incoming connection's user account name.

8. Close all open windows and return to Server Manager.

TOPIC C

Implement Security Activities Throughout the Technology Life Cycle

Technology is not static, and your security strategy shouldn't be static, either. To match the always-in-motion pace of tools, devices, and equipment in your enterprise, you'll need to think of them in terms of where they are in their life cycle. Different phases of this cycle will require different approaches to security, so you'll need to anticipate these changes before they occur to reduce the risks that inevitably come with change. When you do so, you'll be able to put your policy into practice no matter where in its life cycle a piece of technology is.

Systems Development Life Cycle

Technology has a life cycle within the organization: from the initial planning stages before a product is deployed, all the way to its obsolescence. The *systems development life cycle (SDLC)* is the practice of designing and deploying technology systems across this life cycle. It involves a diverse set of resources from the organization, and security is only one part of the SDLC effort when designing and deploying a new technology solution. Large-scale development projects rely on SDLC principles because there are so many human resources, such as architects, developers, and testers to coordinate.

SDLC Phases and Frameworks

Each technology that an organization deploys goes through distinct phases of its deployment. For an SDLC to be effective, you need to integrate information security controls into each step of this process to ensure that risk is minimized across each technology that the organization deploys.

Although the specific methods of SDLC vary, the principles and phases are largely the same: requirements building, project planning, design and development, validation and acceptance testing, deployment and implementation, and post-deployment maintenance. Security-targeted frameworks like the *Security System Development Life Cycle (SSDLC)* and *Security Development Lifecycle (SDL)* incorporate threat, vulnerability, and risk-related controls within the life cycle to achieve systems that are secure by design, rather than secure in a passive and reactive sense. For example, the SSDLC stipulates continuous monitoring for technologies in the maintenance phase of the life cycle to ensure that security controls implemented earlier will continue to be effective.

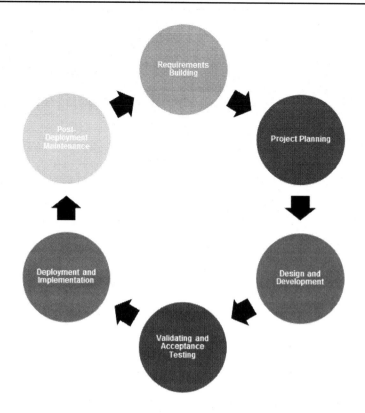

Figure 2–2: The phases of a typical SDLC.

SRTM

A useful tool to track the requirements and interactions of security and the SDLC is the *Security Requirements Traceability Matrix (SRTM)*. The SRTM is a matrix that makes it easy to identify the security requirements of a given system and the actual implementations or tests that can identify whether the requirement has been achieved. SRTMs are designed in such a way as to make it easy for the security professional to identify any gaps in expected security requirements and functionalities. A well-developed SRTM for large security projects provides two-way traceability between requirements and verification tests so that requirements can be traced to tests and vice versa.

The following is an example of an SRTM.

Security Requirement	Source of Requirement	Verification Method
Full system recovery in 24 hours	Business continuity plan	Perform full backup restore on bare hardware in under 24 hours, then test it.
High website availability	Network security policy	Simulate a denial of service (DoS) condition without it taking web servers offline.
Confidential storage of customer information	Legal compliance policy	Perform penetration test on customer information databases with no significant findings.

Emerging Threats and Security Trends

All technology solutions age to a point where their capacities or capabilities no longer fit business needs or meet the security requirements of the enterprise. Across the technology life cycle, security professionals must be concerned with assessing business and technology needs, budget and costs, purchases and implementation of security resources, technical support, ongoing assessment of currently installed technologies, and resource disposal. During this cycle, security assets will eventually become obsolete, and effective planning is necessary to ensure that you either adapt solutions to address emerging threats and security trends, or you replace these assets before they become ineffective. A thorough understanding of the technology life cycle provides the required insight to successfully navigate the process and manage the many security solutions within enterprise security.

End-to-End Solution Ownership

An *end-to-end solution* is an integrated set of hardware and software products, components, and services that meets the business needs and security requirements for an enterprise, as coordinated, implemented, and supported by a single solution provider. This does not mean that all of the components for the solution must be supplied from a single manufacturer. Rather, end-to-end solutions are typically comprised of components and services from multiple manufacturers with whom the solution provider has developed industry expertise. The solution provider also has the integration knowledge to provide end-to-end solution ownership, so that you and your security team have a single point of contact for service and support, and so that you and senior management can be confident that all parts of the solution meet the security requirements of your enterprise.

Security Activities Throughout End-to-End Ownership

It is up to information security to stay involved in the entirety of a solution's useful life cycle within the organization. This will ensure that no gaps in security exist within particular phases of the solution. The following table lists the security activities associated with different phases of the solution's life cycle.

Security Activity	Description
Commissioning	Commissioning is the process of implementing and activating assets and solutions in the end-to-end life cycle. This usually occurs in the very first phases of the solution's life cycle. You should have a good grasp on the solutions at this point, including familiarity with their purposes and functions.
Operational activities	When a new technology is deployed, information security needs to take into account how the day-to-day operational activities of the security organization will change to account for the new solution. This could include changing the current control environment to account for the new solution (e.g., new firewall rules, IDS/IPS signatures), implementing new policies, or performing a penetration test against the system to assess the risk and the changes that are needed. You should undertake these operational activities with a focus on the emerging threat and vulnerability environment, so that you may secure the solution in both the short and long terms.
Maintenance	As systems are maintained, information security has a responsibility to update the control set that exists to minimize risk surrounded by the technology. This can be as simple as applying additional hardening or the latest patches to the system, or as complex deploying new controls (e.g., firewalls) to reduce risk in the system. As part of this process, information security should be working to support the general change management process as it pertains to the technology.

Security Activity	Description
General change management	Change management is the process of ensuring that each change to an information technology environment is tracked, approved, and audited. This process ensures that each system within the environment is in a known state at all times, and that faults introduced by changes can be attributed to the change that was made and reversed to resolve those faults with the least effort and as quickly as possible.
Asset disposal	All technology assets reach the point where they no longer meet business needs or a new solution is put in place to meet those needs. When an asset reaches its end-of-life (EOL), it will most likely need to be destroyed or otherwise disposed of. Certain systems and equipment require their own procedures for proper and secure disposal. For example, an obsolete hard drive will need its sensitive data removed before you dispose of it. It's not enough to simply attach the drive to a computer and format it from an operating system; you may need to use special tools to sanitize the drive, or you may even need to physically destroy it in order to be completely sure no data can be recovered. Other than hardware, you may also need to dispose of software elements like licenses and activation keys.
Decommissioning	Some assets that reach their EOL may be spared destruction, and should instead be retired from use without leaving the enterprise's ownership or control. This is especially true of large and complex physical assets that cannot be easily or feasibly disposed of. Whatever the circumstance, you should make sure that your decommission assets are properly secured in both a physical and virtual sense, as it's likely still possible that they can be reactivated.
Asset/object reuse	Some assets that were decommissioned can be reused at a later time to fulfill an emerging enterprise need. Assets that reach their EOL can also be upgraded to continue to serve a purpose in the enterprise's solutions. These are often cost-effective ways to preserve an end-to-end asset, but you must ensure that you aren't reusing assets that remain obsolete and insecure. Before your organization begins reusing an asset, you should verify that it conforms to the latest security standards set forth by your own policy and the general consensus of the security community.

Asset Management and Inventory Control

Most organizations have massive amounts of technology to keep track of in all phases of the technology life cycle. Managing the hardware, software, and configurations of this technology is a challenging task regardless of the organization's size. *Asset management*, or *inventory control*, is the process of maintaining a detailed record of technology resources for periodic review by network and security administrators. With this record, you can keep track of your resources as they are spread around the enterprise to various places and used by various personnel. Asset management implementation often uses the *radio-frequency identification (RFID)* system to identify enterprise assets like mobile devices for inventory control and tracking purposes.

Other asset tracking technologies, like *geo-location*, can use GPS coordinates to locate lost mobile devices that you have provisioned to employees. You can also implement object tracking and containment technologies like *geo-tagging* and *geo-fencing* to track device usage on the application level and set predefined usage boundaries, respectively. For example, a geo-fenced device may send an alert to an administrator if that device is taken past its preset boundary, like outside the office.

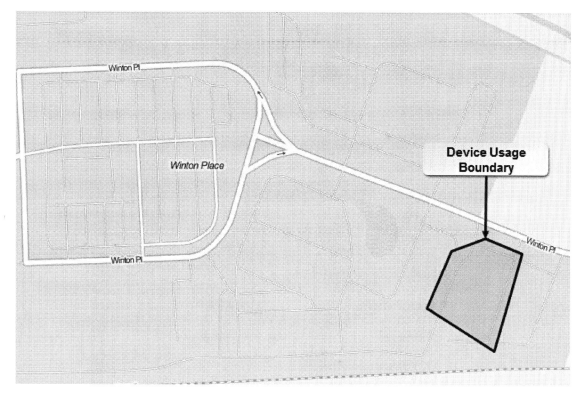

Figure 2–3: An inventory control geo-fence that surrounds an office.

You should understand the importance of asset management in the context of your organization's technology life cycle. In every phase of the cycle, your technology may be in many different states and pass through many different hands. Keeping the technology secure can prove difficult in light of this, which is why you should include considerations for each phase in your management protocols. For example, keep track of who is authorized to use the technology at the planning and design phase, and likewise adapt this to whomever receives the technology when it is deployed. This will aid you in establishing accountability should the technology succumb to its risks.

Software Development Methods

In collaborative software development environments, IT professionals tend to follow an overarching process of designing, developing, and maintaining software. These software development methods are meant to streamline efforts across a life cycle to make a product as efficient and economical as possible. There are several approaches to software development, each with their own structure. Three of the most common methodologies are waterfall, agile, and spiral. Since security is essential to the SDLC, these methodologies likewise bring about their own security implications. You should be aware of these implications so that you may adjust your security design throughout the life cycle.

Method	Description
Waterfall	The phases of a life cycle cascade so that each phase will start only when all tasks identified in the previous phase are complete. There are generally five phases in the waterfall method: requirements, design, implementation, verification, and maintenance. The phases are executed sequentially and do not overlap. The waterfall method is best suited for projects where time is not a significant constraint. Because each phase cannot proceed without an all-clear in the previous phase, this method is economical in that issues found early are much easier and cheaper to fix.
	However, the rigidity of the waterfall method may negatively impact your security efforts. Because requirements change, especially in an ever-evolving threat landscape, the waterfall method cannot account for an incomplete requirements phase that you plan to elaborate on later. In fact, your security concerns may end up changing at any phase of the process, which makes the waterfall method unsuitable for a modular approach.
Agile	This method focuses on adaptive measures in various phases—such as requirements—so that development teams can more easily collaborate and respond to changes. The agile method breaks up tasks incrementally, so that there is no long-term planning, but only short iterations that developers can more easily alter to fit their evolving needs. At the end of each iteration, developers present their progress to stakeholders to receive feedback and input that they can use in proceeding iterations. The agile method is particularly useful in complex, unstable systems whose requirements and design are not easy to predict.
	However, the agile method's focus on rapid development often undermines security. Developers may be releasing new code every week, or even every day. Introducing new, untested functionality at this rate makes it difficult to keep up with vulnerabilities and threat vectors, and security may end up as just an afterthought.
Spiral	Development teams combine several approaches to software development, such as incremental and waterfall, into a single hybrid method. Development is modified repeatedly in response to stakeholder feedback and input, but still follows an overall beginning-to-end structure. This is most useful for large, complex, and expensive projects, as the spiral method imposes risk analysis at each iterative step.
	Despite this, the security issues of its component methods likewise affect the spiral method; once again, incorporating security from the very beginning and at all phases of the development life cycle is a must.

Guidelines for Implementing Security Activities Throughout the Technology Life Cycle

Use the following guidelines to implement security in all phases of your organization's technology life cycle:

- Know the technologies being deployed and their risk profiles.
- Integrate security controls into each phase of the SDLC to minimize risk.
- Use security-minded SDLC frameworks like SSDLC and SDL to achieve security by design.
- Construct SRTMs to trace security requirements and their effectiveness in the life cycle.
- Identify aging technology.
- Adapt solutions to address emerging threats and security trends to keep technology from becoming obsolete.

- Implement security activities like decommissioning, asset disposal and reuse, maintenance, and change management in end-to-end solutions.
- Use RFID, geo-location, geo-tagging, and geo-fencing to exercise asset management and inventory control on all enterprise technology.
- Know the state and ownership of all technology as it goes through its life cycle phases.
- Choose a software development method that suits your project's size, complexity, and mutability.
- Understand the security pitfalls of the waterfall, agile, and spiral methods before using them.

ACTIVITY 2-3
Implementing Security Activities Throughout the Technology Life Cycle

Scenario

Like most other organizations, Develetech has technology that goes through cycles instead of remaining static. Throughout the life cycle of systems, software, networks, and other components, you will need to make sure that security is not ignored. Securing technology once is little better than not securing it at all; you need to anticipate changes in your technology to guarantee that your organization is protected not just now, but in the future.

1. Which of the following are phases or principles of most SDLCs? (Select three.)

   ☐ Validation and acceptance testing.

   ☐ Post-deployment maintenance.

   ☐ Deployment and implementation.

   ☐ Risk mitigation.

2. How will creating a Security Requirements Traceability Matrix (SRTM) help the requirements building phase of your SDLC model?

3. Your IT colleagues have determined that your server hardware is out of date, so they've begun the process of replacing it with more current systems. They've also determined that the old hardware is not salvageable or otherwise of any use, so they move to throw it out. Before they go through with this, what security activity do you need to remind them to take to ensure proper end-to-end solution handling?

4. In asset management, what is the process of creating geographic boundaries to prevent devices from working within or outside of certain areas?

   ○ Geo-location

   ○ Geo-tagging

   ○ Geo-fencing

   ○ Radio-frequency identification (RFID)

5. In software development, whether your team uses a waterfall, agile, or spiral method, what are the best security principles to follow? (Select two.)

   ☐ Implement security measures as issues arise.

   ☐ Incorporate security at the beginning of the development life cycle.

   ☐ Incorporate security at every phase of the development life cycle.

   ☐ Incorporate security after development ends.

Summary

In this lesson, you aided collaboration across many different departments in your enterprise, secured the solutions used in collaboration and communication, and guaranteed that technology in your enterprise is secure throughout all phases of its life cycle. With these skills, you can apply your security in a business-oriented capacity.

Does your company allow BYOD? If yes, what sort of security policies do you have in place? If not, why?

What strategies does your company use for decommissioning or disposing of assets?

 Note: Check your CHOICE Course screen for opportunities to interact with your classmates, peers, and the larger CHOICE online community about the topics covered in this course or other topics you are interested in. From the Course screen you can also access available resources for a more continuous learning experience.

3 Using Research and Analysis to Secure the Enterprise

Lesson Time: 1 hour

Lesson Objectives

In this lesson, you will:

- Determine industry trends and effects on the enterprise.

- Analyze scenarios to secure the enterprise.

Lesson Introduction

A CASP cannot uphold the security of their organization if they do not conduct their own research. Without continual research, you'd be relying on possibly outdated knowledge that could negatively affect the viability of your business. This is due in no small part to the always-changing threat climate, and the similarly dynamic security industry. Likewise, unless you can analyze the systems and other components that make up your enterprise, your research will not provide any valuable insight into how you can improve your security. This is why it is so important to stay up-to-date on both the state of the industry and your own enterprise.

TOPIC A

Determine Industry Trends and Effects on the Enterprise

Like other IT industries, the security industry is always in motion, and what may have been applicable at one point in time could now be obsolete. To make sure these changes don't pass your organization by, you need to determine the ways in which the security industry trends toward certain solutions or practices. This will help you identify the effects these changes have on your enterprise, so that you may adapt and ensure the continued security of your business for the immediate future.

Ongoing Research

Security is an ongoing process, never a finished task. The threats that target your enterprise will not stay static, but will constantly evolve to circumvent your efforts. To stay up-to-date on the current threat and vulnerability climate, it's absolutely vital that you conduct ongoing research into all areas that have the potential to put your business at risk. The more informed you are, the better equipped you will be to meet your organization's diverse business and operational needs.

Before you consult with the wide variety of security resources available, you should be aware of the best practices that guide good research:

- Seek out industry-accepted and vetted sources for information, including major regulatory and standards agencies like the National Institute of Standards and Technology (NIST), SANS, and ISACA.
- Subscribe to a security mailing list like Bugtraq and read up on reported threats frequently.
- Follow social media, like forums and discussion groups, geared toward information security.
- Stay current on discovered vulnerabilities by consulting a database like the *Common Vulnerabilities and Exposures (CVE)* database.
- Follow announcements by security vendors on their websites, especially major vendors like Microsoft® or other vendors you do business with.
- Exercise discretion with unverified sources or untested advice, and beware of social engineering hoaxes.
- Don't settle for one source—corroborate information across several distinct sources.

Figure 3–1: An example of a reputable security resource on the Internet.

A shrewd researcher who keeps these best practices in mind will be able to separate fact from fiction, and be empowered to use shared knowledge to their advantage in the enterprise.

Situational Awareness

The ability to comprehend the business ramifications of constantly evolving threats and vulnerabilities requires a thorough understanding of the enterprise environment. The concept of *situational awareness*, which can be applied to both business and technological aspects of the enterprise, is an understanding or perception of your environment. With this awareness, you can more effectively combat future threats and vulnerabilities.

Situational awareness is an important skill for a CASP to develop through ongoing analysis of data collection logs, use of the latest technologies and systems, and continuous research into new threats and vulnerabilities. For example, say you discover a new vulnerability in the operating system that many of your servers run. You also find an exploit on an Internet threat list that could target these servers. With situational awareness, you're able to survey the impact that an attack could have based on your knowledge of the enterprise network. The way your servers are configured, you determine that this particular exploit could cause a privilege escalation condition, so you move to secure your network and prevent unauthorized access. Constant vigilance makes it easier for you to meet new and emerging challenges.

Situational Awareness Considerations

The following table lists some of the more significant considerations that could affect your level of situational awareness.

Consideration	Description
Emergent threats, issues, and vulnerabilities	The amount of vulnerabilities and the threats that exploit them grows significantly over time, with new ones identified daily. You should improve your knowledge of current vulnerabilities and threats by visiting news sites, security blogs, and consulting the CVE on a regular basis.
Client-side attacks	Web browsers are highly vulnerable to attacks. For example, cross-site scripting (XSS) and privilege escalation exploits are very common due to vulnerabilities in the Java Runtime Environment (JRE) installed on most browsers. Whether it's your own employees, or customers using your website, you should be aware of how these latest client-side attacks can cause security issues in your environment.
Zero day attacks	A zero day attack targets a previously unknown vulnerability that has yet to be patched by the vendor. This is the point when the system's security is at its lowest level, making zero day attacks very difficult to counter. Close communication with vendors and others affected by these vulnerabilities is essential to getting zero day vulnerabilities resolved.

Technology Evolution

When protecting the business, staying up-to-date on the newest threats is only part of the solution. Staying up-to-date on new technologies, security systems, and services is another critical piece. *Technology evolution* is the ongoing process of creative destruction that replaces older technologies and systems with newer ones that more adequately meet changing business needs. Some security technologies that are relatively new and/or emerging in the business world are:

- Continuous monitoring.
- Security information and event management (SIEM).
- Risk intelligence.
- Compliance assessment.

New technologies go through a rigorous testing process as they grow and are developed. The main process that new technologies go through is the *Request for Comments (RFC)* process. The RFC process was designed during the early creation of the Internet to help organize new information and ideas. Based around the idea of peer review, the RFC process itself has evolved over time, and now serves as a testing ground for new ideas and technologies relating to the Internet. Each new proposal goes through a rigorous testing period before the *Internet Engineering Task Force (IETF)* approves these technologies. As a CASP, you should research the RFC proposals that are relevant to your enterprise concerns.

While the RFC process deals with the Internet specifically, another important element of technology evolution is the *International Organization for Standardization (ISO)*. The ISO is designed to help create a series of standards that governments and industries can adhere to in order to have common guidelines for processes and operations at the international level. Each new standard goes through several phases before it is finalized. You'll likely want to ensure that your technology is in compliance with ISO security standards, as most governments and private industries accept its authority in matters of standardization.

Technology Research Groups

Most new technologies these days are developed with a target market in mind, and the security field is no different. New technologies, products, and services that can help secure businesses better and more efficiently are constantly being developed. However, it can be challenging to keep current with new developments, as new releases do not always make it to news sites. In these situations, analyst groups can provide an incredibly valuable service. These groups keep up-to-date on new companies entering markets, and can provide comparisons and contrasts between products and services. Groups such as Gartner (**www.gartner.com**) and the 451 Research Group (**https://**

451research.com) have dedicated analysts that constantly stay in touch with companies in their fields, and provide analysis on these new technologies and services. While analyst groups usually charge for their services, a subscription to these groups can help a CASP stay up-to-date on services that can make their jobs easier.

New Business Tools

Social media and social networking are not just tools for individuals; businesses can also use them to great effect. As our society becomes more connected, businesses must also adapt to the changing technology and connect with their customers. Using social media properly can have a drastic impact on the success of the business, as it allows for more thorough feedback from customers and lets the business communicate directly to individuals. This effectively enhances the organization's presence in the marketplace.

The two social media channels that have the most integration within the business are Facebook and Twitter, and each channel serves a different purpose. Using Facebook can help to keep the business's name in front of customers, and is an excellent place to give discounts for interacting and for updates on what the business is doing. Twitter, on the other hand, is a valuable tool for communicating directly with customers individually. For example, many major airlines and Internet service providers (ISPs) monitor Twitter for tweets complaining about service, and offer speedy support to help make customers' experiences better. While it does require more interaction on the part of the business, using social media in the business strategy can provide exponential benefits.

Another relatively new business tool is end user cloud storage. Apps like Dropbox and OneDrive provide free cloud-based storage space to individuals, while also offering premium subscriptions that increase or altogether remove size limitations. Employees often use these services to back up important work files, or to maintain a repository for easy file retrieval across disparate devices and locations.

Figure 3-2: Social media used as a marketing tool.

Security Implications of New Business Tools

While business tools like Facebook and Twitter can be incredibly powerful and useful, you should not ignore the security implications of integrating them within the organization. It is important that you research the security and privacy features of each tool, especially if your non-security personnel are going to be using them. Public-facing social media websites may provide an otherwise unattainable platform for sharing information, but for a business, this may lead to oversharing of sensitive information. Monitor these social media channels closely, and ensure the employees that use them comply with best security practices, like password length and complexity.

Just as you would research social media, you should identify how certain cloud-based storage apps can impact your enterprise. If a storage service fails to provide adequate levels of encryption, for example, your employees could be placing sensitive information into an insecure offsite environment. This is why you should carefully regulate, through policies and other documentation, how a cloud storage service should and should not be used.

Global IA Industry and Community

There exists a global community of security professionals who seek to protect information through confidentiality, integrity, availability, authenticity, and non-repudiation. This concept is known as *information assurance (IA)*. To safeguard your information properly, you should consult with and participate in this community. The following table outlines some of the components of the IA industry/community that you can glean useful information from.

Component	Description
Computer emergency response team (CERT)	A CERT is a team of security professionals that responds to computer-related incidents that threaten the enterprise. There are several well-known CERT teams, like the CERT Division and the United States Computer Emergency Readiness Team (US-CERT) that partner with diverse industries to enhance their cybersecurity and to disseminate key security information to the public.
Conventions/ conferences	Beyond online sources, there is a wealth of information in face-to-face communications as well. Nearly every week, there are conferences all across the globe in varying sizes, from a few dozen participants to thousands. Each of these conferences has their own focus, and can be incredibly valuable for a CASP. While the line is blurring, there are two main types of security conferences: hacker conferences and business conferences. Hacker conferences are usually more technical and involve the cutting edge of research. Some popular examples are: • DEFCON (**www.defcon.org**) • HOPE (**www.hope.net**) • DerbyCon (**www.derbycon.com**) • ShmooCon (**www.shmoocon.org**) Other conferences and conventions focus on the business impact of various threats and security vulnerabilities. Some examples are: • BlackHat (**www.blackhat.com**) • Source Conferences (**www.sourceconference.com**) • GFIRST **www.us-cert.gov/government-users/collaboration/gfirst**) • SecureWorld Expo (**www.secureworldpost.secureworldexpo.com**) Additionally, some conferences combine both of these flavors into one, creating a blended forum for discussing the latest and most interesting security issues.
Threat actors	Attackers themselves can also be an excellent source of information on the latest security threats. Hacker sites provide insight on the current and emerging threats and vulnerabilities that could affect your enterprise. Some hacker groups post information to social media sites like Twitter to broadcast their exploits. Even attackers that attend conventions might meet and discuss with security professionals about the latest discoveries. Although your motives differ, threat actors essentially use the same weapons and methods to attack a system as you do to protect it. Sun Tzu's adage of "know your enemy" is no less relevant to the world of information security.

Component	Description
Threat intelligence	Threat intelligence is the investigation and collection of emerging threats and emerging threat sources. Companies that provide threat intelligence at the forefront of security research to not only identify attacks, but attackers themselves. The following are examples of services that a CASP may find useful for staying vigilant in a threat climate that is always in motion: • McAfee Global Threat Intelligence (**www.mcafee.com/us/threat-center/technology/global-threat-intelligence-technology.aspx**) • SecureWorks Global Threat Intelligence (**www.secureworks.com/cyber-threat-intelligence/CTU_intelligence/**) • Recorded Future Cyber Threat Intelligence (**www.recordedfuture.com/cyber-threat-intelligence/**) • Verisign iDefense (**www.verisigninc.com/en_US/cyber-security/security-intelligence/threat-intelligence/index.xhtml**)

Security Requirements for Contracts

At some point, every business will need to deal with outside vendors and contractors in order to keep its ever-growing operations efficient and profitable. However, if a business does not go about requesting contractor information and financial quotes in the proper way, that business can end up wasting time and resources on a poorly integrated contract relationship. A CASP should ensure that each phase of this process keeps security in mind, as external contractors are not necessarily exposed to or beholden to the same security policies that internal employees are. Researching just what contract requirements are applicable to your security environment will keep your enterprise from being exposed to an unnecessary amount of risk.

The following table describes each phase of the contract requirement process and how security plays a role.

Phase	Contract Requirement	CASP Involvement
1	*Request for Information (RFI)*	The RFI presents the organization's need that it wants filled, and is distributed to likely contractors. RFIs typically ask candidates for their experience and qualifications to narrow down the search to the most appropriate matches. The RFI stage is occasionally skipped, as some companies prefer to do research on their own. During the RFI process, the CASP may not have a central role but should remain involved to make sure that the information being requested is relevant to security concerns. For example, a government agency will often ask candidates for their security clearance, especially if the relationship will involve handling sensitive information.

Phase	Contract Requirement	CASP Involvement
2	*Request for Proposal (RFP)*	The RFP asks candidates how they will be able to help the business by fulfilling the needs it stated in the RFI. This phase is where the majority of the decision making will be made. Like the RFI, the RFP acts as another way of narrowing down the field of prospective candidates. As a CASP, you should be very involved in this step of the process, especially if the business is evaluating new network or security equipment or services. Although the vendor may be able to provide exactly what your business is looking for at a great price, will their services and equipment create vulnerabilities in your enterprise?
3	*Request for Quote (RFQ)*	The RFQ is where money finally starts to enter into the contract process. After the RFP has narrowed down the final contenders, the RFQ is sent to the remaining candidates to discuss the pricing of the solutions being offered. This step often relies on a lot of back and forth between the business and the proposed competitors to negotiate pricing. At this stage, accountants, procurement officers, and management play a key role as finances are worked out amongst the competing parties; while the CASP's role is less important since they are generally not the financial decision makers. However, a CASP may be involved in the testing of the solution during the trial period, which can fall in the RFQ stage.
4	Agreements	Once the pricing has been negotiated, it is important to ensure that both parties have equivalent expectations for the relationship. This is where service-level agreements (SLAs), operating-level agreements (OLAs), interconnection security agreements (ISAs), and other *interoperability agreements* come into play. Other than choosing the right agreement type, as a CASP, you need to stay current on how these agreements are typically drafted with respect to the security needs of your organization. What new security-related laws do both parties need to conform to? What newly discovered vulnerabilities do you need to account for?

Guidelines for Determining Industry Trends and Effects on the Enterprise

 Note: All Guidelines for this lesson are available as checklists from the **Checklist** tile on the CHOICE Course screen.

Use the following guidelines to help you determine how the evolving security industry can affect your enterprise:

- Consider security to always be ongoing and never finished.
- Conduct research frequently into new threats and vulnerabilities.
- Seek out reputable sources like industry regulators and standards organizations.
- Subscribe to social channels like mailing lists, forums, and discussion groups.
- Stay current on newly found vulnerabilities.

- Exercise discretion when consulting unverified sources.
- Stay aware of your enterprise environment and all of its weak points.
- Know how emerging threats, client-side attacks, and zero day exploits can affect your environment.
- Consult RFC proposals and ISO standards for low-level analyses of technology used in your enterprise.
- Draft policies on proper use of business tools like social media sites and cloud storage services.
- Caution employees against oversharing of sensitive information on social media.
- Choose cloud storage services with adequate levels of encryption.
- Consult services like a CERT or threat intelligence to stay current in the changing security climate.
- Attend security conferences and conventions to exchange ideas with others.
- Follow attacker sites and social media spaces to keep up-to-date on their actions.
- Research potential business partners to incorporate security requirements in contracts.

ACTIVITY 3-1
Determining Industry Trends and Effects on the Enterprise

Scenario

As the Chief Information Security Officer (CISO) of Develetech, you want to make sure that your security systems align with the current security climate. As part of a new initiative, you and your team will do research in various areas to gain a better awareness of your enterprise's security situation. You'll start by finding conferences and conventions you'd like your team to attend, and then you'll find security-minded blogs for them to keep up-to-date on. You'll also look up recent vulnerabilities you suspect might affect your systems, especially since you currently use OpenSSL to secure your web servers. Because Develetech is growing and expanding some of its infrastructure, you'll want to keep pace with evolving technology and its implications so that you'll be prepared for the future. All of this research will keep you and your team from falling behind in an industry that is always moving forward.

---

1. Find upcoming conferences and conventions.
   a) Open Internet Explorer® and navigate to *securityconferences.net*
   b) In the list under **Upcoming Conferences**, verify that several events will be taking place in the near future.
      Note that some events have deadlines for submitting papers and posters.
   c) Select any of the upcoming events to read a short description of that event.
   d) Select the link to the event's website to read more about the event. Try to identify the following information:
      - Where exactly the event takes place.
      - The expected number of attendees.
      - Who will host or be featured as a speaker at the event.
      - What particular subjects are on the docket.
      - Any call for papers, if applicable.
      - How to register for the event.
   e) Repeat this process for any other events that interest you.

2. Find information security blogs.
   a) Navigate to the search site of your choice and search for *security blogs*
   b) Select any of the results and skim some of the blog's most recent articles. Identify the author(s) and evaluate how security subjects are presented. Are the articles objective and free of bias? Do they rely on subjective accounts and experiences? Are they sensationalized? What else can you determine about the author(s)' experience and perspective?
   c) Repeat this process for some of the other blogs that were returned in your search.
   d) Share with the class what you've determined about each blog, and which ones, if any, seem like reputable and useful sources of information.

3. Consult a vulnerability database about the Heartbleed vulnerability.
   a) Navigate to *cve.mitre.org*
   b) From the navigation list on the left side of the CVE home page, under **CVE List**, select the **Search CVE** link.
   c) On the right, from the **CVE List Master Copy** section, select **Search Master Copy of CVE**.
   d) In the **Search Master Copy of CVE** section, in the **By Keywords(s)** text box, type *heartbleed*
   e) Under the text box you just typed in, select **Submit**.

f) Observe the description for the item in the list named **CVE-2014-0160**. A vulnerability exists in older versions of OpenSSL that allows attackers to send malicious packets to a server, potentially exposing sensitive information in plaintext.

g) Select the **CVE-2014-0160** link to get a more detailed look at the issue. Select any of the links in the **References** section to learn what caused the vulnerability and how it affects specific implementations of OpenSSL.

h) Search the CVE for any other specific or general vulnerability that interests you. Share your findings with the class.

4. Research issues related to evolving technology.

a) Navigate to *http://www.gartner.com/technology/research/top-10-technology-trends/*

 Note: If a message box pops up, select **OK**.

b) Identify the most significant emerging technologies of the year.

c) Select any of the article links to read an abstract.

d) Discuss your findings with the class. Will any of these emerging technologies have an effect on your organization's security? If so, how?

5. While Develetech's operations are growing, the marketing team would like to have a greater social media footprint. They plan on sharing information with customers via Twitter, Facebook, and YouTube. What measures should you take to ensure your organization's security when using these business tools? Can you think of any enterprise security incidents that resulted from these tools being used improperly?

6. Develetech is looking to expand its data storage infrastructure by implementing a Fibre Channel solution. This will give the organization greater speed and scalability in accessing and backing up its ever-growing pool of databases. The CEO has already sent out a Request for Information (RFI) to contractors who can provide Fibre Channel equipment and installation. Before he finalizes an agreement with any of the responding contractors, you convince the CEO to let you take time to consider security issues first. What will your focus be during the other contract phases?

7. Close Internet Explorer.

TOPIC B

Analyze Scenarios to Secure the Enterprise

Now that you're aware of the ways in which security and technology trends can affect your operations, you're ready to use techniques to analyze some common enterprise scenarios. These techniques will help you survey your current security state, as well as calculate and assess how changes can alter that state. Using this in-depth analysis of your operations, you'll be much more prepared to improve your security and reduce the risk your enterprise is exposed to.

Baselines and Benchmarks

A *security baseline* is a group of security configuration settings that apply to a particular system in the enterprise. In general, you create a baseline by measuring what the state of a system *should be* using metrics collection and analysis. These metrics should be relevant to the system and should be effective at measuring the performance of its configurations. The baseline is then used as a reference point in future analysis, as it helps you define the optimum level of security for any type of system. Because each baseline configuration is specific to a particular type of system, you will have separate baselines defined for desktop clients, file and print servers, Domain Name System (DNS)/BIND servers, application servers, directory services servers, and many other types of systems.

Related to the security baseline is the *security benchmark*. A benchmark is the current state of a system after it has run through some sort of performance or security-related test. For example, you might monitor your network's bandwidth usage and benchmark its traffic over a 24-hour period. The statistics you gather during this period, such as connection node counts, dropped packet frequency, and common destination points, will all factor into your overall network benchmark. You'll get a good approximation of how your network is performing on a day-to-day basis.

For truly effective analysis, you need to create benchmarks and compare them to baselines. The baseline security configurations for your network may use a network traffic metric to define an approximation of a normal day's web server traffic. When you run your benchmark this week, you notice that it has recorded traffic hitting the web server at an amount that greatly exceeds the baseline. This disparity may lead you to conclude that a DoS condition is likely, and you move to maintain your server's availability. Your comparison of the benchmark to its corresponding baseline has kept you more informed about the security concerns that affect your enterprise environment.

Windows Scan Results

Administrative Vulnerabilities

Score	Issue	Result
	Administrators	More than 2 Administrators were found on this computer.
		What was scanned Result details How to correct this
	Password Expiration	All user accounts (3) have non-expiring passwords.
		What was scanned Result details How to correct this
	Automatic Updates	Automatic Updates are managed through Group Policy on this computer.
		What was scanned
	Incomplete Updates	No incomplete software update installations were found.
		What was scanned
	Windows Firewall	Windows Firewall is managed through Group Policy on this computer and the policy has exceptions configured.
		What was scanned Result details How to correct this
	File System	All hard drives (1) are using the NTFS file system.
		What was scanned Result details
	Autologon	Autologon is not configured on this computer.
		What was scanned
	Guest Account	The Guest account is disabled on this computer.
		What was scanned
	Restrict Anonymous	Computer is properly restricting anonymous access.
		What was scanned
	Local Account Password Test	This check was skipped because user chose not to perform password checks during the scan.

Figure 3-3: A security benchmark report.

Prototyping and Testing

Prototyping and testing enterprise security solutions allows you to model one or more solution scenarios to test hardware and software tools, processes, policies, and procedures. Some or all software prototyping and testing can be carried out in your own enterprise application sandbox, depending on the size and resources of your organization and the business impact of the solution. Alternatively, you can request a prototyping and testing demonstration at vendor facilities, or request that the vendor demonstrate a security solution that another company has installed and that you are considering. A demonstration in a live enterprise environment can provide valuable insight into real-world usage without the added cost of setting up an environment of your own.

When planning a testing strategy, it is important to make sure that all of the key requirements for a new service are tested and evaluated. It is also imperative that a new solution has a breaking-in period before it is placed in a production environment to iron out any quirks that the new business environment might cause. Begin adding more users and load them into the new solution, and monitor it carefully. Look at the problems that this new solution was supposed to solve, and test specific use cases against that new solution. At the same time, continue to increase the amount of stress that the new solution is under.

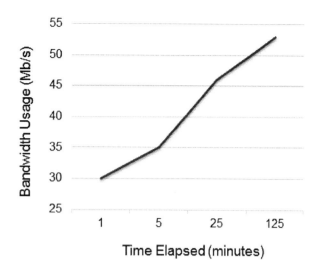

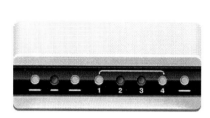

Figure 3–4: Stress testing a network appliance.

Example

You want to test a new network appliance. Using network monitors and packet capturing tools, you can generate an amount of traffic that is capable of pushing the limits of the new appliance. If these limits are well under what you require to maintain your network availability, then you'll know that the appliance should not yet be introduced to your enterprise. On the other hand, you test a different network appliance that fulfills the same basic role and discover that it responds much more strongly to the stress test. This device remains a candidate, and you can continue with more tests before you make a decision. When you prototype and test multiple solutions, you facilitate a safer and more effective security analysis.

CBA

Security solutions that meet the needs of the business must also meet cost-benefit requirements associated with implementing and maintaining them. A *cost-benefit analysis (CBA)* is the process of determining whether the cost of a solution outweighs its benefit to the organization. If it does, then the organization's stakeholders may conclude that the solution is not viable and should be removed or depreciated. So, in searching for hardware and software solutions that will fit your security needs, you will also need to seek out solutions that is priced reasonably and provides sufficient benefits.

ROI and TCO

In performing a CBA, you should calculate a *return on investment (ROI)*. The ROI determines how much money or benefit will be gained in relation to the amount of money that is being spent. When deciding on solutions for the business, ROI is the way to determine what percentage of money will be returned from the solution, and it uses the following equation in its simplest form:

ROI = (Gain from investment / Money spent on investment) * 100

For example, if you spend approximately $1,000 on an intrusion prevention system (IPS), and your IPS halts an intrusion that could have cost you $5,000 in stolen data, then your ROI would be 500%. Although it can be difficult to accurately quantify the gains made from a security investment, having even a general ROI for a given solution can help you present a new solution to the business from a cost-benefit perspective.

In many cases, an ROI is not enough to craft an effective cost-benefit analysis. As you compare one solution with another, you will want to compare the total cost of implementing and maintaining those solutions; that is, the acquisition cost *and* the operating cost. This is a concept called *total cost of ownership (TCO)*. With our IPS example, there might be added costs associated with technical support, license renewal, and server maintenance. The TCO of each solution will allow you to more objectively evaluate costs of similar solutions from different vendors, as well as provide a more accurate picture of their ROI.

 Note: To learn more about determining the utility of a security control, access the LearnTO **Conduct a Cost-Benefit Analysis** presentation from the **LearnTO** tile on the CHOICE Course screen.

Trend Data

As a CASP, one of your greatest strengths will be the ability to stay informed about the general direction of the information security field. While looking at individual events can provide focused information, looking at all of the data as a whole can expose important trends. These trends can help a CASP gain information not only on the threats that the business is currently facing, but also what threats may be coming in the future and what countermeasures are emerging to deal with them. You should be able to analyze and interpret trend data to anticipate the cyber-defense needs of your organization, and stay one step ahead of the attackers.

Figure 3-5: The percentage of vulnerabilities reported in different areas of security over a three-year period.

To notice trends on the horizon, you must constantly absorb new information about technological advances. Attending conferences, listening to podcasts, reading blog posts, and staying engaged on social media all contribute to a larger awareness of the emerging threat and defense climates. While analyst groups and news sources may also discuss what their predictions are for the future, it is up to you, the CASP, to decide what actions to take based on your own high-level research. Identifying trends requires more than just passive absorption of information, however. You need to exercise careful judgment to separate the signal from the noise, and to avoid being tripped up by misleading information, distractions, and other pitfalls of poor critical thinking.

Note: Critical thinking skills are essential to any kind of research and analysis, with security included. For a list of logical fallacies that impede critical thinking, visit **http:// en.wikipedia.org/wiki/List_of_fallacies**

Remember, security should not be reactive, but proactive; this could mean the difference between scrambling to mitigate a security incident and not suffering the incident at all.

Review Existing Security

Before purchasing new solutions, it is important that current security solutions are providing the most benefit possible. Consistent security reviews ensure that the ROI of current security products continues to increase, which will please the business stakeholders, as well as increase the overall security of the organization. You should, at a minimum, conduct yearly internal reviews of security systems and check them against internal security policies to see if the systems continue to meet standards. In some cases, external methods may be necessary to properly verify that your security controls are meeting policy requirements.

Depending on the level of review needed, different solutions are available.

Review Method	Description
Vulnerability assessment	Vulnerability assessments usually incorporate automated tools that run against the entire network. Vulnerability scanners can have high false positive rates, so it is important to manually verify that the results the tool provides are actually risks to the organization.
Penetration test	Penetration tests are a more in-depth assessment method that is performed by an individual or team against the network. Penetration testers can use methods of attack that cannot be simply automated, such as social engineering and physical security assessments.
Full internal audit	Audits will review not only the current systems in place, but also the processes behind those systems. Certain security standards, such as the Payment Card Industry Data Security Standard (PCI DSS), require certified auditors to come onsite and verify that security policies meet their standards. Auditors will often review the results of penetration tests and vulnerability reports to gain a more complete understanding of the environment, and may even require those tests be done if they are not already in place.

Reverse Engineering

Reverse engineering is the process of analyzing a system's structure in order to reveal more about how it functions. In the sense of enterprise security technology, reverse engineering allows you to deconstruct existing solutions to their basest level. Although this process is usually used in the context of software, you can also reverse engineer hardware. Reverse engineering is a valuable tool when dealing with solutions that may no longer be supported by vendors, or when attempting to determine vulnerabilities in a system.

Some solutions are easier to deconstruct than others. For example, the nature of the class files in the Java™ programming language allows them to be easily decompiled into source code. Apps written in Java can therefore be reverse engineered with freely available, easy-to-use tools. However, hardware can be difficult to reverse engineer due to the complexity of integrated circuits and the expensiveness of automated tools.

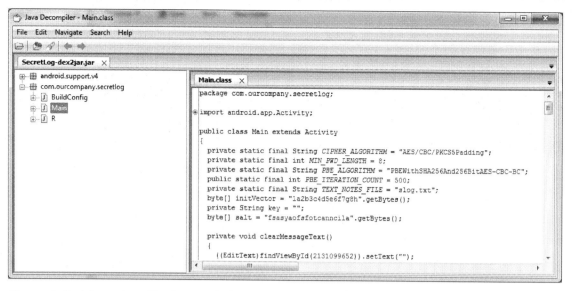

Figure 3-6: A Java class file decompiled to reveal an approximation of its source code.

 Note: To learn more about how you can reverse engineer an app, access the LearnTO **Use Java Reverse Engineering Tools** presentation from the **LearnTO** tile on the CHOICE Course screen.

Solution Attributes

Evaluating the effectiveness and ROI of a solution can be an involved, complex process. If you only think of technology in one-dimensional terms as it relates to your enterprise, then you'll miss crucial factors that could impact your operations. Most solutions have a wide variety of attributes that you should analyze to meet business needs, whether you're implementing new solutions or reviewing ones in place. The following table describes the general attributes of enterprise security solutions.

Attribute	Description
Performance	The performance of a solution is how much work it can accomplish in a given time, or with a certain amount of resources. Performance is often understood as an umbrella term that incorporates other attributes like availability, capability, and latency into one whole benchmark.
Availability	Availability is a fundamental component of security that you should be familiar with. If your solution isn't available or impacts the availability of other systems in your enterprise, then your business needs cannot be met. If servers that host intrusion detection systems (IDSs) routinely go down, then this will defeat the purpose of having a constant, uninterrupted network monitor.
Capability	Capability is what a solution can do within its intended purpose. A firewall, for example, has the capability to allow certain types of data traffic to pass through the firewall while denying other types of data traffic. If your solution is missing a feature that your business needs, it will not be as capable as a different solution.

Attribute	Description
Latency	Latency is the reaction time of a solution. A firewall might be very quick to read and analyze data packets under baseline conditions, but under attack, its processor might be delayed as it keeps up with analyzing and transmitting allowed traffic due to the high volume of rejected traffic. Solutions that lag behind might prove ineffectual against carefully-orchestrated attacks that can quickly devastate an enterprise.
Scalability	Scalability allows a solution to expand with changing conditions. For example, an enterprise risk assessment system that is scalable can measure and report changes in risk as you add or remove devices, applications, and other network resources from the enterprise. Without scalability, a solution that works properly now may become useless in the future as your organization develops.
Usability	Usability refers to how easy or difficult a device or system is to learn and use. For example, a scripting interface for one vendor's routers and switches might have a more user-friendly interface than that of another vendor's. If the learning curve of a solution is too steep, then your employees will have difficulty using it, limiting its effectiveness.
Maintainability	Maintainability refers to how much upkeep or maintenance a solution requires, as well as how easy or difficult it is to maintain the solution. For example, installing updates like patches and bug fixes might be a very easy, automated process in some devices, but a tedious, manual process in others. If your team cannot feasibly maintain a device as it ages, it may be more of a hassle than it's worth.
Recoverability	Recoverability allows a solution to reactivate in the event it crashes or is otherwise deactivated unexpectedly. A database that routinely backs up its data will be able to recover from an attack or accidental crash quickly, while keeping sensitive information from being lost. If certain key solutions have no ability to recover from unforeseen events, they will be a liability to the enterprise.

After-Action Report

An *after-action report (AAR)*, or *lessons learned report (LLR)*, includes an analysis of security events and incidents that can provide insight into directions you may take to enhance security for the future. Not only should you document what happened during an incident and how you responded, but afterward you should also document what this incident means for your security. Essentially, you will be identifying the elements of your security that need improving, and how you can go about improving them in the best way possible. The more you learn from your successes and mistakes, the more fine-tuned your judgment will be. This is an invaluable skill to have, especially if you're called on to solve complex, open-ended problems.

The meat of the after-action report comes in answering a few simple questions:

- First, what actions did you take?
- Is this the optimal solution? In other words, is the solution that you used a stop-gap measure, or is this something that you could reproduce consistently and use as a policy?
- Are there more capable solutions out there?
- How did the teams react to the issue? Could they have solved the incident more quickly or efficiently?
- In the event of the same or a similar incident occurring, how would you respond differently?
- Do the answers to these questions necessitate a change in security policy?

These are just a few of the questions that you should ask when writing an AAR.

Guidelines for Analyzing Scenarios to Secure the Enterprise

Use the following guidelines for your enterprise security analysis:

- Create a separate security baseline for each system.
- Use relevant and effective metrics for measuring configurations in a baseline.
- Routinely conduct benchmarks on systems to see if they align with the security baseline.
- Prototype and test multiple solutions before implementing them.
- Request that a vendor demonstrate a live environment test.
- Determine the return on investment and total cost of ownership of each solution to ensure they meet cost-benefit requirements.
- Collate information from various sources to see high-level trends in security.
- Exercise critical thinking and skepticism before trusting unverified information.
- Review the effectiveness of existing security controls.
- Perform vulnerability assessments, penetration tests, and full internal audits.
- Use judgment to solve difficult problems that do not have a best solution.
- Reverse engineer systems to analyze their behavior, when possible.
- Write an after-action report and detail any lessons learned from an incident.
- Think of questions to ask that pertain to improving your security.
- Analyze security solution attributes to ensure they meet business needs.
- Automate best practice implementation through scripts.

ACTIVITY 3-2
Analyzing Scenarios to Secure the Enterprise

Data Files

C:\093023Data\Using Research and Analysis to Secure the Enterprise\MBSASetup-x64-EN.msi

C:\093023Data\Using Research and Analysis to Secure the Enterprise\DC-baseline.mbsa

Before You Begin

You will be using Microsoft Baseline Security Analyzer (MBSA) to benchmark your domain controller. A baseline scan has already been performed on an ideal domain controller.

Scenario

As Develetech expands its operations and personnel internationally, the IT team is coordinating an effort to establish new domain controllers. As the CISO, you want to ensure that these mission-critical servers are hardened to meet your security standards. Using your company's original, primary domain controller as a baseline, you'll benchmark these new servers and compare them to the baseline. This will allow you to conduct an analysis to determine what needs to change on each new domain controller so that it conforms to your ideal specifications. You will use the Microsoft Baseline Security Analyzer (MBSA) tool to compare your current DC configuration to a baseline that has already been run. You will then analyze the results of this benchmark and identify where you can improve security to match the standard set by the baseline DC.

---

1. Install the MBSA.
   a) Open File Explorer and navigate to **C:\093023Data\Using Research and Analysis to Secure the Enterprise**.
   b) Double-click the **MBSASetup-x64-EN** file.
   c) In the **Open File - Security Warning** message box, select **Run**.
   d) In the **MBSA Setup** wizard, select **Next**.
   e) On the **License Agreement** page, select **I accept the license agreement** and select **Next**.
   f) On the **Destination Folder** page, select **Next** to accept the default folder.
   g) On the **Start Installation** page, select **Install**.
   h) In the **MBSA Setup** message box, select **OK**.

2. View the baseline report within MBSA.
   a) In File Explorer, copy the **DC-baseline** file to **C:\Users\Administrator\SecurityScans**, then close File Explorer.

    Note: You will need to create the **SecurityScans** folder.

   b) On the desktop, double-click the **Microsoft Baseline Security Analyzer 2.3** shortcut to open it.

c) In the **Microsoft Baseline Security Analyzer 2.3** window, in the **Tasks** section, select the **View security reports** link.

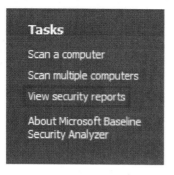

d) On the **Choose a security scan report to view** page, under the **Computer Name** column, select DOMAIN100\SERVER100.

e) Scroll down and review the security issues that the baseline checked for. Read the results for each issue.

Administrative Vulnerabilities

Score	Issue	Result
	Automatic Updates	Updates are not automatically downloaded or installed on this computer.
		What was scanned How to correct this
	Incomplete Updates	No incomplete software update installations were found.
		What was scanned
	Windows Firewall	Windows Firewall is enabled and has exceptions configured. Windows Firewall is enabled on all network connections.
		What was scanned Result details How to correct this
	File System	All hard drives (1) are using the NTFS file system.
		What was scanned Result details
	Autologon	Autologon is not configured on this computer.
		What was scanned
	Guest Account	The Guest account is disabled on this computer.
		What was scanned
	Restrict Anonymous	Computer is properly restricting anonymous access.
		What was scanned
	Administrators	No more than 2 Administrators were found on this computer.
		What was scanned Result details
	Password Expiration	All user accounts that were scanned do not have non-expiring passwords.
		What was scanned
	Local Account Password Test	This check was skipped because user chose not to perform password checks during the scan.

Additional System Information

Score	Issue	Result
	Auditing	Logon Success and Logon Failure auditing are both enabled.
		What was scanned
	Services	No potentially unnecessary services were found.
		What was scanned

3. Scan your domain controller.

a) At the top left of the window, select the **Back** button twice.

b) In the **Tasks** pane, select **Scan a computer**.

c) Verify that your computer name appears in the **Computer name** drop-down list, and uncheck all of the check boxes under **Options** except for **Check for Windows administrative vulnerabilities**.

Options:

- ☑ Check for <u>W</u>indows administrative vulnerabilities
- ☐ Check for wea<u>k</u> passwords
- ☐ Check for IIS administrative <u>v</u>ulnerabilities
- ☐ Check for S<u>Q</u>L administrative vulnerabilities
- ☐ Check for s<u>e</u>curity updates
  - ☐ Configure computers for Microsoft <u>U</u>pdate and scanning prerequisites
  - ☐ Advanced Update Services <u>o</u>ptions:
    - ○ Scan using <u>a</u>ssigned Windows Server Update Services(WSUS) servers only
    - ○ Scan using <u>M</u>icrosoft Update only
    - ○ Scan using o<u>f</u>fline catalog only

d) Select **Start Scan**.

4. Compare your DC benchmark to the baseline.

   a) Select the **Back** button twice and select **View security reports**.

   b) On the **Choose a security scan report to view** page, next to the **Sort order** drop-down list, select the **Click here to see all security reports** link.

   <u>S</u>ort order: | Scan date (descending) ▼ | Click here to see all security reports

   c) From the report list, select the earliest report (the baseline).

   d) At the bottom of the **Microsoft Baseline Security Analyzer 2.3** window, select the **Previous security report** link. ⬛ Previous security report

   e) Switch back and forth between the two reports and compare your benchmark to the baseline. Select any **What was scanned** or **How to correct this** link to view the security recommendations reported by MBSA.

5. What are some of the vulnerable areas of your domain controller that fail to meet the baseline? How could these discrepancies lead to a security issue?

6. Close the **Microsoft Baseline Security Analyzer 2.3** window.

Summary

In this lesson, you researched and determined how the information technology and security industry is evolving, and identified how these changes may positively or negatively impact your enterprise's risk profile. You then analyzed your enterprise operations in the context of common security scenarios, as well as changes brought on by industry trends. Keeping your knowledge of security and technology current, as well as keeping your knowledge of your business operations current, will go a long way toward securing the enterprise in an ever-changing climate.

What security resources do you, or will you, consult in your enterprise duties?

What types of analysis procedures and testing do you do in your enterprise?

 Note: Check your CHOICE Course screen for opportunities to interact with your classmates, peers, and the larger CHOICE online community about the topics covered in this course or other topics you are interested in. From the Course screen you can also access available resources for a more continuous learning experience.

4 Integrating Advanced Authentication and Authorization Techniques

Lesson Time: 1 hour, 45 minutes

Lesson Objectives

In this lesson, you will:

- Implement authentication and authorization technologies.

- Implement advanced identity management.

Lesson Introduction

In the previous lessons, you focused on the conceptual security factors that are under your domain as a CASP. Now, you'll begin to implement specific security techniques and configurations that will keep your enterprise safe from threats. In this lesson, you'll use enterprise-focused authentication and authorization protocols to manage the many users and devices that need to be verified before they are allowed access to your important company resources.

TOPIC A

Implement Authentication and Authorization Technologies

Authentication and authorization are your enterprise's gatekeepers, and they can be implemented in many different ways depending on your business needs. Many companies will have some authentication mechanism for controlling access to specific resources, while structuring that access in levels of authorization. This keeps everyday use of your systems secure continuously. In this topic, you'll implement authentication and authorization schemes that are tailored for enterprise use.

Authentication

Authentication is the method of validating a particular entity or individual's unique credentials. Authentication concentrates on identifying if a particular individual has the right credentials to enter a system or secure site. Advanced authentication covers the complex processes required to authenticate users, grant permissions, and control access to resources across a wide array of interconnected network domains, hardware resources, applications, and services. Even a single organization can have many different logical networks and resources to which access must be strictly granted and provisioned. This gets exponentially more complex as organizations open satellite locations, support remote users, or attempt to combine parts of their networks with other organization's assets.

For instance, enterprises often deal with important and sensitive customer data that needs to be protected from attacks. Within an enterprise, there is the larger potential for breaches and violations, as the demand for information is high and there are more access points through which information can be obtained. At the enterprise level, the cost of poor authentication could be devastating. This is why it is important to take advantage of the frameworks that are available for advanced authentication.

Figure 4–1: Password–based authentication.

Certificate–Based Authentication

In a *certificate-based authentication* framework, certificate authorities (CAs) and digital certificates provide a number of cryptographic guarantees. Servers and clients are able to verify each others' authenticity by requesting digital certificates that prove the subject's identity. For example, a CA issues a web server a certificate, implying that the CA trusts the server. When a client connects to the web server through their browser, they will receive its certificate. If the client trusts the CA, then a web of trust is formed between the three entities, allowing authentication to take place. In this kind of authentication scheme, certificates are often generated for each user and service within a network, who then use the certificates to authenticate a variety of actions, privileges, and requests.

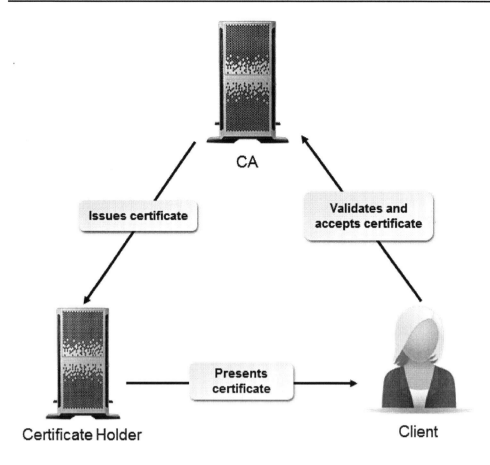

Figure 4-2: Certificate-based authentication.

The use of certificated-based authentication provides a number of strong security properties for an enterprise. First, every client can be assured of the server they are communicating with, and every server can be assured that they are dealing with a legitimate client. Second, the ability to revoke certificates can quickly lock out compromised user accounts or services that would otherwise pose security risks to an organization and its data. Third, the use of certificates avoids security issues present when users are left to provide their own authentication mechanisms, such as passwords, which can be weak or stolen by attackers through a number of attack methods.

 Note: To learn how to establish a CA in your Windows Server 2012 R2 domain, access the LearnTO **Install a Certificate Authority** presentation from the **LearnTO** tile on the CHOICE Course screen.

SSO

Another major advanced authentication technique is *single sign-on (SSO)*. SSO allows a user to authenticate once and receive access to a number of related but independent software systems, without having to sign in again when accessing each specific system. For example, if the Active Directory® service is deployed in a Windows® environment, the user is not prompted to re-authenticate because Active Directory-aware applications retrieve Kerberos service tickets automatically.

 Note: Kerberos is described later in this topic.

SSO has several benefits to an enterprise over traditional separate login systems, and the roaming authentication provided by SSO is performed transparently to the user. The first benefit of SSO is that compromised credentials can be quickly regained by a single action. Similarly, the burden of logging and monitoring user logins can be greatly reduced by having a central server delegate credentials and approve access. Although the process of logging in may seem instant, a large enterprise with many employees will lose time if the employees constantly need to log in to access separate systems. This also makes it easier on the user, as they aren't required to remember as many passwords.

The use of SSO requires a number of security considerations, though, as a compromise of a single set of credentials can lead to access to a number of systems instead of just one. Likewise, if authentication servers become unavailable, the entirety of a system may be unavailable as well. Secure SSO setups, particularly those that are Internet-facing, require multiple levels of authentication before providing full access. Common examples of such authentication include the use of hardware devices such as dongles or smart cards.

Authorization

Authorization is the process of determining what rights and privileges a particular entity has, usually after the system has authenticated them. A system may verify a user's identity, but not all authenticated users must necessarily have access to every resource in the system. For instance, you may delegate permissions for users to access only certain folders on a network share. The manufacturing department may have its own high-level directory on the share, and any users in this department will be authorized to access the directory and all the files contained within. At the same time, a member of the product development department may be denied access to the manufacturing directory.

 Note: Windows Server 2012's Dynamic Access Control (DAC) is an example of a tool that helps administrators implement authorization rules in an enterprise domain.

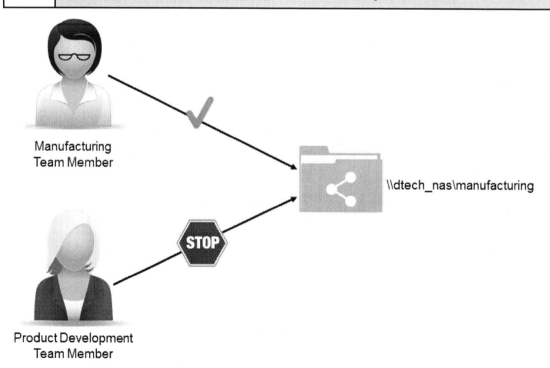

Figure 4–3: Personnel from different departments attempting to access a network share.

Beyond simple authorization schemes, there are several advanced schemes that are useful in an enterprise setting.

OAuth

OAuth is an open authorization framework that enables users to empower an app to act on their behalf, accessing secure application programming interfaces (APIs) (and the resources accessed through those APIs) without sharing their password. OAuth uses a token that is essentially a short string combined with a corresponding secret string.

Traditional web-based applications typically require that users provide a user name and password to authenticate. There are, however, situations when it is not a good idea to use a user name and password for authentication in apps that your enterprise develops. For example, when an app seeks a web or cloud API service, it is not safe to permit the app to store the web service user name and password, because this extends the attack surface to include both the app and the web APIs. Also, passing credentials across the network each time the app makes an API call or establishes a session will also increase risk. OAuth's token-based authentication helps mitigate this risk.

Many major websites and cloud services, like Facebook, Twitter, and Amazon, have adopted OAuth and provide developer documentation on accessing their services through OAuth. In an enterprise setting, this open authorization framework will help limit the exposure of your app users' credentials.

OAuth 2.0

OAuth 2.0 is the most current version, and is not backward compatible with version 1.0. However, OAuth 2.0 may be less secure than version 1.0 because it leaves many factors open to implementation instead of using narrowly defined security protocols.

The OAuth Process

An OAuth token goes through three general steps during the initialization process, each of which has an associated URL (called an endpoint) at the OAuth provider's website, with which the user and app interact to obtain the token. The steps include:

1. **Request**: A client app contacts an OAuth cloud-based provider service to request access to a particular service (called the "scope"). The service has your app redirect the user to the request endpoint, where the user is prompted to provide user credentials.
2. **Authorization**: The user enters login credentials for the service provider website, which will be granted to the client app. The credentials are sent directly to the service provider. If the user has entered the correct credentials, the server replies with a response that authorizes the token and gives the app an authorized request token.
3. **Upgrade**: With the authorized token, the client app issues another request to the service provider. The service provider upgrades the authorized token to an access token, which it returns to the client app. The client app may now use the access token to gain access to the user's resources on the service, within the permitted scope, until the token is revoked by the user.

An HTTP request is sent to the appropriate endpoint to obtain a token or manipulate it. As an example, Google's OAuth endpoints are:

- Request endpoint: **www.google.com/accounts/OAuthGetRequestToken**
- Authorization endpoint: **www.google.com/accounts/OAuthAuthorizeToken**
- Upgrade endpoint: **www.google.com/accounts/OAuthGetAccessToken**

Once acquired, the access token can be used until revoked by the user, which might be a very long period of time.

XACML

Extensible Access Control Markup Language (XACML) is an XML-based standard for access control and authorization. It is a highly flexible language that allows for centralized or distributed management. XACML contains a three-level hierarchy used to place and grant permissions based on access controls:

- Rules—which define the permissions for one action.
- Policies—which are sets of rules that are used in conjunction with one another.
- PolicySet—which are groups of policies that are used together to make decisions.

A rule defines three components: subject, resource, and action. The subject is the entity requesting access to a particular resource. A resource is the service or application to which the subject wants to perform an action. Common actions include database reading or writing, file modification, or resource consumption, such as for data processing.

XACML alleviates the need for applications to specify their own authorization and access control methods. It also has advantages over other access control languages that could be helpful to an enterprise. XACML is extensible, and can easily integrate new policy requirements as they change. It can also reduce inconsistencies in policy implementations as the policies are applied to many resources. For larger enterprises, XACML's ability to create policies that refer to one another is particularly helpful, such as in situations where a resource-specific policy needs to reference a high-level company-wide policy.

XACML Languages

XACML also describes policy and request/response languages. The policy language describes general access control requirements, and the request/response language allows users to create queries about whether a request should be permitted. When users want to access resources, they will request the Policy Enforcement Point (PEP), which is an entity that protects the resources. The PEP in turn will create a request based on the availability of the resource and the action required, and send it to a Policy Decision Point (PDP). The PDP will analyze the request, compare it with some policies, and provide a solution regarding whether access should be granted. The response is sent to the PEP, which allows or denies access to the request.

SPML

Service Provisioning Markup Language (SPML) is another XML-based authorization framework, used primarily for automating and managing the provisioning of resources across networks and organizations. SPML allows for all of the assets assigned to an employee, department, sub-contractor, etc., to be tracked and managed. When access to resources by a particular entity needs to be updated or terminated, SPML-enabled applications will allow management to quickly determine all resources currently available to the entity and change the provisioning automatically.

SPML is used in conjunction with Security Assertion Markup Language (SAML) and XACML to provide secure, automated access to resources by both human users, as well as network-enabled services. Secure deployment of these technologies can save a substantial amount of manual processing time, and can reduce errors associated with human handling of tedious and repetitive tasks.

SPML uses a Requesting Authority, a client that creates service provisioning requests, and sends it to the Provisioning Service Point (PSP), which processes the request and creates or modifies a user account in the target system.

Trust Models

In planning authentication and authorization, a *trust model* defines the relationships between authentication services so that they may accept each other's assertions of users' identities and permissions, when appropriate. Trust models determine how organizations establish relationships between authentication services to authorize different users and groups access to various resources. Trust models are typically based around two types: hierarchical and peer.

In a hierarchical trust model, there is one authority that can verify all other resources under it, and all resources under it implicitly trust that authority. If you request remote access to a host, and that host checks a separate authorization server to see if you have the proper clearance, it is relying on that authority in the hierarchy. The hierarchical model is a quick and effective way of maintaining trust, but if the authority in a hierarchy is compromised, the entire trust in that hierarchy will be compromised. Certificate-based authentication is an example of hierarchical trust.

In a peer trust model, there is no one centralized authority that can verify all resources in the model. Instead, the resources establish a transitive relationship: if resource A trusts resource B, and resource B trusts resource C, then resource A trusts resource C. For example, if you request remote access to a host, and the host can verify that you have already established trust with a separate web server that requires the same level of access, then the remote host will trust you. Peer trust models can avoid a single point of failure like in a hierarchical model using a ticketing system, cached credentials, or other technologies, but they are typically more complex and take more time to operate. Active Directory is an example of technology that can implement peer trust between forests and domains.

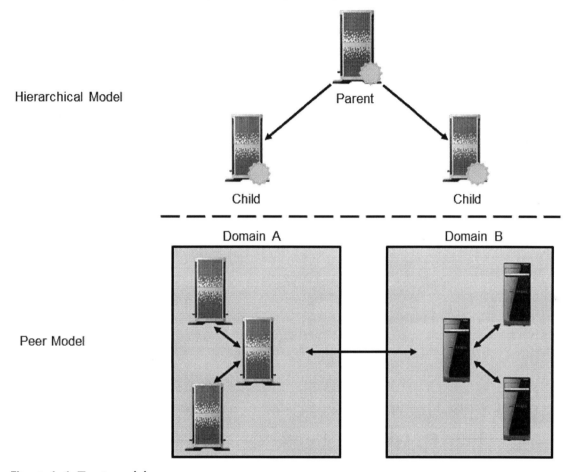

Figure 4-4: Trust models.

RADIUS Configurations

Remote Authentication Dial-In User Service (RADIUS) is an Internet standard protocol that provides centralized remote access authentication, authorization, and auditing services. When a network contains several remote access servers, you can configure one of the servers to be a RADIUS server, and all of the other servers as RADIUS clients. The RADIUS clients will pass all authentication requests to the RADIUS server for verification. User configuration, remote access policies, and usage logging can be centralized on the RADIUS server.

You can configure RADIUS servers using a number of different authentication protocols described in the following table.

Authentication Protocol	Description
Password Authentication Protocol (PAP)	A protocol that sends user IDs and passwords as plaintext. It is generally used when a remote client is connecting to a non-Windows server that does not support strong password encryption. When the server receives a user ID and password pair, it compares them to its local list of credentials. If a match is found, the server accepts the credentials and allows the remote client to access resources. If no match is found, the connection is terminated. Because it lacks encryption, PAP is extremely vulnerable and has been largely phased out as a legacy protocol.
Challenge Handshake Authentication Protocol (CHAP)	An encrypted authentication protocol that is often used to provide access control for remote access servers. CHAP was developed so that passwords would not have to be sent in plaintext. It is generally used to connect to non-Microsoft servers. CHAP uses a combination of message-digest 5 (MD5) hashing and a challenge-response mechanism, and it accomplishes authentication without ever sending passwords over the network. It can accept connections from any authentication method except for certain unencrypted schemes. For these reasons, CHAP is a more secure protocol than PAP. However, CHAP is also considered a legacy protocol, particularly because the MD5 hash algorithm is no longer suitably secure. **Note:** Microsoft's version of CHAP is MS-CHAP and MS-CHAPv2.
Extensible Authentication Protocol (EAP)	A framework that allows clients and servers to authenticate with each other using one of a variety of plugins. Because EAP does not specify which authentication method should be used, it enables the choice of a wide range of current authentication methods, and allows for the implementation of future authentication methods. For example, Microsoft provides EAP use with MS-CHAPv2 in virtual private networks (VPNs). EAP is often utilized in wireless networks and can also be used in wired implementations.
Protected Extensible Authentication Protocol (PEAP)	An extension of EAP and open standard developed by a coalition made up of Cisco Systems, Microsoft, and RSA Security. PEAP encapsulates EAP in an encrypted Transport Layer Security (TLS) tunnel to strengthen its authentication communications. This protects the authentication exchange from man-in-the-middle attacks.
Lightweight Extensible Authentication Protocol (LEAP)	Cisco Systems' proprietary EAP implementation. LEAP features mutual authentication between the client and RADIUS feature, as well as generating Wired Equivalent Privacy (WEP) keys used in wireless communication encryption. LEAP clients can reauthenticate frequently in order to lower the lifespan of the key; however, because WEP is insecure and obsolete, you should avoid using LEAP with WEP.

 Note: These protocols may also be used outside of RADIUS.

Diameter

Diameter is an authentication protocol that improves upon RADIUS by strengthening some of its weaknesses. For example, Diameter has a failover mechanism because it is Transmission Control Protocol (TCP)-based, and RADIUS does not have a failover mechanism because it is User Datagram Protocol (UDP)-based. Additionally, RADIUS does not mandate confidentiality per packet, whereas Diameter does by requiring IPSec and TLS. The name "Diameter" comes from the claim that Diameter is twice as good as RADIUS. Diameter is a stronger protocol in many ways, but is not as widespread in its implementation due to the lack of products using it.

NPS

Network Policy Server (NPS) is a Microsoft Windows Server 2012 implementation of a RADIUS server. It helps in administrating VPNs and wireless networks. NPS was known as Internet Authentication Service (IAS) in Windows Server® 2003.

NAP

Network Access Protection (NAP) is a Windows Server technology that uses RADIUS to evaluate the health state of a host client. Health requirements could mandate that a host be running a particular operating system version, that the host has the latest anti-malware signatures installed, that the host's firewall is enabled, and so on.

LDAP

The *Lightweight Directory Access Protocol (LDAP)* is a directory access protocol that runs over Transmission Control Protocol/Internet protocol (TCP/IP) networks. LDAP clients authenticate to the LDAP service, and the service's schema defines the tasks that clients can and cannot perform while accessing a directory database, the form the directory query must take, and how the directory server will respond. The LDAP schema is extensible, which means you can make changes or add on to it.

Secure LDAP (LDAPS) is a method of implementing LDAP using SSL/TLS encryption protocols to prevent eavesdropping and man-in-the-middle attacks. LDAPS forces both the client and server to establish a secure connection before any transmissions can occur, and if the secure connection is interrupted or dropped, LDAP likewise closes. The server implementing LDAPS requires a signed certificate issued by a certificate authority, and the client must accept and install the certificate on their machine.

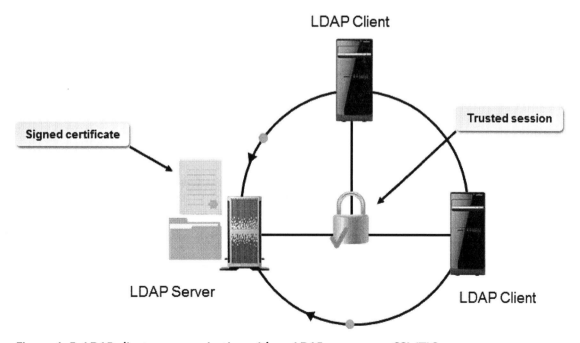

Figure 4–5: LDAP clients communicating with an LDAP server over SSL/TLS.

LDAP Management

Most directory services implementations ship with some management tools of their own. In addition, there are a wide variety of third-party LDAP browsing and administration tools available from both open- and closed-source vendors. Besides preconfigured tools, you can create scripts that use LDAP to automate routine directory maintenance tasks, such as adding large numbers of users or groups, and checking for blank passwords or disabled or obsolete user accounts. The ability to easily and effectively clean up a directory service will go toward reducing its attack surfaces that malicious users would otherwise be able to exploit.

Active Directory

Active Directory (AD) is Microsoft's LDAP-compatible directory implementation. It structures objects within an organization into a hierarchy. An object is a single entity, such as a printer, a user, a computer, or a group, and the attributes for that entity. Objects are grouped into domains, and all the objects for a single domain are grouped and stored on one database. Active Directory allows administrators to centrally manage and control access to objects using access control lists (ACLs). AD allows users to find resources anywhere on the network. It also has a schema that controls how accounts are created and what attributes an administrator may assign to them.

For example, you can grant permissions to a group object to a shared resource like a printer. The users in that group are now authorized to access that printer, and any users outside of the group must also be granted the permissions before they can access the shared printer.

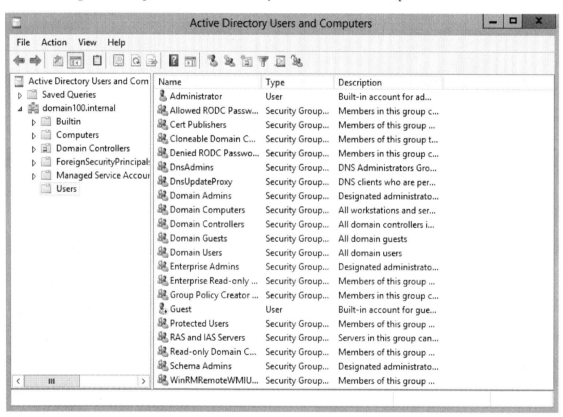

Figure 4–6: User objects stored in an Active Directory database.

Kerberos

AD implementations always use *Kerberos*, an authentication service that is based on a time-sensitive ticket-granting system. It was developed by the Massachusetts Institute of Technology (MIT) to use an SSO method where the user enters access credentials that are then passed to the authentication server, which contains an access list and allowed access credentials. You can use Kerberos to manage access control to many different services using one centralized authentication server. Kerberos' mutual authentication between client and server will help protect the users in your domain from man-in-the-middle or replay attacks.

The Kerberos Process

In the Kerberos process:

1. A user logs on to the domain.
2. The user requests a ticket granting ticket (TGT) from the authenticating server.
3. The authenticating server responds with a time-stamped TGT.
4. The user presents the TGT back to the authenticating server and requests a service ticket to access a specific resource.
5. The authenticating server responds with a service ticket.
6. The user presents the service ticket to the resource.
7. The resource authenticates the user and allows access.

Guidelines for Implementing Authentication and Authorization

 Note: All Guidelines for this lesson are available as checklists from the **Checklist** tile on the CHOICE Course screen.

Use the following guidelines to ensure strong authentication and authorization in your enterprise:

- Research the pros and cons of implementing each authentication and authorization scheme in your enterprise.
- Implement certificate-based authentication in web servers through SSL/TLS.
- Implement an SSO scheme in directory services to streamline user sign in and to ease the burden of having to remember many passwords.
- Implement SSO with multiple levels and factors of authentication to mitigate unauthorized access.
- Use OAuth to secure client credentials that your enterprise app uses to communicate.
- Implement XACML to streamline access control policy integration across the enterprise.
- Implement SPML to securely automate resource provisioning.
- Configure a RADIUS server to use a secure protocol like LEAP, and not insecure protocols like PAP and PEAP.
- Encrypt LDAP communications with SSL/TLS to prevent man-in-the-middle attacks.
- Implement Kerberos in an Active Directory domain to ensure mutual authentication and protect against man-in-the-middle and replay attacks.

ACTIVITY 4–1
Implementing Authentication

Before You Begin

You will be using Network Policy Server (NPS), a network security and management service, and the Routing and Remote Access service (RRAS), which can establish a VPN.

Scenario

You need a way for offsite employees to connect to your internal network, and you've decided on implementing a VPN for that purpose. However, you must secure the access that this VPN enables by implementing authentication techniques for users attempting to connect.

You'll start by installing Microsoft's Network Policy Server (NPS) role, which assists Windows Server environments in managing network security. You'll then register your NPS with Active Directory so that the NPS can compare VPN connection credentials with the credentials stored in the domain directory. Next, you'll install the VPN server, then verify that NPS mandates that it use the strong EAP-MS-CHAPv2 authentication method. With this authentication in place, you can more effectively secure your network against unauthorized access.

---

1. Install the Network Policy Server role.
   a) In the **Server Manager** window, in the **Configure this local server** section, select **Add roles and features**.
   b) In the **Add Roles and Features Wizard**, on the **Before you begin** page, select **Next**.
   c) On the **Select installation type** page, verify that the **Role-based or feature-based** radio button is selected and select **Next**.
   d) On the **Select destination server** page, verify that your server is selected and select **Next**.
   e) On the **Select server roles** page, check the **Network Policy and Access Services** check box and select **Add Features**.
   f) Select **Next** three times.
   g) On the **Select role services** page, verify that the **Network Policy Server** check box is checked and select **Next**.
   h) On the **Confirm installation selections** page, check the **Restart the destination server automatically if required** check box and select **Yes**.
   i) Select **Install**. After installation completes, select **Close**.

2. Register the NPS with Active Directory.
   a) In **Server Manager**, select **Tools→Network Policy Server**.

b)   In the **Network Policy Server** window, in the left pane, right-click **NPS (Local)** and select **Register server in Active Directory**.

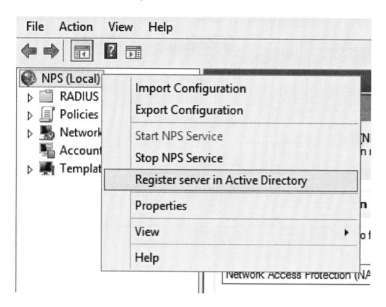

c)   In the **Network Policy Server** message box, select **OK** twice.
d)   Close the **Network Policy Server** window.

3.   Install the Routing and Remote Access role.
a)   In the **Server Manager** window, in the **Configure this local server** section, select **Add roles and features**.
b)   In the **Add Roles and Features Wizard**, on the **Before you begin** page, select **Next**.
c)   On the **Select installation type** page, verify that the **Role-based or feature-based** radio button is selected and select **Next**.
d)   On the **Select destination server** page, verify that your server is selected and select **Next**.
e)   On the **Select server roles** page, check the **Remote Access** check box and select **Next**.
f)   Select **Next** twice.
g)   On the **Select role services** page, check the **DirectAccess and VPN (RAS)** check box and select **Add Features**. Select **Next**.
h)   On the **Confirm installation selections** page, check the **Restart the destination server automatically if required** check box and select **Yes**.

i) Select **Install**. After installation completes, select the **Open the Getting Started Wizard** link.

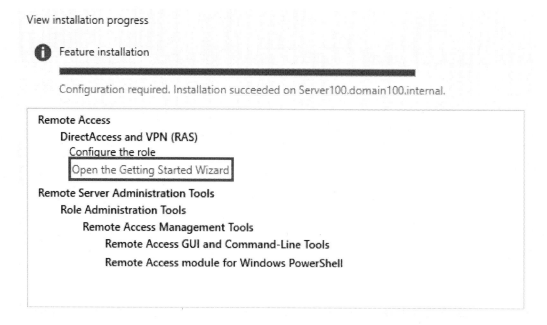

4. Configure Routing and Remote Access to establish a VPN server on your host.
   a) In the **Configure Remote Access** wizard, select **Deploy VPN only**.
   b) In the **Routing and Remote Access** window, right-click your server object and select **Configure and Enable Routing and Remote Access**.

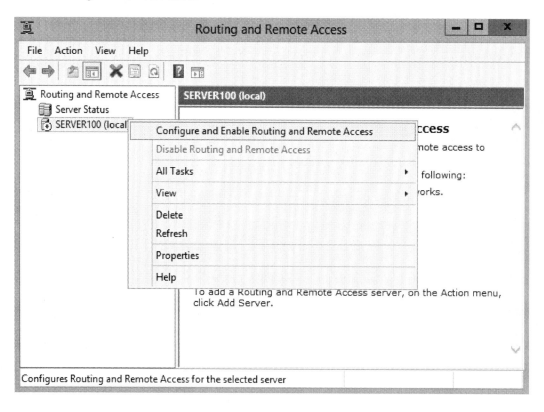

   c) In the **Routing and Remote Access Server Setup Wizard**, select **Next**.
   d) On the **Configuration** page, select the **Custom configuration** radio button and select **Next**.
   e) On the **Custom Configuration** page, check the **VPN access** check box and select **Next**.

f) Select **Finish**.
g) Select **OK** in both message boxes.

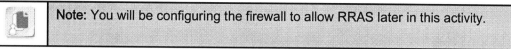

> **Note:** You will be configuring the firewall to allow RRAS later in this activity.

h) In the **Routing and Remote Access** message box, select **Start service**.

5. Configure the authentication protocols that your VPN server will use.

   a) In the **Routing and Remote Access** window, right-click your server object and select **Properties**.
   b) In the **SERVER## (local) Properties** dialog box, select the **Security** tab.
   c) Select the **Authentication Methods** button.
   d) In the **Authentication Methods** dialog box, verify that the check boxes for **Extensible authentication protocol (EAP)** and **Microsoft encrypted authentication version 2 (MS-CHAP v2)** are checked.

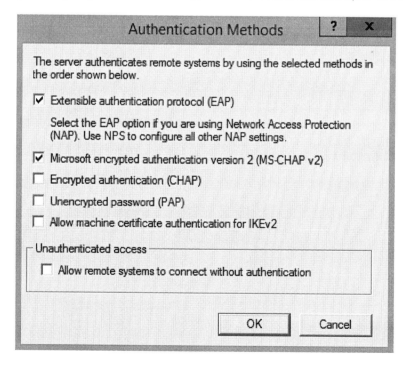

   The NPS will authenticate remote connections to the VPN using Microsoft's MS-CHAPv2 implementation of the EAP framework.

   e) Select **OK** twice.
   f) Minimize the **Routing and Remote Access** window and, if necessary, close the **Add Roles and Features Wizard**.

6. Allow Routing and Remote Access through the firewall.

a) On the desktop taskbar, right-click the **Start** button and select **Search**.
b) In the **Search** box, type *firewall*
c) From the results, select **Allow an app through Windows Firewall**.

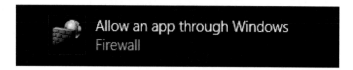

d) In the **Allowed apps** window, scroll down and check the **Routing and Remote Access** check box.
e) If necessary, check the **Domain**, **Private**, and **Public** check boxes for **Routing and Remote Access**.

Allowed apps and features:

Name	Domain	Private	Public
☐ Remote Event Monitor	☐	☐	☐
☐ Remote Scheduled Tasks Management	☐	☐	☐
☐ Remote Service Management	☐	☐	☐
☐ Remote Shutdown	☐	☐	☐
☐ Remote Volume Management	☐	☐	☐
☑ Routing and Remote Access	☑	☑	☑
☑ Secure Socket Tunneling Protocol	☑	☑	☑
☑ Secure World Wide Web Services (HTTPS)	☑	☑	☑
☐ SNMP Trap	☐	☐	☐
☑ SSH Allowed	☑	☑	☑
☐ TPM Virtual Smart Card Management	☐	☐	☐
☐ Virtual Machine Monitoring	☐	☐	☐

Details...   Remove

f) Select **OK**.

Note: You will be able to further configure and test the VPN server in a later activity.

TOPIC B

Implement Advanced Identity Management

Related to authentication and authorization is identity management, which allows you to add, delete, and alter information about each entity that is recorded in your enterprise domain. Through advanced identity management techniques, you can ensure that users and devices retain authentication information where appropriate, even across many disparate systems. In this topic, you'll implement these techniques to both support and reinforce authentication and authorization in your enterprise.

Attestation

In identity management, *attestation* is the technique of verifying that only the individuals who need certain access privileges have those privileges. This helps uphold the security principle of least privilege. The reviewer who verifies this information attests to its accuracy, and such an action may be tracked and logged. The attestation agent is therefore accountable for what they attest to, so that no action on their part can slip through a security audit.

There are two main approaches to attestation: user-focused and resource-focused. In user-focused attestation, the attestation agent monitors the privileges that specific users have. This is useful if you need to investigate privilege removal or addition in response to changes in employment. For example, you may verify added privileges to a recently promoted employee; conversely, you may verify privileges were removed from a demoted employee.

In resource-focused attestation, an attestation agent will look over each application or system and see which users have which privileges. This is useful for enterprises that place a significance on the security of specific resources, especially if those resources are sensitive and vital to business needs. For example, you may verify that a customer records database has a list of users with different levels of access, and that no one user has more access to the database than they absolutely need.

Identity Propagation

Identity propagation refers to the technique of replicating an authenticated identity through various processes in a system. This allows a system with multiple, discrete process layers to accept the same authenticated identity instead of needing to authenticate several different identities. Identity propagation is often employed in mixed environments where services from different vendors must collaborate with one another. These services may differ enough in architecture or design to warrant a unified approach.

Secure identity propagation requires the app to be judicious with the level of authentication it propagates. Certain users need only certain privileges, and no more; so an app developer might need their identity propagated through all processes, but a database administrator might only need propagation through the front-end and the records database. Therefore, your identity propagation methods must be fine-grained enough to accommodate access control and authorization policies.

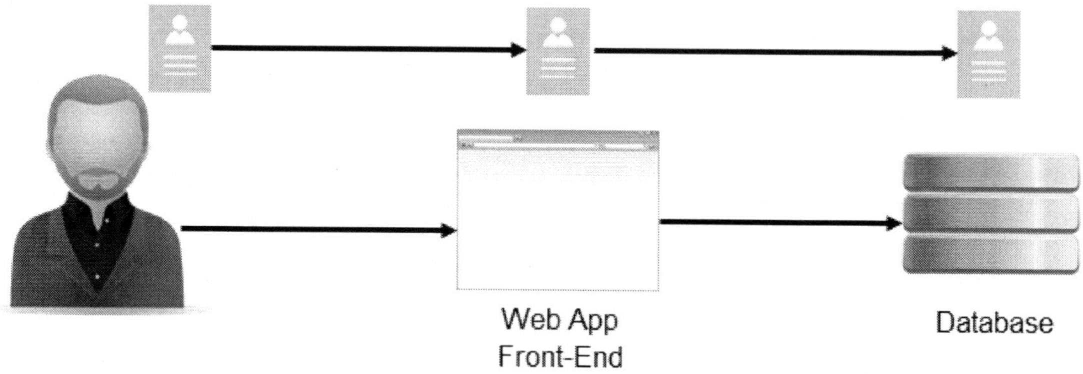

Web App
Front-End

Database

Figure 4-7: Propagating a user's identity through a web application front-end and a database.

Example

Consider a web application that works with customer data. There are various components to this app: the web page front-end that customers see and enter information into; the records database that stores and maintains the customer information; and an intermediary back-end to the app that handles concerns like integrity checks and memory persistence. Each component may require its own authentication, and if all components are developed by the enterprise, this might be a simple affair. However, if each component was developed by an external vendor, it can be more of a challenge for an app to propagate user identities through each one.

Identity Federation

Identity federation is the practice of linking a single identity and its characteristics across many different identity management systems. Identity federation encompasses all of the policies and protocols that contribute to an identity. This provides a centralized identity management structure that eliminates the need for superfluous identity information. Federated identities not only relieve some of the strain on the host, but streamlining a single account for multiple use cases can be, in certain contexts, much more practical and efficient than needing many different accounts.

For example, an enterprise might have several domains or closely integrate with different companies; federating the identity of users across these domains will alleviate the need for each domain to manage its identity separately. This can reduce cost and even lower risk, since account information is centralized instead of replicated across several different domains.

> **Note:** SSO is a subset of identity federation that eliminates the need to sign in more the once. Not all federated identities implement SSO; some require re-authentication at different points.

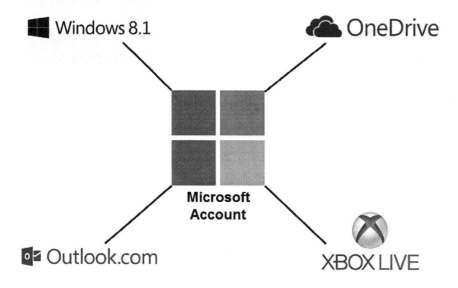

Figure 4-8: A Microsoft account can be used across many different systems.

Identity Federation Methods

There are several different identity management methods that you can implement for a federated environment. The following table lists some of those methods.

Identity Federation Method	Description
Security Assertion Markup Language (SAML)	SAML is an XML-based framework for exchanging security-related information such as user authentication, entitlement, and attributes. This information is communicated in the form of assertions over a secure HTTP connection, which conveys the identity of subjects and authorization decisions about the access level of the subjects. SAML contains components such as assertions, protocol, and binding. Authentication assertions contain information about any acts of authentication or user identity validation, attribute assertions contain information about users, and authorization assertions contain information about the level of access for each user. Clients request assertions from SAML authorities and get a response from them using the protocol defined by SAML.
OpenID	OpenID is a method of authenticating users with certain sites that participate in an OpenID system. This allows them to retain a single account for all participating sites. A user will register with an OpenID system in a given domain like they would with any other account. A site under this OpenID domain will then give the user the option to sign in using this system. The site then contacts its external OpenID provider in order to verify that the login credentials supplied by the user are correct. Internet companies such as Google and Yahoo! use their own OpenID systems.

Identity Federation Method	Description
Shibboleth	Shibboleth is a federated identity method based on SAML that is often employed by universities or public service organizations. In a Shibboleth implementation, a user attempts to retrieve resources from a Shibboleth-enabled website, which then sends SAML authentication information over URL queries. The user is then redirected to an identity provider with which they can authenticate using this SAML information. The identity provider then responds to the service provider (the Shibboleth-enabled website) with the proper authentication information. The site validates this response and grants the user access to certain resources based on their SAML information.
Where Are You From (WAYF)	WAYF is an SSO implementation that is centered around asking users what institution they are from before they are allowed access to a service provider. In WAYF, a user connects to a web resource, which then refers to a WAYF identity management system. The system asks which institution the user is from, which mandates that the user log in to their institution if they are not already. After the user is successfully logged in to their own institution, the WAYF informs the user what identity information will be sent to the service provider. The user must consent before this information is sent. The service provider then decides, based on this information, whether to allow the user access.

Guidelines for Implementing Advanced Identity Management

Use the following guidelines when implementing advanced identity management in the enterprise:

- Implement user-focused attestation in environments where personnel are routinely switching job functions.
- Implement resource-focused attestation in environments where sensitive resources need consistent privilege verification.
- Implement identity propagation in systems that incorporate a mix of vendor processes, especially if those processes are built on different frameworks.
- Ensure that identity propagation has fine-grained control over whose identity gets propagated where to conform to access control policies.
- Implement identity federation to streamline user interactions and identity management within the enterprise.
- Implement identity federation to reduce the cost and the risk associated with multiple identity management systems.
- Use a SAML-based federation framework like Shibboleth to securely manage individual identities.

ACTIVITY 4-2
Implementing Advanced Identity Management

Scenario

Develetech has many different systems across several domains, and to streamline identity management throughout these, you'll consider implementing different techniques. Having these identity management techniques at your disposal could help the enterprise ensure that authentication and authorization are upheld in more complex environments.

1. **What is the process called that would involve verifying the privileges that specific employees possess?**
   - ○ Identity federation
   - ○ Identity propagation
   - ○ Resource-focused attestation
   - ○ User-focused attestation

2. **Develetech has a shared SQL database that stores customer records. There are three different departments that need some sort of access to this database: accounts receivable to generate billing information, sales to update customer records, and the database administrators to perform routine maintenance and oversight. You want to design the SQL database so that identities can propagate through its different functions, streamlining authentication and authorization. What are some of the security concerns involved in this?**

3. **Which of the following identity federation systems asks a user what institution they are from before it grants the user access?**
   - ○ WAYF
   - ○ SAML
   - ○ OpenID
   - ○ Shibboleth

4. **Shibboleth uses which XML-based framework to send authentication information?**
   - ○ XACML
   - ○ SAML
   - ○ DITA
   - ○ SPML

Summary

In this lesson, you implemented advanced authentication, authorization, and identity management techniques, which are common to enterprise settings. The techniques you learned in this lesson will help you manage and verify the identities of users and devices, as well as provide the appropriate levels of access, all to keep unauthorized people or devices from intruding into your enterprise systems.

What authentication and authorization schemes does your company use, and/or which ones are you familiar with?

What identity management techniques do you use on a regular basis, whether for personal or professional use?

Note: Check your CHOICE Course screen for opportunities to interact with your classmates, peers, and the larger CHOICE online community about the topics covered in this course or other topics you are interested in. From the Course screen you can also access available resources for a more continuous learning experience.

5 | Implementing Cryptographic Techniques

Lesson Time: 3 hours

Lesson Objectives

In this lesson, you will:

- Describe cryptographic concepts.

- Choose cryptographic techniques.

- Choose cryptographic implementations.

Lesson Introduction

Authentication and authorization keep unwanted users out of your enterprise operations, but in the event that this defense fails, cryptography will keep those users from compromising your information itself. Cryptography can be a complex subject, but it is nevertheless important that you understand its foundational aspects and how you can use it in your enterprise. The concepts, techniques, and implementations discussed in this lesson will appear time and time again throughout your CASP duties, as cryptography is such a ubiquitous security control. More importantly, you will be equipped to choose the cryptographic procedures that are the best fit for your organization.

TOPIC A

Describe Cryptographic Concepts

Before you implement cryptography in your enterprise, you would do well to understand and identify significant cryptographic concepts. These concepts lay the foundation for what cryptography is and what it can achieve. When you are able to describe them, you will gain a more complete understanding of how encryption is absolutely vital to your enterprise.

Confidentiality

In the context of cryptography, *confidentiality* states that only parties who own the data or who are the intended recipients of sensitive communications are able to read it. For example, an organization may encrypt its storage drives so that only authorized employees can know its contents; employees may send encrypted emails to others so that only they can read it; or a business might transmit personal information like credit card numbers into and out of its network in an encrypted form. Confidentiality, therefore, is one of the most important goals of cryptography, and is likewise an important goal of enterprise security.

Please keep this message secret.

ESXUbp2EXtI69iP0M teLqBE8D15fgcxh8G 6LdCjARiMFN+leW1 +SAoy5md7y/stm

Figure 5-1: A message encrypted so that it cannot be read without the proper key.

Integrity

After the confidentiality of data is secure, *integrity* is the next desired step in cryptography. While confidentiality guarantees that a message being sent from one person to another cannot be read by others, it does not guarantee that the message was not altered since being sent. Integrity goes further by ensuring that no tampering of data occurred. A common example of integrity checking is the use of hashing to verify a file's contents. Downloaded files are often accompanied with their hash so that the end user can verify that the download was successful and was not tampered with. In the field of digital forensics, hashes are used to prove the integrity of collected evidence and that the investigator did not add, delete, or modify evidence.

ESXUbp2EXtI69iP0MteLqB
E8D15fgcxh8G6LdCjARiMF
N+leW1+SAoy5md7y/stm

ESXUbp2EXtI69iP0MteLqB
E8D15fgcxh8G6LdCjARiMF
N+leW1+SAoy5md7y/stm

Figure 5-2: The receiver verifies the encrypted message's integrity.

Non-repudiation

Non-repudiation is the goal of ensuring that the party that sent a transmission or created data remains associated with that data and cannot deny sending or creating that data. You should be able to independently verify the identity of a message sender, and the sender should be responsible for the message and its data. Protocols and algorithms that provide non-repudiation do so by cryptographically binding the identity of the person to the transaction.

Non-repudiation is an important element of forensic analysis. It is also vital to an enterprise from a legal standpoint, as it is one way to determine *accountability*, which is the process of determining who to hold responsible for a particular activity or event, such as a log on.

Figure 5-3: Non-repudiation.

Entropy

In computing, *entropy* is the amount of randomness that can be collected by an operating system and provided to applications. This entropy is then used to generate random data for a number of processes, both cryptographic and not. The more entropy there is in a cryptographic system, the harder it will be to crack. Entropy can come from sources such as specialized hardware, non-uniform data from the running computer, and even from the end user. If you have ever been asked to type on the keyboard or move the mouse while cryptographic keys are being generated, then you have helped create entropy for a cryptographic process.

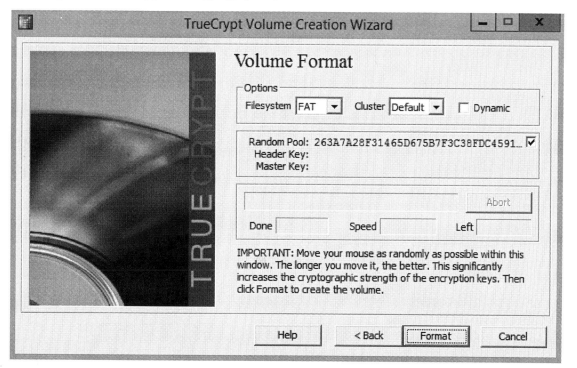

Figure 5-4: Generating entropy for encryption using mouse movements.

Confusion

Confusion is the process of making the relationship between the encryption key and the ciphertext as complex and opaque as possible. Without this property, attackers could selectively generate encrypted versions of plaintext messages and then study their relationship and look for certain patterns. A successful application of this attack could lead to the recovery of the cryptographic key and consequent decryption of the data. Confusion, then, is an important characteristic of a strong cipher.

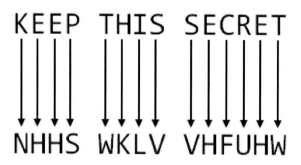

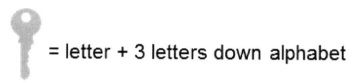

Figure 5-5: Basic confusion using a substitution cipher.

Diffusion

Diffusion is the technique of making the ciphertext change drastically upon even the slightest changes in the plaintext input. This ensures that similar data does not produce similar or repeating information in the resulting ciphertext. Without this property, attackers could selectively determine parts of the message encrypted by the same key. Diffusion is often paired with confusion to describe the characteristics of a strong cipher.

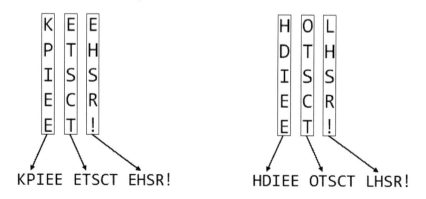

Figure 5-6: A transposition cipher that offers a small measure of diffusion.

 Note: Both confusion and diffusion were first described by Claude Shannon in his seminal article on modern cryptography, *Communication Theory of Secrecy Systems.*

Chain of Trust

A *chain of trust* is established in the relationships that entities in the infrastructure have with one another. This allows security to propagate from the top of the hierarchy all the way through to the bottom. Using *Public Key Infrastructure (PKI)* as an example:

1. The root certificate authority (CA) is at the top of the chain.
2. Each subordinate CA is below it.
3. Each individual PKI entity (server, workstation, etc.) is at the bottom of the chain.

The chain of trust therefore ensures that the confidentiality and integrity of information is valid at every step of the process, as the validity of each component is dependent on the validity of the component that precedes it.

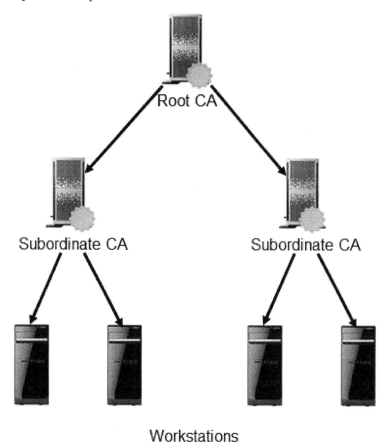

Figure 5-7: The chain of trust in a PKI.

Root of Trust

A *root of trust* is technology that enforces a hardware platform's trusted computing architecture by providing various functions, including:

- Full disk encryption.
- Digital rights management (DRM).
- Detecting and preventing unauthorized changes to software through hashing.

 Note: These concepts are described in greater depth later in the course.

Together, these functions guarantee integrity by preventing someone from modifying the behavior of an environment to an unauthorized state. The root of trust can also be the original entity that establishes a chain of trust.

Steganography

Steganography is an alternative cipher process that hides information by enclosing it in another file such as a graphic, movie, or sound file. Where encryption hides the content of information, but does not attempt to hide the fact that information exists, steganography is an attempt to obscure the fact that information is even present. Steganographic techniques include hiding information in blocks of what appears to be innocuous text, or hiding information within images either by using subtle clues, or by invisibly altering the structure of a digital image by applying an algorithm to change the color of individual pixels within the image. Steganography is commonly employed in the form of digital watermarking to protect copyrighted materials from unlawful use.

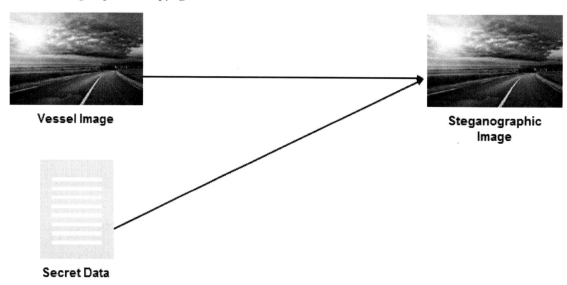

Vessel Image

Steganographic Image

Secret Data

Figure 5-8: Steganography.

 Note: Digital watermarking is discussed in a later topic.

Advanced PKI Concepts

The following table lists some of the more advanced concepts associated with PKI that may factor into your enterprise environment.

PKI Concept	Description
Wild card	A special character used in certificates that can replace any of the other characters in a string. In cryptography, a single wild card certificate can be used to secure a website's domain, as well as all its subdomains. This allows an organization to implement security in all its applications and communications. However, there are security concerns associated with using wild cards to secure your domains. Because the same private key is stored on multiple systems, there is a greater risk that it can be accessed.

PKI Concept	Description
Certificate Revocation List (CRL)	A list of certificates that were revoked before the set expiration date. Each *Certificate Authority (CA)* has its own CRL that can be accessed through the directory services of the network operating system or a website. The client CRL is updated by downloading the updated list from the server.
Online Certificate Status Protocol (OCSP)	An HTTP-based alternative to a CRL for checking the status of revoked certificates. OCSP servers, also called responders, accept a request to check a specific certificate's status. The responder uses the certificate's serial number to search for it in the CA's database. The server then sends the certificate's status to the requester.
	The main advantage of using OCSP over a CRL is that it lowers overhead on the client side. OCSP responses for specific certificate requests contain less data than entire revocation lists. However, because OCSP does not by default encrypt these standard HTTP transmissions, an attacker may be able to glean that a network resource used a specific certificate at a specific time during this OCSP transaction.
Key escrow	An alternative to key backups, key escrow can be used to store private keys securely, while allowing one or more trusted third parties access to the keys under predefined conditions. The third party is called the key escrow agent. For example, in certain situations, a government agency might require private keys to be placed in escrow with the agency. Commercial CAs can also act as escrow agents on a contract basis for organizations that do not want to back up and manage their own private keys.
Issuance to entities	There are a number of considerations regarding issuing certificates to entities when implementing PKI, including:

- Automating certificate requests. Automating makes it easier for users to acquire their own certificates, but it removes control over who gets a certificate from the organization's IT administration. In Windows® environments, certificates are generally deployed through Group Policy.
- Using wild card certificate names or issuing separate certificates to all entities needing them.
- The lifespan of certificates. How long should certificates be valid? When should they expire?
- Does the organization:
  - Develop its own PKI system and CA?
  - Use public certificates?
  - Develop a hybrid system using both options?

PKI Concept	Description
Issuance to entity subgroups (users, systems, and applications)	You should also consider how to handle issuing certificates to specific entity subgroups within the enterprise: • **Users**: These certificates usually have the shortest expiration time, typically one year. The submission and issuance can be automated if issuance central management is too difficult for the organization. Wild card certificates can simplify management, but they can damage accountability and therefore are often not used for issuance to users. • **Systems**: Subordinate CAs, domain controllers, and other systems can use certificates that generally have a long expiration (5 to 30 years). System certificates are easier to manage centrally due to the limited number of affected systems. • **Applications**: Secure Sockets Layer/Transport Layer Security (SSL/TLS), secure email, and other enterprise applications also use certificates, usually with a one- to three-year expiration date. Applications certificates are usually managed centrally. If the applications will only be used by internal entities, an internal CA can manage the application certificates. If the server requires secure communication with any external entities, then the enterprise would need to purchase public certificates.

Cryptographic Applications

There are many ways to apply cryptographic concepts in the enterprise to help secure the confidentiality and integrity of information, but as powerful as encryption can be, it will be useless if it is not implemented properly. Consider the following ways in which cryptography should and should not be implemented in your enterprise.

Proper implementations:

• Choosing an encryption scheme that is considered an industry standard, like Advanced Encryption Standard (AES) or Rivest Shamir Adleman (RSA).
• Employing algorithms with strong key lengths: at least 128-bit for symmetric encryption, and at least 2,048 for asymmetric.
• Storing encryption keys in a key management system.
• Regulating access to this key management system.
• Employing perfect forward secrecy in asymmetric encryption systems.
• Ensuring that data encryption covers all relevant environments in your enterprise.
• Weighing the benefits of encryption with the increase in overhead it brings.

Improper implementations:

• Choosing an obsolete encryption scheme, like Data Encryption Standard (DES), or using one you've created yourself.
• Employing algorithms with weak key lengths, such as 56-bit for symmetric encryption, and 1,024-bit for asymmetric.
• Storing data in insecure and easily accessible locations, either physically or virtually.
• Failing to account for increased cost and overhead.
• Employing encryption in only some of your enterprise's relevant environments.

Cryptographic Methods

The following table describes the two methods used in cryptographic algorithms, along with their known flaws/weaknesses.

Method	Description
Stream cipher	A method of encryption that encrypts data one bit at a time. Each plaintext bit is transformed into encrypted ciphertext. These ciphers are relatively fast to execute and do not require much performance overhead. The ciphertext is the same size as the original text. This method produces fewer errors than other methods, and when errors occur, they affect only one bit. However, stream ciphers can be vulnerable to an attack if keys are used more than once. Another weakness of stream ciphers is that they do not provide a reliable method of ensuring message integrity.
Block cipher	Unlike stream ciphers, this cipher method encrypts data in blocks, often 64-bit in size. It is usually stronger and more secure, but also offers slower performance than stream encryption. Block ciphers are implemented using various modes of operation to establish confidentiality and integrity, depending on the mode chosen. Modes of operation define how a block cipher will repeatedly encrypt single blocks of data in a secure manner. Some common block cipher modes are as follows: • *Electronic Code Book (ECB)*: Each block is encrypted by itself. Each occurrence of a particular word is encrypted exactly the same. This makes ECB a very flawed mode that you should avoid. • *Cipher Block Chaining (CBC)*: Before a block is encrypted, information from the preceding block is added to the block. In this way, you can be sure that repeated data is encrypted differently each time it is encountered. In CBC, if the last block does not reach the block boundary, it must be filled with excess data. This process is called *padding*. • *Propagating or Plaintext Cipher Block Chaining (PCBC)*: Propagates a single bit change in the ciphertext to capture any errors in transmission. • *Cipher Feedback (CFB)*: Allows encryption of partial blocks rather than requiring full blocks for encryption. This eliminates the need to pad a block like in CBC. • *Output Feedback (OFB)*: Converts a block cipher into a stream cipher, which is fed back as input of a block cipher. Because it has no chaining dependencies, OFB does not allow for error propagation. • *Counter (CTR)*: Similar to OFB and uses a counter as input. This ensures that data blocks of the same content do not encrypt to the same value.

Stream Cipher Example

RC4 is the most used and well-known stream cipher. It is used in implementations such as Wired Equivalent Privacy (WEP), BitTorrent®, Microsoft's Remote Desktop Protocol (RDP), and is an optional choice as the cipher to use in a number of applications and protocols that support multiple ciphers. RC4 has a number of security weaknesses though, and protocols relying on RC4 must be aware of these. A prevalent example is WEP, used to secure wireless networks, which was deprecated in 2004 due to its misuse of RC4.

Block Cipher Example

Advanced Encryption Standard (AES) is the most popular block cipher and is used throughout organizations and governments worldwide. It is based on the Rijndael algorithm developed by Belgian cryptographers Joan Daemen and Vincent Rijmen and was adopted by the U.S. government as its standard for symmetric encryption. It has no feasible attacks published against it, and it is very efficient in terms of Random Access Memory (RAM) usage and performance. It can operate with key sizes of 128, 192, and 256 bits.

Cryptographic Design Considerations

The following table lists a number of security implications regarding encryption that you should take into consideration.

Design Principle	Considerations
Strength	Encryption is only as strong as the key that is used to encrypt it. The longer the key length, the harder it will be to break the encryption. Regardless of the method of encryption, the strength of the key will determine the strength of the encryption. Keep in mind that the length of time a certificate is valid may affect its key length, as the longer a certificate lasts, the longer its key needs to stay secure.
Performance	With better encryption strength comes potential performance issues. Using a longer key requires more time to encrypt and decrypt data. Regardless of the encryption method, the encryption protocol used may significantly affect performance. For example, asymmetric encryption is much slower than symmetric encryption.
Feasibility to implement	Older systems may not support the newest encryption protocols and standards. For instance, wireless routers built before 2006 may not support the Wi-Fi Protected Access 2 (WPA2) standard. If all or part of the enterprise is running on equipment that does not support the latest protocols, either encryption may not be feasible to implement or it may require a costly upgrade of equipment just to implement encryption, regardless of the method chosen. Regarding specific encryption protocols, implementing an asymmetric encryption protocol can become a costly endeavor for an organization. Asymmetric systems generally require a PKI setup to operate, which will require that the enterprise either plug into a public PKI system like Verisign® or build their own; either of which can be expensive and require a lot of resources to set up and maintain.
Interoperability	In large, complex systems like an enterprise, there will likely be devices from numerous vendors in use throughout the organization. Different vendors and different devices will behave differently regarding the encryption protocols and standards that you implement. Many devices will just not operate well with other systems when encryption is implemented. You will need to test every existing device and every new device purchased before you deploy your chosen encryption method to discover the potential interoperability issues.

ACTIVITY 5-1
Discussing Cryptographic Concepts

Scenario

You know that cryptography is one of the most important tools in any enterprise's security architecture. Before you implement specific encryption protocols and techniques in Develetech's infrastructure, you'd like to gain a deeper understanding of the fundamental concepts of cryptography. Being able to identify and discuss these topics will better inform your decisions when it comes time to implement cryptographic solutions.

1. In cryptography, what is the purpose of entropy?
   - ○ To generate a great deal of change in ciphertext even, if the plaintext input is altered only slightly.
   - ○ To obscure the relationship between an encryption key and its corresponding ciphertext.
   - ○ To generate a certain amount of randomness with which to strongly encrypt data.
   - ○ To hide information within media like video and audio files.

2. Which of the following concepts guarantees that the sender of a transmission cannot deny having sent it?
   - ○ Integrity
   - ○ Confidentiality
   - ○ Non-repudiation
   - ○ Chain of trust

3. Which statement accurately describes stream ciphers?
   - ○ Faster and less secure than block ciphers.
   - ○ Slower and more secure than block ciphers.
   - ○ Faster and more secure than block ciphers.
   - ○ Slower and less secure than block ciphers.

4. What are some of the key design principles when considering encryption schemes?

5. You're interested in implementing a Public Key Infrastructure (PKI) within Develetech so entities within your domain can exchange cryptographic keys securely. What are some of your concerns about how certificates are issued in this infrastructure?

TOPIC B

Choose Cryptographic Techniques

Now that you have a greater understanding of cryptography's fundamentals, you can take a closer look at the ways in which it is used in the enterprise. The various cryptographic techniques are relevant to specific contexts and provide specialized functions, so choosing the right one is a matter of considering your business needs and situation. In this topic, you'll select the appropriate cryptographic techniques to guarantee confidentiality, integrity, and other security factors crucial to your organization.

Transport Encryption

Transport encryption deals with the secure delivery of data between parties, also referred to as data in transit. It allows users and devices to communicate over untrusted media while still guaranteeing confidentiality, integrity, authenticity, and non-repudiation. Secure network protocols must defend against a wide range of active and passive attacks, and transport encryption is a vital part of mitigating these attacks in any enterprise environment:

- Passive attacks are when a party can monitor a communication in an attempt to glean information from it. For example, eavesdropping on a VoIP call or wardriving a wireless network.

- Active attackers are more dangerous in that they can intercept, modify, add, and remove packets from a network stream and between communicating parties. In order to be secure against both attack types, network protocols must use a range of cryptographic techniques to ensure full security.

  - A *man-in-the-middle attack* is when an active attacker silently tampers with communications between parties. If an attacker can substitute his own key for one of the communicating parties, then they can successfully decrypt the messages of one participant. If the attacker can substitute for both keys, then they can decrypt (and tamper with) the entire conversation. Neither participant in the conversation will notice the attack as the attacker can successfully relay messages between parties.

    A common example of such an attack is rogue web servers or proxy servers with self-signed SSL certificates that trick users into trusting them. All web traffic can then be successfully decrypted by the attacker.

Transport Encryption Protocols

As a CASP, you'll come to recognize the importance of transport encryption in a wide variety of enterprise applications. Customer-facing resources, like websites that handle personal information, often necessitate that data in transit be encrypted. Even enterprise operations that stay internal—like a network administrator's need to remote into a server—are prime candidates for transport encryption. The following protocols are some of the most common ways in which you'll see transport encryption implemented in the enterprise:

- *Secure Sockets Layer (SSL)* and *Transport Layer Security (TLS)* are web-based protocols for securely combining digital certificates for authentication with public key data encryption.
- *Secure Shell (SSH)* is a remote login protocol that uses a variety of encryption methods to keep the session secure.
- *Internet Protocol Security (IPSec)* is an open standard for encrypting transmissions across networks, particularly the Internet.
- *Wi-Fi Protected Access (WPA/WPA2)* is a protocol designed to secure wireless networks through encryption.

Data at Rest Encryption

Data at rest refers to information that does not leave the device on which it is stored. Protecting this data requires a different set of algorithms, protocols, and policies than those of data that traverses computer networks. *Data at rest encryption* is typically implemented in one or more of three general ways: disk, file, and database.

The most common example of data at rest encryption is *full disk encryption*. A large majority of data stored on a hard drive is never transferred over the network, but it is nevertheless still at risk. When dealing with laptops, mobile phones, and other mobile devices, there is a good chance that they will, at some point, either be lost or stolen. Without proper encryption, someone who gains access to the unencrypted device may also be able to access the data. Security measures, such as passwords and PINs, may prevent a casual attacker from accessing data, but nothing short of full disk encryption will completely protect a device's contents. Proper use of full disk encryption, including selecting a strong passphrase, ensures that attackers who steal a device or its hard drive cannot access the plaintext contents. Microsoft's BitLocker® is an example of technology that can implement full disk encryption.

A similar concept to full disk encryption is the encryption of individual files or folders, called *file encryption*. Programs such as *TrueCrypt* allow you to create encrypted containers that can be transferred and stored as regular files. This provides flexibility as the container can be opened and decrypted on any computer with the cryptographic software installed. Microsoft's *Encrypting File System (EFS)* is a feature available for Windows that uses a mix of algorithms to encrypt individual files and folders on the New Technology File System (NTFS) file system architecture.

Lastly, *database encryption* targets just the data stored in a particular database instead of individual files or whole disks. Depending on how a database is implemented, database encryption may incorporate both data at rest and transport encryption.

Hashing

Hashing is one-way encryption that transforms cleartext into ciphertext that is not intended to be decrypted. The result of the hashing process is called a *hash*, hash value, or *message digest*. The input data can vary in length, whereas the hash length is fixed. In a hash function, even the smallest of changes to data can modify the digest considerably, making it much more difficult to deduce the encryption key based on certain patterns. When comparing a value against its hash (to verify the value hasn't been changed), if the hash you generate matches the hash provided with the value, you can be pretty sure the value was not modified.

Hashing has several uses:

- Hashing is used in a number of password authentication schemes. Encrypted password data is called a hash of the password.
- A hash value can be embedded in an electronic message to support data integrity and non-repudiation.
- A hash of a file can be used to verify the integrity of that file after transfer.

Message   Hash Function   Hash

Secret

```
7E32 A729 B122 6ED1
270F 282A 8C63 054D
09B2 6BC9 EC53 EA69
771C E381 58DF ADE8
```

secret

```
2BB8 0D53 7B1D A3E3
8BD3 0361 AA85 5686
BDE0 EACD 7162 FEF6
A25F E97B F527 A25B
```

Figure 5-9: Hashing text using the SHA-256 algorithm.

Password Salting

To offer further security with hashing, a password should be salted. A *salt* is a randomly generated number that is sent along with the password and stored with the relevant encrypted hash value. Salting makes it more difficult for a list of passwords to be cracked, as it protects against pre-computed rainbow tables designed specifically to make mass-cracking of encryption easier. Rainbow tables include a list of hashes for commonly used passwords, and without a salt to complicate the process, an attacker is much more likely to break encryption of credentials. With a salt attached to a hash value, the size of the rainbow table must be increased by such a degree that it becomes infeasible. The salt essentially adds to the length and complexity of a password without requiring that the user memorize it.

Salts can also make dictionary attacks or brute force attacks more difficult to pull off when attempting to crack multiple passwords. Because each password has its own salt, the attacker must include each individual salt with his password guess along with the hash value. Hashing can drain computational resources quickly, so this can slow an attacker down considerably.

Salts are often employed in web apps to account for the possibility of an SQL injection exposing password hashes. People often use the same password in different accounts across multiple sites or systems, and when a salt is added to the hash, an attacker will be unable to know this by simply seeing identical hashes.

Hash Functions

The strongest hash functions conform to the following rules:

- It should not be possible to generate plaintext data based on a certain hash value, meaning the function should have *pre-image resistance*.
- It should not be possible to modify plaintext data without also changing its hash value, meaning the function should have *second pre-image resistance*.
- It should not be possible to produce two different plaintext input values that have the same resulting hash, meaning the function should have *collision resistance*.

 Note: It is impossible for a hash function to be completely resistant to collisions, as the number of different possible hashes is limited by the function's bit size. In other words, there are an infinite amount of unique inputs, and only a finite amount of unique hashes.

Different Hash Algorithms

There are many different kinds of hash algorithms that you may choose to employ when encrypting your data. Each function may differ based on size and its resistance to certain attack types. The most common functions are message-digest 5 (MD5) and Secure Hash Algorithm-1 (SHA-1). MD5 uses a 128-bit hash value and is often used to verify data integrity. Recent attacks on MD5 have shown that it is vulnerable to collisions.

SHA-1 uses a 160-bit digest and is an updated version of SHA-0, which contained an exploitable error in its algorithm. The SHA function was created by the National Security Agency to protect sensitive government data. SHA-1 has been attacked before, and is not entirely secure. SHA-2, and later SHA-3, were created to further strengthen the security of the SHA function.

Key Stretching

Key stretching is a technique that strengthens potentially weak cryptographic keys, such as passwords or passphrases created by people, against brute force attacks. In key stretching, the original key is enhanced by running it through a key-stretching algorithm. Enhanced keys are usually larger than 128 bits, which makes them harder to crack via a brute force attack.

When a key is stretched, the time that it takes to hash each password is increased by a specific value, so it will take an attacker at least that long to try each key, assuming they are using similar hardware. A password that once took a second to hash can be stretched to take two seconds, which would double the attacker's time requirements. This may prove to be a useful deterrent, as the amount of time it takes to try each key may make a brute force attack infeasible. Key stretching often adds overhead, so like other security techniques, you will need to balance performance concerns with your need for confidentiality.

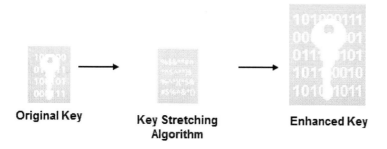

Original Key   **Key Stretching Algorithm**   **Enhanced Key**

Key stretching makes it harder to crack passwords and passphrases.

Figure 5-10: Key stretching.

Key stretching techniques include:

- Repeatedly looping cryptographic hash functions.
- Repeatedly looping block ciphers.
- Where the key is used for a cipher, configuring the cipher's key schedule to increase the time it takes for the key to be set up.

Key-Derivation Functions

One popular approach to key stretching is to use a key-derivation function:

- *Password-Based Key Derivation Function 2 (PBKDF2)* is part of the Public Key Cryptography Standards from RSA Laboratories. This key derivation function uses five input parameters to create a derived key:
  - A pseudorandom function such as a hash, cipher, or hash message authentication code (HMAC).
  - The master password used to generate derived keys.
  - A cryptographic salt, or random data added to a password or passphrase to counter against certain attacks.
  - A specified number of iterations for the function to loop.
  - The desired length of the derived key.

- *Bcrypt* is a key-derivation function based on the Blowfish cipher. Like PBKDF2, it uses a cryptographic salt, but it also adapts over time by increasing the iteration count. There are implementations of bcrypt for Ruby, Python, C, C#, Perl, PHP, Java, and other languages.

Digital Signatures

A *digital signature* is a message digest that has been encrypted again with a user's private key. Asymmetric encryption algorithms can be used with hashing algorithms to create digital signatures. The encrypted hash is attached to the message as the digital signature. The sender provides the receiver with the signed message and the corresponding public key. The receiver uses the public key to decrypt the signature to reveal the sender's version of the hash. This proves the sender's identity, because if the public and private keys did not match, the receiver would not be able to decrypt the signature. The receiver then creates a new hash version of the document with the public key and compares the two hash values. If they match, this proves that the data has not been altered.

 Note: Digital signatures support message integrity because if the signature is altered in transit, the receiver's version of the hash will not match the original hash value. They support non-repudiation because the specific encrypted hash value is unique to the sender.

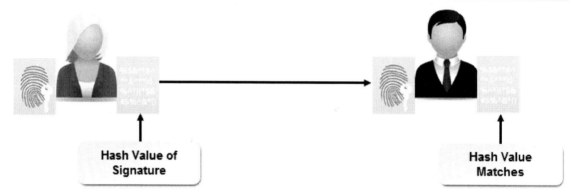

Hash Value of Signature

Hash Value Matches

Figure 5-11: A digital signature.

Digital signatures are particularly valuable in an enterprise environment where authenticity, data integrity, and non-repudiation are vital to the handling of sensitive documents. For example, a financial institution must be absolutely certain that any request to change a customer's account is legitimate. Furthermore, the arbiter of this request must be able to verify that its contents have not been tampered with (for example, requesting that funds be transferred to an attacker's account instead of the intended recipient's). And, for liability purposes, the arbiter must have a guarantee that the sender has no grounds to later deny sending the request.

Encryption of the Hash

It is important to remember that a digital signature is a hash that is then itself encrypted. Without the second round of encryption, another party could easily:

1. Intercept the file and the hash.
2. Modify the file.
3. Re-create the hash.
4. Send the modified file to the recipient.

Code Signing

Code signing is the method of using a digital signature to ensure the source and integrity of programming code. Applications available on the Internet can potentially cause damage to a system. Therefore, it is important to verify the author's identity before installing the application on a computer or any other device.

The software developer or publisher signs the data using their private key and sends the message and a digital certificate to the receiver. Upon receipt of the message, the receiver uses the sender's public key to verify the sender's identity. Though code signing ensures the integrity of code, it cannot prevent hackers from distributing malicious software. Even a hacker can request a certificate, sign a virus, and publish it on the Internet as authentic software. This is considerably more difficult to pull off when using public CAs, so the users in your enterprise should be aware that they should only run software programs that have signatures from known or trusted publishers.

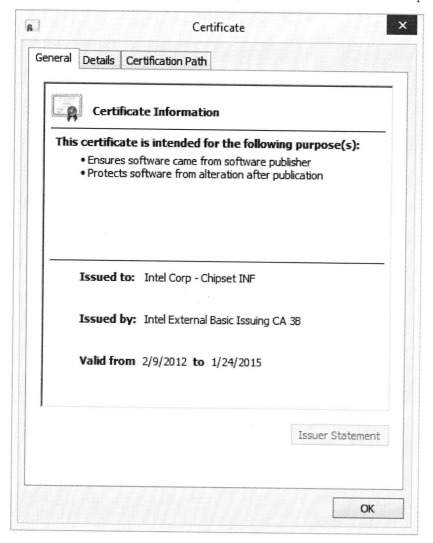

Figure 5-12: The certificate for a signed application.

Example

You created an application and signed it before publishing it on the Internet. Your app's users, in the process of downloading the application, will find your digital signature attached to the app and understand that the code has not been altered. When you later release an update with the same key signature as the original software, users will automatically trust the update.

Pseudorandom Number Generation

A *pseudorandom number generators (PRNG)* is an algorithm that can produce pseudorandom numbers, which are numbers that approximate randomness without being truly random. These pseudorandom numbers are based on an initial state, called the seed state. The seed state is simply a number that defines what will be the first stage of the number generation. The seed state will then be passed through a mathematical formula in order to output a pseudorandom number. Cryptographic key generation tends to use pseudorandom numbers.

True randomness is actually achievable through specialized hardware that gathers data from certain physical phenomena. Examples of these include measuring radioactive particle decay, detecting photons passing through an area in a certain time, measuring atmospheric noise, and other discernible data generated from physical events.

While these generators are the best source of truly random numbers, they are not always practical for the following reasons:

• They can take a long time to gather enough entropy.
• They require integration into software systems.
• They can be cost prohibitive.

A PRNG will always produce the same pseudorandom number sequence when given the same seed state. Therefore, the *seed* must be truly random and it must be kept secret. If a seed that was used to generate a cryptographic key is compromised, the key can be regenerated on demand by attackers.

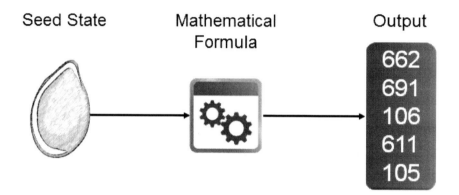

Figure 5-13: A PRNG that uses a seed state based on atmospheric noise to generate a sequence of pseudorandom numbers between 1 and 1,000.

Examples

Two of the most known PRNGs are the Mersenne Twister and Fortuna. The Mersenne Twister is not considered safe for cryptographic purposes, while Fortuna is able to produce pseudorandom number streams suitable for cryptographic operations.

Perfect Forward Secrecy

Perfect forward secrecy (PFS) is a characteristic of session encryption that ensures if a key used during a certain session is compromised, it should not affect previously encrypted data. This is a very desirable trait, as long-term keys, such as public/private key pairs, shared keys, and others, are at risk of exposing all data encrypted with them if the key is compromised.

In cryptographic systems without PFS, data that was previously captured by an attacker can be vulnerable to decryption at any point in the future if the long-term keys used during the communication are compromised.

Two real-world examples of this include:

• Decryption of previous HTTPS traffic through the compromise of a web server.
• Decryption of previously sent and received emails through the compromise of a user's desktop or laptop.

Obtaining PFS requires that long-term keys are only used to derive ephemeral (per-session) keys and that the same ephemeral key is never used twice to generate other keys. By never using the same key twice, an attacker who compromises a session key or long-term key can only decrypt one piece of information, such as one packet of a network stream or one conversation.

PFS is a standard function of the SSH and Off-the-Record Messaging (OTR) protocols, and is optional in the IPSec and TLS protocols. Despite its significant benefit to security, the vast majority of websites that use TLS do not fully incorporate PFS. There is minor overhead involved in PFS communication, but it is usually not prohibitive enough to justify leaving it out of a TLS-enabled website.

Heartbleed and the Importance of PFS

In April 2014, a member of Google's security team discovered that *OpenSSL*, a popular open-source implementation of the SSL/TLS protocol, had been vulnerable to a devastating exploit for more than two years. An attacker could use this exploit to retrieve plaintext user names, passwords, and even the cryptographic keys themselves.

This bug was named *Heartbleed*, and it affected hundreds of thousands—or about 17%—of the Internet's trusted, secure web servers. Although it would not have solved the problem and attackers would still be able to glean sensitive information, PFS would have greatly mitigated its effect. Any keys an attacker could have gleaned with the exploit would only be valid for that particular session. Without PFS, an attacker could use these keys to unlock encrypted communications from the past, putting a great deal more information at risk.

Guidelines for Choosing Cryptographic Techniques

 Note: All Guidelines for this lesson are available as checklists from the **Checklist** tile on the CHOICE Course screen.

Use the following guidelines to choose when and how to implement cryptographic techniques in your enterprise:

- Implement transport encryption when sensitive data is transmitted across your network or to some external network like the Internet.
  - Use SSL/TLS protocols on all web servers that exchange sensitive information, especially if your web servers are accessed by customers.
  - Use SSH when remotely logging in to servers and other machines on your network to establish a secure interface.
  - Use IPSec in other network communications, such as when outside users need to tunnel into your enterprise network through a VPN.
  - Secure any wireless network traffic in your enterprise with the WPA2 encryption standard.
- Implement data at rest encryption when sensitive data is archived on devices in your organization.
  - Encrypt an entire disk when everything on that particular storage medium needs to be secured.
  - Encrypt individual files and folders when only specific data on a disk needs to remain confidential.
  - Encrypt any database that stores sensitive information for a more practical approach than full disk encryption.
- Use encryption suites with key stretching algorithms, especially if the default key length is not of sufficient length (128 bits).
- Use key-derivation functions like PBKDF2 and bcrypt to strengthen key generation in apps that your enterprise develops.
- Use a strong hash function like SHA-2, and avoid flawed functions like MD5 when storing passwords in a database or checking file/message integrity.
- Ensure that password hashes are salted to mitigate the threat of rainbow tables and other cracking attempts.
- Digitally sign sensitive documents to ensure authenticity and integrity when they are transmitted across your organization.

- Sign the code of any applications your organization develops to guarantee its legitimacy.
- Reduce overhead by choosing a cryptographic algorithm that incorporates a pseudorandom number generator.
- Ensure that the seed state of a PRNG is generated in a truly random fashion.
- Implement secure communication protocols like TLS and SSH using a suite that fully supports perfect forward secrecy.
- Ensure that you are running a post-Heartbleed fix version of OpenSSL (1.0.1g or higher) if it is used in your organization.

ACTIVITY 5-2
Choosing Cryptographic Techniques

Data File

develetech_social-engineering-policy.doc

Before You Begin

Adobe® Reader® XI is installed and a copy of **develetech_social-engineering-policy.doc** is on your desktop. You will work with a partner in this activity. You should also have some method of transmitting files to your partner, such as a Universal Serial Bus (USB) drive or an email address.

Scenario

You're prepared to disseminate your Social Engineering Awareness Policy to Develetech's help desk staff. However, because of the nature of the very phenomenon your policy is about (deception through the abuse of human trust), you want to put your policy into practice by guaranteeing its authenticity and integrity. After all, if your help desk staff consults a document that has been altered from its intended vision, misleading information could cause them to inadvertently compromise business operations. Likewise, your employees need a guarantee that the policy is sanctioned by you and you only; otherwise, they have little reason to trust its authority.

To ensure these important security concepts, you will digitally sign the policy document. First, you'll use the master document to create a PDF of the policy. In Adobe Reader, you'll create a new, self-signed certificate to attach to the PDF. This certificate will have all of the pertinent identity information, as well as the cryptographic keys to validate the signature. You'll then install the certificate on all help desk workstations and send each help desk employee a signed copy of the policy PDF. Your help desk staff will be able to verify the authenticity and integrity of the document, and they can safely consult it in their day-to-day duties.

 Note: You and your partner will play the roles of both the CISO and the help desk staffers during this activity.

---

1. Open the Social Engineering Awareness Policy and save it as a PDF.
   a) From the desktop, open **develetech_social-engineering-policy** in Microsoft® Word.
   b) On the ribbon, select **FILE→Export**.
   c) On the **Export** page, select the **Create PDF/XPS** button.
   d) Save (publish) the file to the desktop as *<YOUR NAME>_develetech_social-engineering-policy* making sure to replace **<YOUR_NAME>**.
      The PDF opens in Adobe Reader.
   e) Close Word.

2. Begin signing the document with your digital signature.
   a) Scroll down to the last page of the PDF document.

b) From the pane on the right, select the **Sign** tab, then select **Work with Certificates**.

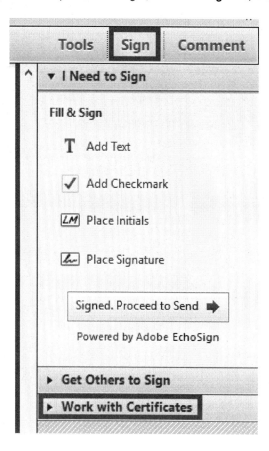

c) Under **Work with Certificates**, select **Sign with Certificate**.
d) In the **Adobe Reader** message box, select **Drag New Signature Rectangle**.
e) Using your pointer, drag a rectangle in the blank space under the **Revision History** section.

7.1.1 Document revised (date, version and author): _____

 Note: The exact placement and dimensions of the rectangle aren't important for this activity.

3. Create your digital signature.
    a) In the **Add Digital ID** wizard, select the **A new digital ID I want to create now** radio button, then select **Next**.

b) On the next page of the wizard, verify that **New PKCS#12 digital ID file** is selected. Select **Next**.

c) On the next page of the wizard, enter the following information into the blank fields, making sure to use your own name:

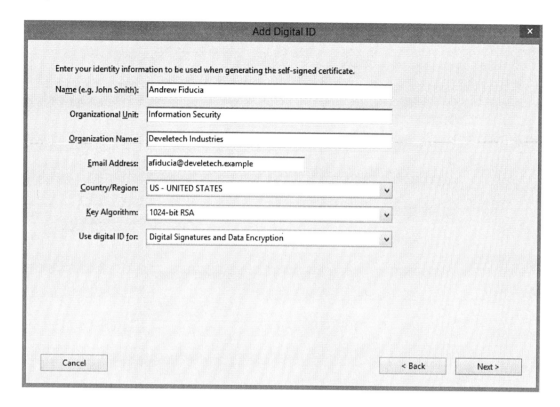

> **Note:** Remember, use your own name in both the **Name** and **Email Address** fields.

d) Select **Next**.

e) On the next page of the wizard, select **Browse**. Navigate to the desktop and save the file there with the default name.

f) In the **Password** and **Confirm Password** fields, enter *!Pass1234*

g) Select **Finish**.

h) In the **Sign Document** dialog box, in the **Password** text box, type *!Pass1234*

i) Check the **Lock Document After Signing** check box, then select **Sign**.

j) Save the document, overwriting the previous one.

k) Verify that you have successfully signed the document.

Andrew Fiducia

Digitally signed by Andrew Fiducia
DN: cn=Andrew Fiducia,
o=Develetech Industries,
ou=Information Security,
email=afiducia@develetec
h.example, c=US
Date: 2014.06.26 11:21:34
-04'00'

l) Close Adobe Reader.

4. Send your certificate (.pfx) file and your policy document PDF to your partner.

5. Install your partner's certificate.
   a) After you've received your partner's files, double-click to open their .pfx certificate.
   b) In the **Certificate Import Wizard**, on the **Welcome to the Certificate Import Wizard Page**, verify that **Current User** is the store location and select **Next**.
   c) On the **File to Import** page, verify that the file path to your partner's certificate is correct, then select **Next**.
   d) On the **Private key protection** page, enter *!Pass1234* as the password, then select **Next**.
   e) On the **Certificate Store** page, verify that **Automatically select the certificate store based on the type of certificate** is selected, then select **Next**.
   f) On the **Completing the Certificate Import Wizard** page, select **Finish**.

   g) Select **OK** to confirm that the import was successful.

6. View your partner's signature.
   a) Open your partner's policy document PDF in Adobe Reader.
   b) If necessary, in the **Trusted Certificates Update** dialog box, select **OK**, then select **OK** again.

c) Verify that a message appears at the top of the document that says the document has been signed and that all signatures are valid.

d) To the right of this message, select the **Signature Panel** button.

The **Signatures** panel opens to the left of the document.

e) In the **Signatures** panel list, right-click **Rev. 1: Signed by <partner's name and email address>** and select **Go to Signature Field**.

f) In the **Adobe Reader** message box, select **OK**. Verify that you can see your partner's signature.

7. Validate your partner's signature.

a) Right-click the signature and select **Validate Signature**.

b) In the **Signature Validation Status** message box, verify that the signature is valid and signed by your partner, and that the document has not been modified since the signature was applied.

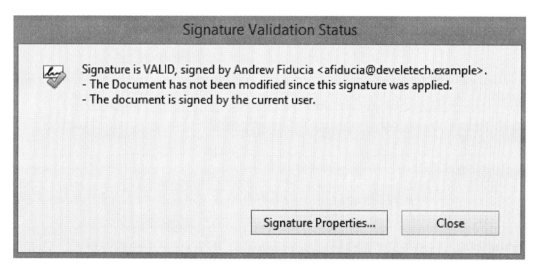

c) Select **Signature Properties**.
The **Signature Properties** dialog box provides more information about this self-signature, including that its certifier does not allow changes to be made to the document, and that the time of signing is based on the signer's local clock. The time of signing is also listed.

8. View more details about the certificate used by your partner to sign the document.

a) In the **Signature Properties** dialog box, select **Show Signer's Certificate**.

b) Select the **Details** tab.

c) In the **Certificate data** list, view your partner's certificate information. Verify the following information:

 Note: In the list, you can select each item to get a more detailed description.

- The **Signature algorithm** used is a combination of the SHA1 hash function and the RSA public key cryptography system.
- The **Subject** and **Issuer** contain your partner's name and Develetech company information.
- The **Validity ends** date implies that the certificate is valid for five years after it was first issued.

- The **Public key** is generated with RSA and is a 1,024-bit hexadecimal value.
- There is a **SHA1 digest** and **SHA1 digest of public key** in hexadecimal format.

d) When you're finished, select **OK**, then **Close**. Close Adobe Reader.

TOPIC C

Choose Cryptographic Implementations

The general techniques used in cryptography are included in industry standard protocols and suites. These solutions tend to target certain networking channels or implementations, like email, remote shell, and web browsing, to offer a complete cryptographic package. This eases the burden on security professionals like yourself from having to incorporate cryptographic techniques on an individual or case-by-case basis. In this topic, you'll choose these implementations to address the needs of the business. Doing so will help you streamline enterprise security, particularly in the areas of confidentiality and integrity.

DRM

Digital rights management (DRM) is technology that attempts to control how digital content can and cannot be used after it is sold. In many DRM schemes, this means providing protection against unauthorized copying of copyrighted works, like documents, media, software, and many other forms of digital content. DRM often uses algorithms to encrypt data, and only those users or devices with the proper decryption key may be able to access or copy that data successfully.

DRM may be useful for an enterprise that publishes intellectual property, as DRM will likely limit customers' ability to share their purchased content with others. For example, an online music service may encrypt songs a user downloads so that only specific software or hardware with the decryption key can play that music. The service can prevent the user from copying the song, as well as set an expiration date for when the user can no longer play the file. However, DRM like this can be bypassed. A user may simply use recording software to record the song as it plays, then save that recording to a DRM-free file.

Watermarking

Digital watermarking is a DRM mechanism that uses steganographic techniques to embed data within media to enforce copyright protection. Data is embedded in a file so that certain hardware or software platforms can validate its authenticity. The hidden data may include information about its source for identity purposes, such as the copyright owner and the media distributor.

Watermarking does not directly prevent users from copying data; rather, it serves to alert distributors or users to any unauthorized content that the system detects. For example, a music distributor may change a song in a way that is imperceptible to human hearing, while still identifying the distributor as its source. This could be used to prove that unauthorized sharing of content has taken place. Keep in mind that certain software can remove a digital watermark from virtual media like audio and video files, while leaving the rest of the media relatively intact.

SSL/TLS

Secure Sockets Layer (SSL) and Transport Layer Security (TLS) are security protocols that combine digital certificates for authentication with public key data encryption.

SSL/TLS generally provides the security guarantees of authenticity, integrity, and confidentiality:

- **Authenticity**: The protocol uses public key cryptography to authenticate the server and client. Also, there is typically a certificate authority which is used during this step to verify the public key sent by the server to the client.
- **Integrity**: The protocol uses a *message authentication code (MAC)* to provide integrity of the data sent. This prevents a malicious user from tampering with the communications.

- **Confidentiality**: The protocol uses symmetric cryptography with a negotiated shared key to encrypt and decrypt messages between the client and server. This provides confidentiality because the shared key is only known to the client and server, as they have the public and private keys necessary to encrypt and decrypt the channel on which the shared key was agreed.

Because of these security guarantees, SSL/TLS has become the de facto protocol for protecting HTTP traffic through web browsers. Before you consider SSL/TLS, keep in mind that the major weak point of SSL/TLS encryption is the certificate authority. A certificate's validity depends on the state of the CA, and if the CA is compromised, that entire trust relationship is compromised. This is particularly difficult to control when the focus is on the Internet, as private organizations must rely on the few public authorities that web browsers implicitly trust. Intranet web servers, on the other hand, can integrate with enterprise CAs that you have control over, and subsequently, are responsible for.

Examples

Virtually all organizations that allow customers to exchange sensitive financial data with their web servers implement some form of SSL. Online banking, for example, is a particularly strong candidate for the protocol as thousands of customers may be depositing, withdrawing, and transferring funds into and from their accounts electronically every single day. Even websites that do not face the public Internet will benefit from SSL/TLS if they routinely handle sensitive information. For example, a university might have its own intranet website set up for students to use on campus. Even though access is limited, the university will want to prevent students from being able to hijack other students' sessions.

TLS vs. SSL

Although they are often used in conjunction with one another, SSL is a predecessor of TLS. The latest versions of TLS are more flexible and secure than SSL, but TLS is not backwards compatible with SSL. Very few websites actually implement the most up-to-date version of TLS.

After SSL version 3.0, the next update was renamed TLS 1.0 and brought minor changes to the protocol. TLS 1.1 added protection against attacks that exploit the CBC mode of block cipher operation. TLS 1.2, the current version as of May 2014, replaced the combination hash function MD5-SHA-1 with the more secure SHA-256, as well as adding support for AES.

SSH

Secure Shell (SSH) is a protocol used for secure remote login and secure transfer of data. To ensure security, the entire SSH session, including authentication, is encrypted using a variety of encryption methods. SSH is the preferred protocol for working with File Transfer Protocol (FTP) and is used primarily on Linux® and UNIX® systems to access shell accounts. Microsoft® Windows® does not offer native support for SSH, but it can be implemented by using a third-party tool such as PuTTY.

 Note: SSH is meant to replace Telnet, an older remote login protocol that lacks encryption.

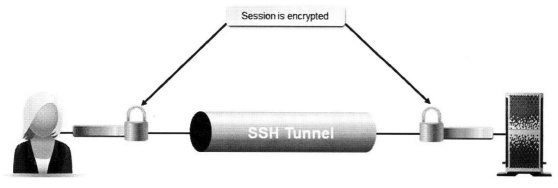

Figure 5-14: Using an SSH tunnel to remotely access a web server.

In the enterprise environment, SSH is often used to log into and execute commands on a remote host like a file server. For example, a network admin may open a shell to a rack-mounted server that has no display or is located offsite. This gives the admin an interface to the particular server where they can manage that server's processes from their own desktop workstation. The encryption that SSH provides will secure this communication from any eavesdropping, and since perfect forward secrecy comes standard with SSH, any past communications will remain secure if the current session key is compromised.

PGP and GPG

Pretty Good Privacy (PGP) is a publicly available email security and authentication utility that uses a variation of public key cryptography to encrypt emails: the sender encrypts the contents of the email message and then encrypts the key that was used to encrypt the contents. The encrypted key is sent with the email, and the receiver decrypts the key and then uses the key to decrypt the contents. PGP also uses public key cryptography to digitally sign emails to authenticate the sender and the contents.

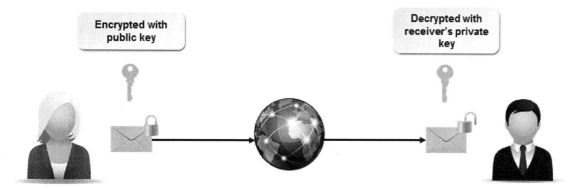

Figure 5-15: PGP encryption.

PGP is a viable method of ensuring authenticity and integrity in email communications across an enterprise. Be aware, however, that PGP generally requires additional end-user plugins and software to operate. This may make it less attractive to a large enterprise that needs to account for significant end-user integration and management.

GNU Privacy Guard (GPG) is a free, open-source version of PGP that provides equivalent encryption and authentication services. It supports a wide variety of cryptographic algorithms, including RSA, AES, SHA, and Triple Data Encryption Standard (3DES). GPG is compliant with current PGP services and meets the latest standards issued by the Internet Engineering Task Force (IETF).

 Note: GNU refers to the GNU General Public License (GPL), a widely adopted licensing system that allows free use, sharing, and modification of software that is under license. GPG is licensed under version 3 of the GNU GPL.

S/MIME

Secure/Multipurpose Internet Mail Extensions (S/MIME) is another email-based encryption standard that adds digital signatures and public key cryptography to traditional *MIME* communications. MIME defines several advanced characteristics of email messages that had previously been unavailable, including the ability to send text in character sets other than ASCII and the ability to send non-text file attachments. S/MIME provides assurances of confidentiality, integrity, authentication, and non-repudiation, and is built into most modern email clients.

Although similar, S/MIME differs from PGP in a couple key ways. In S/MIME communications, both the sender and receiver rely on the same certifying authority, rather than exchanging keys in advance. In PGP, each party establishes their own trust and can adjust key usage according to their agreed-upon wishes. S/MIME is also more easily administrated than PGP in an enterprise environment, as it relies on centralized management rather than requiring end users to install specific plugins.

 Note: To learn how to create digital certificates to use in email encryption, access the LearnTO **Create an S/MIME Certificate** presentation from the **LearnTO** tile on the CHOICE Course screen.

Guidelines for Choosing Cryptographic Implementations

Use the following guidelines when choosing cryptographic implementations:

- Implement DRM to protect intellectual property from unauthorized use and sharing.
- Keep in mind that DRM can be bypassed.
- Use watermarking to embed identity information in a media file.
- Keep in mind that watermarking can also be bypassed.
- Use SSL/TLS for secure web communications, preferably the latest versions of TLS.
- Use SSH instead of a protocol like Telnet to execute remote commands on a host.
- Implement PGP and GPG for email encryption, but be aware of the extra software and plugins necessary.
- Use S/MIME email encryption to interface with a CA and streamline administration.

ACTIVITY 5–3
Choosing Cryptographic Implementations

Data Files

C:\093023Data\Implementing Cryptographic Techniques\BvSshServer-Inst.exe

C:\093023Data\Implementing Cryptographic Techniques\putty-0.63-installer.exe

Before You Begin

You will work with a partner in this activity. You will be running the Bitvise SSH Server and using PuTTY as an SSH client to create a secure shell to your partner's server. Your server's firewall has been preconfigured to allow SSH traffic over port 22.

Scenario

Your network administrators will need to access Develetech's various servers throughout the day, and it will be much more efficient and convenient for them to adjust settings from a remote terminal. However, opening up remote access to sensitive hosts can invite a great deal of risk to your organization, so you'll want to make sure that the remote protocols you use protect the confidentiality and integrity of your network communications.

You decide to implement Secure Shell (SSH) remote protocol technology, which will help prevent eavesdropping and tampering of transmissions by encrypting the remote access sessions. You'll install SSH on your servers and configure a specialized account for remote terminal access. You'll also verify the strength of the encryption algorithms the SSH server supports and adjust security settings, like blocking failed login attempts and creating an IP address whitelist of acceptable remote workstations. You'll then test your remote connection with PuTTY, a Windows-based SSH client. Lastly, you'll confirm that any remote SSH activity is logged for later review.

---

1. Install the SSH server.
   a) Open File Explorer and navigate to **C:\093023\Implementing Cryptographic Techniques**.
   b) Double-click the **BvSshServer-Inst** file.
   c) In the **Open File - Security Warning** dialog box, select **Run**.

d) In the **Bitvise SSH Server 6.07 Installer** dialog box, check the **I agree to accept all the terms of this License Agreement** check box and select **Install**.

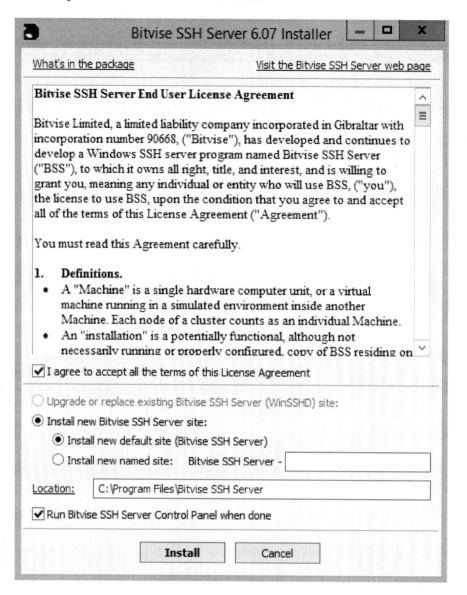

e) In the **Bitvise SSH Server Edition Selection** dialog box, select **Standard edition**, then select **OK**.
f) After the installation completes, select **OK**.

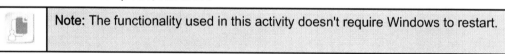

Note: The functionality used in this activity doesn't require Windows to restart.

2. Add a Windows account to the SSH server.
   a) In the **Bitvise SSH Server Easy Settings** dialog box, verify that the **Listening port** is **22** and **Open Windows Firewall** opens ports to the local subnet.

b) At the top of the dialog box, select the **Windows accounts** tab.

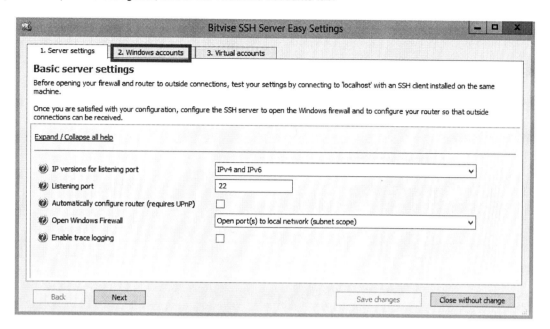

c) In the **Simplified Windows accounts** page, if necessary, uncheck the **Allow login to any Windows account**.
   This will ensure that only the accounts you specify will be allowed SSH access.

d) At the bottom-left of the window, select the **Add** button.

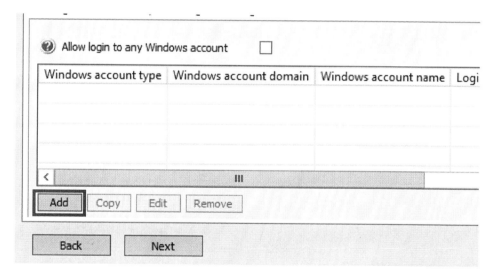

e) In the **Adding new entry to Simplified Windows accounts** dialog box, to the right of the **Windows account name** text box, select the **lookup** link.

f) In the **Select User or Group** dialog box, in the **Enter the object name to select** text box, type *SSHclient* and select **Check Names**.

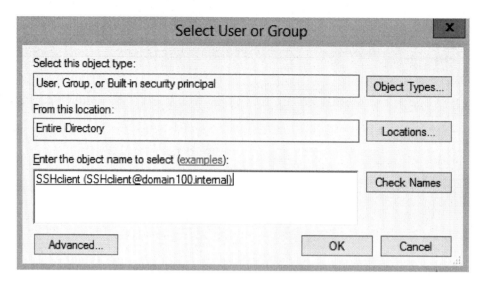

g) Select **OK**.
h) Verify that this account has login, file transfer, terminal, and port forwarding access, and select **OK**.

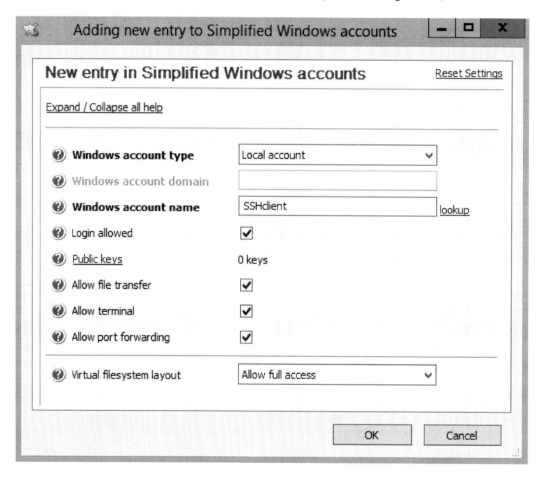

i) Verify that the SSHclient account is now listed, then select **Save changes**.
j) In the **Bitvise SSH Server - Initial Settings Confirmation** message box, select **Save settings**.

3. Verify advanced security settings on the SSH server.

a) In the **Bitvise SSH Server Control Panel** window, select the **Edit advanced settings** link.

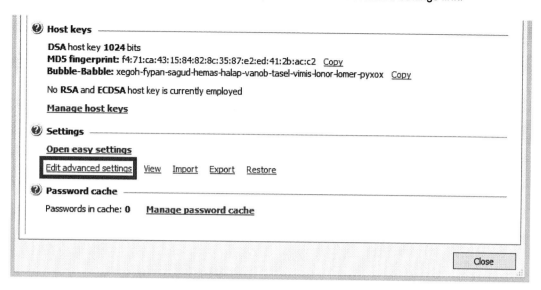

b) In the **Bitvise SSH Server Advanced Settings** window, in the navigation pane, under **Server**, select **Logging**.

c) Verify that the SSH server will record logs in both the Windows Event Log and a separate text file. By default, Bitvise SSH Server logs errors and warnings to the Windows Event Log, while logging errors, warnings, and information to its own text file.

d) From the navigation pane, under **Algorithms**, select **Encryption**. By default, Bitvise SSH Server supports strong encryption algorithms like AES and 3DES.

4. Change SSH session security settings.

a) From the navigation pane, select **Session**.

b) Change the **Maximum login attempts** to *2* After two unsuccessful login attempts, the SSH server will terminate the client's connection.

c) Change the **Login attempt delay (s)** to *10*

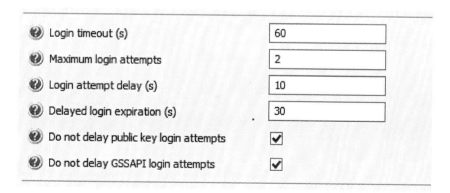

The client must wait 10 seconds after the first attempt fails to try to log in again.

d) Scroll down and select the **IP blocking - white list** link.

e) Select **Add**.

f) In the **Adding new entry to IP blocking - white list** dialog box, in the **IPv4 address**, enter your partner's IP address.

g) Select **OK**, then verify that your partner's IP address is whitelisted. The SSH server will not automatically block login attempts originating from this IP address. An IP address is automatically blocked if it fails too many login attempts. The default threshold is 20 attempts.

h) Select **OK**.

5. Start your SSH server.
   a) In the **Bitvise SSH Server Control Panel** window, select the **Start Server** link.

> **Bitvise SSH Server 6.07**
> Copyright (C) 2000-2014 by Bitvise Limited.
>
> **EVALUATION** - 30 days remaining
> **Apply activation code** to remove evaluation time limit.
>
> **Please purchase within 30 days of initial installation.**
> See www.bitvise.com/ssh-server for purchasing instructions.
>
> Bitvise SSH Server service is **stopped**   **Start Server**   Startup type: Automatic
> Open log folder viewer

   b) In the **Confirm Windows Firewall Open For Local Network Only** message box, select **Start Server**.
   c) Verify that the Bitvise SSH Server service is **running**.

> **Bitvise SSH Server 6.07**
> Copyright (C) 2000-2014 by Bitvise Limited.
>
> **EVALUATION** - 30 days remaining
> **Apply activation code** to remove evaluation time limit.
>
> **Please purchase within 30 days of initial installation.**
> See www.bitvise.com/ssh-server for purchasing instructions.
>
> Bitvise SSH Server service is **running**   **Stop Server**   Startup type: Automatic
> Open log folder viewer

6. Install the PuTTY SSH client.
   a) In File Explorer, navigate to **C:\093023Data\Implementing Cryptographic Techniques**.
   b) Double-click the **putty-0.63-installer** file.
   c) If necessary, in the **Open File - Security Warning** dialog box, select **Run**.
   d) In the **Setup - PuTTY** wizard, select **Next**.
   e) On the **Select Destination Location** page, select **Next**.
   f) On the **Select Start Menu Folder** page, select **Next**.
   g) On the **Select Additional Tasks** page, check the **Create a desktop icon for PuTTY** check box and select **Next**.
   h) On the **Ready to Install** page, select **Install**.
   i) After installation completes, uncheck the **View README.txt** check box and select **Finish**.

7. Establish an SSH connection with your partner's server.
   a) From the desktop, double-click PuTTY.
   b) In the **PuTTY Configuration** window, in the **Category** navigation pane, under **Connection**, select **SSH**.

c) In the **Encryption cipher selection policy** list box, verify that PuTTY prioritizes the AES algorithm, which Bitvise SSH Server supports.

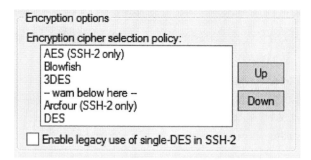

The algorithms below the **warn below here** line are insecure and will produce an alert if used to encrypt the session.

d) From the navigation pane, select **Session**.

e) In the **Host Name (or IP address)** text box, type your partner's IP address and select **Open**.

f) In the **PuTTY Security Alert** message box, select **Yes** to trust the host and add its key to the cache.

8. Log in to the remote terminal session.

a) At the **login as** prompt, enter *SSHclient*

 Note: SSHclient is a preconfigured account on the Windows domain.

b) At the prompt, enter *!Pass1234* as the password.

 Caution: Be careful when inputting the password, as the characters will not appear for you to check.

```
login as: SSHclient
SSHclient@192.168.36.100's password:
```

You are successfully logged in to your partner's server under their SSH client account.

9. Test the SSH terminal functionality.

a) At the prompt, enter *cd C:* to change to the **C** directory.

 Note: This character is a backslash.

b) Enter *mkdir test*

```
Microsoft Windows [Version 6.3.9600]
(c) 2013 Microsoft Corporation. All rights reserved.

C:\Users\SSHclient>cd C:\

C:\>mkdir test

C:\>
```

c) Wait for your partner to do the previous substep, then open File Explorer on your own host and check your **C** directory for the **test** folder that they just created.

d) Delete the **test** folder, then close File Explorer.

    e) At the SSH command prompt, enter **exit** to log out and close PuTTY.

10. Review the connection logs.

    a) In the **Bitvise SSH Server Control Panel** window, select the **Activity** tab.

    b) Verify that the **Activity log** page shows connection and disconnection events from a PuTTY client using the SSHclient account.

    c) Select the **Open log folder viewer** link at the top-right.

    d) In the **Bitvise SSH Server Log Folder Viewer** window, double-click the most recent log file to open it in Notepad.

       The log file is in XML format and has recorded various information about the SSH session, including:

       • Your partner's whitelisted IP address that was used to establish the connection.

       • The account and access information your partner used to log in.

       • Various session and key exchange transmissions.

11. Stop Bitvise SSH Server and close the application.

    a) Close Notepad, then close the **Bitvise SSH Server Log Folder Viewer** window.

    b) On the **Bitvise SSH Server Control Panel**, select the **Server** tab.

    c) Select the **Stop Server** link.

    d) Select the **Close** button.

    e) On the desktop taskbar, select the **Show hidden icons** button, then right-click the **Bitvise** icon and select **Exit Control Panel**.

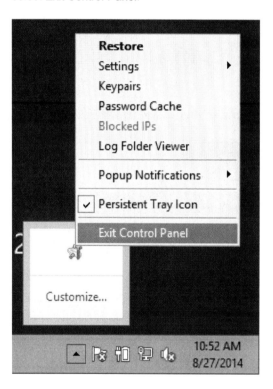

Summary

In this lesson, you described the fundamentals of cryptography, as well its goals for the benefit of the enterprise. You then chose specific cryptography techniques to implement to secure your information's confidentiality, integrity, and non-repudiation. Lastly, you selected protocols that provide various cryptographic techniques in comprehensive, easy-to-deploy packages. With this thorough understanding of encryption, you'll be able to secure your enterprise's information and communications in some of the most effective ways possible.

Where would you find the various cryptographic techniques used in your business?

What cryptographic implements do you use in your business? Which implementations would you like to use?

 Note: Check your CHOICE Course screen for opportunities to interact with your classmates, peers, and the larger CHOICE online community about the topics covered in this course or other topics you are interested in. From the Course screen you can also access available resources for a more continuous learning experience.

6 Implementing Security Controls for Hosts

Lesson Time: 3 hours, 30 minutes

Lesson Objectives

In this lesson, you will:

- Select host hardware and software.

- Harden hosts.

- Virtualize servers and desktops.

- Implement cloud augmented security services.

- Protect boot loaders.

Lesson Introduction

You've discussed and implemented the all-important techniques of authentication, authorization, and encryption. Now you'll focus your security efforts on the four major systems that make up information technology in an enterprise: hosts, storage, network, and applications. In this lesson, you'll begin by looking at the hosts in your domain. Hosts are the individual devices that communicate within your network, and the security of each device is fundamental to the security of your business operations as a whole. Any single device left unprotected can be all of an attack surface a malicious user needs to compromise your network, your data, and your business. So, you'll consider some of the common security challenges that enterprise hosts face, and then choose the best controls to implement.

TOPIC A

Select Host Hardware and Software

Selecting the appropriate host hardware and software will allow you to start your host security procedures on the right track. If your environment runs on systems that natively provide at least some level of security, you will have an easier time keeping that environment as a whole protected. In this topic, you will consider several different hardware and software solutions that provide host security, and select the appropriate ones based on your enterprise needs.

HSM

A *hardware security module (HSM)* is a physical device that enforces encryption and access control capabilities in a computer. HSMs are typically plugged into a port on the computer, like a Universal Serial Bus (USB), and prevent the execution of external programs that attempt to tamper with the computer. The HSM can respond to tampering a number of ways, including logging the action, triggering an alarm, or locking down the system entirely.

Figure 6-1: A USB flash drive with HSM functionality connected to a server.

HSMs typically verify the integrity of data on a computer through message authentication codes (MACs). For example, when an authorized user makes changes to an employee's salary in a database full of employee financial information, the HSM creates a MAC of that valid input. If a user or program asks the HSM to scan a salary value and its MAC is incorrect, the HSM will identify that the database has been tampered with. The HSM itself secures the key that it uses to construct the MAC, so it should be infeasible for the attacker to reproduce that valid MAC. This makes it important for the HSM to conduct secure key management to both create and maintain cryptographic keys.

HSMs typically have a standardized user interface for easy programming and customization. Aside from integrity verification, HSMs can be used as a secure key generator and storage container for a certificate authority (CA) in a public key infrastructure. HSMs can also take on key generation in applications that use Secure Sockets Layer/Transport Layer Security (SSL/TLS) to accelerate the process. HSMs also support scalability in an expanding enterprise infrastructure through clustering and load balancing. However, one drawback of HSMs is that they can be prohibitively expensive for smaller organizations.

TPM

Trusted Platform Module (TPM) is a hardware-based encryption specification that allows secure cryptoprocessors to generate cryptographic keys to be used to authenticate hardware, encrypt disks, enforce digital rights management (DRM), or for any other encryption-enabled application. TPM can also be used as a Basic Input/Output System (BIOS) security method by using full disk encryption apps such as BitLocker® to secure the operating system's volume. Several major PC manufacturers provide TPM-integrated microprocessors with their products.

Figure 6–2: A TPM cryptoprocessor.

Trusted OS

A *trusted operating system (trusted OS)* is an operating system that security professionals have examined to see whether or not it meets a certain standard based on the *Common Criteria (CC)*. The CC is a set of standards developed by a group of governments working together to create a baseline of security assurance for a product. When a trusted OS is used, an organization's claims of having a "secure" product can be evaluated and judged. Anything tested is then given an *Evaluation Assurance Level (EAL)* rating from 1 to 7 that states the level of secure features offered by the system. One key to this process is that it evaluates the security features that an operating system offers, not those that are implemented by default. This means it is still the responsibility of the organization to implement the available security features.

In typical trusted OS implementations, the operating system will isolate its resources and services from applications that run on the OS to offer a strong defense against potential exploits. Effective trusted OS implementations also categorize levels of access through various roles, and prevents root level roles from being an attack surface for a malicious user to take advantage of. Trusted OSs should also abide by the principal of least privilege in doling out rights to users and groups. You would generally implement a trusted OS when the data that your operating system will support is highly confidential, such as trade secrets, research and development, and classified government systems.

Examples

Some examples of trusted operating systems that have been CC certified include:

- Oracle® Solaris 11.1

- Red Hat® Enterprise Linux® 6.2
- Microsoft® Windows Server® 2008 R2
- Apple® Mac OS® X 10.6

 Note: A full list of all CC-certified products, including operating systems, is available at **www.commoncriteriaportal.org/products/**

Endpoint Security

An *endpoint* is any host that is exposed to another host in a communication channel. This can refer to servers and workstations, but also includes portable endpoint storage devices such as thumb drives. The proliferation of these devices means that unauthorized endpoint access has become a major concern for security professionals. To prevent unauthorized endpoint access and potential exploits, endpoint security software configures host devices to allow only authorized endpoint devices to connect to other hosts in a network. Typical endpoint security software provides security administrators with tools that address a variety of different security issues.

Endpoint Security Software

The following table describes various endpoint security software solutions that you can implement in your enterprise.

Endpoint Security Control	Description
Anti-malware	Malware is any malicious or unwanted software that can cause damage to a host in a number of ways. Anti-malware software uses different methods to scan a host for the presence of known or potential malware, and then seeks to either isolate it from the rest of the host or remove it outright. Anti-malware is typically broken up into two categories: • **Antivirus**: This brand of anti-malware software tends to target viruses, worms, Trojan horses, and rootkits. Antivirus solutions are critical to a defense-in-depth enterprise strategy because, if by some chance a virus should evade detection by one of your other security measures, you may be able to stop it at the host level. While viruses, worms, Trojan horses, and rootkits are all different manifestations of malware, they all fall into the same family and possess signatures that make them detectable, especially once they're known. Signature-based antivirus solutions look for the specific characteristics of a virus to detect their presence in a host. They can also be heuristic-based, examining the normal operations of a system and looking for anomalies and abnormalities. • **Anti-spyware**: Unlike the malware mentioned earlier, spyware focuses on secretive information gathering without the user's knowledge. In fact, the less disruptive spyware is to the machine, the more likely it will evade detection. Spyware can be difficult to detect and remove since often there are specific procedures for removing it that may be different from one tool to another. This is why a successful anti-spyware strategy will include spyware detection and removal tools like Spybot - Search & Destroy® and HijackThis, more secure browsers (e.g., Internet Explorer® is the most widely targeted and exploited browser while Mozilla Firefox®, Google Chrome™, and Safari® currently possess fewer vulnerabilities), and user training and awareness. The last point is important when users have any sort of administrative control over their own host machines and have permission to install software.
Spam filters	Since spam is ubiquitous, having a defense-in-depth strategy against spam is critical and spam protection can be multi-layered. Most network solutions will have a spam filter at the mail server level, attempting to protect the organization as a whole. By utilizing a spam filter at the host level, any spam that gets through the network level detection can be potentially caught and removed before it ever gets to the user. Spam filters use a number of different approaches for removing unwanted email, including determining if the email is coming from a known spammer (blacklisting), or looking at the content of the email and determining if it has the markings of spam. Unsolicited email is a breeding ground for viruses and information gathering scams. As such, it is more than just a nuisance, but rather a genuine security threat that you should address in your host environments.

Endpoint Security Control	Description
Patch management	Patch management is the practice of monitoring for, obtaining, evaluating, testing, and deploying software patches and updates. As the number of computer systems in use has grown over recent years, so has the volume of vulnerabilities and corresponding patches and updates intended to address those vulnerabilities. So, the task of managing and applying them can be very time-consuming and inefficient without an organized patch management system. Especially for third party software, use a patch management system to ensure that every host application is running with the latest security requirements and updates issued by manufacturers. Patch management software is also useful for rolling back a patch to a previous version in the event that the new patch opens up vulnerabilities.
Host-based intrusion prevention system (HIPS)/ host-based intrusion detection system (HIDS)	A HIPS/HIDS monitors a specific system to look for anomalies in behavior. These anomalies can be anything from odd browser behavior to a process trying to change a file. They examine various resources of the system and determine whether that component is behaving appropriately and, if it isn't, the HIPS/HIDS acts on that. A HIDS is passive and will simply notify the administrator that an anomaly has occurred, whereas a HIPS is more advanced and will actively attempt to halt the behavior to prevent damage or unauthorized access. Either control is an excellent tool for security professionals to use at endpoints in their organization.
Data loss prevention (DLP)	DLP is a software solution that detects and prevents sensitive information in a system from being stolen or otherwise falling into the wrong hands. The software actively monitors data in any state—whether in use or at rest—and detects any unauthorized attempts to destroy, move, or copy that data. If any suspicious activity is detected, some DLP software is able to block users from interacting with data in specific ways. For example, a security administrator might put a DLP system in place on a host to detect any attempt to send confidential files on that host over email, and then prevent that email from reaching its destination. In this respect, data loss prevention has the opposite goal of an intrusion detection/prevention system (IDPS); instead of focusing on inbound attacks, DLP software protects outbound data.
Host-based firewalls	While a network firewall is designed to protect the entire infrastructure, a host-based firewall has the much smaller task of protecting the individual computers it is installed on. They allow for individual configuration on that host; while the network firewall may need to require certain types of traffic, the host firewall can limit traffic to only those protocols and ports that are necessary. As part of a defense-in-depth strategy, host-based firewalls also provide the advantage of being able to prevent malicious software from trying to send information from an infected host. They also provide another layer of security should there be a compromise of the network firewall. Examples of host-based firewalls include the Linux®-based IPTables, the Microsoft® Windows® integrated firewall, Zone Labs ZoneAlarm®, Norton Personal Firewall, COMODO, and Kaspersky™.

Endpoint Security Control	Description
Log monitoring	With an increased number of hosts in an environment, event logs can become too much for any individual administrator to handle. While logs are an excellent resource, they're most helpful to a human reviewer when that reviewer knows what they're looking for. Log monitoring software automates the review process by periodically checking logs created by a host, be they from an operating system, application, or any other component, and looks for anomalies or known unwanted behavior. If the monitoring software detects these conditions, it will alert an administrator. Unlike a HIPS/HIDS, log monitoring software does not analyze runtime behavior, it monitors only what is recorded in output.

Guidelines for Selecting Host Hardware and Software

 Note: All Guidelines for this lesson are available as checklists from the **Checklist** tile on the CHOICE Course screen.

Use the following guidelines to select the host hardware and software solutions for your enterprise.

- Implement an HSM on hosts that need strong assurances of integrity, like databases.
- Use an HSM to generate and store keys for a CA in a PKI.
- Use an HSM to take on SSL/TLS key generation overhead to accelerate the process.
- Consult the Common Criteria for certified operating systems.
- Consult each OSs' EAL for more information on the security features it provides.
- Implement a trusted OS that can properly isolate resources and services from apps.
- Implement a trusted OS that removes root level access to reduce its attack surface.
- Implement anti-malware software like antivirus and anti-spyware at each endpoint in your network.
- Use monitoring software like log monitoring and HIDS to detect anomalous behavior on hosts.
- Use prevention software like HIPS and host-based firewalls to stop incoming attacks.
- Use DLP software to prevent hosts from losing or transferring sensitive data.
- Implement spam filters to avoid security incidents from successful phishing attempts.
- Implement patch management software to automate the process of staying up-to-date on security fixes.

ACTIVITY 6-1
Selecting Host Hardware and Software

Scenario

When it comes to hosts in your environment, you'll want to select the appropriate hardware and software that aids security. Develetech may only have the budget or management resources for a certain type or amount of solutions, but understanding the role of each solution will make it easier for you to choose what's best for the organization.

---

1. What is endpoint security software that detects and actively stops anomalous behavior on a host?

   ○ DLP

   ○ Host-based firewall

   ○ HIDS

   ○ HIPS

2. Which of the following are functions of patch management software? (Select three.)

   ☐ Obtaining updates from a repository.

   ☐ Deploying updates to multiple hosts in a network.

   ☐ Monitoring host health after updates have been applied.

   ☐ Rolling back updates to a previous version.

3. Develetech has a huge amount of host security and event logs that analysts must comb through to perform auditing duties. The current process of viewing logs is inefficient and unproductive. What kind of software solution would you suggest the company implement to streamline auditing? Why?

4. How does an HSM typically ensure the integrity of data? What other security functions can an HSM provide?

5. What are some of the common security characteristics of trusted operating systems?

TOPIC B

Harden Hosts

Now that you've incorporated secure hardware and software solutions in your enterprise, it's time to harden the rest of your hosts. The hardening process can involve industry-tested configurations, as well as your own custom configurations, to optimize the security of each host in your network. Without reinforcing security at the host level, the data on the host, as well the host itself, could be compromised. This topic will help you ensure that your individual devices and equipment are protected from risk and common threat types.

Security and Group Policy Implementation

Before you can begin to directly harden hosts in your enterprise, you need a plan of action. The various security policies you've drafted should now start focusing on the individual workstations, servers, and other devices that populate your security domain. These host hardening policies will give you perspective on what you need to accomplish your business and security goals, as well as allow you to troubleshoot security controls for hosts.

Group policies, for example, allow you to apply a set of security guidelines to a large number of hosts. This alleviates administration and allows for a wide variety of user-based security controls including password lockout schemes and password requirements, as well as system-based controls like system auditing. By means of policy management, you can integrate restricted interfaces that provide users with access only to those things that are absolutely necessary to their tasks and nothing more.

Successful hardening of hosts is not just in the hands of security professionals like yourself, though. Many attacks can be prevented through end-user training on best security practices. Teach your employees ways to keep the hosts safe while using them, including locking and/or shutting down their computers when they are away from them; ignoring spam and other illegitimate email communications; and keeping careful track of mobile devices. Establishing such practices in an end user policy is an important step in actively protecting enterprise property.

Standard Operating Environment

Once you have decided on the operating system to use in your environment, preferably a trusted OS, you should then develop a consistent configuration baseline for that operating system. This allows you to limit the amount of administration necessary, and it also creates a consistent security environment where the same configuration can be used from host to host. When updates are necessary, you can apply them to all systems rather than having to perform individual patch and update management. Additionally, it will be easier for you to scale your security controls and adapt to new threats and vulnerabilities.

A standard operating environment in your enterprise will consist of many different configurations that depend on your business needs and the function of the host itself. For example, you may configure your employee workstation environments to restrict what kinds of apps the employees can download and use on these workstations. This process is called application whitelisting and blacklisting. An *application whitelist* is a list of apps that you specifically allow the host to access or work with in some way. Apps that are not explicitly listed are by default blocked on that host. Conversely, an *application blacklist* is a list of apps that you specifically block on the host. Any apps that are not on this list are by default allowed on the host.

Whitelists vs. Blacklists

Whitelists tend to be more ideal than blacklists; it's virtually impossible for you to know *every* app that you don't want on a host, so maintaining a blacklist won't stop any unknowns out there from running on the host. Apps on a whitelist, on the other hand, are apps you know and trust. It's almost always better from a security perspective to accidentally block a legitimate app than it is to accidentally allow a malicious app.

Command Shell Restrictions

The majority of end users have no need for access to command shells/command prompts and other administrative tools on their machines. It is more likely that their use of these features would create a problem rather than facilitate correcting one. By means of the policies mentioned previously, you can eliminate access to these features for all but those with necessary administrative control of the host. This will greatly decrease the chances that an end user will accidentally cause a problem and increase the host's attack surface.

In specific implementations, you may choose to restrict specific commands or restrict access to the command shell entirely. If the host's operating system defaults to allowing an insecure command protocol like Telnet, it would be worthwhile to turn off this service. Some computers, especially those used by customers in demonstrations, should block command shells from executing on guest accounts.

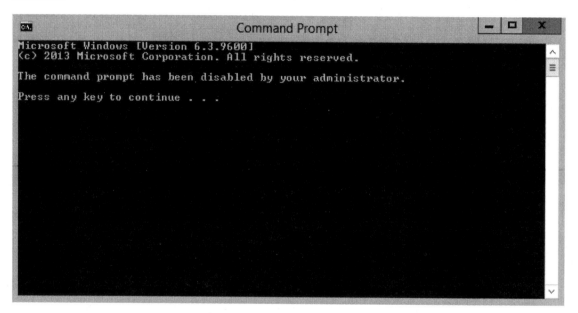

Figure 6-3: Command prompt disabled on a host.

 Note: To learn how to prevent users from accessing the command prompt on a Windows host, access the LearnTO **Disable the Windows Command Prompt** presentation from the **LearnTO** tile on the CHOICE Course screen.

Patch Management

As you've seen, patch management is an integral part of host security. Patches are inevitable, and they cover a wide variety of systems and components. As part of your host hardening strategy, you should integrate patch management software and configure it based on the context of each host. Mission-critical hosts might need to be treated differently than less critical ones. A misapplied patch on the former could significantly weaken its defenses and allow attackers to exploit newly introduced vulnerabilities. Even security fixes pushed by a vendor may unintentionally leave the host insecure if those fixes strip the host of the strong security configurations you've already put in place.

To effectively maintain the strength of host configurations, many organizations have taken to creating official patch management policies that define the who, what, where, when, why, and how of patch management for that organization. A patch management program might include:

- An individual responsible for subscribing to and reviewing vendor and security patches and updating newsletters.
- A review and triage of the updates into urgent, important, and non-critical categories.
- An offline patch test environment where urgent and important patches can be installed and tested for functionality and impact.
- Immediate administrative push delivery of approved urgent patches.
- Weekly administrative push delivery of approved important patches.
- A periodic evaluation phase and full rollout for non-critical patches.

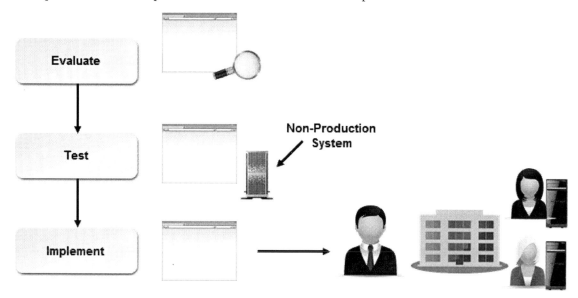

Figure 6–4: A system for patch management.

Out–of–Band Communication

There are various interfaces that hosts use to communicate with each other, and these can be out-of-band or in-band. *Out-of-band* communication refers to communication that operates outside of normal channels. For example, a network interface controller (NIC) on a host can be put out-of-band, and the host will use this NIC as a dedicated interface with which to send or receive data that is separate from normal network communications. Configuring out-of-band NICs, access control lists (ACLs), management interfaces, and data interfaces provides administrative functionality that an in-band interface would typically not have:

- Reset a host if the main communications channel fails.
- Rebooting a host that is shut down.
- Reinstalling a host's operating system.
- Mounting physical media like DVDs.
- Accessing a host's BIOS.
- Monitoring hardware components like fans and power supplies.

Using dedicated interfaces with out-of-band communications isolates key functionality from the rest of network communications, which may make it more difficult for an attacker to compromise the hosts in your enterprise if they are able to compromise the in-band channels.

Peripheral Restrictions

In computing, a *peripheral* is any device that connects to a host computer but is not considered a fundamental part of it. Peripherals can be everything from input devices like a mouse and keyboard, to output devices like monitors and speakers. They can also refer to external storage media like thumb drives and external hard drives. Peripherals are essential to most computing environments, but they can nevertheless be abused by an opportunistic threat. When you control what peripherals your hosts use, and how the hosts use them, then you'll add another layer of defense to your hardening process.

For example, a remote server doesn't need a dedicated mouse and keyboard, nor does it need a dedicated monitor. An administrator who remotes into a server does so from their own workstation that has these peripherals. The administrator is authenticated and maintaining a secure connection from that workstation; an attacker who can physically access input and output peripherals plugged directly into the server doesn't necessarily need to compromise the remote session to breach security. This is why you should be judicious in how you treat peripheral usage on your various hosts.

Communications Protocols Used by Peripherals

Beyond the simple control of choosing to allow or disallow certain peripherals, you should also consider the communications protocols that these peripherals often use. The peripherals themselves aren't the only source of risk; the way in which they communicate can also be a security issue. The following table describes three common peripheral communications protocols and their associated security concerns.

Communications Protocol	Security Concerns
Universal Serial Bus (USB)	USB is the most common peripheral communications protocol, and it can provide advanced functions like power and data transfer. Because of these capabilities and their ubiquity, USB ports are often the threat vector for a great number of attacks on hosts, including data exfiltration, spreading malware, and capturing keystrokes. Nearly every modern desktop or laptop comes with multiple USB ports for easy plug and play. What's more, USB drives containing sensitive information are often lost or stolen, which presents great risk to an organization whose employees transfer data using these thumb drives on a daily basis. Since it is difficult to control the physical security of such small and portable devices, you should consider encryption as the most plausible way to combat this risk. Otherwise, your policy should severely restrict employee use of USB thumb drives in the workplace.

Communications Protocol	Security Concerns
Bluetooth	Bluetooth® is a wireless communications protocol with a 30-foot transmission limit. This protocol is commonly used to exchange data between devices that are within close proximity, like a wireless headset receiving audio transmitted from a smartphone in the user's pocket. There are a couple of attacks that specifically exploit vulnerabilities in the Bluetooth protocol: *Bluejacking* is an attack in which an attacker sends unsolicited messages from one Bluetooth device to another. These messages can lead to device malfunctions or even propagate viruses, including Trojan horses. To control for this type of attack, you should configure Bluetooth-enabled devices to reject anonymous contacts and run in non-discoverable mode. *Bluesnarfing* is an attack in which an attacker gains unauthorized access to information on a Bluetooth-enabled device. Unlike bluejacking, access to wireless devices such as smartphones, tablets, mobile phones, and laptops by bluesnarfing can lead to the exploitation of private information, including email messages, contact information, calendar entries, images, videos, and any data stored on the device. Beyond ensuring that the Bluetooth transmissions are using encryption, you could also implement encryption on the device's end as well.
FireWire	FireWire® is the name that Apple® gives to IEEE 1394, a peripheral communications interface comparable to USB in terms of function. Because FireWire is much less popular than USB, it does not possess the same level of risk. However, the ability for a user to easily transfer data between devices using FireWire is still a concern. Additionally, because of the way in which some implementations of FireWire map different physical memory spaces in hardware instead of software, an attacker may be able to attach a FireWire device to a host machine and retrieve cryptographic keys stored in physical memory addresses.

Full Disk Encryption

Full disk encryption is a powerful technique for hardening hosts that need entire volumes to remain confidential instead of just individual files or databases. While a host may benefit from these lower-level encryption techniques, full disk encryption has its share of advantages:

- Esoteric memory like swap space and temporary files are included with full disk encryption.
- Users don't need to remember what individual information to encrypt.
- Destroying all data on a disk in case of an emergency is as quick and simple as destroying the key.

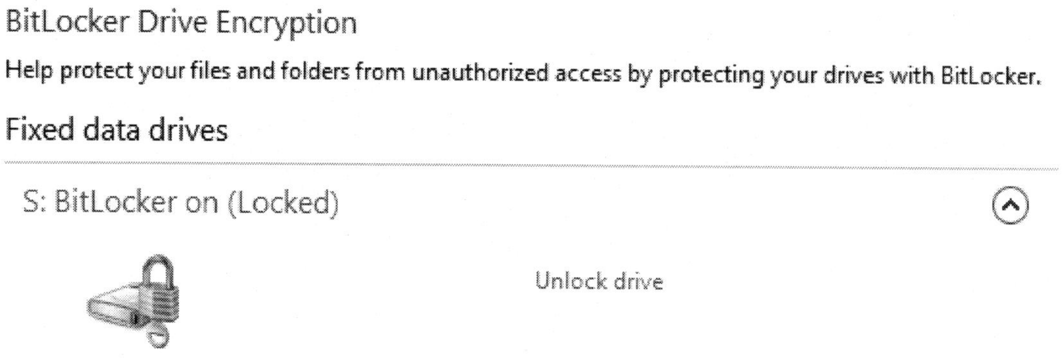

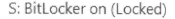 BitLocker Drive Encryption

Help protect your files and folders from unauthorized access by protecting your drives with BitLocker.

Fixed data drives

S: BitLocker on (Locked)

                                      Unlock drive

Figure 6-5: A disk encrypted with Microsoft's BitLocker.

Keep in mind that disk encryption often brings with it a significant amount of overhead, as entire volumes need to go through the encryption process. This is particularly a concern if you intend to encrypt large or numerous storage media. Depending on how vital a storage medium is to your business, you may find that the total cost of ownership (TCO) outweighs the need for such a thorough solution.

Cold Boot Attack

While full disk encryption is a strong host hardening method, it is susceptible to at least one kind of attack. In a *cold boot attack*, a malicious user with physical access to a computer with an encrypted disk may be able to retrieve encryption keys after starting the computer from its off state. When the operating system loads, the attacker may be able to scan the system's Random Access Memory (RAM) to find the keys that were stored temporarily in memory and not just on the disk itself. Although RAM is volatile, it can take several minutes after losing power before data is completely erased. This highlights the need for strong physical security policies to work in tandem with other areas of security.

Guidelines for Hardening Hosts

Use the following guidelines when hardening hosts in your enterprise:

* Incorporate tools that enforce your existing security policies.
* Install a standard operating environment on all secure hosts and whitelist software that is allowed to run in that environment.
* Restrict shell commands per user or per host for least privilege purposes.
* Implement patch management software that will allow you to test software updates, and then deploy them efficiently.
* Restrict host access to peripheral protocols like USB, Bluetooth, and FireWire.
* Implement full disk encryption on sensitive host storage media as long as you can manage the increased overhead.

ACTIVITY 6-2
Hardening a Windows Host with Patch Management

Before You Begin

You will be using Windows Server Update Service (WSUS), Microsoft's patch management tool.

Scenario

You'd like to have more control over how patches, hotfixes, and other updates are applied to the hosts in your enterprise environment. Particularly, Develetech's Windows Server hosts require meticulous management of the updates that Microsoft regularly publishes. The default Windows Update service is inadequate, as not all of these updates necessarily apply or are relevant to your hosts and their roles. You need to be judicious in what kind of changes you allow to the endpoints in your network.

The Windows Server Update Service (WSUS) is a patch manager that focuses on updates to hosts running Microsoft products and services. You'll use WSUS to set rules about what types of updates your host server downloads and installs, and to what environments, services, and software they apply. With this fine-grained control over your update deployment, you'll be more prepared to secure your endpoints against unnecessary or potentially incompatible changes to your host software, while at the same time ensuring that the hosts receive all of the essential bug and security fixes.

---

1. Add the WSUS role to your server.

    a) In **Server Manager**, select **Add roles and features**.

    b) In the **Add Roles and Features** wizard, select **Next** three times.

    c) On the **Select server roles** page, check the **Windows Server Update Services** check box and select **Add Features**.

    d) Select **Next** four times.

    e) On the **Content location selection** page, verify that the **Store updates in the following location** check box is checked.

    f) In the text box, type *C:\WSUS-Updates* and select **Next**.

    > If you have a drive formatted with NTFS and at least 6 GB of free disk space, you can use it to store updates for client computers to download quickly.
    >
    > If you need to save disk space, clear the check box to store updates on Microsoft Update; downloads will be slower.
    >
    > If you choose to store updates locally, updates are not downloaded to your WSUS server until you approve them. By default, when updates are approved, they are downloaded for all languages.
    >
    > ☑ Store updates in the following location (choose a valid local path on Server100.domain100.internal, or a remote path) :
    > ```
    > C:\WSUS-Updates
    > ```

    g) On the **Confirm installation selections** page, check the **Restart the destination server automatically if required** check box and select **Yes**.

h) Select **Install**. After installation completes, select the **Launch Post-Installation tasks** link.

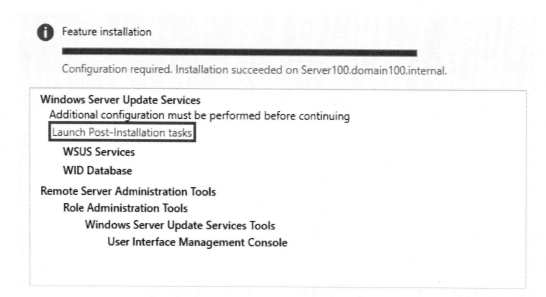

 Note: It may take a few minutes for the installation and the post-installation tasks to complete.

i) Wait for the text in the details pane to turn from **Please wait while your server is configured** to **Configuration successfully completed**, then select **Close**.

2. Verify WSUS synchronization options.
   a) Select **Tools→Windows Server Update Services**.
   b) In the **Windows Server Update Services Configuration Wizard**, select **Cancel**.

 Note: The wizard window might not be visible. Select its icon on the taskbar to bring it forward.

 Note: Synchronization is required to progress through the wizard. Initial synchronization to Microsoft's servers can take a very long time, so it is skipped in this activity.

c) From the navigation pane on the left, expand your server object and select **Options**.

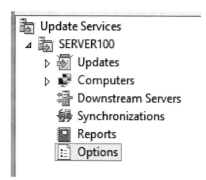

d) In the details pane, select **Update Source and Proxy Server**.

e) In the **Update Source and Proxy Server** dialog box, verify that **Synchronize from Microsoft Update** is selected.

   WSUS will receive updates directly from Microsoft's servers.

f) Select **OK** to close the dialog box.

3. Configure update classifications and the products they target.

   a) In the details pane, select **Products and Classifications**.

   b) In the **Products and Classifications** dialog box, verify that some of the older generation products are checked.

   Only updates for these products will synchronize with the WSUS server. More products would be available if you were to synchronize, such as in the following screenshot.

   c) Select the **Classifications** tab.

   d) Verify that **Critical Updates**, **Definition Updates**, and **Security Updates** are all checked. Select each one to learn more about how Microsoft defines these classifications.

e) Check the **Update Rollups** check box, then select **OK**.

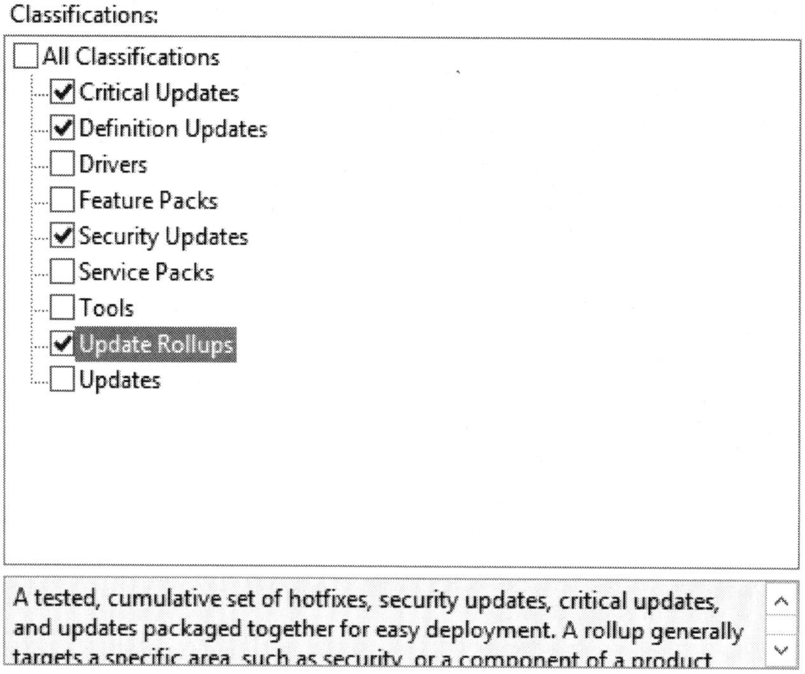

Classifications:

☐ All Classifications
  ☑ Critical Updates
  ☑ Definition Updates
  ☐ Drivers
  ☐ Feature Packs
  ☑ Security Updates
  ☐ Service Packs
  ☐ Tools
  ☑ Update Rollups
  ☐ Updates

A tested, cumulative set of hotfixes, security updates, critical updates, and updates packaged together for easy deployment. A rollup generally targets a specific area, such as security, or a component of a product

Only updates that fit these classifications will synchronize with the WSUS server.

4. Get an overview of your available updates.
    a) From the navigation pane, select **Updates**.

b) Verify that the **Overview** separates updates by classification as well as status. Because you didn't synchronize, your overview will not show any updates. The following screenshot is what the **Overview** might look like after synchronization.

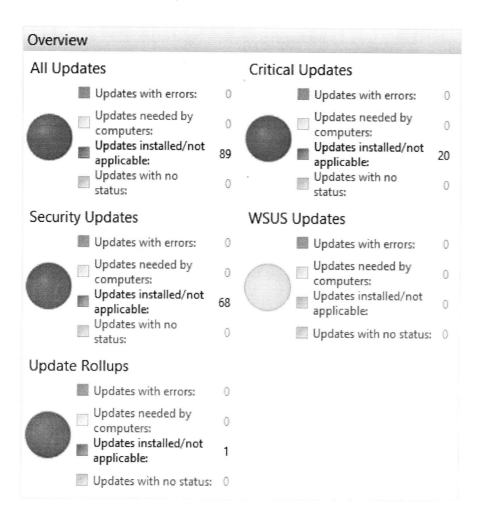

c) Close the **Update Services** window.

TOPIC C

Virtualize Servers and Desktops

Many enterprises are turning toward virtualization to streamline their host setups, as management of physical devices can be an unwanted difficulty. This is especially true of organizations that need host environments that they can readily deploy and redeploy across a variety of business contexts. However, like any physical machine, virtual servers and desktops are susceptible to risk. In this topic, you'll consider the unique pitfalls associated with virtualizing hosts, and you'll use certain security techniques to ensure that your virtualized hosts meet the standards set by your enterprise.

Virtualization Platforms

Virtualization is the process of creating a simulated environment of computing technology that already exists in its actual form. A *virtual machine (VM)* is software that can virtualize computer hardware, operating systems, applications, and other computing environments. Multiple VMs can run on a single host that provisions its hardware resources to each virtual machine. There are many different platforms and software solutions available for an enterprise to use to virtualize its environments.

Hardware virtualization platforms provide an enterprise with the opportunity to consolidate all of its environments onto one physical server workstation, which can simplify control and reduce energy consumption. Some examples of hardware virtualization platforms are:

- Hyper-V® from Microsoft®.
- VMware® ESX® from VMware, Inc.
- Oracle® VM Server from Oracle.

Operating system-level/container-based virtualization allows a single OS kernel to run several isolated user instances. This can help administrators more easily manage resources and keep one virtualized instance from interfering with others on the kernel. Some examples of operating system-level virtualization platforms are:

- Oracle® Solaris Containers.
- Docker from Docker, Inc.
- LXC, an open source platform.

Application virtualization abstracts software from the operating system it runs on. This is useful for hosts running newer operating systems that need to run legacy applications. These legacy applications can now execute as if they are interfacing with an older operating system that they are compatible with. Examples of platforms that provide application virtualization are:

- App-V from Microsoft®.
- VMware® ThinApp® from VMware, Inc.
- Citrix XenApp® from Citrix Systems®.

Hypervisors

Server virtualization is achieved through two different methods, each with their own security advantages and disadvantages. One such method is by using a hypervisor. A *hypervisor* is the layer of software that separates the virtual software from the physical hardware it runs on. Hypervisors manage resources on the physical host and provide them to multiple virtual environments. This enables a great deal of additional flexibility and increases the efficiency of hardware utilization by running multiple guest systems on a single host system, each operating as an independent system.

Hypervisors can be further broken down into two basic types: type I and type II. Type I hypervisors run on *bare metal*, that is, they run directly on the host's hardware when managing the guest virtual environments. In this sense, the hypervisor is integrated into the host's operating system. Because the hypervisor is directly linked to the host's hardware, it is relatively fast; likewise, there is less of an attack surface for a malicious user to compromise.

Type II hypervisors, on the other hand, actually run as an application on top of the host machine's operating system. This adds another level between the hypervisor and the bare metal. This is primarily useful for personal devices or production devices that are not dedicated to virtualization. Type II hypervisors are typically slower than type I, and they add an extra layer of complexity to virtual machine management. This means that the OS the hypervisor runs on is itself an entirely new attack surface that you must secure. Otherwise, an attacker could compromise the OS, bypass the hypervisor, and attack the hardware directly.

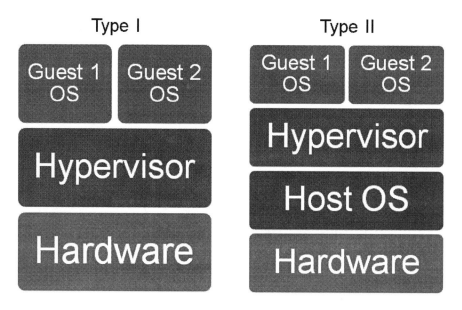

Figure 6-6: Hypervisor types.

Container-Based Virtualization

The other method of virtualizing servers is *container-based virtualization* technology, also called *operating system-level virtualization*. In this method, a physical host runs its own operating system, and on that operating system are individual containers that run isolated systems. Even type I hypervisors can add significant processing overhead, but container-based virtualization tends to be even more efficient at managing resources because each guest does not install their own operating system; rather, there is only one operating system on the host that provisions what each container needs. This has a positive effect on the availability of virtual systems, with the downside being that the containers must be using the same operating system as the host.

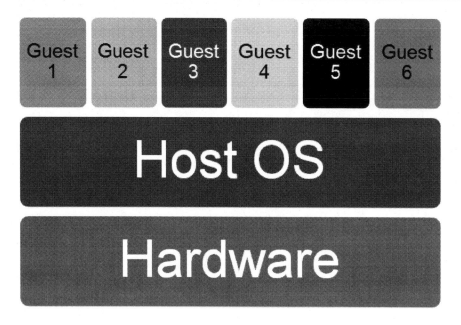

Figure 6-7: Container-based virtualization.

VDI

Virtual desktop infrastructure (VDI) uses desktop virtualization to separate the personal computing environment from the user's physical machine. In VDI, a desktop operating system and applications are run inside the VMs that are hosted on servers in the virtualization infrastructure. The VMs running desktop operating systems are referred to as virtual desktops. There are three main VDI deployment models, as described in the following table.

Deployment Model	Description
Hosted	Hosted virtual desktops are generally provided by a third party that manages the entire virtualization infrastructure and simply provides desktop services on demand.
Centralized	In this model, all VDI instances are hosted on a virtualization infrastructure within the enterprise. All VM images are stored centrally. When a user requests a desktop instance, a new instance is created from an existing image and delivered to the remote user over the enterprise network.
Synchronized	Synchronized or remote virtual desktops expand on the capabilities of centralized virtual desktops by adding the ability to continue working in a disconnected state without requiring network connectivity. This model requires more local computing resources than other VDI deployment models.

Security Implications of VDI

There are several advantages to using VDI over a non-virtual desktop:

- Desktop provisioning and administration is simplified.
- Desktop security and data protection is simplified.
- Providing secure remote access to enterprise desktop environments is easier.
- The cost of deploying new applications is lower.
- Downtime in the event of hardware failures is reduced.

Likewise, the following are disadvantages of using VDI:

- If the network is not managed properly, this will introduce a security risk.
- Supporting peripheral devices like printers can be challenging.
- Supporting complex or media-rich applications can be difficult.
- Building and managing VDI environments adds complexity.
- Network interruptions can lead to downtime and lost productivity.

Terminal Services

A terminal service enables a client to connect remotely to a server using minimal hardware. This client is referred to as a *thin client*, as it offloads most of the processing workload to the server it connects to. Software called a *terminal emulator* emulates the various input functions that a user can take advantage of, which usually consists of just a keyboard, mouse, and a monitor. The emulated terminal on the server provides the thin client with the means to remotely interface with the server.

Terminal emulation is a common means of remotely accessing virtual machines, especially those in a centralized VDI configuration. The main concern with terminal emulation is choosing a terminal emulation program that communicates over secure protocols. Remoting into a virtual desktop over Telnet, a communication protocol without encryption, is highly insecure. Using a emulator with Secure Shell (SSH), on other hand, will provide strong encryption to protect terminal commands in transit from a thin client to a server. Secure terminal emulators will help in preventing man-in-the-middle attacks when users in your enterprise communicate with VMs.

Application Delivery Services

Similar to terminal emulation is the idea of application delivery services, known as *application streaming*. In application streaming, a thin client requires as little of the application's resource as possible to interact with the application, as it is hosted on a server. Such applications are typically run from a networked VM that centralizes the streaming process independent from the client. This has the advantage of increased efficiency, as the VM will only provide the client with what it absolutely needs to complete a certain task within the application. This on-demand service alleviates the burden of each client locally, storing all of an application's resources when they only ever use a small part of them.

Like with terminal emulation, you should ensure that application streaming is done through encrypted sessions. To satisfy availability needs, you also need to make sure that your network infrastructure can handle the demand for application streaming.

 Note: Both terminal services and application delivery services are sometimes referred to as presentation virtualization.

vTPM

Virtual Trusted Platform Module (vTPM) is able to extend TPM functionality to operating systems and applications running in virtual machines on a host with TPM hardware. VMs in this virtualization model can take advantage of TPM's cryptographic functionalities on the software level. Instances of vTPM are strongly tied to a corresponding VM, so if that VM migrates, so too should the vTPM instance. This allows the vTPM instance to retain the confidentiality and integrity of data that is contained within it as the VM migrates.

Another security concern of vTPMs is their ability to establish and maintain chains of trust from physical to virtual TPM. Some software might need to differentiate between the semantics of a physical TPM and a virtual one; otherwise, key and certificate signing may not be successfully validated.

VM Vulnerabilities

There is an inherent risk in running multiple guest systems within a virtualization infrastructure. Each guest system added introduces an additional threat vector and increases the attack surface area to the virtualization environment as a whole. There are several risks associated with running multiple guest systems that are compounded if the guest systems cross mixed security levels. The following table describes some of the major vulnerabilities associated with co-mingling hosts with different security requirements.

Vulnerability	Description
VM escape	In a VM escape, an attacker executes code in a VM that allows an application running on the VM to escape and interact directly with the hypervisor. VM escape could give the attacker access to the underlying host operating systems and thereby access to all other VMs running on that host machine. This is one of the most serious threats to virtual security.
Privilege elevation	In privilege elevation, an attacker exploits a design flaw or oversight in an operating system or application to obtain higher-level privileges and access to resources that they would normally not be able to access. In a virtualized environment, an attacker with elevated privileges could access the host machine and do anything an administrator could do to both the host machine and the VMs running on that host.
Live VM migration	In some situations, you may need to move a virtual machine from one physical host to another with no impact to the VM's availability. This is called live VM migration. Platforms like Hyper-V and VMware's vMotion provide this functionality. However, live migration can be exploited by attackers. Hypervisors without proper authentication and integrity protocols may allow an attacker to migrate VMs to their own machine, or migrate the VMs to a victim machine, overloading it with a denial of service (DoS) attack.
Data remnants	Data remnants are leftover information on a storage medium even after basic attempts have been made to remove that data. Because virtual machines are an abstraction of a physical environment and not the real thing, it is difficult to ensure that data you delete on the VM will truly sanitize that data from its physical source. This is similar to the idea that simply emptying an OS's trash bin will not completely erase the data from the hard drive; an attacker may still be able to retrieve the remaining bits before they are overwritten. For virtual machines, this is primarily a concern during the de-provisioning process, as every bit of data involved in the virtual instance may not be completely gone from physical storage.

Guidelines for Virtualizing Servers and Desktops

Use the following guidelines when implementing virtualizing in your enterprise:

- Choose a virtualization platform that fulfills your business need for certain environments.
- Consider the security implications of hypervisor types, and whether the additional attack surface of type II is worth the risk.
- Consider using a container-based VM instead of a hypervisor if each guest only needs the same operating system as the host.
- Choose a VDI deployment model that most aligns with your business needs.
- Prepare to offer support for peripherals and complex media-rich apps in VDI solutions.
- Manage network resources provisioned for your VDI carefully to ensure availability.
- Use secure communication protocols like SSH when emulating a terminal on a remote machine.

- Ensure that application streaming is using encrypted protocols to prevent man-in-the-middle attacks.
- Choose a vTPM solution that can successfully maintain chains of trust in key and certificate signing.
- Address common VM vulnerabilities like VM escape, privilege elevation, live VM migration, and data remnants in your architecture.

ACTIVITY 6-3
Virtualizing Servers and Desktops

Data Files

C:\093023Data\Implementing Security Controls for Hosts\VirtualBox-4.3.12-93733-Win.exe

C:\093023Data\Implementing Security Controls for Hosts\kali-linux-1.0.9a-amd64.iso

Before You Begin

You will use Oracle VM VirtualBox to create a virtual instance of Kali Linux on your Windows host. Kali Linux is an operating system that comes pre-packaged with many useful security tools.

 Note: Kali Linux was preceded by a Linux distribution called BackTrack.

Scenario

You plan to soon conduct various tests on the security of your systems at Develetech. You've identified Kali Linux as an operating system that includes a great deal of penetration testing tools, vulnerability assessment programs, and other security utilities that will help ensure your enterprise is safe from threats. However, you don't want to dedicate separate hardware on which to run Kali Linux, so you decide to virtualize the operating system on an existing host environment. This will make it easier to set up and manage Kali Linux or any other environments you later decide to incorporate.

However, hosts running these virtual machines are still exposed to risk, so you'll configure security settings in the virtual hosting process. You need to ensure that the VM is hidden from the outside network and that, in the event that an attacker takes control of the VM, they cannot in turn compromise the host it runs on.

---

1. Install VirtualBox.
    a) Navigate to **C:\093023Data\Implementing Security Controls for Hosts**.
    b) Double-click the **VirtualBox-4.3.12-93733-Win.exe** file.
    c) In the **Oracle VM VirtualBox 4.3.12 Setup** wizard, select **Next**.

d) On the **Custom Setup** page, select **Next** to accept the default installation parameters.

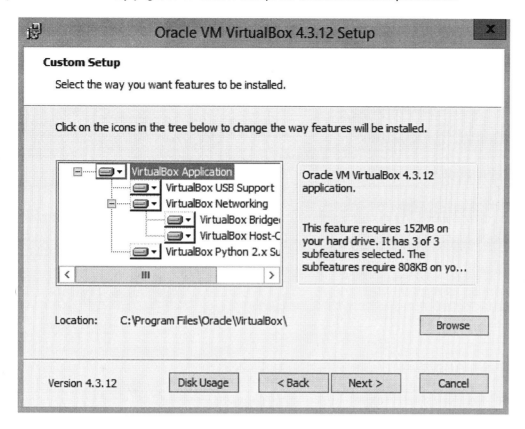

e) Select **Next** to accept additional install options.
f) Select **Yes**.
   VirtualBox will reset your network connection during installation.
g) On the **Ready to Install** page, select **Install**.
h) In the **Windows Security** dialog box, select **Install**.
i) After installation completes, select **Finish** to launch VirtualBox.

2. Create the virtual machine profile.
   a) In the **Oracle VM VirtualBox Manager** window, select the **New** icon.

   b) In the **Create Virtual Machine** dialog box, in the **Name** text box, type *Server##-Kali* where *##* is your unique student number.
   c) From the **Type** drop-down list, select **Linux**.

d) From the **Version** drop-down list, select **Other Linux (64-bit)**.

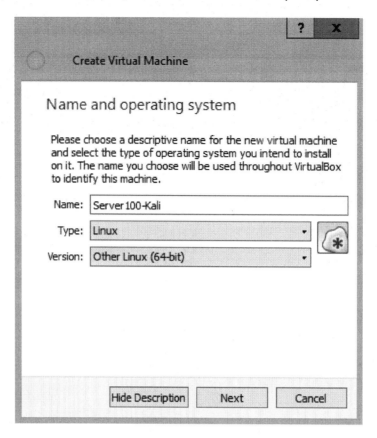

e) Select **Next**.

f) On the **Memory size** page, in the **MB** spin box, double-click and type *2048* and then select **Next**. This will allocate 2 GBs of RAM to the virtual machine.

g) On the **Hard drive** page, select **Create** to create a hard drive for the virtual machine.

h) On the **Hard drive file type** page, verify that **VDI (VirtualBox Disk Image)** is selected and select **Next**.

i) On the **Storage on physical hard drive** page, select **Next** to dynamically allocate drive space.

j) On the **File location and size** page, select **Create**.

k) Verify that the VM profile was created.

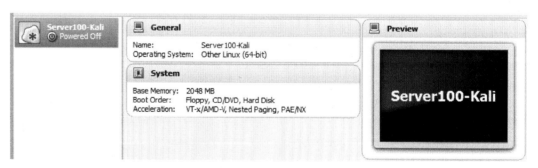

3. Verify the virtual machine profile's security configurations.

a) With your **Server##-Kali** profile selected, select the **Settings** button.

Settings

b) In the **Server##-Kali – Settings** dialog box, on the **General** page, select the **Advanced** tab.
c) Verify that **Shared Clipboard** and **Drag'n'Drop** are disabled.

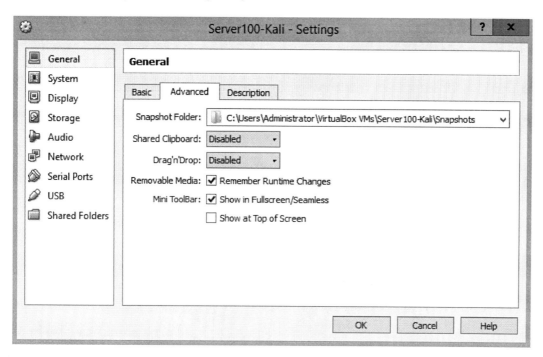

When enabled, users can copy data between the host and the VM guest based on its setting. An attacker who accesses the guest may then be able to read from or write data to the host. Disabling these features reduces the host's attack surface.

d) From the navigation pane, select **Display**.
e) Verify that the **Enable 3D Acceleration** check box is unchecked.

Video drivers used in 3D acceleration are often insecure, and software that accesses these drivers could compromise the OS. Additionally, a guest with 3D acceleration enabled could access program code involved in the VirtualBox host process, which it could use to crash the virtual machine.

f) From the navigation pane, select **Network**.
g) Verify that the **Attached to** value is **NAT**.

In NAT mode, VirtualBox acts as a router between the host and guest VM. VirtualBox secures the guest VM by forwarding its network communications through the host. The guest VM is therefore invisible and unreachable from outside of this virtual subnet.

h) Select **OK**.

4. Load Kali Linux into the virtual machine profile.
   a) Select the **Start** button.

b) In the **Select start-up disk** dialog box, select the **Choose a virtual optical disk file** button.

c) Navigate to **C:\093023Data\Implementing Security Controls for Hosts** and open **kali-linux-1.0.9a-amd64**.
d) Select **Start**.

e) In the **Server##-Kali [Running] - Oracle VM VirtualBox** window, with **Live (amd64)** selected, press **Enter**.

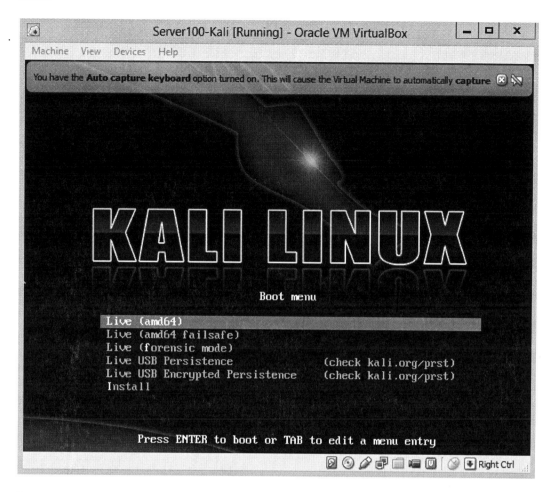

This will create a live instance of Kali Linux instead of going through the more time-consuming process of installing it.

f) After Kali Linux loads, verify that you are logged in to the desktop.

g) If necessary, close the warnings at the top of the VM window.

 Note: It will be easier for you to work in the VM if you expand the window or switch to full-screen. You can switch to full-screen by selecting **View→Switch to Fullscreen**.

h) At the top of the Kali Linux desktop, select the **Iceweasel** icon.

 Note: Iceweasel is a rebranded version of Mozilla® Firefox® web browser.

    i) In Iceweasel, navigate to **www.google.com** and verify that you can connect.

    j) Close Iceweasel.

5. Shut down the virtual machine.

    a) In the virtual machine toolbar, select **Machine→Close**.

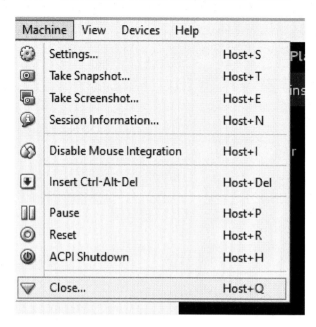

    b) In the **Close Virtual Machine** dialog box, if necessary, select **Save the machine state**.

    c) Select **OK**.

    VirtualBox saves the current state of the virtual machine and then closes it.

    d) Close the **Oracle VM VirtualBox Manager** window.

TOPIC D

Implement Cloud Augmented Security Services

While providing your own security services to hosts in your enterprise is a good idea, you nevertheless have the option to rely on cloud-based solutions for specific functionality. This is often an attractive choice for businesses that need to outsource this functionality for financial or management reasons. What's more, the communal nature of cloud-based security services can actually be more beneficial than if you relied on in-house-developed solutions, as consensus may drive a better product. In this topic, you'll take a look at some of the security services that cloud companies provide to their clients, and determine how best to implement these services in your enterprise.

Cloud Services

Described in the following table are the three general services that cloud computing provides to enterprises.

Service	Description
Software	*Software as a Service (SaaS)* refers to using the cloud to provide applications to users. This service eliminates the need for users to have the software installed on their computers and for organizations to purchase and maintain software versions. Examples include Microsoft® Office 365™, Salesforce®, and Gmail™.
Platform	*Platform as a Service (PaaS)* refers to using the cloud to provide virtual systems, such as operating systems, to customers. Examples include Oracle® Database, Microsoft® Windows® Azure™ SQL Database, and Google App Engine™.
Infrastructure	*Infrastructure as a Service (IaaS)* refers to using the cloud to provide access to any or all infrastructure needs a client may have. This can include data centers, servers, or any networking devices needed. IaaS can guarantee quality of service (QoS) for clients. Examples include Amazon® Elastic Compute Cloud®, Microsoft Windows Azure Virtual Machines, and OpenStack™.

 Note: Some service types overlap, and some organizations offer suites that encompass more than one service type.

Cloud Security Services

Many enterprises turn to cloud providers for their security needs. Instead of shouldering the responsibility of building, maintaining, and hosting security technologies, the enterprise offloads those responsibilities onto a third party. This allows the enterprise to function at optimum efficiency while still protecting its assets.

While reputable cloud providers incorporate security at all levels of their service, the client usually has no other option but to trust the provider's word. However, some cloud providers give their clients overt tools with which the client may actively improve their security. These tools can be in the form of PaaS, IaaS, or SaaS; the actual implementation will vary depending on the enterprise's business needs and any existing weak points in its security architecture. In addition to lightening the load on hosts in an enterprise network, the distributed nature of cloud services can also serve to more effectively analyze and reach a consensus on security issues, as many enterprises will be participating and sharing data in the same environment. Likewise, this highlights the risk you take in relying on cloud providers for your security services, as you do not have complete control over every element that may adversely affect your systems.

Hash Matching

Hash matching is a technique that cloud providers use in some of the security services they offer to their clients. The service runs a cryptographic hash function on data that the client sends to the service. The resulting hash of each piece of data is compared with known hash values to detect any matches. This is primarily used in scanning technology like antivirus, anti-spam, and vulnerability scanning. Instead of hosting these tools locally, the enterprise can enlist a cloud provider to take on the overhead involved in running this software for each host.

Cloud antivirus and anti-spam solutions can use the enterprise's Internet connection to remotely scan data on a host and look for hash matches. The hashed data is compared to known virus or email content values in a signature-based analysis. If matches are detected, the cloud software can alert an administrator or take steps to remove the virus or block the spam, depending on how the enterprise has the service configured. Besides saving on computing resources, enterprises benefit from cloud antivirus and anti-spam software because it is always current and doesn't require you to constantly download signature database updates.

Cloud providers can also go beyond basic antivirus and anti-spam solutions by offering more in-depth vulnerability scanning services. These services use hash matching to check host operating systems, firmware, apps, and more for known weak points. These weak points are usually matched to a vulnerability database like NVD, and to predefined industry standards and best practices. Cloud-based vulnerability scanning helps enterprises perform a more complete security analysis of their environments without needing to configure or assign resources to a local solution.

Keep in mind that all three of these cloud solutions have the potential to expose vulnerability information to an unauthorized audience if the provider you choose does not implement the proper security on their end. Transport encryption is particularly crucial to keep communications with the cloud confidential.

Events	More details	Date/Time ▼	Status
Scan	Scanning: Critical ...	9/8/2014 11:01 AM	Finished
Cookie detected Unknown name	Location: C:\Users...	9/8/2014 10:58 AM	Deleted
Cookie detected Cookie/Mediaplex	Location: C:\Users...	9/8/2014 10:58 AM	Deleted
Cookie detected Cookie/onestat.com	Location: C:\Users...	9/8/2014 10:58 AM	Deleted
Cookie detected Cookie/Serving-sys	Location: C:\Users...	9/8/2014 10:58 AM	Deleted
Cookie detected Unknown name	Location: C:\Users...	9/8/2014 10:58 AM	Deleted
Cookie detected Cookie/Casalemedia	Location: C:\Users...	9/8/2014 10:58 AM	Deleted
Cookie detected Cookie/Apmebf	Location: C:\Users...	9/8/2014 10:58 AM	Deleted
Cookie detected Cookie/QuestionMarket	Location: C:\Users...	9/8/2014 10:58 AM	Deleted
Cookie detected Cookie/Serving-sys	Location: C:\Users...	9/8/2014 10:58 AM	Deleted
Cookie detected Unknown name	Location: C:\Users...	9/8/2014 10:58 AM	Deleted
Cookie detected Cookie/PointRoll	Location: C:\Users...	9/8/2014 10:58 AM	Deleted
Scan	Scanning: Critical ...	9/8/2014 10:50 AM	Started
Computer vaccinated		9/8/2014 10:49 AM	Vaccinated

Figure 6-8: Cloud antivirus software using hash matching to detect unwanted files.

Examples

Examples of cloud antivirus solutions include: Panda Cloud Antivirus, Immunet®, and HitmanPro 3.

Examples of cloud anti-spam solutions include: McAfee® SaaS Email Protection & Continuity, Mimecast®, and AppRiver SecureTide™.

Examples of cloud vulnerability scanners include: Tripwire® SecureScan, Nessus® Enterprise Cloud, and QualysGuard®.

Sandboxing

Sandboxing is a technique that isolates untrusted data in a closed virtual environment to conduct tests and analyze the data for threats and vulnerabilities. Sandbox environments intentionally limit interfacing with the host environments to maintain the hosts' integrity. Sandboxes are used for a variety of purposes, including testing of application code during development and analyzing potential malware.

The analysis of files uploaded to a sandbox can include determining whether or not the file is malicious, how it might have affected certain systems if run outside of the sandbox, and what dependencies it might have with external files and hosts. Sandboxes offer more than traditional anti-malware solutions because you can apply a variety of different environments to the sandbox instead of just relying on how the malware might exist in your current configuration.

Cloud-based sandboxes offer a community-built approach to collecting and analyzing data for potentially unwanted behavior. As multiple enterprises share suspicious data with the sandbox, the analysis of that data can quickly inform other enterprises of the results. Enterprises that actively use this service benefit from always up-to-date malware signatures and vulnerability identification. This saves the enterprise on both resources and time.

Be aware that oversharing information can be a security concern for any enterprise that relies on a third party to analyze its data. You need to be careful about what types of data you send to the cloud sandbox for analysis, because if the cloud provider is breached, an attacker could use this analysis to identify vulnerabilities in your infrastructure.

Figure 6–9: Analyzing a file in a cloud–based sandbox.

Examples

Examples of cloud-based sandboxes include: Sourcefire® Advanced Malware Protection, Voonami™ Sandbox Cloud, and Skytap® Cloud.

Content Filtering

Content filtering is a technique that restricts what types of content a user is allowed to access. The enterprise will typically place these restrictions on Internet content that it deems inappropriate or a security risk. For example, an enterprise might not allow an employee's browser to run a Java™ plugin as it connects to Internet websites from the company network. This protects the employee's host machine from the vulnerabilities associated with the Java plugin. You can implement content filtering on a host-based level, or you can push policies network-wide.

Cloud-based content filtering solutions centralize and streamline the process of filtering out unwanted Internet content. This filtering can be both outbound and inbound, as the enterprise may want to prevent its users from transmitting certain types of content to remote servers. The cloud provider may use its own criteria for blocking content based on its clients' general needs, like a school that wants to prevent its students from accessing adult content when browsing the web, or the enterprise can integrate its own policies with the cloud service to run a custom filtering program. Cloud content filtering can also use anti-malware tactics to identify and block malicious code from entering the network and infecting its hosts.

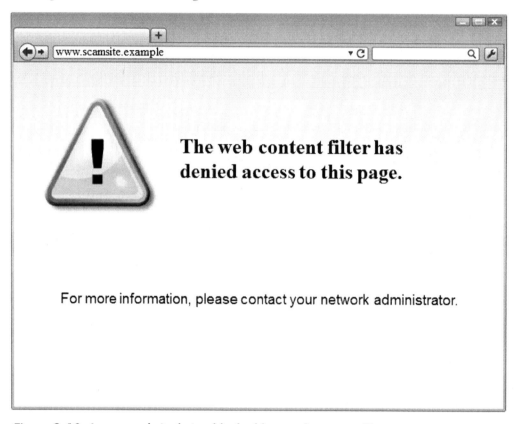

Figure 6-10: A scam website being blocked by a web content filter.

Examples

Examples of cloud-based content filtering solutions include: Symantec™ Web Security.cloud, Webroot® Web Security Service, and Barracuda Web Security Service.

Guidelines for Implementing Cloud Augmented Security Services

Use the following guidelines when implementing cloud augmented security services.

- Become familiar with the various cloud service types.
- Look for cloud providers that engage in hash matching of malware signatures to outsource anti-malware processes.
- Take advantage of cloud-based sandboxes that offer safe, isolated analysis of files and vulnerabilities.
- Be wary of oversharing data and information in cloud sandboxes.
- Use cloud software that filters out unwanted content on your domain, preventing users from accessing certain websites.

ACTIVITY 6-4
Implementing Cloud Augmented Security Services

Scenario

The CEO of Develetech sees the cloud as a cost-effective way to solve some of the enterprise's security needs. Instead of relying on its own hardware and software that it must purchase, manage, and maintain, Develetech can transfer this burden to the cloud provider. You've identified some host-directed security services that could benefit the organization, and you'd like to implement the ones that are the best fit.

1. One of Develetech's options is to offload anti-malware and anti-spam scanning to a cloud provider. What are the advantages and disadvantages to relying on cloud hash matching for these services?

2. How can a cloud-based sandbox help Develetech test its internally developed applications?

3. What situations can you think of that could warrant cloud content filtering for Develetech?

TOPIC E

Protect Boot Loaders

An often overlooked, but still important, component of host security is boot loader protection. Most, if not all, of the hosts in your environment will run on computing architecture that boots into an environment through firmware such as BIOS and Unified Extensible Firmware Interface (UEFI). It is important that you secure this foundational aspect of devices in your domain, as an unprotected boot loader or firmware can invalidate your efforts to harden the actual operating system environment on a host. So, you'll implement some relevant security measures that keep a host from booting into an insecure environment.

BIOS

The *Basic Input/Output System (BIOS)* is a standard for firmware interfaces that is stored on a computer motherboard's ROM chip. When a computer with BIOS is powered on, the BIOS firmware is the first to run; this allows it to test the various hardware components in a computer, as well as run a boot loader so that an operating system can start. The BIOS has access to the ports used by basic hardware input devices like a mouse and keyboard. Users can also load up a BIOS interface instead of an operating system to make system-level changes to various processes. For several decades, BIOS has been the dominant standard in the home and enterprise computer industry.

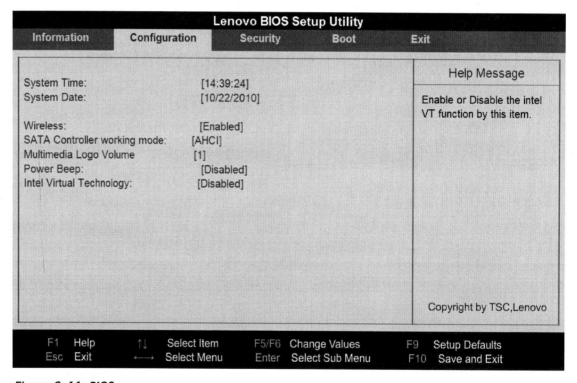

Figure 6-11: BIOS.

UEFI

Unified Extensible Firmware Interface (UEFI) is a new technology that is aiming to replace the ubiquitous BIOS by bringing with it several key advantages. UEFI runs faster than BIOS, can operate within a greater amount of memory, can access disk drives of currently unattainable sizes, and can access more hardware types.

Another strength of UEFI is security. BIOS chips have proven vulnerable to virus and rootkit attacks that can force the BIOS to malicious code. Depending on the malware itself, this code could grant a user elevated privileges, allow them to read physical memory, take control of the system before the OS is even booted, and corrupt the BIOS chip itself. UEFI can mitigate these risks by implementing a protocol called secure boot.

Secure Boot

Secure boot is an optional UEFI feature that prevents unwanted processes from executing during the boot operation. This is because all processes must be signed with a digital signature that the UEFI validates before they can execute at boot time. If the UEFI cannot validate a particular digital signature, it will not boot the corresponding process. This addresses malware-related vulnerabilities in the BIOS, as the malware will likely not have a valid digital signature. Valid signatures are stored in a database in memory.

While this can offer a good deal of protection against boot loader exploits, it can also constrain your ability to customize the boot operation on your systems. If you wish to run software or hardware at boot that the secure boot database doesn't recognize, you'll need to update that database or contact the hardware vendor and ask them to add these to the database. Hosts that still run the BIOS alongside UEFI can enter into the BIOS and disable the secure boot protocol, but some OS implementations like logo-certified Windows® RT 8.1 do not allow you to do this.

Secure boot is supported by a number of operating systems, including Windows® 8/8.1, Windows Server® 2012, and several Linux® distributions.

Measured Launch

Some TPM implementations, like *Trusted Computing Group (TCG)* and Intel's *Trusted Execution Technology (TXT)*, assist in guaranteeing that a trusted OS stays trusted by booting into a safe environment. To determine an operating system's state, the TPM will measure various aspects of the environment. These measurements can be of application code, system configuration, data structures, the current state of memory, and other factors that could affect the environment. In a *measured launch*, each resource is measured and then validated against a list of expected measurements. If the resource's measurements do not meet pre-defined policy, the measured launch will mark the host as untrusted.

Measurements used in a measured launch are hashed and placed in special registers to prevent tampering. The measurement of each module forms part of a chain of trust, as the measurements begin at the root and verify one module after another.

Measured launch is useful for protecting against integrity violations and malicious system alteration. Because it is able to measure system processes at such a low level, and before the operating system starts, the launch can verify the security of a host's BIOS or hypervisor. When these become untrusted, the host is no longer part of the larger pool of trusted computers.

IMA

The *Integrity Measurement Architecture (IMA)* is another TPM-based method of verifying trusted computing. IMA is an open source Linux subsystem that works with the operating system kernel to measure a file before it is loaded. The measurement is hashed and stored, then the TPM can validate the hash against a list of expected values for evidence of tampering. If the file is not a match, the IMA will not allow it to load or execute.

Like secure boot and measured launch, IMA protects hosts in a trusted computing environment from integrity violations that could compromise the trusted pool as a whole.

ACTIVITY 6-5
(Optional) Protecting Boot Loaders

Scenario

You want to implement hardware-based security services to protect your hosts' boot loaders from loading malicious or unwanted components. Any host compromised by these components could in turn compromise your trusted computing architecture. To secure the boot loading process, you decide to turn on the TPM-based modules in the BIOS that will measure a system's launch and detect any anomalies. This will ensure that each host boots into a secure environment, and any host that fails to meet security standards will be removed from the trusted pool.

1. Boot into your computer's BIOS/UEFI.

   a) Restart or shut down your computer.

   b) When the computer first starts back up, before Windows boots, press the appropriate key to enter into the BIOS/UEFI.

2. Explore the BIOS/UEFI for measured launch and secure boot options.

   a) In the BIOS/UEFI, look for a tab called **Advanced** or **Security**.

    Caution: Don't make any changes to the following settings. This could cause system instability.

   b) On this tab, look for an option or section that deals with the CPU. For example, there may be an option called **CPU Setup**. This option may take you to another page.

    Note: There may also be a **Security** section within the **Advanced** tab.

   c) Look for a setting that allows you to enable or disable TCG or TXT. These settings may also be called by their full names: Trusted Computing Group and Trusted Execution Technology, respectively.

   These settings use Trusted Platform Module (TPM) to boot the computer into a known safe environment. This process is also called a measured launch.

    Note: In some configurations, the setting may simply be called TPM or measured launch.

   d) If you're using UEFI, look for an option called **Secure Boot**. This is usually located on the **Boot** tab, but may be available on the **Security** or **Advanced** tabs.

   This option ensures that the processes that execute at boot time are all signed with valid digital signatures. This helps prevent malicious code from tampering with crucial boot processes that could compromise the entire host.

3. Exit the BIOS/UEFI and boot back into Windows.

   a) Press **Esc** to return to the main menu.

   b) Exit the BIOS/UEFI *without* saving. This option is generally accessible through a keyboard shortcut listed at the bottom of the screen, or through the **Boot**, **Exit**, or **Save & Exit** tabs.

   c) When Windows loads, sign in as Administrator and return to the desktop.

Summary

In this lesson, you implemented security on your host environments. You began by selecting security-enabled host hardware and software, then you hardened the hosts in your enterprise through various techniques. You then addressed the unique security challenges of virtualization, and took advantage of cloud security services to protect your hosts from risk. Lastly, you secured the base of a host's software—its booting systems—to prevent your hosts from loading insecure environments. When you combine all of these controls and techniques together, the hosts in your enterprise will be much safer from the numerous attack vectors that threaten their security.

What hosts in your enterprise need to run on a trusted OS or other standard operating environment?

Does your company use security services provided by a cloud vendor? If so, which services?

Note: Check your CHOICE Course screen for opportunities to interact with your classmates, peers, and the larger CHOICE online community about the topics covered in this course or other topics you are interested in. From the Course screen you can also access available resources for a more continuous learning experience.

7 Implementing Security Controls for Enterprise Storage

Lesson Time: 1 hour, 30 minutes

Lesson Objectives

In this lesson, you will:

- Identify storage types and protocols.

- Implement secure storage controls.

Lesson Introduction

After hosts, the next enterprise system you'll secure is storage. Storage solutions may routinely interface with hosts, applications, and the network, but their unique function of holding data at rest is a significant component to many businesses. While you may harden hosts or protect software and communications, doing so is usually in service of the data your enterprise has in its possession. If the data itself is not likewise secured, nor the protocols that handle it in storage, then your security efforts will be dangerously incomplete. In this lesson, you'll secure the many storage solutions available to ensure that the data itself cannot be compromised if other enterprise systems fail.

TOPIC A

Identify Storage Types and Protocols

There are many different storage solutions available to businesses. The factors involved in choosing the right solution are usually the size of the business, its budget, and what exactly it needs to store. Before you can implement any sort of controls to harden your storage solutions, you need to identify the common types and protocols that pervade the industry. Then, you'll consider each solution's security concerns to assess what may or may not be right for your organization. Identifying each storage type and protocol will make implementing security controls a much easier task in the future.

Virtual Storage

The cost of hardware and maintenance on physical storage has prompted many organizations to look to virtual solutions. Storage virtualization allows network administrators greater flexibility when it comes to managing and deploying storage technologies for the end user. Virtual storage also makes data migration a more seamless process, and administrators will be able to avoid the network disruption that can come from moving physical hardware around an enterprise infrastructure.

Security Implications of Virtual Storage

The general risks involved in virtualization are also a factor in virtual storage. You should consider the security of your virtual storage like you would any virtual environment. Consider the following security implications:

- **Unauthorized access**: The hosts that run virtual storage environments must be hardened from attack, otherwise an attacker may be able to alter, delete, or retrieve the data that the host's virtual machine (VM) runs.
- **VM escaping**: An attacker may be able to break out of the virtual environment and directly affect the host. This could allow the attacker to compromise the data on this VM, or even all of the data in the entire virtual storage pool.
- **Data remnants**: A virtual storage environment that you de-provision may not completely wipe its data from physical storage. If any sensitive data remains, an unauthorized user could gain access to it.

Cloud Storage

Another way in which enterprises are addressing the problem of physical storage is through cloud storage solutions. Instead of managing physical storage infrastructure within the enterprise itself, administrators may work with a third party that provides the actual storage through an Infrastructure as a Service (IaaS) cloud service model. These cloud storage services are virtual, allowing the service provider to allocate resources based on their enterprise clients' needs. There are several advantages to choosing cloud storage for the enterprise:

- Data can usually be accessed from anywhere.
- Management of hardware, as well as backups and support, are outsourced, limiting the amount of necessary support personnel required for the system.
- Storage is often very cheap because the provider likely has the capability to store enormous amounts of data.
- Collaboration between people is made easy and can be done from a wide variety of devices.

Security Implications of Cloud Storage

Although it is an attractive option for a number of reasons, cloud storage is not without its pitfalls. Consider the following security implications of choosing a cloud storage solution:

- **Control**: The biggest issue with outsourcing anything is the loss of control over it. The data is no longer in an internally controlled facility. The maintenance and support are handled by people outside of the organization, and there are people with administrative access to all of the data who are not part of the organization. Cloud providers may also undergo business changes like a merger, which could lead your organization to lose even more control over its data. Additionally, if you stop doing business with a provider, there's no guarantee that they won't still retain your data in some form.
- **Compliance**: Since data is not under your organization's direct control, you must consider the impact of how the data is stored. You should strongly consider working with providers who are willing to be subjected to audits and security certification processes.
- **Data segregation**: Storage providers using shared solutions will provide their services to other clients, and you must make sure that your enterprise data is not shared or stored with these other parties. At a minimum, encryption should be standard to minimize the crossover of data in any way.
- **Contingency**: Like any business, cloud storage providers can fail. If a cloud service provider should go out of business, both the client and the provider should have contingency plans in place.
- **Forensics and investigations**: A shared storage solution like cloud storage means that data from one organization could be stored with that of other organizations. Because of this complexity, it may be difficult, if not impossible, to perform an investigation should a security breach occur. This is an issue that you should discuss with the cloud provider during the contract phase.

Data Warehousing

Data warehousing is the process of analyzing and reporting on data in storage, usually consolidated from multiple sources. Data that is sent or modified in storage passes through a warehouse system where it is analyzed based on a number of possible factors. Management can use this analysis to create trend reports and get a better picture of their data and how it is stored in the enterprise. Data warehouses are therefore useful in putting stored data into a business-oriented perspective so that key personnel can make more informed decisions. Data warehouses may also ensure the quality of data by detecting corrupted data, and potentially fixing it.

Security Implications of Data Warehousing

Because data warehouses tend to consolidate data from many different sources, they are an attractive target to an attacker looking to steal, alter, or make data unavailable. You should therefore consider the following security issues associated with warehousing data:

- **Access control**: Data warehouses that span many different departments or subdivisions of an enterprise need to restrict employees in each category by only giving them access to data that they absolutely need. Contractors, partners, and other external clients may also access your data warehouse, so you should also control for their permissions.
- **Compliance**: Data warehouses often store customer personally identifiable information (PII), and you need to make sure that your solution implements all applicable security and privacy laws.

Data Archiving

Data archiving is the process of moving data into separate storage once it is no longer used on an active basis. While older data may not serve an immediate purpose to an enterprise, it can nevertheless still be important to retain. A data archive will be necessary for organizations that need to keep this older data in case it needs to be referenced in the future, or the organization may be required to keep the data for compliance purposes. This is often seen in organizations in the scientific or health services industries. Data archives are almost always isolated from day-to-day storage solutions, so as to minimize the chance that this older data is accessed in the event that current data stores are breached.

Security Implications of Data Archiving

While data archiving is important for many organizations, the immense amount of data archived may bring with it an increased amount of risk to an organization. Consider the following security implications of archiving data:

- **Reliability**: Administrators tend to focus their availability efforts on current in-use data stores, rather than archived data that they may not touch for a long time. However, disk failures and other malfunctions are still as much of a concern, so administrators need to frequently test archived systems and implement redundancy and fault tolerance where possible.
- **Physical security**: Data archives are not just isolated virtually, but often physically, too. You need to ensure that any additional locations that contain these archives have the proper physical security controls in place, like access-controlled doors and surveillance cameras.
- **Compliance**: Like warehoused data, archived data often includes PII and will likewise need to conform to all applicable laws and regulations.

NAS

Network-attached storage (NAS) is a category of self-contained devices that are designed specifically for file storage and file sharing on local area networks (LANs). They are designed to connect directly to the LAN and receive their own IP address (or, in some cases, multiple addresses).

NAS solutions generally run their own simplified operating system (usually a stripped down version of Linux®/UNIX®) and use various file storage protocols that allow them to interact with other network operating systems. The most common of these protocols are:

- *Network File System (NFS)*, an older network protocol that is predominant in communicating with Linux/UNIX environments.
- *Server Message Block (SMB)*, a common protocol used in communication with Windows®-based network environments and also supported by Apple® and most Linux/UNIX environments. File sharing on the typical Windows desktop is over SMB. Modern implementations of SMB are also referred to as *Common Internet File System (CIFS)*.

A NAS device will usually have its own web-based management interface available across the local intranet and provide its own local permissions or integrate with a network authentication service such Active Directory®. They always include at least one hard drive, most often in some type of redundant array of independent disks (RAID) configuration that allows for a combination of hard drives to be used. Typically, NAS devices contain multiple slots for hard drives that can easily be removed and replaced.

The primary advantage of NAS is that it's streamlined for one purpose: file storage. Rather than deal with an entire server and operating system running many different processes and causing computing overhead, NAS devices can provide a dedicated, high-speed solution for network storage. NAS devices are also relatively inexpensive compared to other storage solutions available on the market—this makes a NAS ideal for smaller organizations with limited resources.

Security Implications of NAS

As NAS devices are designed to run over your network, there are various security implications you need to be mindful of when implementing this type of storage solution in the enterprise.

- **User permissions**: If a user's credentials are compromised by an unauthorized user, there is nothing stopping them from accessing privileged data on the NAS, since it simply appears as one or many network shares. Careful consideration of access control and account management principles like least privilege, separation of duties, complex passwords, and changing administrator passwords are vital.
- **Physical security**: NAS devices are typically not very large since they consist of minimal hardware and slots for hard drives. They could easily be victims of anything from accidental damage and resets to actual theft. As a result, as with other servers, they should be confined to a protected, limited-access server room.
- **Maintenance**: Though they possess simplified operating systems and are mostly firmware-based, NAS solutions should be included in the patch and update program for the network. Vendors may release security solutions, as well as performance upgrades, to the software running on a NAS, and you should not overlook them in this process.
- **Network security**: Since NAS devices are network devices, you should monitor the traffic in and out of them as part of the network security scheme.

SAN

A *storage area network (SAN)* is a high-speed, private network of storage devices all linked together to create one large storage resource. Numerous storage devices including hard disk arrays, tape libraries, and optical devices can be combined to act as storage for other systems. To the servers that use it, however, the SAN just looks like another local drive, as if it was just another hard drive in the machine. The server simply hands data off to the SAN and allows the SAN to manage the storage of that data behind the scenes. The devices in a SAN communicate and rearrange data amongst one another and the entire process is unknown to the original server.

One of the primary advantages of a SAN is scalability. The SAN is its own abstracted network of devices, so you can attach a nearly unlimited number of hard drives or other storage media to increase its size and it is completely transparent to the systems that use the SAN. A SAN is also its own private network, segmented from the rest of the network so it isn't hampered by user traffic or other network bottlenecks. It also uses a specialized architecture that is designed to make the storage network more efficient. Because SANs run on private networks, it is difficult for an attacker to directly access them. In fact, data is isolated on a SAN based on the source, so even if an attacker compromises a Windows machine and manages to gain access to the SAN data for that machine, they won't be able to access the data that belongs to a UNIX system attached to the SAN.

Security Implications of SAN

Despite its advantages, SANs are not impervious to being compromised. As a CASP, you should be aware of the following security implications when using a SAN:

- **User permissions**: Just like NAS storage scenarios, if a user compromises a system that uses the SAN (such as a server), they would be able to access data that is associated with that server from the SAN. Make sure to set the proper permissions and always apply the principle of least privilege.
- **Physical security**: As with any critical system, both accidents and intentional sabotage are important considerations. You should limit physical access to the SAN and its components to necessary personnel in a protected, secure area.
- **Management interface**: The SAN itself will have Ethernet or serial port access for direct management. If possible, create a private, separate intranet or virtual local area network (VLAN) for management of the SAN to help limit access to the SAN management controls. Because user authentication is required to access the SAN management console, you should ensure that complex passwords and other strong user authentication principles are implemented.
- **Encryption**: To further protect the data on a SAN, encrypt the data while it is stored on the SAN, so that even a sophisticated attack or theft would result in the attacker accessing encrypted data rather than clear blocks of storage.

- **Shared storage**: Logical partitions on a SAN are assigned a *logical unit number (LUN)* to differentiate them from one another, and hosts are mapped to specific LUNs for storage. However, host devices may be able to see LUNs other than those directly associated with them. As a result, devices may accidentally try to write data to logical devices they are not supposed to. In the case of a Windows system, it will try to label every LUN it sees. If it successfully labels a LUN that belongs to a UNIX-like system, it could render it unreadable by the original machine. You can mitigate this by using LUN masking.

 Note: LUN masking is discussed in the next topic.

vSAN

A *vSAN* is a virtual implementation of a storage area network that uses Fibre Channel switches to segment SANs, so that they can only communicate over the ports they are attached to. This protects the vSAN's data because all of the processing and storage of its data is isolated from the rest of the physical SAN. Likewise, network traffic that is disrupted on one vSAN will not be disrupted on the other vSANs that are independent of that particular virtual network.

Security Implications of vSAN

Before implementing a vSAN in your enterprise, be mindful of the following security implications:

- **Unauthorized access**: The host machine must be secured to protect it from unauthorized access to the virtual SANs running on it. If an attacker gains root- or system-level access to a host machine, then all vSANs and the data and applications stored on them could be compromised.
- **VM escaping**: Like other virtual implementations, vSANs are susceptible to VM escaping. An attacker could use a guest VM to gain access to and alter the host kernel and central processing unit (CPU). Once the attacker has escaped the virtual machine, then all common threats and attacks against host machines can be applied to the virtual machines as well.

iSCSI

The *Internet Small Computer System Interface (iSCSI)* is a protocol implementing links between data storage networks using Internet protocol (IP). This protocol is designed to extend across wide area networks without needing any new infrastructure. Users can enter commands and remotely manage data servers from great distances, and iSCSI can centralize data storage so that the information is not bound to individual servers. Although useful primarily for smaller organizations, iSCSI implementations can't match the speed and efficiency of an infrastructure-overhauling storage technology like Fibre Channel.

An iSCSI architecture is comprised of *initiators*, which are iSCSI client machines, and *targets*, which are iSCSI storage devices or applications. Each iSCSI client is assigned an *iSCSI Qualified Name (iQN)*, which is an initiator node name similar to a Media Access Control (MAC) address that is used to identify each client in the architecture.

Security Implications of iSCSI

Because it runs over Transmission Control Protocol/Internet protocol (TCP/IP), iSCSI is likewise exposed to much the same threats as the rest of the network. More specific security implications of iSCSI are as follows:

- **User permissions**: Users accessing the data should only be given permission to access data that is essential to their tasks and no more (least privilege). User accounts need to be appropriately guarded, passwords need to be secure, and permissions should always be carefully assessed.

- **Encryption**: iSCSI operates as a cleartext protocol, which means data is not encrypted as it moves. Since it uses Ethernet standards to transmit data, an unauthorized user may be able to eavesdrop on the iSCSI network and capture and reconstruct traffic. Therefore, you should implement encryption at other layers of the protocol stack, such as by using Internet Protocol Security (IPSec).
- **Authentication**: Devices on an iSCSI SAN verify each other by means of their iQN, but this process can easily be spoofed. One way to decrease the risk is by implementing Challenge Handshake Authentication Protocol (CHAP), which requires initiators and targets to supply a correct user name and password before a connection will be made. While this alleviates some of the risk, CHAP is not a wholly secure protocol and is vulnerable to a variety of attacks.
- **Isolation**: In most scenarios, the only thing separating the iSCSI SAN from the rest of the network is some form of physical or virtual network segmentation. Since both the SAN and the regular LAN use the same protocols for communication, if someone were to misconfigure the network setup in some manner, the SAN could become easily accessible to the regular network, and this change could go undetected. You should consider segmenting the iSCSI SAN physically from the rest of the network to prevent this issue from arising.

FCoE

Fibre Channel over Ethernet (FCoE) allows traditional Fibre Channel protocols to use high-speed Ethernet networks to transmit and store data. This protocol decreases the infrastructure cost of cabling, as well as lowers the amount of physical hardware devices that are required, like network interface cards (NICs) and switches. Likewise, power and cooling costs may be reduced.

FCoE is designed to allow all of the functionality provided by the upper OSI level Fibre Channel packets, but packages and ships them over an Ethernet infrastructure rather than Fibre Channel hardware. Standard Ethernet, however, is not suited for this kind of data. Only the latest versions of Ethernet with upgraded standards to provide low latency, better quality of service (QoS), and other features that are typically associated with a protocol like Fibre Channel are adequate.

Security Implications of FCoE

Like other SAN solutions, FCoE has its own security implications:

- **Eavesdropping**: Now that all traffic (TCP/IP and Fibre Channel) is passed over Ethernet, there is only one wire to monitor for intruders. This can be a concern because, in many default Fibre Channel configurations, the data crosses the network unencrypted and an intruder could rebuild data from captured frames.
- **Denial of Service (DoS)**: Another concern associated with the shared Ethernet standard is the potential for a DoS. Typically, the completely segmented Fibre Channel SAN is very difficult to attack. Now that Fibre Channel and TCP/IP are sharing one network, an intruder simply has to execute a TCP/IP-based DoS attack, and it will impact all network bandwidth.

ACTIVITY 7-1
Discussing Enterprise Storage Types and Protocols

Scenario

Develetech has opened a new office for its finance department. The employees in this department will need routine access to many different account records and other transactional data. As the CISO, you've been called to give your input on the potential storage solutions that the rest of management is considering. Discussing the security implications of each solution will help management decide what is best for Develetech, and keep the enterprise's risk to a minimum.

1. What are some of the security implications of cloud storage that you need to consider before choosing that solution?

2. Which of the following typically describes a NAS? (Select two.)
   - ☐ Ideal for smaller organizations.
   - ☐ Uses the iSCSI protocol.
   - ☐ Uses the Fibre Channel protocol.
   - ☐ Uses the CIFS protocol.

3. Develetech manages thousands of online transactions a day on its store and needs a storage solution that will manage its accounts data, purchasing transactions, and payroll information. This storage solution is mission critical, needs to be readily available, and needs to allow for extremely minimal downtime. Cost is not an issue and the solution must be very fast. What type of storage solution would you recommend, and why?

4. True or False? By default, iSCSI encrypts network traffic.
   - ☐ True
   - ☐ False

5. What are some of the pitfalls of enabling Fibre Channel to run over Ethernet?

TOPIC B

Implement Secure Storage Controls

You've identified the various storage types and protocols you're likely to see in an enterprise setting, and now you'll address their unique security issues by implementing controls. You can apply many of these controls to multiple solutions, and some controls may be more viable with certain protocols or types than others. Whatever your configuration may be, you'll be able to keep the storage solutions in your enterprise safe from unauthorized users reading, retrieving, modifying, or erasing sensitive data.

Snapshots

A *snapshot* is a static view of data at a specific point in time, taken to mark the last "good" version of that data. Snapshots work as a real-time rollback mechanism to this last good version. The reference point created by a snapshot is compared to the current state of the data. If the data changes, the snapshot software will make a copy of the data in its previous form. You may then roll your data back to this previous state, if necessary.

Snapshots are particularly useful as a quick means of backing up storage media in the event of a security breach or data corruption, as traditional backups involve copying large amounts of data, which may take longer than you'd like. Keep in mind, however, that the efficacy of snapshots is dependent on how often they are taken. If many changes were made to a database since the last snapshot, and you need to roll some of those changes back, you'll have to roll back all of them since the last snapshot.

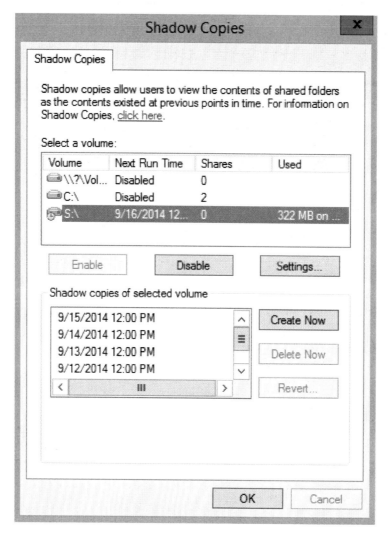

Figure 7-1: Microsoft's Shadow Copy taking a snapshot of a drive every day at noon.

Shadow Copy

Shadow Copy is Microsoft's implementation of snapshots in its Windows Server® operating system environments.

Deduplication

Deduplication is data compression technology that eliminates redundant data in storage. Storage solutions offer massive amounts of space, and often, users will store the same file repeatedly in numerous locations. As a result, processes like routine backups will end up using storage space to copy the same file to multiple locations in the backup. With data deduplication techniques, automated processes look for repetitive blocks of data and, rather than storing the same piece of data in more than one location, it saves it only once. In all the other locations, it simply makes a reference to the file rather than actually storing another copy.

This can greatly reduce storage needs and make storage solutions faster. It may even serve a security purpose by limiting the amount of areas where sensitive data is stored. However, deduplication may actually present a security risk because it removes redundant data, resulting in the loss of a redundancy that may be in place for a reason (for example, having multiple backups of a file). You must exercise caution and consider how a deduplication control will impact your storage systems.

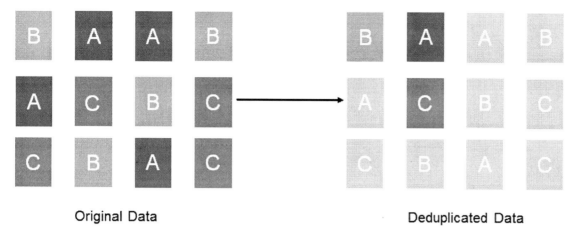

Original Data   Deduplicated Data

Figure 7–2: Data being deduplicated.

Dynamic Disk Pools

Dynamic Disk Pools (DDP) refers to an algorithm that dynamically distributes storage resources like data, protection information, and spare capacity across a pool of drives. This enables each logical drive to share its resources with the rest of the drives in the pool. Like a RAID setup, DDP offers redundancy in the event of drive failure; however, DDP is often much faster when rebuilding a failed drive. This is because, as resources are distributed across the entire pool, DDP uses every drive in the pool in the rebuilding process. Even the rebuilding process may expose drives to failure, so DDP improves data protection over traditional RAID implementations by taking less time to rebuild failed drives.

LUN Masking and Mapping

The process of assigning LUNs to identify hosts in a SAN is called *LUN mapping*. Because hosts in a SAN may see LUN numbers they are not associated with, and overwrite data to logical devices they are not supposed to, *LUN masking* was created to prevent this compromise of data. LUN masking forces hosts to authenticate, and their presence is only revealed to the LUNs they are assigned to.

This technique is used primarily to prevent the accidental corruption of data and is implemented at the *host bus adapter (HBA)* level of a SAN. If an attack compromises the HBA, LUN masking will be left vulnerable.

HBA Allocation

iSCSI technology allows for multiple host bus adapters to be in one single machine, and each port can be configured, automatically or manually, to handle only certain types of traffic. For example, you could configure one port on a server to be solely dedicated to storage tasks and communication. This process is known as *HBA allocation*. Shaping the flow of network traffic through HBA allocation may help you optimize performance and increase availability.

Multipath

Older network specifications like Small Computer System Interface (SCSI) were limited to single buses through which devices could communicate. *Multipath* is a method of enhancing the availability of devices in SAN networks by ensuring that no single point of failure, like a lone SCSI bus, exists in the communication channel. Multipathing provides more than one route to data, allowing data to take different routes depending on how heavy the traffic is on the primary route. It also monitors for the possibility of problems on one route and automatically adjusts to another route. Because availability is such a major part of security, and a single point of failure can be a huge risk to an enterprise, multipath is vital to any SAN implementation.

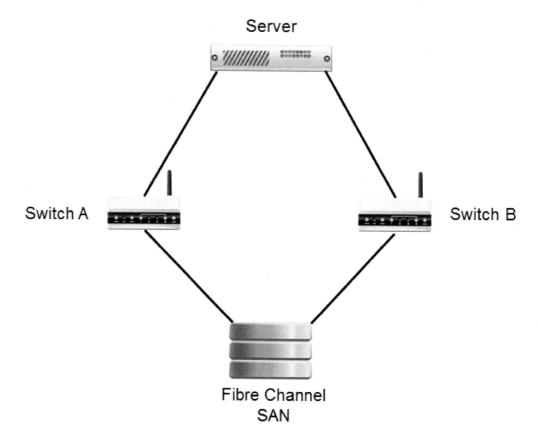

Figure 7-3: A server with two HBAs in a multipath configuration to a Fibre Channel SAN.

Offsite and Multisite Replication

In *offsite replication*, an organization creates backups and redundancy of its data and moves that data outside of its network. This can be done through networked solutions, or an organization may outsource this process to a cloud company. The process may be continuous, or the organization may schedule replication for specific points in time. Replication helps guarantee that data is consistent and that fault tolerance is in place should a disaster occur. Placing this replication in an offsite location further helps guarantee that backed up data is separated from the main operational network, and that a breach of that network will not necessarily compromise the availability of the replicated data stores. An organization can then use this offsite backup to quickly recover from an incident.

A similar concept is *multisite replication*, in which data is backed up across many different locations in a distributed manner. This is often necessary for big data, as it exceeds sizes that an individual site may not be able to handle. As data is replicated in more than one location, this may prove useful should a single offsite data store be compromised.

Storage Encryption

As you've seen, encrypting sensitive data is a must for any organization, and data in storage is no exception. Storage encryption encompasses a variety of methods that all help to guarantee confidentiality and integrity in specific elements of data storage. The following table describes how each method can provide essential security to your data at rest.

Encryption Method	Storage Security Relevance
Disk	The drives that hold stored data may benefit from being encrypted entirely to guarantee that all data is covered. Keep in mind, however, that this will increase processing overhead.
Block	Block-level encryption encrypts all of the data stored in solutions that use standards like Fibre Channel and iSCSI by encrypting blocks of data in fixed sizes. This tends to provide better performance than full disk encryption.
File	File-level encryption protects the individual files that the database stores data in. This is particularly useful for instances where data is replicated, as certain database files need to remain confidential as they are transmitted and stored elsewhere.
Record	Individual records in a database may be encrypted to protect that specific data without needing to encrypt the entire disk, block, or file. This may save you increased overhead costs associated with higher-level encryption.
Port	Encrypting specific ports will keep data communicated across those ports in a network confidential. Databases that routinely send and receive data across networks can benefit from this, but keep in mind that the data is only encrypted in transmission, and that additional encryption will need to be in place to secure the data in storage.

Guidelines for Ensuring Secure Storage Management

 Note: All Guidelines for this lesson are available as checklists from the **Checklist** tile on the CHOICE Course screen.

Use the following guidelines to ensure security in your data storage solutions:

* Implement multipath routing in SAN solutions to ensure availability of storage.
* Take regular snapshots of data stores for backup purposes.
* Use deduplication to eliminate unwanted redundancies in data.
* Use DDP to ensure drive reliability in the event of disk failure.
* Ensure that your SAN uses LUN masking to prevent accidental overwriting of data.
* Shape the flow of traffic to your storage solution through HBA allocation.
* Consider replicating your data to individual or multiple offsite locations to have an isolated backup.
* Consider which storage encryption method is the best fit for your needs, given your performance and confidentiality requirements.
* Use many of these controls simultaneously, if possible.

ACTIVITY 7-2
Implementing Secure Storage Controls

Before You Begin

You will be using BitLocker Drive Encryption, a disk encryption service provided by Microsoft. You will also be using Microsoft's Shadow Copy, a storage snapshot service. There is a volume labeled **STORAGE (S:)** on your computer and a **develetech_social-engineering-policy.doc** file on your desktop.

Scenario

Develetech is a large company that stores and maintains data sets relevant to many different facets of its business. A significant amount of this data at rest is considered confidential and meant for certain eyes only. Because it's infeasible to encrypt each file individually, you decide that implementing disk-level encryption is your best bet at keeping unauthorized personnel from accessing sensitive information. Using Microsoft' BitLocker Drive Encryption, you'll start by moving the source Word document for the social engineering policy into a separate storage volume, and then encrypt that volume. This way, those without knowledge of the password should not be able to compromise the policy document if it ever needs to be rewritten and/or republished.

Still, if the encryption key is leaked, or if an attacker gains access to the computer while the drive is unlocked, this defense could be rendered useless at stopping an attack. This storage volume and future volumes will be holding mission-critical data that the enterprise cannot afford to lose or be changed in malicious or negligent ways. To uphold the volume's integrity in case of a breach or accident, you will use Microsoft's Shadow Copy service to create a read-only snapshot of the storage volume. You will schedule Shadow Copy to take a snapshot every day, and you'll test its reversion feature to see how a storage volume can easily be returned to a safe and secure state.

---

1. Move the policy document to storage.

a) From the desktop, right-click **develetech_social-engineering-policy.doc** and select **Cut**.

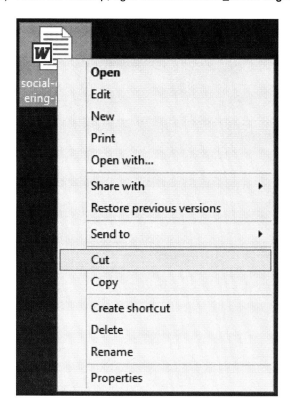

 Note: Make sure you are selecting the Word document file and not the PDF.

b) Open File Explorer, then right-click the **S** volume and select **Paste**.
c) Open the storage volume to verify that the document is there, then return to **This PC**.

2. Install the **BitLocker Drive Encryption** service.
   a) In the **Server Manager** window, in the **Configure this local server** section, select **Add roles and features**.
   b) Select **Next** four times.
   c) On the **Select features** page, check the **BitLocker Drive Encryption** check box.
   d) In the **Add Roles and Features** dialog box, select **Add Features**.
   e) Select **Next**.
   f) Check the **Restart the destination server automatically if required** check box.
   g) In the **Add Roles and Features** message box, select **Yes**.
   h) Select **Install**.
      Windows Server 2012 restarts.
   i) Log back in.
   j) In the **Add Roles and Features Wizard**, select **Close**.

 Note: There may be a delay before the wizard reappears.

3. Encrypt the **S** storage volume.
   a) Open File Explorer.

b) Right-click **STORAGE (S:)** and select **Turn on BitLocker**.

 Note: If no option to turn on BitLocker appears, restart your computer and try again.

c) On the **Choose how you want to unlock this drive** page, check **Use a password to unlock the drive**.
d) In the **Enter your password** text box, type *!Pass1234* and in the **Reenter your password** text box, type *!Pass1234* again.
e) Select **Next**.
f) On the **How do you want to back up your recovery key?** page, select **Save to a file**.
g) In the **Save BitLocker recovery key as** dialog box, select **Local Disk (C:)**, and then select **New folder**.
h) Type *blkey* and then press **Enter**.
i) Double-click **blkey** to open the folder, and select **Save**.
j) In the **BitLocker Drive Encryption** message box, select **Yes**.

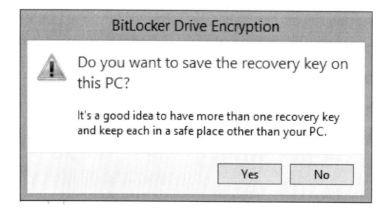

In a production environment, you would most likely also save the recovery key onto a removable drive. You could use Active Directory's key archival service.

k) Select **Next**.
l) On the **Choose how much of your drive to encrypt** page, select **Encrypt entire drive** and then select **Next**.
m) Select **Start encrypting**.
n) If necessary, in the notification area, from the **Show hidden icons** menu, select the **BitLocker** icon.

o) Verify that BitLocker is encrypting the drive.

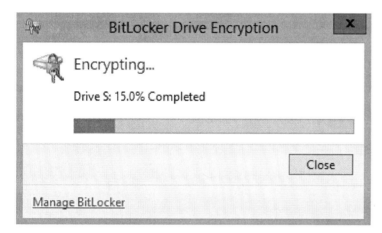

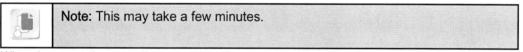

Note: This may take a few minutes.

p) When the encryption operation completes, if necessary, select **Close**.
q) Examine the **File Explorer** window.

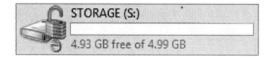

The drive icon for **S** now shows a lock on it.

4. Configure the Shadow Copy location and size limit settings.

a) Right-click the **S** volume and select **Configure Shadow Copies**.

b) In the **Shadow Copies** dialog box, with the **S:** volume highlighted, select **Settings**.
c) In the **Settings** dialog box, verify that the **Storage area** will be located on same volume (**S**). Because the volume is encrypted, the snapshot must be saved to that same volume.

d) Next to **Maximum size**, select **No limit**.

The snapshot will only be limited by the amount of available space on the **S** volume.

5. Schedule Shadow Copy creation for every day at noon.
    a) Select **Schedule**.
    b) From the **Schedule Task** drop-down menu, select **Daily**.
    c) In the **Start time** spin box, set the time to **12:00 PM**.

d) Verify that the **Schedule Task Daily** spin box is set to every **1** day.

```
┌─────────────────────────────────────────────────────────────────┐
│                            S:\                          [ ? ] [ X ]│
│ ┌─────────┐                                                        │
│ │Schedule │                                                        │
│ ├─────────┴──────────────────────────────────────────────────┐   │
│ │                                                              │   │
│ │  1. At 12:00 PM every day, starting 7/21/2014          [ v ] │   │
│ │                                                              │   │
│ │                              [   New   ]    [  Delete  ]     │   │
│ │                                                              │   │
│ │  Schedule Task:           Start time:                        │   │
│ │  [ Daily          v ]     [ 12:00 PM   ][^v]  [ Advanced... ]│   │
│ │  ┌─ Schedule Task Daily ──────────────────────────────────┐ │   │
│ │  │   Every  [ 1    ][^v]  day(s)                           │ │   │
│ │  └────────────────────────────────────────────────────────┘ │   │
│ │                                                              │   │
│ │  [✓] Show multiple schedules.                                │   │
│ │                                                              │   │
│ │                              [   OK   ]    [  Cancel  ]      │   │
│ └──────────────────────────────────────────────────────────────┘ │
└───────────────────────────────────────────────────────────────────┘
```

e) From the drop-down list at the top, select the second schedule item, then select **Delete**.

   This will remove the second instance in the default schedule so that only the schedule you just created will run.

f) Select **OK** twice.

6. Manually take a snapshot of the volume.

   a) In the **Shadow Copies** dialog box, with the **S:** volume selected, select **Create Now**.
      Shadow Copy creates a read-only snapshot of the volume.

b) Verify that the **Used** column shows how much space the Shadow Copy takes up, and that the **Shadow copies of selected volume** text box lists the Shadow Copy by its date and time.

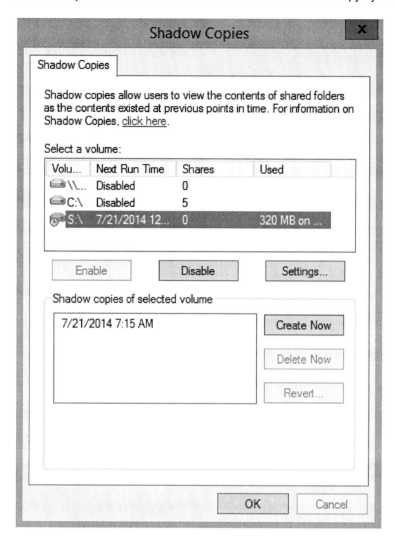

c) Select **OK**.

d) If necessary, right-click in File Explorer and select **Refresh** to see that the **S** volume has added space for the Shadow Copy.

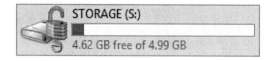

7. Make a change to the storage volume.

   a) Open the **S** volume and open up the policy document in Word.

   b) Make any change you wish to the document and save it, then close the document.

    Note: You may also change the name of the document, delete the document, or move other files onto the **S** volume.

   c) Return to **This PC**.

8. Test Shadow Copy's reversion feature to revert the volume to the snapshot you manually took.

   a) Right-click the **S** volume and select **Configure Shadow Copies**.

b) With the **S:** volume selected, in the **Shadow copies of selected volume** text box, select the date and time of the snapshot.

c) Select **Revert**.

d) In the **Volume Revert** message box check the **Check here if you want to revert this volume** check box and select **Revert Now**.

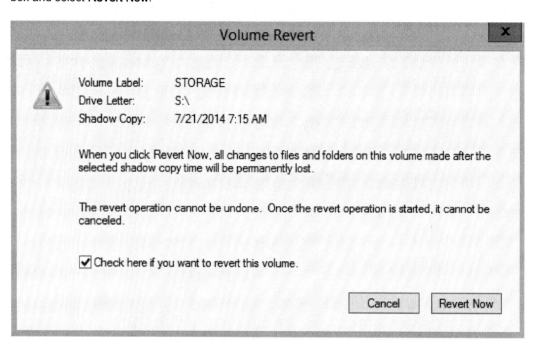

e) After the reversion process completes, select **OK**.

f) Open the **S** volume and observe that whatever changes you made were reverted to the snapshot you took.

g) Close File Explorer.

Summary

In this lesson, you identified the usefulness of the many storage types and protocols available to enterprises, as well as assessed each type or protocol's security challenges. Then, you implemented security controls in your enterprise storage configuration to keep your sensitive data from being unduly exposed to risk. Storage security is important to many organizations, especially those that routinely archive confidential information, so being equipped to respond to threats will help keep that information in the state it should be.

What storage types are most prevalent in your organization, and what security concerns do you have about them?

What security controls do you currently implement in your storage solutions, and what controls would you like to add?

 Note: Check your CHOICE Course screen for opportunities to interact with your classmates, peers, and the larger CHOICE online community about the topics covered in this course or other topics you are interested in. From the Course screen you can also access available resources for a more continuous learning experience.

8 Analyzing and Implementing Network Security

Lesson Time: 3 hours

Lesson Objectives

In this lesson, you will:

- Analyze network security components and devices.

- Analyze network-enabled devices.

- Analyze advanced network design.

- Configure controls for network security.

Lesson Introduction

The next enterprise system is its network, the way in which all users and devices can communicate with each other. This communication and interaction brings with it a great deal of complexity, so understanding security in this context is as important as ever. In this lesson, you'll secure your network by identifying the advantages and disadvantages of various devices and design principles, and then you'll put this analysis into practice through various controls. Using what you've learned, you'll be more equipped to apply this security to your enterprise's communications and ensure the confidentiality, integrity, and availability of your network.

TOPIC A

Analyze Network Security Components and Devices

Like host and storage systems, you should begin your network security procedures by first identifying common components and devices. Analyzing these solutions will give you an overview of each one's strengths and weaknesses in the area of security, and you'll be better informed when it comes time to harden your enterprise network with them.

Unified Threat Management

Unified threat management (UTM) refers to a system that centralizes various security techniques—firewall, anti-malware, network intrusion prevention, URL filtering, content inspection, malware inspection, and more—into a single appliance. In addition, UTM security appliances usually include a single console from which a security administrator can monitor and manage various defense settings. UTM was created in response to a number of difficulties that administrators face in deploying discrete security systems; namely, managing several complex platforms as well as meeting the significant cost requirements. UTM systems help to simplify the security process by being tied to only one vendor and requiring only a single, streamlined application to function. This makes management of your organization's network security easier, as you no longer need to be familiar with or know the quirks of each individual security implementation.

Figure 8-1: Unified threat management combining the functionality of various security techniques into one device.

Nevertheless, UTM has its downsides. When defense is unified under a single system, it creates the potential for a single point of failure that could affect an entire network. Discrete security systems, if they fail, might only compromise that particular avenue of attack. Additionally, UTM systems can struggle with latency issues if they are subject to too much network activity.

NIDS

A *network intrusion detection system (NIDS)* is a system that primarily uses passive hardware sensors to monitor traffic on a specific segment of the network. It cannot analyze encrypted packets because it has no method for decrypting the data. It can sniff traffic and send alerts about anomalies or concerns. Like a host-based intrusion detection systems (HIDS), NIDS uses one of two analysis techniques: anomaly-based, in which it compares network traffic against a baseline and looks for significant deviations; and signature-based, in which it looks for specific threats that are listed in a database. NIDS is useful in automating what would otherwise be a tedious process for network administrators.

NIDS can run on a target machine monitoring its own traffic or other machines in a network monitoring all network traffic. You would typically place an NIDS at a strategic point within your network to analyze behavior that centers around a sensitive asset. For example, you might place web servers behind a firewall, and use an NIDS to monitor traffic that attempts to breach the firewall. Another particular use for an NIDS is rogue machine detection. A *rogue machine* is any unknown or unrecognized device that is connected to a network, often with malicious intent.

Because it can monitor all incoming and outgoing network traffic, an NIDS can cause issues with network speed. This is why it is important to place the NIDS strategically, and not necessarily force it to monitor all traffic on the network. Another disadvantage of NIDS is that it can only scan for attacks while they occur, and by the time it raises an alert to the network, the attack may have already harmed the system. NIDS is also limited in its ability to separate noise generated by bad packets from actual uncorrupted signals; this can lead to a high number of false positives.

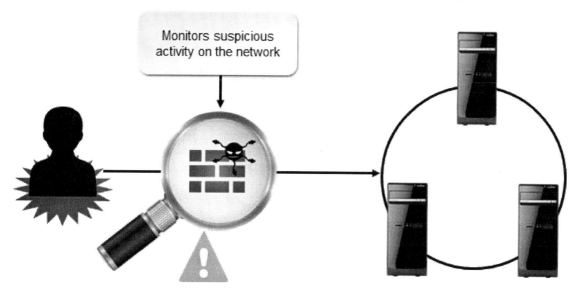

Figure 8–2: A NIDS detecting suspicious activity on a network's firewall.

 Note: To learn more about identifying anomalous behavior on your network, access the LearnTO **Set Up a Network Intrusion Detection System** presentation from the **LearnTO** tile on the CHOICE Course screen.

NIPS

A *network intrusion prevention system (NIPS)* is an extension of an NIDS in that it that monitors suspicious network and system traffic, sends a warning if suspicious traffic might constitute an attack, and also reacts in real time to block the traffic. An advantage of using NIPS over NIDS is that it can regulate traffic according to specific content, because it examines packets as they travel through the NIPS. Blocking traffic may involve dropping unwanted data packets or resetting the connection. This is in contrast to the way a firewall behaves, which blocks IP addresses or entire ports based on your explicit instructions.

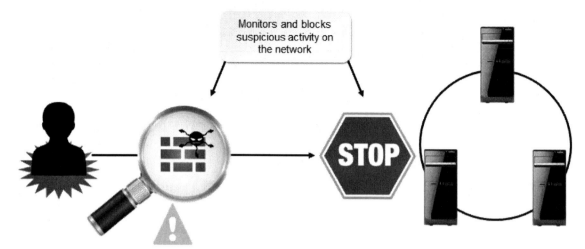

Figure 8-3: A NIPS detecting and blocking suspicious activity on a network's firewall.

Like an NIDS, you should place an NIPS strategically around your network to optimize its effect and reduce network overhead. NIPS are also vulnerable to false positives if not carefully configured to your environment. This can have a much more harmful impact on your enterprise than if you were using an NIDS, as the false positive alert will actively stop legitimate traffic, lowering your network's availability. This is why you need to be fully aware of your network's day-to-day functions, so that you may configure your NIPS to allow the types of traffic that you know to be legitimate. One additional downside to using an NIPS is cost: while many NIDS applications, like Snort®, are free of charge, NIPS will typically run you tens of thousands of dollars.

 Note: The information security industry is phasing out the use of NIDS/IDS systems in favor of NIPS/IPS, as NIPS/IPS is a more complete solution.

 Note: The National Institute of Standards and Technology (NIST) and others in the industry use intrusion detection and prevention systems (IDPS) as an umbrella term to refer to all solutions that both passively detect and actively block unwanted activity.

Inline Network Encryptor

An *inline network encryptor (INE)* is a device that ensures the confidentiality and integrity of data in transit between secured networks that have an intermediary unsecured network. The INE device is situated just outside the secure network, and any data sent by the secured network through the unsecured network must pass through the device first. The INE encrypts the data, then passes it to a perimeter router, which then passes it to the unsecured network. The unsecured network then sends the data to the destination network's perimeter router, where it passes the data on to a receiving INE device. This device decrypts the data before it passes it on to the destination network.

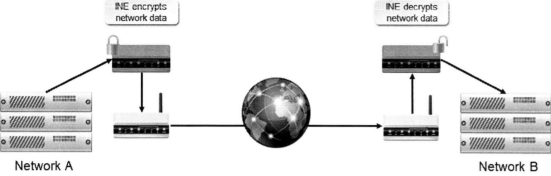

Figure 8-4: An INE setup.

While INEs can be a useful tool in an organization that needs a layer 3 solution to send data over an unsecured network, they do have their drawbacks. Depending on the technology used, bandwidth becomes an issue as less powerful INEs can limit data throughput to unacceptable levels, depending on your organization's size and activity. If your network is constantly sending data to another network through an unsecured intermediary like the Internet, encryption of every data packet will likely add a significant amount of overhead. More powerful INEs claim to accommodate high bandwidth networks with 10+ Gb/s throughput, but these devices are very expensive.

 Note: While similar in function, virtual private networks (VPNs) tend to connect individuals to networks whereas INEs connect whole networks to other networks.

Example

INEs are often used by government agencies to send sensitive information between their disparate networks over an unsecured network like the Internet. Data packets are sent over IP communications often using the Internet Protocol Security (IPSec) protocol to encapsulate data in a way that is invisible to the end user. The National Security Agency (NSA), for example, develops and uses High Assurance Internet Protocol Encryptor (HAIPE) devices based on an enhanced version of IPSec that uses strong cryptographic algorithms and can quickly be de-provisioned to destroy cryptographic keys.

Security Information and Event Management

Security Information and Event Management (SIEM) solutions provide real-time or near real-time analysis of security alerts generated by network hardware and applications. SIEM solutions can be implemented as software, hardware appliances, or outsourced managed services. SIEM technology is often used to enhance incident response capabilities by providing expanded insights into intrusion detection and prevention through aggregation and correlation of event data across multiple incidents.

SIEM products are excellent tools that can help an enterprise streamline its network security administration. Productivity in the areas of log analysis and auditing of network systems is likely to increase, as SIEM solutions will help administrators more easily identify problems that would otherwise take them a very long time to detect. This is especially crucial in responding to a security breach where every second counts.

SIEM Capabilities

A typical SIEM implementation will provide a number of capabilities to your enterprise, as listed in the following table.

Capability	Description
Aggregation	A primary function of a SIEM solution is to aggregate event and log data from multiple disparate systems while providing a single vantage point from which to process the data.
Correlation	The power of SIEM technology and the true benefits of scale are realized when strong correlation capabilities are used to link common events, attributes, and data together, forming a more complete picture of important events.
Alerting	A SIEM implementation performs automated analysis of incoming event data and has the ability to generate alerts that notify administrators of specific conditions or events.
Visibility	The aggregated data collected by a SIEM solution is usually combined and presented in dashboard-style view, giving administrators a single view from which to view patterns of events and activity.
Compliance	SIEM applications can be employed to automate the gathering of compliance data and produce reports that meet governance and auditing requirements.
Data retention	As a byproduct of collecting and aggregating large amounts of event data, the SIEM solution usually has the capability to store historical data and facilitate correlation of data over time. This capability is critical for event analysis and forensics, and can also meet data retention needs for compliance requirements.

Network-Attached HSM

Hardware security modules (HSMs) are useful for more than just host or storage security. Network-attached HSMs can provide cryptographic services for communications architectures like cloud computing and virtualized environment deployments. This is beneficial to large-scale enterprises that need to centralize the way in which keys for multiple connected hosts are managed. Instead of attaching separate devices to each individual host, the network HSM can act as a standalone device for increasing the scope and scalability of cryptographic services in your organization.

To increase scalability, network-attached HSMs typically partition themselves to provide isolated encryption containers for hosts that need to work with specific protocols or implementations. This allows the individual HSM to be the root of trust for the many different implementations that use these encrypted containers. However, multiple hosts can still attach to a single partition, if need be.

Application and Protocol Aware Technologies

There are other assorted network security technologies that are application and protocol aware. An application aware technology is able to recognize applications connected to it and collect information on the state of those applications. This allows the technology to better maintain and optimize its operations. Likewise, protocol aware technologies can identify and analyze various protocols and standards used in communication with networks.

The following table describes some examples of application or protocol aware technologies used in networking.

Technology	Description
Web application firewall (WAF)	WAFs implement traditional firewall functionality like input and output filtering in the web application itself. This allows the firewall to control the application for any incoming or outgoing network traffic that does not meet a pre-defined policy.

Technology	Description
Next-generation firewall (NGFW)	Next-gen firewalls go beyond traditional firewall functionality by operating at the application layer and protocol stack. This allows the NGFW to initiate deeper packet inspection to detect unwanted network communications that target the higher levels. These types of threats are becoming more and more common, and traditional firewalls are ill-equipped to handle them.
Intrusion prevention system (IPS)	An IPS will often need to analyze the behavior of specific applications or protocols to detect anomalies in how they communicate with other systems in the network. With this information, a properly configured NIPS can take the necessary steps to block malicious activity while reducing false positives.
Passive vulnerability scanners	Some passive vulnerability scanners have the ability to report on application or protocol-specific information to help identify where weak points exist in a network. This application or protocol-specific information can give administrators a better idea of how vulnerabilities are introduced in their network, and how they can go about fixing them. Unlike more active scanners like an IPS, passive scanners are less likely to interfere with normal network operations.
Database activity monitor (DAM)	A DAM is a database security utility that runs independently from the database and serves to monitor and report on activities. This monitoring is usually performed continuously and in real-time. DAMs have the ability to monitor networked applications to validate end-user authentication.

Virtual Networking and Security Components

Just as hosts can be virtualized, so too can networks. Networking components like switches, routers, wireless controllers, firewalls, and proxies can all be integrated as software into a virtual environment. The virtual environment decouples these network components from their actual hardware and runs them as an abstraction; this allows administrators to configure network services and protocols to work on virtualized platforms in the enterprise.

There are several reasons why you might choose to virtualize your network. Managing the flow of large amounts of data as it traverses an actual network can be very difficult from both an administrative and operational perspective. In a virtual network, administrators can more easily control the flow of specific data to reduce the load on physical network devices. Using virtualization, you can consolidate these physical devices so that they work together to streamline network performance for whatever your use case may be. Additionally, virtual local area networks (VLANs) help security administrators by segmenting virtual machines (VMs) on different networks and restricting resources used by each port and user on the virtual network, providing them with more fine-grained control than they would have in a normal LAN.

However, one drawback of virtualized networks is that their topology can become difficult to manage in very large, complex enterprise networks.

Device Placement

The placement of devices in your network should be a critical concern in maintaining its security. At its most basic level, the network is usually divided into internal resources and external resources with a filter in between that detects intruders and exploits and defends the network against attack. This wall is commonly called the perimeter and can be comprised of firewalls, routers, and switches or a device that contains the functionality of all three. More advanced threats to network security require defenses to also be placed inside of the perimeter, creating a defense-in-depth strategy.

Proper device placement is about more than just its virtual location within the topology of your network, however. No amount of security configurations will keep a server safe if a thief can simply steal your UTM device from the premises. This makes physical security just as much of a necessity as its virtual complement, even though it is often overlooked. Place key network devices where their physical access can be both monitored and controlled.

 Note: Keep in mind that device placement, whether virtual or physical, may end up affecting network performance.

Guidelines for Analyzing Network Security Components and Devices

 Note: All Guidelines for this lesson are available as checklists from the **Checklist** tile on the CHOICE Course screen.

Use the following guidelines to analyze network security components and devices.

- Consider that UTMs will make management of devices easier, but will also create a single point of failure in your network security.
- Strategically place any NIDS where they will offer the most protection and cause the least amount of network disruption.
- Investigate how an NIPS will impact your network in the event of false positives.
- Investigate how much of a bottleneck an INE will be on your network before implementing it.
- Determine how the many capabilities of a SIEM can help you monitor your network appliances.
- Determine if multiple hosts would benefit from a centralized network-attached HSM, rather than multiple host-based solutions.
- Investigate the usefulness of devices that can monitor and defend your network on its higher levels.
- Determine if virtualizing your network will streamline its administration.
- Place devices logically around and in your network with respect to where they can best uphold CIA.
- Place network devices physically where you can easily monitor and control their access.

ACTIVITY 8-1
Analyzing Network Security Components and Devices

Scenario

There are many different network devices, each with their own security strengths and weaknesses. Like host and storage solutions, Develetech wants you to analyze network devices to find out which ones are the best fit for the organization. This will ensure that the network stays secure without sacrificing availability or slowing down bandwidth.

1. Develetech might implement a UTM to centralize various utilities that secure the network. However, what are the drawbacks of using a UTM? (Select two.)

   ☐ It is difficult to manage.

   ☐ It creates a single point of failure.

   ☐ It can have latency issues.

   ☐ It is difficult to update.

2. Develetech wants some way to prevent a breach compromising the network. What solution, NIDS or NIPS, would you suggest, and why?

3. Which of the following security devices provides a real-time analysis of alerts generated by network components?

   ○ HSM

   ○ SIEM

   ○ INE

   ○ WAF

4. What does it mean for a security device to be application aware? How does an NGFW benefit from being application aware?

5. What are the advantages of virtualizing a network? (Select three.)

   ☐ You can more easily control the flow of specific data.

   ☐ You can consolidate physical devices to increase performance.

   ☐ You can more easily restrict resources used by each port.

   ☐ You can more easily manage the network's topology in a large, complex environment.

6. Your team has established firewalls, an NIDS, and other security devices around your network perimeter. This topology is very secure against virtual threats from external—and even internal—attacks. However, their task of securing the network is not yet done. What else do you need to remind them of with regard to the security of these devices?

TOPIC B

Analyze Network-Enabled Devices

You've analyzed networking devices that are commonly found in enterprise settings, but there are other devices out there that you may not think of as being relevant to networking. From an information processing standpoint, these devices are typically less complex than the computers you work with everyday; however, modern technology has made it possible for them to integrate with your wider network for streamlined communication. In your duties as a CASP, these devices may fall under your security purview, so it's important that you analyze the ways they can affect your network.

Building Automation Systems

A *building automation system (BAS)* is a system that monitors and controls various operational resources in a building, including lighting systems, power systems, ventilation, alarms, plumbing, and miscellaneous physical security systems. These resources are all networked and linked under a central management system so that building administrators can more easily make changes to or view the status of these crucial mechanisms.

Aside from the ease of management involved in being able to control potentially large physical resources, a BAS can save the enterprise time and money on maintenance or repairs that can be avoided through proper monitoring and control of the resources. Security systems like alarms and access control doors can also be under the domain of a BAS, and administrators can make policy-based adjustments when needed.

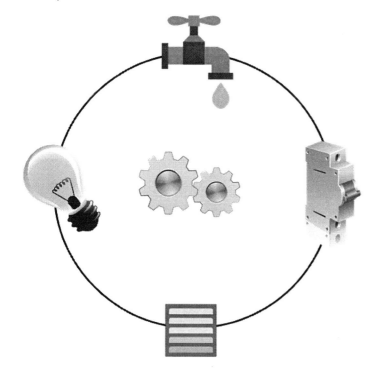

Figure 8-5: A BAS controlling various infrastructure systems.

Nevertheless, the fact that these devices are networked under a centralized control system brings with it an increased amount of risk to an enterprise. While attackers are typically more familiar with computer assets and may find more value in targeting them, your building systems are no less vulnerable to the same kind of attacks that take advantage of familiar networking protocols. Some

BASs use the Simple Network Management Protocol (SNMP) to communicate; this protocol is susceptible to a number of spoofing, sniffing, and brute force attacks. An attacker who compromises the BAS can abuse its high level of control by damaging building equipment or rendering it inoperable. Because certain security systems are often under the control of a BAS, these attacks can inflict more than just an immediate financial loss—they could compromise the physical security of the premises. It is therefore important for you to understand the risks involved in implementing a BAS.

HVAC Controllers

Heating, ventilation, and air conditioning controllers (HVAC controllers) are elements of a BAS that regulate comfort levels in a physical environment. Many HVAC controllers are automated; they monitor the current state of an HVAC device and compare it to a baseline. If the current state does not align with the intended state, then the controller will compensate in the appropriate manner. For example, if the building's temperature falls below 68 degrees, the heating system will kick in until the building's temperature meets that threshold, at which point it will either turn off or maintain its operations.

Figure 8-6: A heating and cooling controller.

However, networked HVAC controllers can also interface with a BAS to allow a person to manually control its operations. This allows the building manager or other qualified personnel to receive alarms in case of an incident, and respond directly without needing to physically configure the device. Like the BAS it interfaces with, controllers are susceptible to the same types of attacks that are the result of poor security protocols. Specifically, the damage an attacker can do to HVAC systems can create an unreasonable or even hazardous working environment for the enterprise's on-site employees. Besides the human element, an attacker could use a compromised HVAC controller to damage temperature- and ventilation-sensitive equipment like servers. Always-on, powerful hardware tends to run hot, which is why server rooms almost always require some form of careful temperature control to prevent overheating. An attacker could turn off the mechanisms that cool the server room, overheating the machines and possibly damaging the hardware.

Example

One example of a networked HVAC controller is the Nest Learning Thermostat, a Transmission Control Protocol/Internet protocol (TCP/IP) temperature regulation device that can download updates to its software from the Internet, as well as allow users to remotely control the temperature of their buildings using a Wi-Fi connected smartphone or similar device.

Sensors

Complementing a BAS and any of its controllers are networked sensors; devices that can actually measure the state of physical phenomena and report them to other relevant nodes in the network. Sensors in HVAC systems measure temperature, but sensors can also respond to things like sound, air pressure, smoke, steam, pollution, and many other physical phenomena. Sensors often interface with their corresponding controller to communicate information about an environment instantly to the controller or the human personnel who operates it. Unlike controllers, sensors need discrete hardware platforms that can actually respond to physical stimuli, and often these platforms must be numerous and spread out across a large area. This makes them particularly challenging to set up in a network, even if that network is wireless.

Figure 8–7: A smoke detector includes sensors.

As part of a BAS, sensors are likewise vulnerable to the same threats. An attacker who can take over a building's sensors can much more easily cause a physical emergency to go undetected or unannounced to the proper personnel. Likewise, the attacker may be able to create a false alarm to divert attention and resources away from the real intrusion vector. Another point of concern is the software that these sensors use to communicate. Many are bundled with stripped-down operating systems that provide the necessary functionality and not much more. If these operating systems aren't or can't be hardened, they will be another attack surface for a malicious user to exploit.

Physical Access Control Systems

A BAS implementation might include support for physical access control systems like doors, locks, card readers, biometric scanners, mantraps, and other physical barriers that keep unauthorized personnel out. These systems are typically automated based on pre-defined access policies. Networked systems can also allow an administrator to adjust these controls instantly from a central management platform. If, for example, an ex-employee tries to enter the building through an automated mantrap and still has working credentials, an administrator can manually override this automation and configure the mantrap to deny the ex-employee access.

Figure 8-8: A fingerprint scanner.

Networked physical access can be very convenient for administrators and building managers, but it carries the risk that can affect any other automated system. In this case, these controls are directly linked to the enterprise's security rather than existing primarily for some other purpose, like an HVAC system. While it is true that virtual security is weak without physical security, the reverse could be also be said of networked physical systems. If attackers compromise the computer network, they can also render certain physical obstacles ineffectual.

Scientific and Industrial Equipment

Scientific and industrial equipment can be networked for increased productivity and management. Like other services in a network, this equipment can respond to a number of commands, as well as efficiently report information to many other nodes in the network. While typical implementations use older serial communications to connect to individual hosts, some scientific and industrial equipment is being switched to TCP/IP networks for increased flexibility.

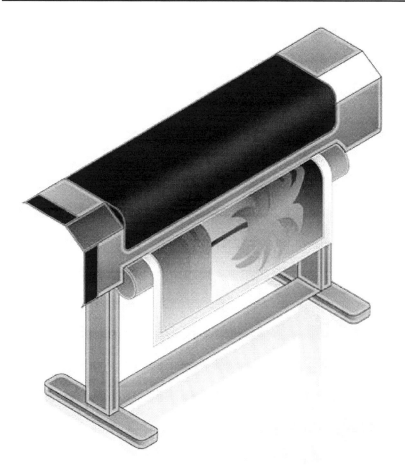

Figure 8-9: An industrial printer.

Because the volatility and cost of such equipment places a great amount of risk on the organization, the mechanisms that control them need to be secured from unauthorized access. Many research operations rely heavily on the accuracy of their findings, and if the equipment they use has been tampered with because of a poorly secured network, then their funding may have been wasted and their important research compromised. Likewise, industrial plants and warehouses use a lot of older equipment that may not communicate securely over the control network; if an attacker can take over or sabotage this equipment, this could have a significant financial impact on the enterprise. Industrial equipment, because it is so large and often unwieldy, can also be a danger to personnel from a safety standpoint. Even if it is not their intent, a malicious user can still cause physical harm by controlling dangerous industrial equipment.

Stuxnet

Stuxnet was a computer worm discovered in 2010 that was designed to attack the automation involved in machinery and other industrial equipment that ran specific software on Windows® operating systems. Stuxnet allowed controllers to send remote commands to infected equipment, as well eavesdrop on its operations. This worm underscored the importance of establishing a security framework for industrial control systems and the devices they oversee.

A/V Systems

Audio/visual systems like televisions, projectors, microphones, speakers, lighting, and other multimedia are sometimes just as connected as a workstation or server would be in an enterprise. For example, a hotel or other building open to customers might have televisions running in their lobby that constantly cycle through different programming depending on where they are and what time of day it is. If these TVs are networked, personnel can easily deploy this programming to all of the devices at once, instead of needing to physically program each one individually.

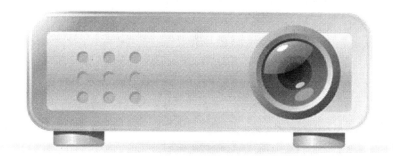

Figure 8-10: A projector.

The interconnection of audio/visual devices, of course, means that network security governance must expand to accommodate these devices. While they tend not to hold sensitive information or control any sort of environment functions, a compromised audio/visual device can still be a headache for an enterprise. Many businesses rely on these systems in meetings and presentations, and if those important business processes are disrupted, the business itself could suffer as a result. Additionally, many devices like smart TVs boast Internet connectivity, which could be yet another attack surface that could put the enterprise at risk.

IP Video

An *Internet Protocol video camera (IP camera)* is a device that is used for surveillance of an area and actively transmits data to and from networks like the Internet. This separates the IP video camera from traditional closed-circuit television (CCTV) cameras, which are limited in the extent of their transmission. IP cameras are essentially high-quality webcams created to be used exclusively as surveillance tools for enterprise physical security.

Figure 8-11: An IP video camera.

IP cameras have a number of advantages over traditional CCTV surveillance. Like any IP-enabled network device, the camera can encrypt its payload with a number of different protocols to ensure the confidentiality and integrity of the signal it is transmitting. Security personnel can access the video feed from an IP camera from essentially anywhere that has Internet access, allowing them to remotely monitor an area for threats. IP cameras also easily accept remote commands transmitted by a controller to do a variety of actions, including panning, rotating, and zooming.

The bandwidth required to transmit and store live video feeds can be detrimental, however. From a confidentiality and integrity standpoint, transmissions that fail to incorporate appropriate transport encryption can fall victim to snooping and man-in-the-middle attacks, allowing a malicious user to both see the video feed and possibly alter it. Wirelessly networked cameras are particularly vulnerable to these attacks.

Guidelines for Analyzing Network-Enabled Devices

Use the following guidelines to analyze network-enabled devices:

*   Understand the protocols that link any building automation system in your enterprise.
*   Identify each element of a BAS that has a networked interface.
*   Identify the capabilities of HVAC controllers and how they can be used in malicious ways.
*   Map all networked sensors to get an overview of their logical and physical topology.
*   Ensure that networked sensors are running hardened software.
*   Have redundant sensors in place in the event of device failure.
*   Determine your enterprise's need to have physical access control systems networked.
*   Identify each access control point and how it can be managed from a centralized system.
*   Assess the risks involved in networking expensive and mission-critical scientific equipment, as well as dangerous industrial equipment.
*   Determine how each audio/visual device in your enterprise can communicate, especially to a wider network like the Internet.
*   Determine if your network bandwidth can accommodate IP camera surveillance systems.
*   Identify how an attacker can snoop on or spoof surveillance video from an IP camera.
*   Consider that a traditional analog camera might be a better choice, but keep in mind that even these can be connected to networked devices like DVRs.
*   Identify other peripheral devices that may be networked in your enterprise, like printers, scanners, etc.

ACTIVITY 8-2
Analyzing Network-Enabled Devices

Scenario

Although not commonly thought of in the realm of security, network-enabled devices like physical building systems nonetheless require your attention. At Develetech, you'll review any such systems for security vulnerabilities that could harm your property, and you'll also analyze physical access control equipment like locked doors and cameras that are more easily managed in a networked environment. Having interconnected equipment makes administration much more convenient, but gives attackers another opportunity to cause damage. Securing these devices is just as important to your organization's well-being as securing its computers.

---

1. If Develetech chooses to implement a BAS, specifically with HVAC controllers and sensors, what are some of the security concerns you should raise?

2. You're worried that some guests or unauthorized employees might use an administrators' smart card to gain access to the locked server room. How can you ensure that your security team has the tools necessary to deny access to the server room on-the-fly, or quickly revoke an administrators' authorization after their smart card has been stolen?

3. What control is vital in securing an IP camera from eavesdropping?
   - ○ Logging
   - ○ Configuration lockdown
   - ○ Storage encryption
   - ○ Transport encryption

TOPIC C

Analyze Advanced Network Design

Beyond the physical components or devices that facilitate security in your network, you need to make sure the network is secure in its actual design. A network architecture that fails to account for security puts the business at risk, even if its individual components boast security features. Quite a few of the more advanced design protocols are new and emerging, so it's vital that you analyze how their security implications could aid or hinder your enterprise network. This can be a challenge for any CASP, as there may not yet be a consensus from which to solicit help. Nevertheless, in this topic, you'll analyze the design of your network architecture with respect to these advanced protocols and technologies.

Remote Access

Remote access, whether it's through desktop sharing, remote assistance, remote file/directory access, or simple terminal emulation, exposes a great deal of resources, data, and systems to the wider world. Therefore, you should develop threat models that identify resources that may be exposed to remote access attacks. As these are identified, you will be better equipped to implement access control and only give employees access to what they absolutely need. Additionally, the VPN your employees use to tunnel into your internal network through the Internet should be secured with a strong tunneling protocol like Layer 2 Tunneling Protocol (L2TP) with IPSec encryption.

Figure 8-12: Using a VPN to tunnel through the Internet and remotely access a private server.

Other secure protocols, like Secure Shell (SSH) and Secure Sockets Layer/Transport Layer Security (SSL/TLS), can also aid in remote access. SSH allows a user to open a secure command interface to remote systems using encryption. This prevents snooping on network communication from client to server by ensuring the confidentiality of the data being communicated. SSL/TLS may be used for remote access to lower the administrative effort needed to deploy solutions to each individual system. With SSL/TLS remote access, a user can securely connect to network resources by simply using a browser. Like SSH, the remote communications are encrypted to prevent confidentiality issues.

Examples

For desktop-related remote access, Microsoft's Remote Desktop Protocol (RDP) grants a user a graphical user interface (GUI) with which to remotely control a server's desktop. When using RDP, you should ensure that transport encryption is enabled to prevent any man-in-the-middle attacks. Similar to RDP, one of the most popular desktop sharing programs is RealVNC's Virtual Network

Computing (VNC®) application. VNC is not secure by default; you should enable transport encryption to verify that your remote connection is secure.

IPv6 and Associated Transitional Technologies

Internet Protocol version 6 (IPv6) is the version of the Internet Protocol (IP) designed to succeed IPv4 as available IPv4 addresses are being exhausted. The last top-level block of IP address space was assigned in February 2011. IPv6 provides a much larger pool of available IP addresses by increasing the IP address space from 32 bits to 128 bits. The practical addressable space of IPv4 addresses is roughly 4.3 billion IP addresses. By comparison, IPv6 provides about 340 trillion, trillion, trillion addresses—enough for more than a billion IP addresses for every square millimeter of Earth's surface.

2001:A153:00F1:0000:0000:E2EE:0D55:H120

2001:A153:F1::E2EE:D55:H120

Figure 8-13: A hexadecimal IPv6 address and its abbreviated form.

 Note: IPv6 addresses are abbreviated by eliminating leading zeroes in each group, and by representing consecutive groups of zeroes with two colons (::). Double colons can only appear once in an address.

Internet Protocol Security (IPSec) was originally developed for IPv6, and was later back-ported to IPv4. In general, IPv6 provides better native security than IPv4 by having built-in support for encryption. IPv6 also includes new efficiency features, such as simplified address headers, hierarchical addressing, support for time-sensitive network traffic, and a new structure for unicast addressing. However, IPv6 is not compatible with IPv4.

It is also important to be aware of IPv6 network traffic even if the network is not intended to support IPv6 traffic. Attackers may use IPv6 as a transport mechanism due to the fact that older security technology may be compatible with IPv6 traffic or even aware of its existence.

Network Authentication

A crucial element of any network's design is the authentication methods that you choose to use. There is not necessarily one best solution for all situations, and the right fit for your enterprise will depend heavily on your business needs. Smaller enterprises might find traditional user name/password authentication sufficient, but this will likely not be enough for a large, complex enterprise to stay secure.

In many network configurations, multifactor authentication is particularly effective. For example, you may require that users who connect to your private wireless authenticate with a smart card, as well as provide their company user name and password at an access point. This prevents unauthorized users from compromising a single authentication factor and easily gaining access to your network. You can also guarantee mutual authentication through a ticketing system like Kerberos, so that both parties can be certain of who they are communicating with. This is particularly useful in network communications where servers and clients require an equal amount of trust between each other, like when a privileged user needs to access and transmit sensitive company data to a network share.

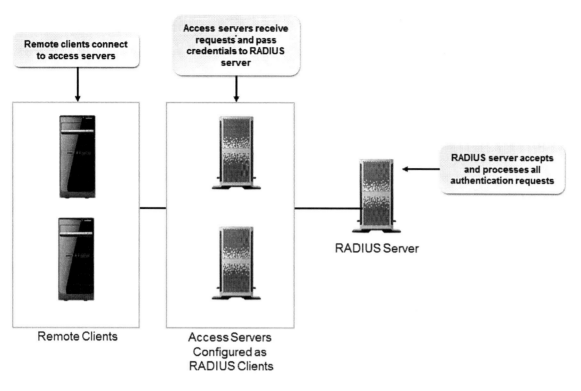

Figure 8-14: RADIUS is a protocol that includes network authentication.

802.1X

802.1X is an Institute of Electrical and Electronics Engineers (IEEE) standard used to provide a port-based authentication mechanism over a LAN or wireless LAN. For wireless communications, 802.1X uses the 802.11a and 802.11b protocols. 802.1X also encapsulates frames in the Extensible Authentication Protocol (EAP) to provide user authentication for a service like Remote Authentication Dial-In User Service (RADIUS).

In designing your network for security, you'll want to ensure that users and devices can only attach to the network in the first place if they've been authenticated. This is especially true for wireless networks, as they offer easy non-physical access across an open area. You can take advantage of the 802.1X standard to regulate access and block unwanted or unknown users.

In the 802.1X process, the user asking for permission to connect will need to rely on the authentication service to verify their credentials, and 802.1X is what communicates these requests and makes the decision to either accept or reject the request. If the authentication is successful, the access point enables the relevant traffic (such as TCP/IP) for the user. If authentication does not succeed, the user will only be allowed to receive traffic over the 802.1X protocol, effectively locking them out. This keeps unauthenticated users and devices from attaching to your network.

Mesh Networks

A *mesh network* is a type of network topology in which all nodes are directly connected to all other nodes. Every node will act as a relay to all other nodes in the network. This is common in wireless networks, as a wired mesh network will require a significant amount of cabling that will only grow as new nodes are added.

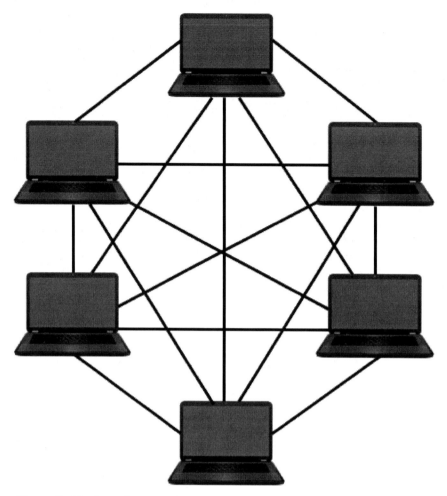

Figure 8–15: A mesh network.

Mesh networks can reliably transfer information from node to node. If one node malfunctions, the rest of the nodes in the network can fall back on a secondary routing path that bypasses the affected node. This keeps the malfunctioning node from interrupting data transfer, as the rest of the network will still be able to transmit the data to every other healthy node using a different route. Likewise, mesh networks can ensure that each node is carrying its own weight, which allows the nodes to keep the network available in high-traffic situations. The nodes in the mesh also have dedicated lines of communication instead of needing to constantly switch, so they can achieve a measure of security as information will more reliably reach its intended destination and no other.

Despite these advantages, mesh networks can be very costly and difficult to administer, especially in wired implementations. Even wireless mesh networks are difficult to construct, and often require that each node install accompanying software. Your ability to build and maintain your network in terms of cost and labor should influence whether or not you decide to go with a mesh topology.

Examples

The following are real-world examples of mesh networks:

- Devices using the ZigBee® specification.
- City-wide wireless networks.
- Laptops created for the One Laptop per Child (OLPC) initiative.
- Devices used by the U.S. military in field operations.

Software-Defined Networking

Software-defined networking (SDN) is an attempt to simplify the process of administrating a network by separating systems that control where traffic is sent from systems that actually forward this traffic to its destination. This allows a network administrator to directly program the control systems without needing to also focus on the forwarding systems. Network administrators can more easily manage the flow and logistics of their network, and adjust traffic on-the-fly based on their needs.

The SDN architecture is more flexible than a traditional network design, as it can reduce the effort and cost involved in rescaling a network. The high-level approach of SDN gives administrators a more complete and holistic picture of their network, enabling them to more quickly and efficiently respond to a breach or adapt to the enterprise's evolving business needs.

Despite its advantages, SDN may be vulnerable to certain attacks. If an attacker compromises the connection between the controller and forwarding device, they may be able to more easily initiate a Denial of Service (DoS) condition on the entire network because of how control is centralized. The attacker may also be able to access the controller itself, giving them a great deal of unauthorized privileges over the network. This means that the connection between the controller and its forwarding devices must be secured using a protocol like SSL/TLS.

Examples

Although SDN is still quite new and has yet to see widespread adoption, some cloud service providers like Amazon and Rackspace® are using SDN in their Infrastructure as a Service (IaaS) products. With the flexibility of SDN, these cloud providers can more easily scale their networking services to their customers' needs.

Cloud-Managed Networks

Some cloud service providers offer products to their customers that allow them to manage their network configurations from anywhere in the world with an Internet connection. The cloud controller that administrators use to manage their networks can provide many different features, like deploying access points, monitoring traffic, changing access control configurations, setting up firewalls and other security solutions, altering data flow, and more.

Despite its convenience, positioning the network controller in the cloud can have unwanted consequences. If the cloud provider is disrupted, then the controller will be unable to communicate with its devices, and the network itself will be inoperable. The risk of losing availability comes with every cloud service, but the significant impact of this risk might outweigh the benefits. Some cloud service providers recognize this risk and only put management software in the cloud, not the controller itself. In this case, if the cloud goes down, the network will stay operational.

Cloud-managed networks are most often deployed by organizations like universities that need a centralized way to manage their relatively large wireless networks that serve many people.

Guidelines for Analyzing Advanced Network Design

Use the following guidelines to analyze advanced network design:

- Establish secure protocols like SSH and SSL/TLS for remote access.
- Enable transport encryption on remote applications like RDP and VNC.
- Be aware that IPv6 is not backwards-compatible with IPv4.
- Investigate what technologies in your network support IPv6, even if they don't actively use it.
- Implement strong authentication methods, like multifactor and mutual, in your network's design.
- Implement 802.1X, especially in wireless networks, to force users to authenticate before they can even connect to your network.
- Construct your network around a mesh topology if you can meet the financial and administrative costs.

- Secure connections between controller and forwarding device in SDN architectures.
- Avoid using cloud network management solutions that put the controller in the cloud.

ACTIVITY 8-3
Analyzing Advanced Network Design

Scenario

The design of your network at Develetech is just as important as the specific devices you choose to implement. Being able to analyze design concepts like IPv6, mesh networking, software-defined networking, and more, will help you take a holistic approach to securing your network.

---

1. What are some of the advantages that IPv6 has over IPv4? (Select three.)
   - ☐ A much larger address space.
   - ☐ Backward compatibility.
   - ☐ Built-in encryption support.
   - ☐ Greater network management efficiency.

2. Develetech is planning on setting up a VPN that will allow employees to access the network from home. Which type of tunneling protocol should the VPN employ for optimum security?
   - ○ PPTP
   - ○ L2TP
   - ○ L2TP/IPSec
   - ○ PPP

3. How can the 802.1X protocol help Develetech uphold network authentication?

4. Develetech's network engineers have raised concerns that the company's current configuration is putting the network at risk of unacceptable downtime. They suggest converting to a mesh configuration to solve this problem. What are your thoughts and concerns?

5. What are some of the security implications of using SDN and cloud-managed networking?

TOPIC D

Configure Controls for Network Security

You've analyzed network security components and devices, and done the same for your overall network architecture. Now you'll implement the controls that can keep your network safe from intrusion and other threats. These controls fulfill a wide variety of security standards and business needs, so, as usual, how you configure them will depend on the context of your own enterprise. Regardless, you'll most likely find ways to incorporate several of the following controls into your network's day-to-day functions.

Network Baselining

Before you begin to implement specific security controls tailored toward certain aspects of your network, you need to capture the state of your network as a whole. As you know, baselining is a valuable method for setting security standards that your systems need to meet to address enterprise concerns. More than just hosts, applications, and other areas of your business will benefit from baselining efforts; your network is sure to benefit as well, considering how vital communications are to any operation. Unless you craft an ideal security image of what your network should look like, you may not know how vulnerable you are to new and unknown threats.

As part of your efforts to protect the enterprise, you should implement secure configurations and baselining of network and security components.

Configuration Lockdown

As you configure your network to establish a security baseline, you'll want to protect that configuration itself. After all, if anyone with access to a server can simply reconfigure it, then your baseline is essentially useless as you cannot rely on it. To protect the integrity of your configurations, you need to implement *configuration lockdown*. When configurations are locked down, they cannot be altered in any way that you specify, such as a user installing custom software or editing the registry on a server. Even if the intent is not malicious, configuration lockdown will prevent undesired actions from compromising the state of your network.

Configuration lockdown can even block administrators from making unwanted changes. People with privileged access are capable of making mistakes, and if you can guarantee the solidity of your configuration, you may not even need to take the risk that an administrator will change something they shouldn't have.

Change Monitoring

Change monitoring is the process by which some mechanism focuses on watching a system for any alterations to your configured baseline, and then logs, audits, and alerts the proper personnel to this change. If, for example, someone manages to attach a rogue access point to your network, the change monitor will detect this; it may then analyze the event itself and determine the proper course of action, or you may configure the monitor to simply alert you of the change so that you can respond manually. Either way, change monitoring will prevent more subtle threats to your network from going undetected. Even if the network isn't overtly threatened right away, you can remove the threat before it even has a chance to. Change monitoring keeps you from losing sight of how your network evolves over time.

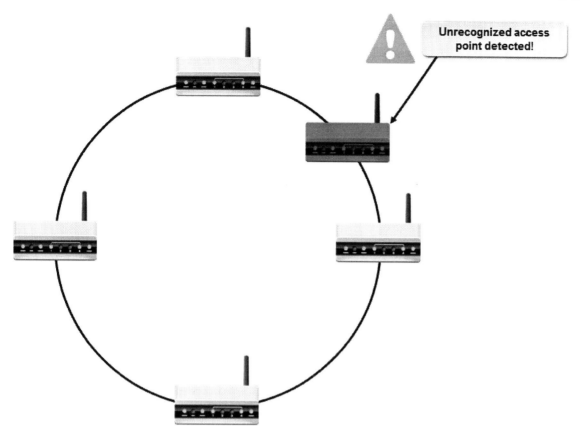

Figure 8-16: Detecting a change in a wireless network configuration.

Availability Controls

From a networking standpoint, good availability controls can mean the difference between a fully functioning enterprise and one that struggles to rebuild following an incident. Part of your baselining procedure should include methods of keeping data both accessible and resistant to failure. For example, you can install uninterruptible power supplies (UPS) that maintain power to your network devices. In the event of a power outage, the UPS will keep a reserve of power ready for the devices; this way, the network can continue to serve its users without interruption for several minutes until power is restored.

You can also take advantage of availability controls by establishing redundant network devices as part of your baseline. You may include more switches and routers in your network configuration than is necessary to run it normally, simply to have fallback devices that will prevent users from being cut off if the default devices fail or are compromised.

Load Balancer

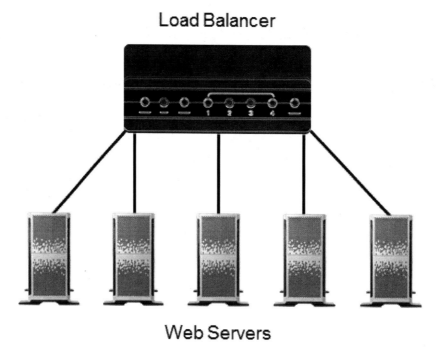

Web Servers

Figure 8-17: A load balancer ensuring the availability of a group of web servers.

ACLs

An *access control list (ACL)* specifies which objects in a system have which permissions. In networking, devices like routers and switches may grant or deny access to certain resources based on an incoming or outgoing connection's IP address or port number. In this case, the ACL acts like a firewall in that it establishes a baseline for what traffic can go where. However, ACLs of this type are less complex than firewalls and typically place less strain on the network.

In your network, you may place ACLs on devices that communicate with external networks. This will protect your network from unknown or unwanted traffic, as well as help you secure ports that are vulnerable to attackers.

DMZ

The method of tailoring ACLs to create security zones in your network can be achieved through a *demilitarized zone (DMZ)*. The DMZ is the private network segment that is located between two ACL-enabled routers or firewalls and made available for public access. A DMZ enables external clients to access data on private systems, such as web servers, without compromising the security of the internal network as a whole. The external router enables public clients to access the service; the internal router prevents them from connecting to protected internal hosts.

DMZs are most beneficial to the enterprise when they protect sensitive assets that rely heavily on outside access. Other than web servers, this can include Domain Name System (DNS) servers, remote access servers, and File Transfer Protocol (FTP) servers. A customer who accesses resources on your website will filter through the external router based on less restrictive blocks that you put in place. These are often blocks to ports that are unnecessary in the context of a web server or whatever resource you're protecting. While the customer is accessing your website, the internal router actively blocks their connection from routing to the rest of the network based on the fact that the DMZ cannot initiate new connections to your LAN. This allows the customer to gain access to the website, and nothing more.

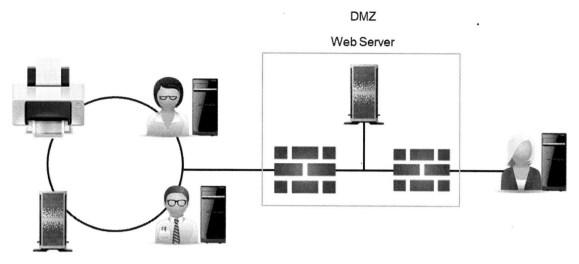

Figure 8-18: A web server in a DMZ.

Separation of Critical Assets

Beyond DMZs, you should establish security zones in your network that separate critical assets from one another. *Virtual LANs (VLANs)* logically segment nodes in a network from other portions of the network. This allows you to group hosts in your network based on a number of factors, including who typically accesses them, how often they access them, and the significance of the role that they play in business operations.

This segmentation can help delay an attack or other incident through a defense-in-depth strategy. If every critical asset in your network is on the same LAN without any segmentation, then a compromise of that single LAN will lead to the compromise of every asset. To reduce this single point of failure and the subsequent great risk to your organization, you can segment assets on their own VLANs. For example, databases that contain sensitive enterprise transactions can be grouped in a VLAN separate from public-facing web servers grouped in their own VLAN. If an attacker launches a DoS against the web servers, it will be easier for you to restrict the DoS to that VLAN and protect the availability of the databases in the other VLAN. When you separate your critical assets, you equip yourself with the means to stop an incident from spreading through your network.

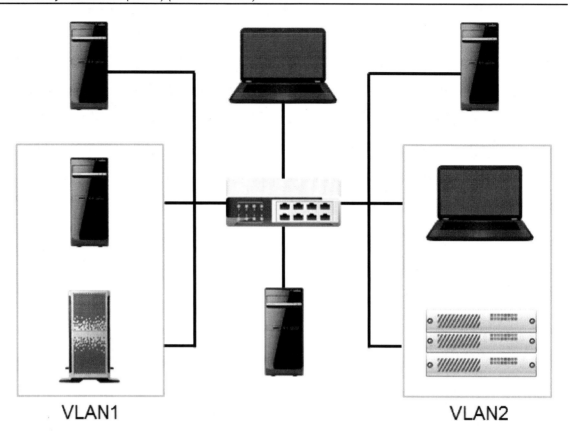

Figure 8-19: Separating assets into different VLANs.

Data Flow Enforcement

Simply guaranteeing confidentiality in transmissions will not necessarily keep your whole network safe. Attackers may still be able to take advantage of transport encryption to disrupt the flow of data. This is why you must implement more complex network security solutions for data flow. Sensors and monitors, for instance, can capture the size and frequency of all packets transmitted over the network, giving you the network flow data you need to analyze the traffic in your enterprise. Additionally, network monitors can record all transmission on a host-by-host level. A forensic investigation will benefit from this analysis, as you can accurately pinpoint the source and destination of relevant traffic over a given time period. Likewise, network flow data will help you craft a network baseline and detect anomalous traffic usage that deviates from this baseline.

Flow data is useful for seeing your network from a high level, but what if you need to enforce a security policy in individual transmissions? For this, you'd need a solution that scans the actual content of encrypted data, not just its metadata. One such solution is *SSL inspection*, a technique of monitoring the contents of HTTPS traffic to detect threats in the encrypted payload. SSL inspection technologies decrypt a transmission before it reaches its destination, inspect its data for malware or anything else that does not conform to pre-set policy, and then re-encrypts the data and passes it along to its destination. SSL inspection can be used to trigger alerts based on certain keywords, reject or allow certain packets over others, or other related forms of content filtering.

 Note: SSL inspection can be considered a white hat (ethical) version of a man-in-the-middle attack.

 Note: Microsoft® Forefront® is an example of software that offers data flow enforcement in enterprise networks.

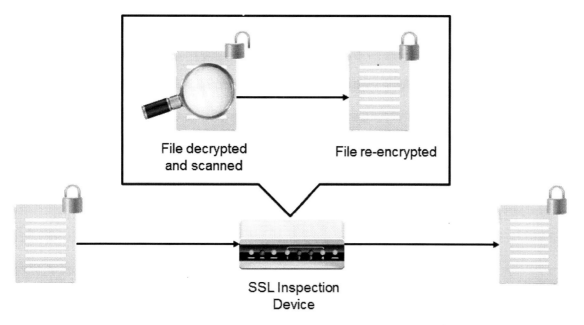

Figure 8-20: SSL inspection.

Network Device Configuration

A network is only as secure as the devices that sustain it. The advanced configuration of routers, switches, and other network devices is an important step in securing the network as a whole. The following table describes some of the parameters involved in advanced device configuration.

Advanced Configuration Parameter	Description
Transport security	TLS is a cryptographic protocol used to provide communication security to data being transported over networks. TLS is used to encrypt communication, ensure its integrity, and prevent eavesdropping. While typically used in client-server applications, TLS has also been implemented as an alternative to IPSec to provide encryption in VPNs. You can also use SSH as a comparable transport security method to gain remote management access to network devices.
Trunking security	Trunking security is a security mechanism in connected network switches (the trunk) that enables switch ports on any switch that is connected to the trunk to deny access through the port based on the media access control (MAC) address of an offending device connected to the switch. You can block a device on the network at layer 2 to effectively prevent all communication by the device through any network switch. The switches connected to the trunk will all block the device based on the MAC address or network hardware address. This prevents the device from propagating malicious traffic across the trunk to other switches, and thus other parts of the network.
Route protection	Route protection is a security method implemented in routers to ensure that there is always an available path between routers for data delivery. Route protection is an important security feature for circumstances in which a route is blocked due to DoS attacks, or there is a failure in an upstream network.

Network Access Control

Network Access Control (NAC) is a general term for the collected protocols, policies, and hardware that govern access on device network interconnections. NAC provides an additional security layer that scans systems for compliance and initiates remediation techniques for any issues that do not meet policy standards.

One such remediation path that NAC policies can take is a quarantine. In a quarantined network, a device that does not meet enterprise standards is routed to a specific VLAN that performs the necessary updates, while being segmented from the rest of the network. This keeps the device in a controlled environment (sometimes called a VLAN "jail") until it is deemed fit for communication with the larger network.

You should deploy a NAC policy according to your organization's needs based on three main elements: authentication method, endpoint vulnerability assessment, and network security enforcement. For example, your NAC may only allow a user from the production department access to the production file share if that user has the proper anti-malware software installed on their device. This ensures that the malware vulnerabilities associated with each endpoint are mitigated through access control.

> **Note:** Network Access Protection (NAP) is the Microsoft implementation of NAC.

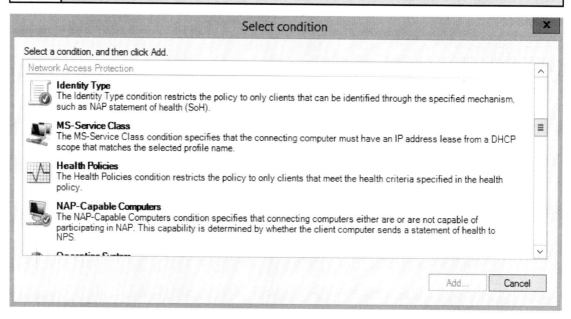

Figure 8–21: NAP conditions.

Critical Infrastructure and Industrial Control Systems

The concept of *critical infrastructure* refers to resources that, if damaged or destroyed, would cause significant negative impact to the economy, public health and safety, and security of a society. Different governments categorize critical infrastructure in different ways, but the following assets provide resources that are necessary for a society to function:

- Water supplies
- Electricity generators
- Food producers
- Health services
- Transportation services
- Telecommunication services

- Security and defense services

Many of the aforementioned services and more are supported through networked *industrial control systems (ICSs)*. ICSs employ various control systems to support communications between critical infrastructure assets.

SCADA

One type of ICS is a *supervisory control and data acquisition (SCADA)* system. A SCADA network typically supports critical infrastructure facilities such as electric, gas, and water utilities by sending remote control signals to industrial assets used by these utilities. The SCADA also receives information about the state of these assets to analyze or troubleshoot any problems they may be experiencing. For example, an engineer may use a SCADA system to receive information about the pressure and volume of water in a tank at a treatment plant, while also using the SCADA to adjust those factors to run the tank more efficiently.

Historically, SCADA networks were isolated from the rest of the enterprise network and from the Internet as a whole. As a result, many SCADA systems were not designed originally with strong security controls in mind as the perceived threat of malicious activity was thought to be low.

As data communication networks have become more widespread in recent history, connections between SCADA networks and more traditional enterprise networks have started to appear. SCADA systems and networks are now more likely to be considered part of the enterprise network as a whole. This presents a new set of challenges for the security professional who must secure the enterprise network. SCADA systems and networks employ unique protocols and systems to connect, communicate, and transfer data. You must assess these new protocols and systems and securely integrate them into your enterprise environment that is either directly or indirectly connected to industrial control systems.

Network Management and Monitoring Tools

As a CASP, it is necessary for you or your team to constantly monitor and manage your enterprise network. There are a variety of different management and monitoring tools out there, and to get the most complete view of the network, you may need to use several different tools. Microsoft® Message Analyzer is an example of monitoring software that can analyze packets sent over your network to help you isolate traffic-related problems. SolarWinds® User Device Tracker can help you manage devices attached to your network so you can more easily filter out potentially malicious hosts. The Spiceworks™ suite of network administration tools facilitates efficient and secure routing across various devices. However you need to manage and monitor your enterprise network, there are plenty of tools out there with varying costs and effectiveness.

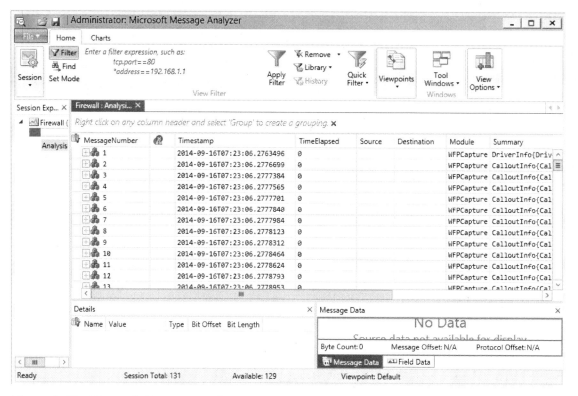

Figure 8-22: Microsoft Message Analyzer.

Guidelines for Configuring Controls for Network Security

Use the following guidelines when configuring security controls for your network:

- Implement secure configuration and baselining of network and security components.
- Lock down security configurations that shouldn't change without the proper authorization.
- Implement change monitoring to detect alterations to your network that would otherwise go unnoticed.
- Implement availability controls like UPSs and redundant network devices.
- Implement ACLs at the network device level to define where traffic is allowed and where it isn't on your network.
- Construct DMZs around sensitive public-facing resources like web servers and FTP servers.
- Separate critical assets using VLANs to prevent a single point of compromise in your network.
- Use network sensors and monitors to see a high-level view of data flows in your network.
- Use SSL inspection to verify that individual data transmissions conform to your policy.
- Configure network devices like switches and routers using transport security, trunking security, and route protection.
- Establish NAC systems to enforce security policies for hosts attaching to your network.
- Integrate SCADA protocols in any enterprise operations that network with industrial control systems.
- Choose network management and monitoring tools that fulfill your security and business needs.

ACTIVITY 8-4

Configuring Controls for Network Security

Before You Begin

Network Policy Server (NPS) and a VPN is already set up and running.

Scenario

You've already set up the VPN server, and now you want to impose more access controls to safeguard your network against attack. You'll limit the VPN to only allow authenticated domain users access so that no outside personnel without the proper credentials can tunnel into the network. In addition to controlling who can access the VPN, you'll control *when* they can access it. To ensure that the response to a security breach or other network malfunction is timely, you'll only allow VPN access during typical work hours, while completely denying access on the weekends.

---

1. Allow domain users to access your VPN server.
   a) In **Server Manager**, select **Tools→Network Policy Server**.
   b) Expand **Policies**, right-click on **Network Policies**, and select **New**.
   c) In the **New Network Policy** wizard, in the **Policy name** text box, type *VPN Policy* and select **Next**.
   d) On the **Specify Conditions** page, select **Add**.
   e) In the **Select condition** dialog box, select **User Groups**, then select **Add**.

   Groups

    Windows Groups
   The Windows Groups condition specifies that the connecting user or computer must belong to one of the selected groups.

    Machine Groups
   The Machine Groups condition specifies that the connecting computer must belong to one of the selected groups.

    User Groups
   The User Groups condition specifies that the connecting user must belong to one of the selected groups.

   f) In the **User Groups** dialog box, select **Add Groups**.

    g) In the **Select Group** dialog box, in the **Enter the object name to select** text box, type **Domain Users** and select **Check Names**.

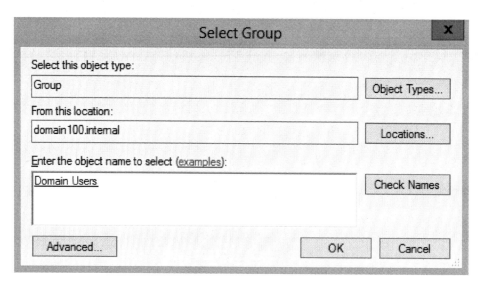

    h) Select **OK** twice.
       Every user account in the domain is given access to the VPN server.

2. Specify a time of day restriction for access to your VPN.
    a) On the **Specify Conditions** page, select **Add**.
    b) In the **Select condition** dialog box, select **Day and Time Restrictions**, then select **Add**.
    c) In the **Day and time restrictions** dialog box, select the **Permitted** radio button.
    d) In the calendar, click and drag your mouse pointer across all of the Sunday grid, then select the **Denied** radio button.
    e) Do the same for all of Saturday.
    f) Using the calendar, only permit access on Monday through Friday from 8:00 AM to 5:00 PM.

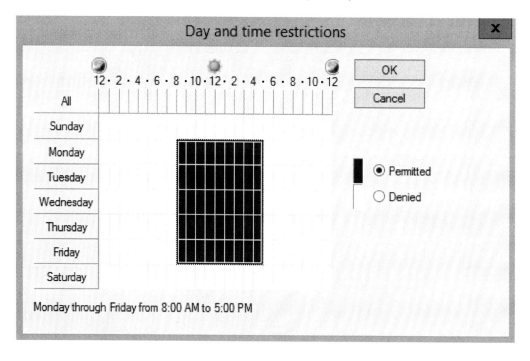

    g) When the calendar is set, select **OK**.
    h) Select **Next** twice.

3. Configure EAP-MSCHAPv2 authentication and a VPN port constraint.

   a) On the **Configure Authentication Methods** page, select **Add**.

   b) In the **Add EAP** dialog box, select **Microsoft: Secured password (EAP-MSCHAP v2)** and select **OK**.

   c) Uncheck all of the **Less secure authentication methods** check boxes and select **Next**.

   d) On the **Configure Constraints** page, in the **Constraints** list, select **NAS Port Type**.

   e) Under **Common dial-up and VPN tunnel types**, check the **Virtual (VPN)** check box and select **Next**.

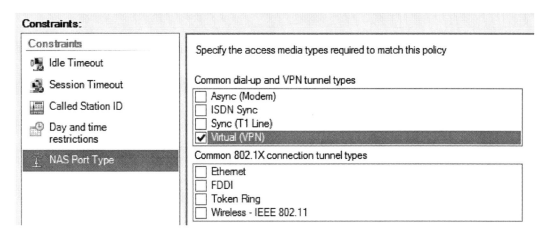

   f) On the **Configure Settings** page, select **Next**.

   g) On the **Completing New Network Policy** page, verify your policy conditions and settings, then select **Finish**.

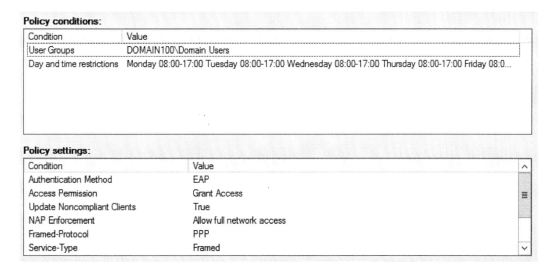

4. Set up a VPN connection to your instructor's server.

   a) From the desktop taskbar, right-click the **Start** button and select **Control Panel**.

   b) In the **Search Control Panel** text box, type *network*

c) Select the **Network and Sharing Center** link.

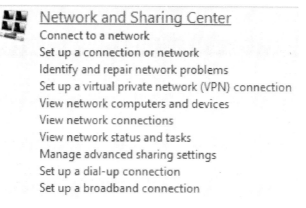

d) In the **Network and Sharing Center** window, select the **Set up a new connection or network** link.
e) In the **Set Up a Connection or Network** wizard, select **Connect to a workplace**, then select **Next**.
f) On the **How do you want to connect?** page, select **Use my Internet connection (VPN)**.
g) On the **Type the Internet address to connect to** page, enter your instructor's IP address.
h) Select **Create**.

5. Verify that you can connect to the instructor's VPN server.
a) In the **Network and Sharing Center** window, select the **Change adapter settings** link to the left.

b) In the **Network Connections** window, right-click the **VPN Connection** adapter and select **Properties**.
c) In the **VPN Connection Properties** dialog box, select the **Security** tab.

d) In the **Authentication** section, select **Use Extensible Authentication Protocol (EAP)** and, verify that **Microsoft: Secured password (EAP-MSCHAP v2)** is selected in the drop-down list.

e) Select **OK**.

f) Right-click the **VPN Connection** adapter and select **Connect / Disconnect**.

g) In the **Networks** pane that pops up, select **VPN Connection** and select **Connect**.

h) Type *Administrator* as the user name and *IPass1234* as the password.
    You are now connected to your instructor's VPN server.

6. Change your time of day policy and verify that you are unable to connect to the VPN.

   a) Return to the **Network Policy Server** window and, if necessary, select the **Network Policies** folder.

   b) Right-click your **VPN Policy** and select **Properties**.

   c) In the **VPN Policy Properties** window, select the **Conditions** tab.

   d) Select the **Day and time restrictions** entry and select the **Edit** button.

   e) Change the restriction so that only Saturday is permitted, or any time other than your current time.

   f) Select **OK** twice.

   g) Attempt to connect to your instructor's VPN again.
       You are denied access, indicating that the time of day restriction is successful.

   h) Close any open windows except for **Server Manager**.

Summary

In this lesson, you analyzed networking security devices. You also analyzed non-computer devices that are network-enabled. You then considered the design of your network's architecture in terms of security, and lastly, you configured specific controls that help protect your network from threats. This thorough analysis and implementation of network security is yet another significant component of your overall enterprise risk management (ERM) strategy.

What are your thoughts on networked non-computer technology like surveillance cameras, sensors, HVAC controllers, etc.? Would you network these devices in your own organization? Why or why not?

What sort of network security controls do you currently implement in your enterprise?

 Note: Check your CHOICE Course screen for opportunities to interact with your classmates, peers, and the larger CHOICE online community about the topics covered in this course or other topics you are interested in. From the Course screen you can also access available resources for a more continuous learning experience.

9 | Implementing Security Controls for Applications

Lesson Time: 2 hours

Lesson Objectives

In this lesson, you will:

- Identify general application vulnerabilities.

- Identify web application vulnerabilities.

- Implement application security controls.

Lesson Introduction

The last major enterprise system you'll secure is applications. Applications enable a great deal of functionality for both your employees and your users, and both will likely come to depend on these apps for their day-to-day activities. Whether they work with their own personal information or your company's sensitive data, your users must trust that these apps are secure. Likewise, you must ensure that your own systems are not exposed to an unnecessary amount of risk due to poor programming and software design. Not all enterprises develop their own applications, but even if yours uses third-party software, you'll be more informed when it comes to choosing a secure solution for your business.

TOPIC A

Identify General Application Vulnerabilities

Applications can be vulnerable to exploits in numerous ways. These vulnerabilities are general enough that they can affect many different kinds of applications, even ones programmed in different languages. It's important that you recognize the various ways in which an attacker can compromise your software, and by extension, other systems within your enterprise.

Insecure Direct Object References

In programming, a *direct object reference* is a reference to the actual name of a system object that the application uses. If an attacker is able to manipulate a parameter that directly references an object, they can craft that parameter to grant them access to other objects they are unauthorized to access. For example, a call to a SQL database may request account information by directly referencing the `acctname` parameter. An attacker may replace the `acctname` parameter with a different account name or number, which would grant them access to that account if the object reference is insecure.

Direct object references are typically insecure when they fail to verify whether or not a user is authorized to access a specific object. This is why it's important to implement access control techniques in applications that work with private information or other types of sensitive data.

Error and Exception Handling

An important aspect of an application's security is how that application handles unexpected errors and exceptions. Application developers cannot reasonably account for every possible way a user or attacker may interact with an application which could result in an error. This is why the key defense mechanism for any application is how it responds to unexpected errors, a technique called *exception handling* or *error handling*. Because errors can cause app failures, they can lead to holes in the security of an app. An attacker may attempt to execute an SQL injection or buffer overflow on your app by targeting inputs. If your app lacks proper exception handling, it is vulnerable to these threats.

When an exception is encountered, the application should be capable of either gracefully recovering with effective exception handling or presenting a meaningful message to the user. However, if a message is presented to the user, it should not include overly verbose debugging information or system-generated responses. An attacker can use such messages to assist them in troubleshooting the exploit attempt and further their attack. In other instances, an attacker may be capable of retrieving sensitive information within the messages themselves, providing a possible sensitive data exfiltration channel.

Server Error in '/' Application.

Conversion failed when converting from a character string to uniqueidentifier.

Description: An unhandled exception occurred during the execution of the current web request. Please review the stack trace for more information about the error and where it originated in the code.

Exception Details: System.Data.SqlClient.SqlException: Conversion failed when converting from a character string to uniqueidentifier.

Source Error:

An unhandled exception was generated during the execution of the current web request. Information regarding the origin and location of the exception can be identified using the exception stack trace below.

Stack Trace:

```
[SqlException (0x80131904): Conversion failed when converting from a character string to uniqueidentifier.]
   System.Data.SqlClient.SqlConnection.OnError(SqlException exception, Boolean breakConnection) +1948826
   System.Data.SqlClient.SqlInternalConnection.OnError(SqlException exception, Boolean breakConnection) +4844747
   System.Data.SqlClient.TdsParser.ThrowExceptionAndWarning(TdsParserStateObject stateObj) +194
   System.Data.SqlClient.TdsParser.Run(RunBehavior runBehavior, SqlCommand cmdHandler, SqlDataReader dataStream, Bul
   System.Data.SqlClient.SqlDataReader.HasMoreRows() +157
   System.Data.SqlClient.SqlDataReader.ReadInternal(Boolean setTimeout) +197
   System.Data.SqlClient.SqlDataReader.Read() +9
   System.Data.Common.DataAdapter.FillLoadDataRow(SchemaMapping mapping) +78
```

Figure 9-1: An overly verbose error message.

Try...Catch Statements

One of the advantages found in managed code programming languages like Java™, C++, and Python™, is their ability to provide good exception handling support. In Java, for example, whenever you suspect a statement might cause an exception, you'd wrap it in a `try` statement and end with a `catch` statement. The code within the `try` is considered *protected*. The `catch` explicitly defines which exception is expected, and if that exception occurs within the protected statement, the proceeding `catch` block is executed. A `catch` block often contains a statement that outputs an error message to the user. This both prevents an exception from compromising your app and informs the user that they have made a mistake.

Example

The following is a simple example of `try...catch` functionality in Java:

```
int a = 3;
int b = 0;
try
{
    int c = a / b;
}
catch (ArithmeticException e)
{
    System.out.println("Can't divide by zero!");
}
```

The arithmetic expression in the `try` block is expected to throw an exception, so the program executes the `catch` block if an arithmetic exception does occur. The `catch` block will print an error message to the user that they cannot divide by zero.

Privilege Escalation

Privilege escalation occurs when a user is able to obtain access to additional resources or functionality which they are normally not allowed access to. One of the most common scenarios is when a normal user is able to exploit some vulnerability on a system to gain administrator or root level privileges. There are actually two distinct types of privilege escalation: vertical and horizontal.

Vertical privilege escalation, also called *privilege elevation*, occurs when a user can perform functions that are not normally assigned to his or her role or explicitly permitted. A lower privilege application or user gains access to content or functions that are reserved for a higher-privileged-level user such as root or an administrator.

Horizontal privilege escalation occurs when a user accesses or modifies specific resources that they are not entitled to. For example, an attacker may be able to manipulate input parameters in a vulnerable application to obtain other app users' private data.

Privilege escalation attacks demonstrate why following the principle of least privilege is vital, even in app development. When you fail to be discreet in handling privileges, attackers will jump at the opportunity to exploit your app and compromise its other users. Since data corruption and app crashing can provide a vector for attackers to escalate privileges, you should also implement the buffer overflow mitigation techniques described later in this topic.

Example

Jailbreaking an iOS® device is an example of vertical privilege escalation in which a user bypasses an Apple® device's built-in digital rights management (DRM) to give themselves greater access to the operating system.

Improper Storage of Sensitive Data

Many applications have access to or must store sensitive information. These applications tend to store this data in either a database or on a file system somewhere. The types of sensitive information applications may have access to include passwords, credit card numbers, account records, customer data, and even proprietary company information. The most popular method for securing this sensitive information is through encryption. The popularity of encryption in application libraries and languages has made integrating encryption into applications simple, but developers still tend to make mistakes in their implementations. The amount of protection offered by standard encryption functions can sometimes be overestimated or misunderstood, leading to implementation weaknesses or missing security controls.

A few common mistakes to avoid when implementing encryption in apps are as follows:

- Failure to identify and encrypt critical data.
- Insecure storage of encryption keys, encryption certificates, and passwords.
- Improper handling of sensitive data in volatile memory.
- Choosing a poor source of randomness, such as a timestamp, for seeding a pseudorandom number generator for key, token, or certificate creation.
- Usage or implementation of a weak or homebrewed algorithm.
- Failure to include support for secure encryption key exchanges.

Buffer Overflows

A *buffer overflow* vulnerability occurs when an application copies user-inputted data into an allocated memory buffer that is not large enough to accommodate it. The destination buffer is overflowed, which results in adjacent memory being overwritten with the user's inputted data. Depending upon the type of buffer being overflowed, an attacker may be able to exploit a buffer overflow vulnerability to gain control of the application and execute arbitrary code. The attacker could use this arbitrary code execution to perform unauthorized actions such as adding a user to a system, opening up a socket connection to a system shell, or crashing the application. One of the most recognizable buffer overflows is a *stack overflow*. A stack-based buffer overflow involves overwriting the return address of a function on the system stack to alter the execution of an application.

| O | V | E | R | F | L | O | W | | |

Figure 9-2: The letter "W" is beyond the assigned memory's buffer.

There are various techniques that can counteract the threat of buffer overflows. Something as fundamental as choosing one programming language over another may mitigate buffer overflow issues. For example, C does not provide any built-in mechanism for checking if data will overwrite the boundaries of a buffer, whereas Java contains standard libraries that will perform bounds checking to prevent buffer overflows. However, changing languages may be infeasible in an environment that relies heavily on legacy code, so it's imperative that you know where the weaknesses in your apps are.

 Note: To learn more about mitigating buffer overflow vulnerabilities in C-based programming, access the LearnTO **Protect Against Buffer Overflows** presentation from the **LearnTO** tile on the CHOICE Course screen.

Example

The Code Red computer worm discovered in 2001 exploited a buffer overflow vulnerability in version 5.0 of Microsoft's Internet Information Services (IIS).

Canaries

Canaries are a technique used to alert an app to the possible overwriting of a buffer and a resulting overflow condition. Canaries are known values that are placed between buffers. If an overflow occurs, the canary will corrupt first, and the inability for the app to verify the canary value will alert it to an overflow. Like canaries used in coal mines, canary values are a warning system.

Integer Overflows

An *integer overflow* is a particular type of buffer overflow. In an integer overflow, an application attempts to store a number in a variable type that is not large enough to store that number. For example, you know that computers can only process and store binary data represented as a 1 or 0. An 8-bit integer means that the computer has allocated eight spots for this integer to be stored and is represented by the maximum value of 11111111, or 255 (in decimal). If you attempt to store an integer with a value greater than 255 at this location, the buffer will overflow, causing the registers to roll over.

Like standard buffer overflows, integer overflows can cause an app to over-allocate memory and eventually crash. If, for example, an application makes the assumption that a variable will always contain a positive value and the value is stored as a signed integer type, an overflow would cause this number to wrap and become negative, leading to unintended behaviors.

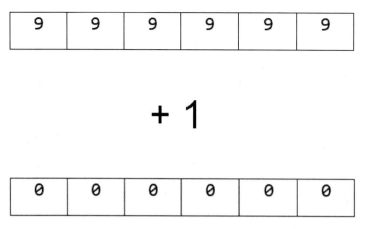

Figure 9–3: The number 1,000,000 exceeds the allocated six digits, causing an integer overflow.

The countermeasures you use for buffer overflows are also generally applicable to the integer variety. Using a programming language that does bounds checking will help you automate the prevention process, and canaries can also help detect the integer overflow condition. Designing your app around sanity checks and strictly defining protocols will make it easier for you to identify areas in your code that are susceptible to integer overflows.

Memory Leaks

A *memory leak* is the result of an application allocating memory and then not cleaning that memory up by freeing it when it is no longer required for usage by the application. Memory leaks are a common programming error in unmanaged code programming languages like C and C++, as the application developer is responsible for managing allocated memory within the application. Memory leaks are not as prevalent in managed code programming languages such as Java, as these languages have built-in memory management and garbage collection functionalities.

In most cases, a memory leak will start out small but over time begin to consume a large amount of system memory resources, resulting in the application crashing and, in the worst cases, the system crashing. If identified by an attacker, they can exploit a memory leak through a Denial of Service (DoS) attack so that users are not able to access the app or the system it runs on. Integer overflows may also cause memory leaks.

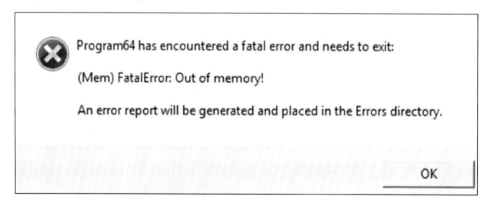

Figure 9–4: An error message indicating a memory leak.

The memory leak countermeasures you implement will depend on the programming language you are using. In general, you should make extensive use of testing before deployment. With enough stress testing, you will find it easier to pinpoint when and how memory leaks occur so that your app will be ready for publishing. Some debugging tools, like WinDbg, can safely attack an app in testing to identify memory leaks.

Memory Leak Example

The following example is written in pseudocode and is describing a program at a high level. This part of the program displays several navigation buttons to the user, and depending on what button they press, the program will take them to the intended page:

```
When a button is pressed:
        Allocate some memory, which will be used to remember the current page
reference
        Put the page reference into allocated memory
        Is the target page the same as the page the user is currently on?
          If yes, do nothing
          Otherwise:
             Call the target page
             Release the memory used to remember the page reference
```

In this example, if you're on the home page and you select the home button, memory will begin to leak. This is because the allocated memory is only released when a different page is called, and not when the app calls the one you're currently on. Although it may not be a common occurrence, if you make the mistake of pressing the home button enough times, the app will eventually run out of memory and crash.

Race Conditions

A *race condition* occurs when the resulting outcome from execution processes is directly dependent on the order and timing of certain events. If these events fail to execute in the order and timing intended by the developer, then the race condition becomes a bug and a potential vulnerability. Because race conditions often depend on unknown variables, they can be very difficult to detect and mitigate.

A *time of check to time of use (TOCTTOU)* race condition occurs when there is a change between when an app checked a resource and when the app used the resource. This change invalidates the check. An attacker that can identify a TOCTTOU vulnerability will attempt to manipulate data after it has been checked but before the application can use this data to perform some operation. For example, if an application creates a temporary file to store a value for later use, and an attacker can replace this file between the time it is created and the time it is used, then the attacker is exploiting a TOCTTOU vulnerability. The goal of this attack is to gain control of the application and/or control application results.

To protect against race condition and TOCTTOU exploitation, ensure that your app is developed so that processes are not sequentially defined unnecessarily. Additionally, you can implement a locking mechanism to make sure that your program has exclusive access to a resource when it needs it, preventing other processes from accessing or altering the same resource. For example, a file locking mechanism will restrict access to the relevant file while it is being used by an app. Locks should take place before the check so that the resource is guaranteed to be the same when it is used.

Resource Exhaustion

Resource exhaustion is a type of DoS vulnerability that occurs when an application does not properly restrict access to requested or needed resources. If an attacker is able to consume enough of an important resource, such as network bandwidth or central processing unit (CPU) time, the application will no longer be able to perform its normal operations and may crash. In many cases, this is the simplest attack to carry out against an application, and is often difficult to prevent.

If an application or other system is designed to be failopen—that is, access restrictions are lifted in the event of a failure—then resource exhaustion becomes especially problematic. In this situation, an attacker may be able to take control of a system after initiating the DoS.

To protect against resource exhaustion, limit the amount of resources that any one user can allocate with your app. Likewise, you can limit the number of simultaneous resource requests (throttling), and you can cache commonly accessed data. It's also very important that you design your app so that resource exhaustion triggers a failsafe—not a failopen—condition.

Geo-tagging

Geo-tagging is the process of actively adding geographical identification metadata to an app or its data. Geo-tagged media can include photographs, recorded video, Short Message Service (SMS) texts, and more. For example, when a user takes a photograph using their camera app, the app's geo-tagging functionality may add any of the following information to the image file's metadata:

- The latitude and longitude of the user when they took the photo.
- The specific place name of where the user took the photo.
- The altitude of the user when they took the photo.
- The user's compass direction when they took the photo.

Geo-tagging almost entirely relies on information gathered through Global Positioning System (GPS). Since GPS functionality is ubiquitous in mobile devices like smartphones and tablets, apps that engage in geo-tagging are almost always marketed toward mobile platforms and their users. Of course, this kind of information has inevitable security consequences. Users will upload a photo they took to the Internet, completely unaware that this public image contains the exact coordinates of where they live. Many apps fail to even tell their users about geo-tagging, much less tell them how to turn the feature off. The effect this can have on privacy is not just felt by average users, but by organizations as well. If your employees need to meet in secret, away from competitors and unauthorized personnel, an app on their mobile phones may transmit their coordinates and give away their location.

When it comes to geo-tagging, the best policy may be to simply not include it in your app's development. If for whatever reason you feel geo-tagging is a must in your app, you should make sure to educate its target users on the potential dangers of geo-tagging. If your app is public-facing and its users are not in your employ, then you should, at the very least, warn users when geo-tagging is turned on and allow them to turn it off.

Example of Geo-Tagging as a Security Risk

Four U.S. Army helicopters were destroyed by Iraqi insurgents in 2007 because U.S. soldiers had taken geo-tagged photographs of the helicopters and posted them on the Internet. The insurgents used the metadata in these images to pinpoint the exact location of the helicopters inside the military base.

Data Remnants

If your application works with sensitive data, it may not sufficiently handle file deletion. While users may be able to delete files created by your application, it may keep headers or pointers associated with those files in memory. These headers could reveal metadata about the file that the user deleted, such as file format, size, author, and more, while pointers may allow an attacker to recover data directly from unsanitized memory addresses.

Applications may also store temporary files in directories that the user is unaware of, but that an attacker may be able to exploit before they are removed. If an application doesn't have exclusive access to the temporary files it creates, or if it fails to remove them after the application closes, then it will be easier for an attack to glean information present in those files.

ACTIVITY 9-1
Identifying General Application Vulnerabilities

Scenario

Develetech is in the stages of developing an app for internal use, but which also has public-facing elements. This app will allow employees to instantly look up product information, as well as share insights into their work on Develetech's public facing website, and various social media platforms. Like all apps, this one will be susceptible to a number of vulnerabilities unless you incorporate security throughout the design process. Being able to identify these potential vulnerabilities will help your development team keep the app and its users safe.

---

1. Develetech purchased an app that its employees use on a daily basis, and most employees have non-administrator access to its features. However, an attacker is able to use their normal employee credentials to acquire administrator permissions. What vulnerability is present in the application?

   ○ Buffer overflow

   ○ Integer overflow

   ○ Horizontal privilege escalation

   ○ Vertical privilege escalation

2. As your development team begins designing the new app for the company, there are a few security concerns you'd like them to be conscious of so that the app doesn't present any unreasonable risk. One of those concerns is error and exception handling. What do your developers need to keep in mind when incorporating this technique?

3. Which of the following describes a vulnerability in which an attacker exploits the time between when an application checks a resource and when it actually uses the resource?

   ○ TOCTTOU

   ○ Memory leak

   ○ Resource exhaustion

   ○ Data remnants

4. As expected, Develetech's app development team is planning on designing the app with storage encryption functionality to protect any sensitive information that it handles. To make sure that this security initiative is successful, what are some of the pitfalls that the development team should avoid when incorporating storage encryption?

5. Your employees will primarily use your app on mobile devices like smartphones and tablets. Using the app, you want them to be able to upload photos they take to public galleries on Develetech's website, but you're concerned that the metadata in these photos will give away too much information to competitors, especially the whereabouts of management and sales staff. What security precautions would you suggest either the app's developers or the app's users take?

TOPIC B

Identify Web Application Vulnerabilities

Certain vulnerabilities affect web applications more often than they do offline programs. Exploits of this nature tend to target browser-based defects in programming, whether from the client side or server side. Identifying where web-based applications are vulnerable will help save your enterprise from needing to redeploy the apps your clients and employees rely on, and it could save your development team from needing to completely redesign the app.

SQL Injection

Almost every web application employs a database backend to store whatever kind of information that it needs to operate. To gain access to the information stored within the database, the application may use *Structured Query Language (SQL)* to communicate. SQL is one of the most widely used languages that applications use to speak to the database to perform four basic functions. These functions include: selecting data from the database, inserting data into the database, deleting data from the database, and updating data within the database. In an *SQL injection* attack, an attacker can modify one or more of these four basic functions by adding code to some input within the web app, causing it to execute the attacker's own set of queries using SQL.

To identify SQL injection vulnerabilities in a web app, an attacker must test every single input to include elements such as URL parameters, form fields, cookies, POST data, and HTTP headers. The simplest and most common method for identifying possible SQL injection vulnerabilities in a web app is to submit a single apostrophe and then look for errors. If an error is returned, the attacker will look to see if it provides them with SQL syntax details that can then be used to construct a more effective SQL injection query. If the single apostrophe returned an error message, the attacker may also try submitting two apostrophes, and if no error is returned, then the input being tested is most likely vulnerable to SQL injection. Attackers may also carry out injections by using the SQL wildcard character (%) to look for a large amount of data sets, or they may submit a mathematical expression equivalent to the expected value to expose some vulnerability within the app.

Example

An organization's public-facing web app uses simple HTML forms and CSS to ask for a user name and password to access the app. This web app accesses a SQL database of credentials to validate the user name and password input. If you have a user, *John*, with a password of *!Pass1234*, then the following is what a typical SQL query would look like:

```
SELECT * FROM tbl_user WHERE username = 'John' AND password '!Pass1234'
```

This SQL query would return all instances within the database where the user name *John* and the password *!Pass1234* were found.

An attacker begins his injection by inserting a single apostrophe into the user name form field, and the *!Pass1234* password he has discovered beforehand. This results in the following SQL query:

```
SELECT * FROM tbl_user WHERE username = ''' AND password '!Pass1234'
```

Notice that there are now an odd number of apostrophe characters, which would result in an error being returned by the database server. The attacker now knows that they need to complete the SQL statement with a syntactically correct query. To do this, the attacker uses a value that is always true, such as "1=1", and then uses the built-in capability to insert inline comments within the query by inputting the "--" characters. The "--" characters are used within the SQL language to denote comments, and the SQL database query engine will ignore anything following them. This is what the SQL injection exploit string "'or 1=1--" would look like when the attacker inserts it into the user name form field:

```
SELECT * FROM tbl_user WHERE username = '' or 1=1--' AND password '!Pass1234'
```

The SQL syntax is now correct, and the database will not return an error if this SQL statement were sent to it. Instead, the database will return every single one of its lines, since the "1=1" statement is always true.

Real-World Example

In 2008, three attackers perpetrated an SQL injection attack that compromised over a hundred million credit card numbers, most prominently from Heartland Payment System's databases. This was one of the largest breaches in the history of cybercrime.

SQL Injection Mitigation

To protect against SQL injections, you may implement a blacklist or whitelist of statements. A blacklist will outright deny certain statements you know to be exploitable. However, there could be plenty of exploitable statements you are unaware of, so a whitelist of acceptable values may offer more security. You can also use *prepared statements*, also called *parameterized statements*, to create a template with which certain constants are substituted when the command is run. A correctly implemented prepared statement will plan out ahead of time how SQL queries are executed, so user inputs such as quotes and comment characters will not compromise the SQL statement that is already compiled.

Session Management

Session management is a fundamental security component in the majority of web applications. Session management enables web applications to uniquely identify a user across a number of different actions and requests, while keeping the state of the data generated by the user and ensuring it is assigned to only that user. Session management is particularly important when it comes to user authentication, as it is required to ensure the integrity of the user and the data generated by the user while interacting with the web application. Because of the key role session management plays in web applications, it has become a prime target for attackers.

Session Fixation and Session Prediction

Sessions are typically attacked one of two ways: session fixation and session prediction. *Session fixation* is forcing a user to browse a website in the context of a known and valid session. An attacker attempting a session fixation attack needs to force an already known session onto the targeted user. To carry out this attack, an attacker can manipulate the methods sessions normally assigned to a user such as providing alternative inputs to web applications via GET requests. Some web applications assign these values via GET requests directly to the user's cookie for backward compatibility reasons. An alternative, and more popular, method for carrying out a session fixation attack is to use a cross-site scripting (XSS) attack to set the session cookie directly with a client-side scripting language such as JavaScript®.

Session prediction attacks focus on identifying possible weaknesses in the generation of session tokens that will allow an attacker to predict future valid session values. If an attacker can guess the session token, then the attacker can take over a session that has yet to be established. A session token must be cryptographically random to be secure, and it must not reveal any information about the session client. In addition, proper session management dictates that apps limit the lifespan of a session and require re-authentication after a certain period of time.

Example

1. An attacker comes across a website (**http://insecure.example**) that does not properly validate its sessions.
2. The attacker sends the victim the following link to fixate the session ID: **http://insecure.example/?SID=MY_SESSION_NOW**.
3. The victim, unaware of the danger, selects the link and logs in to the website.

4. The attacker navigates to **http://insecure.example/?SID=MY_SESSION_NOW** and is granted full access to the victim's account on the site.

XSS

In a *cross-site scripting (XSS) attack*, an attacker takes advantage of scripting and input validation vulnerabilities in web apps to attack legitimate users in three different ways.

In a *stored attack*, the attacker injects malicious code or links into a website's forums, databases, or other data. When a user views the stored malicious code or clicks a malicious link on the site, an attack is perpetrated against the user.

In a *reflected attack*, the attacker crafts a form or other request to be sent to a legitimate web server. This request includes the attacker's malicious script. The attacker sends a link to the victim with this request, and when the victim clicks on this link, the malicious script is sent to the legitimate server and reflected off of it. The script then executes on the victim's browser.

In a *Direct Object Model (DOM)-based attack*, malicious scripts are not sent to the server at all; rather, they take advantage of a web app's client-side implementation of JavaScript to execute their attack solely on the client.

Examples

Many prominent websites have been vulnerable to XSS attacks, including Yahoo!®, Google™, Twitter, Facebook, and YouTube™. One of the most well-known worms that spread XSS attacks was the Samy worm that affected MySpace in 2005. Within a day, the worm had infected over one million profiles.

XSS Mitigation

The best method for discovering XSS vulnerabilities within web applications is through full source code reviews. When reviewing the source code of the web application, you should look for inputs that are not validated and sanitized. It is also a good idea to inspect the validating and sanitizing routines themselves, as these routines may be insufficient. In many cases, just reviewing the client-side source code can identify possible XSS vulnerabilities, as some web application developers will rely on client-side languages such as JavaScript to validate and sanitize strings within web applications.

Another resource you may want to check are public repositories, as many web applications are built on top of other content management applications and will tend to reuse code to perform tasks within a custom application. Fuzzing is another common technique for finding XSS vulnerabilities within web applications. This method places a test string in all inputs to see what the web app generates, and checks that output for signs of scripting vulnerabilities.

XSRF

In a *cross-site request forgery (XSRF or CSRF) attack*, an attacker takes advantage of the trust established between an authorized user of a website and the website itself. This type of attack exploits a web browser's trust in a user's unexpired browser cookies. Websites that are at the most risk are those that perform functions based on input from trusted authenticated users who authenticate automatically using a saved browser cookie stored on their machines. The attacker takes advantage of the saved authentication data stored inside the cookie to gain access to a web browser's sensitive data.

This functionality is found on most web pages and is allowed when a user logs in to access account information. If, when logging in, the user selects the **Remember Me** option, then a cookie is saved and accessed the next time they visit that web page. For example:

1. A victim logs in to their banking website **bank.example** choosing the **Remember Me** option.

2. **Bank.example** stores the victim's authentication data inside a cookie.

3. An attacker sends the victim an email message with a link inside it. The link is disguised as something innocuous, but really points to: **http://www.bank.example/transfer? from_acct=victim&to_acct=attacker&amount=1000**.

4. The victim logs out of **bank.example**, checks this email message, and selects the link.

5. **Bank.example** trusts the user and fulfills the request in this link, transferring money to the attacker.

XSRF attacks are extremely difficult to detect and perform forensics on, since the attack is carried out by the user's browser just as it normally would be if the user themselves made the request. It is almost impossible to distinguish a successful XSRF attack from normal user activity.

XSRF Mitigation

Prevention of XSRF attacks is extremely difficult, as the requests tend to look very similar to those made by a user of a web application performing normal actions within the application itself. One effective solution, if implemented correctly, is to request user-specific tokens in all form submissions. When a web app generates a link or form that allows a user to submit a request, the application should include a hidden input parameter with a common name such as "XSRFToken." The value of this token must be randomly generated in a way where an attacker cannot guess it. If the token can be guessed, then either the algorithm or the implementation is flawed, leaving the web app vulnerable to XSRF attacks.

Other general session management techniques, like limiting session duration, may provide a small level of security. HTTP request header verification has proven to be an unreliable defense against XSRF, as attackers can easily create custom headers for requests.

Clickjacking

Clickjacking occurs when an attacker tricks a client into clicking on a web page link that is different from where they had intended to go to. After the victim clicks the link, they may be redirected to what appears to be a legitimate page where they input their sensitive information. A clickjacking attack can also redirect a user to a malicious web page that runs harmful scripts in a user's browser.

Clickjacking is often made possible by framing, which delivers web content in HTML inline frames, or iframes. An attacker can use an iframe to make it the target of a link that is defined by other elements. When a user selects the link, they could, for example, start inputting their credentials while an invisible iframe is the one accepting the values.

Example

1. An attacker posts a video to a victim's Facebook feed. Embedded in the video, behind the **Play** button, is an invisible frame that sends a Facebook Like request.

2. The victim clicks on the video's **Play** button, inadvertently selecting the embedded button behind it.

3. The victim then Likes something that they hadn't intended to.

Clickjacking Mitigation

A technique to protect against iframe abuse is called *frame busting*. Frame busting involves forcing a page to the top of the frame, which removes the malicious iframe loaded on a site. One way to implement this technique is by using the following JavaScript code:

```
if ( top != self ) { self.location = top.location ; }
```

Keep in mind that this is a basic frame busting technique designed to protect against simple framing abuse. More advanced iframe attacks will require more advanced JavaScript countermeasures.

Most modern browsers also support the X-Frame-Options defense, which you can implement on your site to define response headers that automatically prevent other sites from framing content. Using the **DENY** value prevents any site from framing content, using **SAMEORIGIN** denies every site except the same page from framing content, and **ALLOW-FROM** can be used to whitelist certain pages. However, to be truly effective, this header must be deployed to every page in a domain.

 Note: To learn more about how malicious users execute clickjacking attacks, access the LearnTO **Recognize Clickjacking Threats in iframes** presentation from the **LearnTO** tile on the CHOICE Course screen.

Cookies

When a client browser makes a connection with a web-based application, the application often transmits a temporary *session cookie* to the browser so that the web server can track the user and specific details about that user. The web server can also save and re-use a *persistent cookie* in subsequent sessions to preserve user-specific application preferences, to log the user in automatically with stored authentication information, and to track visitor statistics for the website or web app.

As both types of cookies are susceptible to attacks, and may even be used in conjunction with other attacks like XSRF, you must ensure secure cookie storage and transmission.

Cookie Hijacking and Cookie Poisoning

Because session cookies are generally configured and transmitted across the communications channel between the client and the server as a simple text file, an attacker can hijack a cookie to inject malicious code that they can use to take control of the session. Once the session is hijacked, the attacker can propagate a DoS attack against the web app or sign in to the web app using the victim's name, the client computer, or both. To counter *cookie hijacking*, you can encrypt cookies during transmission, delete cookies from the client's browser cache when the client terminates the session, and design your web app to deliver a new cookie with each new session between the app and the client's browser.

Cookie poisoning modifies the contents of a cookie after it has been generated and sent by the web service to the client's browser so that the newly modified cookie can be used to exploit vulnerabilities in the web app. To counter cookie poisoning, you should validate the input of your web app to account for tampered-with cookies, encrypt cookies during transmission and storage, and delete cookies from the browser cache when the client terminates the session.

Cookie Security Attributes

If your web app works with cookies, you should be familiar with the various cookie attributes that may offer your clients protection from a number of attack vectors.

Cookie Attribute	Description
Secure	Instructs the client's web browser to only send the cookie if the request is being sent over a secure channel, such as HTTPS. By setting this attribute, your web app will aid in protecting the cookie from being passed over unencrypted requests and sniffed by an attacker. Note that if a web application can be accessed over both HTTP and HTTPS, then there is still a chance that a cookie will be sent over plaintext.
HttpOnly	Aids in preventing attacks such as XSRF, as it disables access from client-side scripts such as JavaScript to the cookie. The major issue with this attribute is that not all browsers support this functionality and may outright ignore this attribute.

Cookie Attribute	Description
Domain	Is compared against the domain of the server in which the URL is being requested, as cookies can only be accessed from domains or sub-domains specified in this attribute.
Path	Specifies the URL path for which the cookie is valid. The path attribute is only checked after the domain attribute has been verified. If the domain and path attributes are valid, then the cookie will be sent in the request.
Expires	Is used to set persistent cookies that expire at the set date within this attribute. By setting this attribute, the browser will continue to maintain and use this cookie until it expires. Once the expiration date has been reached, the browser will delete this cookie. If this attribute is not set, then the cookie is considered a session cookie and will be deleted when the web session ends.

ACTIVITY 9-2
Identifying Web Application Vulnerabilities

Scenario

Aside from its general purpose app, Develetech is also developing a web app that allows customers and employees to more easily interface with the company's website. Web apps often bring a unique set of challenges to security, so you need to be able to identify vulnerabilities specific to web apps to keep yours from being exploited.

1. The web app includes support for several different social features, including forums that customers can use to discuss Develetech's products and any technical issues they may be having. You've received reports that several forum users have had their accounts hijacked. These hijacked accounts started spamming the forums, which led to them being banned. In your investigation, you noticed that all of the users that were impersonated had either commented on or simply visited a specific forum thread. In this thread, a user invoked an HTML script in their comment. This could be a(n):

   ○ XSRF attack

   ○ Stored XSS attack

   ○ Reflected XSS attack

   ○ DOM-based attack

2. Develetech's web app integrates with an SQL database that holds customer records; what are the possible consequences of a successful SQL injection attack?

3. True or False? Session prediction is an attack in which an attacker forces an already known session onto a target user's browser.

   ☐ True

   ☐ False

4. Which one of the following HTML elements is abused in a clickjacking attack?

   ○ Comments

   ○ Tables

   ○ Forms

   ○ iframes

5. You want to communicate to your web app development team that insecure cookie handling can be a security issue for your users. What can you tell them about both session and persistent cookies?

TOPIC C

Implement Application Security Controls

Now that you've identified how apps are vulnerable to a wide array of exploits, it's time to implement controls that will mitigate these vulnerabilities. Whether web-based or not, the apps you use in your organization will benefit from these techniques.

Application Security Design Considerations

Before you choose to implement specific controls in your enterprise, you must understand the three major philosophies of application security: security by design, security by default, and security by deployment. These philosophies will help inform the security-conscious choices you make in all steps of the development process, whether your app is web-based or not.

Philosophy	Description
Security by design	Application security should be incorporated from the very start of the software development process, not as an afterthought or as bolted-on technology. This philosophy includes expanding application requirement definitions and specifications to incorporate security, such as protecting sensitive data from being processed or stored by the application. This also includes incorporating security-focused testing in addition to common functionality and unit testing while the application is being developed. An app that is secure by design may, for instance, take an aggressive posture against buffer overflows by mandating that apps use certain bounds checking techniques in all instances where data is written to a buffer. For web apps, security by design might require input validation techniques be used in all HTML forms, especially those that are susceptible to SQL injection.
Security by default	The default installation and initial configuration of an application should be secure. This means that a default installation should not require additional hardening and configurations by the end user to secure the application. This philosophy encourages disabling features that are not commonly used within the application to reduce the applications attack surface. For example, a web app that is secure by default might disable geo-tagging unless the user manually enables it. In this case, the user's expectation of privacy is assumed, and if the user truly wants their photos geo-tagged, they will take the necessary steps to enable it themselves.
Security by deployment	How and where an application is deployed in an environment is extremely important to application security. An application should be deployed in the most secure fashion, which in most cases reflects a defense-in-depth strategy. This includes deploying and configuring security controls outside of the application, such as firewalls and intrusion prevention systems (IPS). These controls serve as additional layers of security to protect the application and reduce the overall attack surface of the application. Deployment may also refer to how apps are made available to the general public. If your app is primarily web-based, will you require that customers authenticate before they can access it? In the event of patches and other bug fixes, how will you push these changes to a live system without disrupting the availability of your app?

Security Through Obscurity

Another philosophy you may have heard of is *security through obscurity*. Security through obscurity focuses primarily on attempting to hide the existence of vulnerabilities from others. Instead of decreasing an attack surface, an app that employs this philosophy counts on attackers being unable to even discover its flaws. This is a very weak and insufficient stance to take, as the discovering of a vulnerability is almost never a matter of *if*, but almost always a matter of *when*. Skilled hackers have proven time and time again that flaws in applications and systems will not go unnoticed for long. For these reasons, you should never rely solely on security through obscurity to protect your app.

Input Validation

Input validation involves ensuring that the data entered into a field or variable in an application is within acceptable bounds for the object that will receive the data. Input data should be within the size constraints of the memory location that will store it, be formatted in the expected way, and make sense in the context for which it will be used. If a given piece of input data cannot meet these standards, it should be considered invalid and should not be processed.

For example, say an input field on a web page asks for a date. An unvalidated input could allow an attacker to submit a chunk of text that is actually malicious code intended to exploit a vulnerability in the server or operating system software. Proper input validation would check to see if the submitted value is in the expected format (for example, mm/dd/yyyy for a date input). If the format is not correct, validation fails and the value is not recorded.

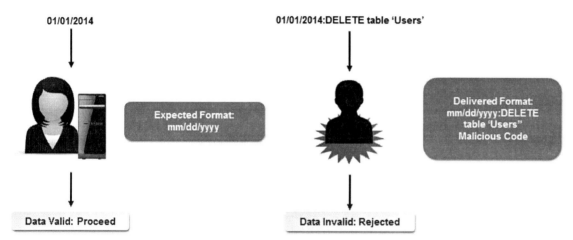

Figure 9–5: Input validation thwarting an attacker.

Input validation is critical to application security as most application vulnerabilities involve some form of malformed or tainted input. XSS and SQL injections are probably the two most popular web application attacks that exploit input validation vulnerabilities. Input validation vulnerabilities can make it possible for an attacker to carry out injection attacks to create, read, update, or delete any arbitrary data available to the application. In the worst-case scenario, these flaws could enable an attacker to completely compromise the application and even the underlying system.

Fuzzing

Fuzzing, also known as *fault injection*, is a testing method used to identify vulnerabilities and weaknesses in applications by sending the application a range of random or unusual input data and noting any failures and crashes that result. Fuzzing can find memory leaks or other bugs in an app, and allows developers to address any faults that are found in the code. This type of testing is usually performed in the final phases of the application development process.

A fuzzing tool targeting a desktop or mobile app may test inputs like buttons and text fields on an app's user interface (UI), whereas a fuzzer targeting web apps may attempt to inject fault in forms and RPC requests. Fuzzing is most useful for finding simple bugs, and rarely is able to find complex glitches in an app's execution.

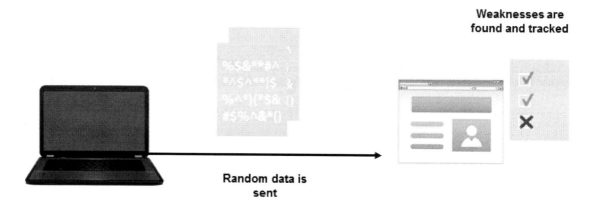

Figure 9-6: Testing input vulnerabilities in a web app.

You should consider this type of testing on any application that transmits sensitive data and performs online transactions. Although it should not replace human code reviews and other forms of debugging, fuzzing is an excellent addition to a developer's app hardening tactics.

Application Sandboxing

Application sandboxing is a security technique used to segregate an application from other applications and data on a system. An application launched in a sandbox cannot edit operating systems files like the Windows registry or modify files on the user's hard disk. This severely limits or restricts the ability for a malicious application to carry out actions on the system itself. The application sandbox provides a secure environment for an application to execute in its own space and creates a virtual barrier around that application to protect the system, data residing on the system, and other applications.

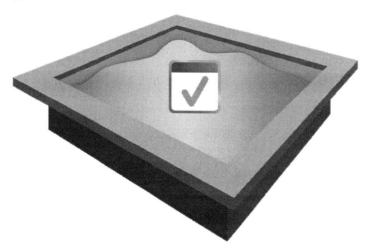

Figure 9-7: Testing an application in a sandbox.

For developers, sandboxing can be very useful during the testing phase. A tester will be free to experiment with an app and not expose the company's wider systems to undue risk if the code is isolated. Also, if the app runs in a sandbox for final deployment, you can provide a secure environment for your app's users by preventing malicious software from interfering with your app.

Examples

The application Sandboxie is an example of a Windows®-based sandbox that allows end users to execute programs and applications in a sandboxed environment. Any Windows application can be executed inside Sandboxie, eliminating the need for the application itself to support application sandboxing. Applications such as Internet browsers, instant messenger applications, chat applications, email readers, games, and even peer-to-peer networking applications can be executed in Sandboxie to provide an additional layer of protection against attacks aimed at exploiting these common applications.

For example, if Internet Explorer® is run inside a Sandboxie sandbox, successful exploits performed by malicious websites will not compromise the system itself and will restrict the compromise to that specific instance of Internet Explorer running. Once the end user finishes using the Internet Explorer application and closes the sandbox, all the information and data associated with that instance of the application will be removed from the system. Additionally, if the malicious website attempted to exploit a vulnerability within Internet Explorer that performed a malicious action like establishing an open and listening socket for the Windows shell, Sandboxie would stop this action from being carried out and inform the end user of this activity.

Some mobile operating systems, such as Android™ and Windows® Phone, automatically place installed apps in a virtual machine sandbox when they run. Apps on the device cannot communicate with each other unless authorized—either by the user, or by the app, depending on the OS and the app's implementation.

Application Security Frameworks

An *application security framework* is a framework that can be embedded into standard application and system development processes to make it easier for a security manager to oversee development from a security standpoint. The goal of an application security framework is to build in security from the very beginning of the application's life cycle (security by design). Most software development life cycles (SDLC) have application security frameworks already built in. For SDLCs that do not have an application security framework built in, there is most likely an application security framework that can be tailored to support the SDLC.

App security frameworks typically incorporate industry-accepted approaches to development, standard libraries that facilitate secure coding, and web services security for interaction with web apps.

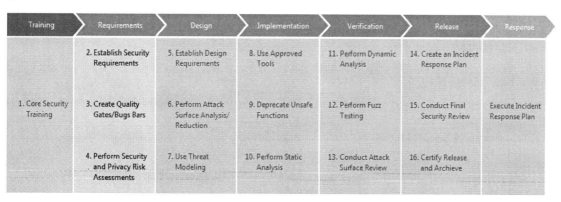

Figure 9-8: Microsoft's SDL framework.

SDL

Microsoft's Security Development Lifecycle (SDL) is an example of an industry-accepted application security framework that can be tailored or modified to support a wide range of SDLCs, including the traditional waterfall method and the currently popular agile method. The original Microsoft SDL appears to have been designed with the waterfall model in mind, as it clearly follows a step-by-step process to traverse the different elements within the SDL until the final stage is reached. However, this SDL has also been modified with iterative steps to support a more fluid and dynamic development process as seen with the agile method. When applying the SDL to the agile method, only specific pieces or portions of the SDL are executed, based off the phase of the project.

Standard Libraries

Standard libraries are sets of functions, methods, algorithms, subroutines, templates, variables, and data structures that are made available to a programmer in every implementation of a programming language. These libraries can be described in the programming language specification or can be determined by a more informal acceptance of the programming languages community. The problem is that some standard library functions can be used inappropriately, or in ways that may introduce security issues with the program being developed. For example, some of the C programming language standard library functions can be exploited and should be considered insecure by default, as they do not check for proper buffer size. There are usually secure alternatives to these functions, however.

Insecure and Secure C Functions

The following C library functions are insecure: `strcat()`, `strcpy()`, `sprintf()`, `vsprintf()`, `bcopy()`, `scanf()`, and `gets()`.

Secure alternatives for these standard library functions include: `strlcat()`, `strcat_s()`, `strlcpy()`, `strcpy_s()`, `sprintf_s()`, `vsprintf_s()`, `memcopy()`, `scanf_s()`, and `gets_s()`.

WS-Security

Web services security (WS-security) is an extension to the Simple Object Access Protocol (SOAP) that enforces confidentiality and integrity in web communications, as well as defining how security tokens are used to identify a user. WS-security primarily uses XML syntax for digital signatures and specifies how Extensible Markup Language (XML) content is encrypted. Unlike Secure Sockets Layer/Transport Layer Security (SSL/TLS), WS-security is meant to provide end-to-end security in that integrity and confidentiality are guaranteed even after a communication is sent from its source. In apps that use web services to communicate, WS-security can be a useful framework for protecting messages in transit across the Internet. However, WS-security adds a significant amount of overhead and may not be justifiable depending on your app and implementation.

Secure Coding Standards

Secure coding standards define the rules and guidelines for developing secure software systems. Writing secure code is an essential part of the secure software development process. When you enforce secure design principles and application frameworks in code, you will help save your enterprise from being drained of its time and resources by security incidents that could have been avoided.

Specific standards will differ based on the programming language used and the functionality that the app provides. Here are some general coding standards to implement in development:

- Incorporate input validation and sanitation filters for all fields that accept data at the client. This is a key area of vulnerability for new and existing applications.
- Maintain an organized and consistent version control database so that rollbacks to prior versions are possible if new code has major errors.
- Incorporate an ongoing peer review of code logic and coding practices to identify security weaknesses and to reinforce secure coding practices. Include user testing as part of code review tactics.
- Leverage user testing to examine error message output and exception messaging. Revise the code and messages for exception and error handling.
- Encrypt vulnerable data that will transmit across communications pathways.
- Stay up-to-date on the latest exploits and vulnerabilities for programming languages used in development.
- Consider all application inputs that use SQL query formats as untrusted.

- Incorporate the latest compilers for program code to mitigate vulnerabilities between language versions.

 Note: One resource you can use to stay up-to-date on programming language vulnerabilities is WhiteHat Security's annual website statistics report (**www.whitehatsec.com/resource/ stats.html**).

DAM

Databases contain valuable information about an enterprise and tend to be the main target for internal threats and data leakage. The database activity monitor (DAM) tracks all user, administrator, and third-party activities and enforces policies to limit access to databases either partially or completely.

Aside from monitoring direct user access to a database, DAM systems can also implement application monitoring services. If your enterprise employees use an intermediary app to access a database, this service will be able to provide accountability for the users, as well a fraud detection mechanism to alert security personnel to abuse of privileged access. Whereas a normal implementation of an app that accesses a database may aggregate client connection information (including identity), an app that is designed with application monitoring will be able to identify all end users to validate their authorization. This is a particularly important security control for an enterprise that needs to conform to certain data governance requirements like Payment Card Industry Data Security Standard (PCI DSS), the Health Insurance Portability and Accountability Act (HIPAA), the Sarbanes-Oxley Act (SOX), and the Federal Information Security Management Act (FISMA).

DAMs may also be useful in detecting SQL injections and similar types of application attacks. For instance, the DAM can create a baseline from which to identify any abnormal or deviant SQL-related input that uses an app as a database attack vector.

WAF

Implementing web application firewalls (WAFs) in your network may help secure your applications even after they have been developed. The application layer input/output security offered by WAFs can be extended into two advanced categories: distributed and cloud-based.

Distributed WAFs propagate throughout a network infrastructure and do not need to rely on a single device to function. This increases the WAF's scalability and is helpful for large virtual infrastructures that see application traffic in great volumes.

Cloud-based WAFs take advantage of a centralized and collaborative infrastructure to improve detection of unwanted traffic targeting web apps. They aid an organization in offloading resources that would otherwise need to be dedicated to the WAF to the cloud. This is ideal for organizations that cannot support the additional hardware and software required to implement WAFs in their network. The organization's application layer traffic is sent over the Internet to this cloud-based WAF, where it is either allowed or blocked based on how the WAF is configured.

Client–Side Processing and Server–Side Processing

Client-side processing is the set of activities performed within the browser or on the client computer as part of the interaction with the web application and data set for the application that are resident on the server. *Server-side processing* is the set of activities performed at the server computer and which are delivered to and interact with the client computer. Generally speaking, server-side processing sends web page data from the server to the client browser. Client-side processing interprets and renders the web page so that it is displayed within the browser at the client computer.

In some situations, developing your app for processing data on the client-side is more ideal than processing it server-side, and vice versa. Client-side processing tends to relieve the strain on servers and offloads overhead to the client, whereas server-side processing is usually more secure as it is under your control. For example, the following languages and techniques are attractive to developers because they require the client to process data:

- JavaScript®, a popular client-side scripting language that can interact directly with a web page's HTML (including HTML5), including altering it in several ways.
- JavaScript Object Notation (JSON), a subset of JavaScript that is used in the representation state transfer (REST) style of web application architecture.
- Asynchronous JavaScript and XML (AJAX), a technique which can combine either XML or JSON (AJAJ) with JavaScript to send and receive data to a server without changing the web page on the client. XML is often formatted with the SOAP specification.
- Browser extensions like ActiveX®, Java Applets, and Adobe® Flash®.

However, because the client has control over this processing, the data cannot be fully trusted and is highly susceptible to XSS and XSRF attacks, among others. Proper state (session) management is essential to secure the communications between client and server in your web app, especially when it comes to authentication and authorization. It's also important to understand that choosing client-side over server-side processing may mean that you end up sacrificing security for performance.

Guidelines for Implementing Application Security Controls

 Note: All Guidelines for this lesson are available as checklists from the **Checklist** tile on the CHOICE Course screen.

Use the following guidelines when implementing controls for application security:

- Ensure that your applications are secure by design, default, and deployment.
- Use input validation techniques to test applications for vulnerabilities in how they process user input.
- Use fuzzing techniques to detect faults in an application's behavior.
- Test applications in sandboxes to isolate them from hosts in production.
- Construct your app with a security framework like SDL to streamline the security implementation process.
- Use standard programming libraries that offer secure functions and other coding elements.
- Implement a DAM to monitor applications that interface with databases in your network.
- Implement a WAF to control application-layer traffic in your network.
- Balance the performance boost of client-side processing with the security of server-side processing where feasible.

ACTIVITY 9-3
Implementing Application Security Controls

Data File

C:\093023Data\Implementing Security Controls for Applications\Input Validation Demo.url

Before You Begin

You will be using a PHP and HTML test form provided by **w3schools.com**. This is a basic web form and accompanying source code that demonstrates input validation techniques.

Scenario

The app development team at Develetech has begun work on a new customer-facing web app. The app is intended to be a way for customers to easily offer feedback or ask support questions concerning the products that they buy from the company. The information the customers input into the app will likely be sensitive in nature, and may contain personally identifiable information (PII). To guarantee your customers' experience with your website is protected, you'll want to make sure that the development team is designing the app with security in mind.

Before you bring your requirements to the app development team, you'll want to start testing some of the security controls that are available for applications; in particular, input validation. Input validation is a crucial technique for web apps because of how easily and often attackers are able to carry out code injections and scripting exploits through poorly validated forms. You'll examine PHP and HTML code that creates a basic web form for users to input information. You'll test its input validation techniques and identify how the form controls for XSS attacks and other unnecessary inputs could jeopardize the app or its users' information. With this knowledge, you'll have a better sense of what needs to go into a web app to secure how it handles user input.

---

1. Open the PHP test code and observe the properties of the form's different fields.

    a) Navigate to **C:\093023Data\Implementing Security Controls for Applications** and double-click **Input Validation Demo.url** to open the web page in Internet Explorer.

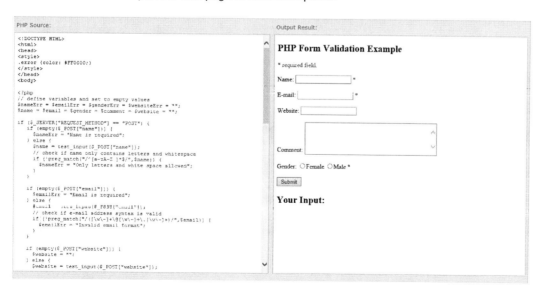

b) Verify that the column on the left under **PHP Source** holds the HTML and PHP source code for the **Output Result** on the right.

```
PHP Source:

<!DOCTYPE HTML>
<html>
<head>
<style>
.error {color: #FF0000;}
</style>
</head>
<body>

<?php
// define variables and set to empty values
$nameErr = $emailErr = $genderErr = $websiteErr = "";
$name = $email = $gender = $comment = $website = "";

if ($_SERVER["REQUEST_METHOD"] == "POST") {
    if (empty($_POST["name"])) {
        $nameErr = "Name is required";
    } else {
        $name = test_input($_POST["name"]);
        // check if name only contains letters and whitespace
        if (!preg_match("/^[a-zA-Z ]*$/",$name)) {
          $nameErr = "Only letters and white space allowed";
        }
    }
```

The HTML markup at the bottom creates the form, which asks the user for basic input types like their name, email, website, etc. The PHP code above it (in red) uses five `if ... else` statements (one for each field) to impose certain constraints on what a user can input into each field. These constraints are:

- The **Name**, **E-mail**, and **Gender** fields are all required. If input for any of these fields are empty, they will return a `<field>Err` variable with the appropriate warning (e.g., `$nameErr = "Name is required";`).
- The **Website** and **Comment** fields are optional. If input for either of these fields is empty, they will return the value without error (e.g., `$website = "";`).
- The **Name** field must only contain letters and whitespace, otherwise it will return an error.
- The **E-mail** field must be in the format of **X@X.X**, where **X** is any alphanumeric character or a hyphen, otherwise it will return an error.
- The **Website** field, if used, must be in the format of **www.X.Y**, where **X** is any alphanumeric character or certain symbols, and **Y** is any character. Otherwise, it will return an error.
- The **Comment** field, if used, can contain any characters. No errors will be returned.

The PHP code at the very bottom of the source code will echo the user's inputs back to them on the same page.

2. Test the form's validation with different inputs.
   a) In the form, under **Output Result**, in the **Name** text box, type text that includes non-alphabetic characters and select the **Submit** button.
   b) Verify that the form detects your unacceptable input and tells you what is required for that field.

Name: |John' | * Only letters and white space allowed

   c) Verify that the form also marks the **E-mail** and **Gender** fields as required, as you did not fill them out before submitting.
   d) Replace the text inside the **Name** field with valid characters.
   e) In the **E-mail** field, type an invalid email address (without an **@**, for example). Select a **Gender** radio button and select **Submit**.
      You are presented with an **Invalid email format** message.

f) Replace the email with one that is formatted correctly and select **Submit**. Verify that there are no errors on the page.

3. Verify that the form escapes special characters to prevent XSS exploits.

a) In the source code, scroll to the following HTML markup.

```
<h2>PHP Form Validation Example</h2>
<p><span class="error">* required field.</span></p>
<form method="post" action="<?php echo htmlspecialchars($_SERVER
["PHP_SELF"]);?>">
    Name: <input type="text" name="name" value="<?php echo $name;?>">
    <span class="error">* <?php echo $nameErr;?></span>
    <br><br>
    E-mail: <input type="text" name="email" value="<?php echo $email;?>">
    <span class="error">* <?php echo $emailErr;?></span>
    <br><br>
    Website: <input type="text" name="website" value="<?php echo $website;?>">
    <span class="error"><?php echo $websiteErr;?></span>
    <br><br>
    Comment: <textarea name="comment" rows="5" cols="40"><?php echo $comment;?
></textarea>
    <br><br>
    Gender:
    <input type="radio" name="gender" <?php if (isset($gender) &&
$gender=="female") echo "checked";?> value="female">Female
    <input type="radio" name="gender" <?php if (isset($gender) &&
$gender=="male") echo "checked";?> value="male">Male
    <span class="error">* <?php echo $genderErr;?></span>
    <br><br>
    <input type="submit" name="submit" value="Submit">
</form>
```

b) Verify that the `form method` tag has a PHP echo statement containing `$_SERVER["PHP_SELF"]`

```
<form method="post" action="<?php echo htmlspecialchars($_SERVER
["PHP_SELF"]);?>">
```

The PHP server sends the form data you submitted back to the page itself, so that you receive any errors on the same page.

c) Verify that the `$_SERVER["PHP_SELF"]` code is wrapped in an `htmlspecialchars()` function.

This functions converts special characters into HTML entities. For example, **<** would become **&lt**. Without this, an attacker could execute an XSS attack by passing an HTML tag into the page, where it will be executed in the user's browser. This is especially harmful when an attacker exploits JavaScript.

For example, a user could send the following URL link to a victim: **http://www.example.com/ info_form.php/%22%3E%3Cscript%3Eprompt('Enter payment info')%3C/script%3E**

The page would translate the last part into:

```
<script>prompt('Enter payment info')</script>
```

which would pop up a prompt on the user's computer asking them to input their payment info.

However, the `htmlspecialchars()` function would convert those less than and greater than characters into HTML entities as such:

```
&lt;script&gt;prompt('Enter payment info')&lt;/script&gt;
```

This prevents the script from executing, and the XSS attack is thwarted.

4. Test the form's additional input validation techniques.

a) Verify the PHP `test_input` function directly above the HTML markup.

```
function test_input($data) {
    $data = trim($data);
    $data = stripslashes($data);
    $data = htmlspecialchars($data);
    return $data;
}
```

Aside from escaping the special characters as before, this function will strip the input data of any slashes and trim out any excess characters like new lines.

b) In the form itself, in the **Comment** field, type *Validating*

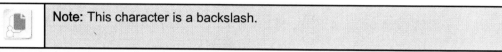

Note: This character is a backslash.

c) Press enter to begin a new line, then type *Forms*

```
Validating\
Forms
```

Comment:

d) Select **Submit**.

e) In the **Your Input** section, verify that your comment was stripped of its backslash and the new line you added.

Your Input:

John
email@address.com

Validating Forms
male

5. Close Internet Explorer and File Explorer.

Summary

In this lesson, you identified the ways in which your enterprise's apps may be vulnerable to malicious or accidental threats. This includes general vulnerabilities that affect most apps, no matter their function, and vulnerabilities that tend to be relevant only to web-based apps. After that, you implemented security controls to fix both general and web-based vulnerabilities. Whether you outsource the apps your enterprise uses, or develop them in house, you will be prepared to address the risks they may pose to your organization.

What are your experiences with vulnerabilities in the applications that you or your enterprise uses?

Does your enterprise develop its own applications or have any control over the development of applications it uses? What sort of security controls have you put in place, or what controls would you like to see put in place?

 Note: Check your CHOICE Course screen for opportunities to interact with your classmates, peers, and the larger CHOICE online community about the topics covered in this course or other topics you are interested in. From the Course screen you can also access available resources for a more continuous learning experience.

10 | Integrating Hosts, Storage, Networks, and Applications in a Secure Enterprise Architecture

Lesson Time: 2 hours, 45 minutes

Lesson Objectives

In this lesson, you will:

- Implement security standards in the enterprise.

- Select technical deployment models.

- Secure the design of the enterprise infrastructure.

- Secure enterprise application integration enablers.

Lesson Introduction

Now that you've implemented controls for each of the four main enterprise systems, it's time to tie them all together into one complete architecture. Integrating each system into this architecture will require your security focus, because even though you secured each individually, placing them all into a larger defense-in-depth framework will come with its own set of challenges. These challenges are highly dependent on the ways in which you configured your systems and how these systems should interact with one another. So, you must integrate your hosts, storage, networks, and applications in a way that will support both your business needs and your security policies.

TOPIC A

Implement Security Standards in the Enterprise

The systems you integrate with your enterprise environment should be able to reach baseline standards first. This will prevent any one of these systems from becoming a weak link in your organization. In this topic, you'll implement industry standards and related security requirements in your enterprise.

Standards

No matter what component of information technology your enterprise implements, each has a set of known and accepted standards that you should follow. Adherence to standards set by recognized organizations like the International Organization for Standardization (ISO), the Internet Engineering Task Force (IETF), the International Electrotechnical Commission (IEC), and the American National Standards Institute (ANSI) is vital to not only establish and maintain interoperable business relationships with other enterprises, but to help your organization more easily integrate ever-changing security technologies and solutions.

However, not all standards work in harmony with each other. You'll likely come across competing standards that may offer opposing solutions to the same essential problem. This is often the case with new and emerging technology. After all, standardization is a collaborative process that takes time—sometimes several years after the technology is released. For example, Advanced Encryption Standard (AES) is a standard adopted by the United States government for symmetric cryptography, whereas Triple Data Encryption Standard (3DES) is a symmetric cryptography standard that offers similar guarantees of security for many organizations. Ultimately, when it comes to competing standards, you must take advantage of your skills in research and analysis to determine the best practice for your enterprise. The choice of which standards to adhere to is not just a matter of selecting the strongest or cheapest option; you must also consider factors like support, scalability, and interoperability.

Categories of Standards

Standards come in many different forms, and you should be aware of how the industry perceives them. You should consult the expert consensus on standards as you consider which ones to implement. The efficacy and usefulness of any standard is very much dependent on how the relevant industry responds to it. If enough organizations choose not to adopt a standard, then it will lose support and become less of a viable option. A *de facto standard* is accepted by the industry as a result of its early dominance in a marketplace that had previously seen a lack of standards. These usually haven't undergone any formal standardization process. Once the appropriate standardizing bodies confirm the standard, it is considered official, or a *de jure standard*.

Another category of standards you should be mindful of is the *open standard*. There is much debate as to what should qualify as an open standard, but generally, it refers to standards that are publicly available and impose limited amounts of licensing restrictions. The level of openness of each standard varies, and some communities only consider a standard to be truly open if it can be acquired, used, and extended without restriction. However they are defined, open standards that are meant to facilitate collaboration and peer review.

Interoperability Issues

Interoperability is important, but there are some issues involved that should not escape your attention. If you plan on implementing new solutions to your current systems, then this could cause issues with legacy systems. Some legacy software and hardware is very rigid in its interoperability; it may only work properly in the exact right environment that it has been working in for a long time. Even if the legacy systems do work with current systems, their outdated protocols and standards could compromise the current systems' security. For example, a legacy operating system may be unable to take advantage of Secure Shell (SSH) encryption for remote execution, instead relying on the insecure Telnet protocol. This makes it essentially useless from a security standpoint, especially if your changing business needs necessitate that communications are encrypted.

It's also worth considering where these solutions are coming from. In-house developed solutions typically have an easier time interoperating with each other, as the enterprise has likely programmed them specifically for this purpose. Commercial, vendor-supplied solutions may have varying security standards that make it difficult for you to maintain them in your organization. Customized commercial products might alleviate some of these problems by providing you with the opportunity to adjust them for your own enterprise needs.

Lastly, the applications you work with, whether in-house or vendor-supplied, might not successfully interoperate if they all do not meet certain requirements. A web interface app that allows users to alter records in a database might use specific units that the database app doesn't recognize. This could lead to the apps failing to function properly or crashing altogether, resulting in lost availability.

Data Flow Security

As enterprises evolve, it is common for business requirements and standards to evolve as well. As a CASP, you should understand the implications these changing needs can have on your systems and the potential impact to the security of the enterprise as a whole. As new hosts, applications, and other elements are introduced into the environment, priorities for performance and availability may change. The need for these changes is particularly evident in the flow of data across your network architecture. It is therefore up to you to secure data flows to meet changing business needs.

There are two common methods to control data flow security:

- *Traffic shaping*, also known as *bandwidth shaping*, is the practice of prioritizing the flow of packets over the network to meet quality of service (QoS) requirements, speed up or delay particular packets, increase available bandwidth, or otherwise ensure network or protocol performance. Traffic shaping is most often implemented by slowing down packets of one or more types to allow packets of another type to flow through the network unencumbered.
- *Virtual circuits* are part of a routing technique that connects endpoints logically through a provider's network. These logical paths are assigned to identities rather than physical locations, and can be either permanent or switched. Most virtual circuits provide some level of reliability built into the connection via error correction and automatic re-transmittals.

Guidelines for Implementing Standards in the Enterprise

> **Note:** All Guidelines for this lesson are available as checklists from the **Checklist** tile on the CHOICE Course screen.

Use the following guidelines to implement standards in your enterprise:

- Consult standards organizations like ISO, IETF, IEC, and ANSI.
- Research competing standards and analyze their differences.
- Decide which standard is more of a fit for your enterprise based on factors such as security strength, cost, support, scalability, and interoperability.
- Research industry perspectives on new and emerging standards.
- Keep in mind the difference between de facto and de jure standards.
- Research and contribute to open standards.
- Thoroughly document your standards policies and procedures, and secure that documentation.
- Test legacy systems for their interoperability with current and new systems.
- Determine whether commercial solutions can successfully meet your security standards.

- Ensure that apps in your enterprise are tested for their interoperability with one another.
- Implement traffic shaping to reduce network overhead.
- Implement virtual circuits to reinforce your network's reliability.

ACTIVITY 10-1
Implementing Security Standards in the Enterprise

Scenario

Enterprises should rely on the collaborative standards-making process to ensure a strong foundation of security, and Develetech is no different in that regard. You'll consider the different standards that are out there, and how they can help shape your own security strategies to help mitigate risk in your enterprise.

1. What are some of the important factors to consider when choosing security standards to implement in the enterprise?

2. Since taking on the role of CISO of Develetech, you've updated the company's security standards to meet enterprise risk management (ERM) requirements. With these standards in mind, what sort of interoperability issues might there be in legacy systems?

3. How can data flow security methods help a company like Develetech uphold enterprise standards for network availability?

TOPIC B

Select Technical Deployment Models

Integration is best achieved through deployment models, which typically define the purpose, scope, and function of various systems and components. Deployment models can ensure that your systems are incorporated into your enterprise in a way that facilitates security. They may also present unique vulnerabilities. In this topic, you'll review the security considerations of key deployment models and select the ones that offer the best security for your organization.

Deployment Models

A *deployment model* is a framework for defining how a particular system will be put to use in an organization. Part of that definition may include ideas such as:

- Where a system will be hosted, both physically and virtually.
- How you will treat the security of information storage and transmission for that system.
- How you will integrate the system with or isolate it from other systems, where appropriate.
- How to adapt the system to changes in business operations, such as:
  - Insourcing systems that were once offloaded to a third party, so as to retain more control over them.
  - Outsourcing daily management tasks (managed services) to increase productivity and decrease expenses.
  - Establishing partnerships with third parties to achieve common marketplace goals.

Cloud and Virtualization Hosting Options

Cloud computing and virtualization technologies can be deployed using six basic methods, each with their own security considerations. The following table describes those methods.

Deployment Model	Description
Private	Private cloud services are usually distributed by a single company or other business entity over a private network. The hosting may be done internally, or it may be done offsite. With private cloud computing, organizations can exercise greater control over the privacy and security of their services. This type of delivery method is geared more toward banking and governmental services that require strict access control in their operations.
Public	Public cloud computing is done over the Internet by organizations that offer their services to general consumers. With this model, businesses are able to offer subscriptions or pay-as-you-go financing, while at the same time providing lower-tier services free of charge. Because public cloud computing relies on the Internet, security is always a concern.
Community	When multiple organizations share ownership of a cloud service, they are deployed as a community cloud. This is usually done to pool resources for a common concern, like standardization and security policies. Community hosting is most secure when the organizations involved have strong interoperability agreements in place.

Deployment Model	Description
Hybrid	Hybrid cloud computing combines two or more of the aforementioned deployment methods into one entity. The advantage to this approach is best realized in organizations that depend on internal cloud services in their operation, but also offer computing services to the general public.
Single tenancy	A single tenancy virtual environment provides different virtualized software instances for each user. These environments are optimal for privacy as instances are not shared with other users. However, single tenancy environments must be updated individually, meaning that you cannot deploy essential security fixes to every environment quickly.
Multi-tenancy	Multi-tenancy virtual environments implement a single instance of virtualized software that serves multiple clients at once. This streamlines the software provisioning process and can save an organization or cloud provider on cost. However, multi-tenancy solutions are often more difficult to manage because of their complexity, and implementing data isolation becomes a challenge in an environment that shares the same resource pool with multiple tenants.

Elastic Cloud Computing

The value proposition of any cloud computing service is to pay-as-you-go and to pay only for what you use. It also implies that cloud computing is elastic: that the services provided will grow or shrink depending on the need for them, and that those services can grow independently of one another if the need grows independently. For example, if an enterprise needs more storage for a database, storage space should be able to grow with that need without affecting or reconfiguring the other services being provided.

Elastic cloud computing has much the same security concerns as inelastic cloud models. However, because resources in an elastic cloud model are pooled among many clients, and that pool is constantly changing, there is an increased possibility that one organization's data is being exposed to another. There may also be a risk to your availability if the software that autoscales the resource pool size is poorly programmed or implemented.

Data Remnants in the Cloud

As more data is stored or transmitted digitally, especially in a cloud computing environment, it has become harder to purge or destroy data without leaving behind some traces of data remnants (the residual representation of data that remains even after the data itself has been removed or erased). Within a large-scale shared infrastructure, such as a public cloud provider, it is possible—and in fact, likely—that storage resources will be re-used by multiple organizations.

There are several techniques to prevent unwanted access to data remnants:

- Deleting the data before decommissioning a system. This offers minimal protection.
- Overwriting data—often with random 1s and 0s—before decommissioning. This offers strong protection in modern hard drives, but older media like floppy disks may require several overwriting passes. Bad sectors in flash memory like Universal Serial Bus (USB) thumb drives and solid state drives (SSDs) may still leave remnants even after several overwrite passes.
- Encryption of the data prior to storage, so that any data remnants are hidden. This offers the best protection for sensitive data, as even if remnants are recovered, they will be incomprehensible to anyone without the proper key.

Other methods such as degaussing or physical media destruction are not viable methods with a cloud provider because the client organization will not typically have physical access to the storage media.

Note: To learn how to avoid remnant data when disposing of or decommissioning a hard drive, check out the LearnTO **Completely Erase Data from a Disk** presentation from the **LearnTO** tile on the CHOICE Course screen.

Data Aggregation

Data aggregation is the technique of mining various sources to collate information on individuals or organizations. Aggregated data may be useful for organizations that want to get a higher-level, conceptual view of their own data as it exists in multiple forms. This is designed to help organizations see how their operations shape trends in their data. The organization can then change their business processes if they feel these trends indicate an unwanted direction, or they could keep the status quo if the data indicates a positive direction.

Despite these benefits, data aggregation can pose a very large risk to an enterprise, especially if its data is hosted by a cloud provider. The cloud provider might not just share this data with your enterprise, but could also sell the data to third parties for marketing research purposes. Even if the cloud provider does not engage in this behavior, the act of aggregating data itself could still leave your enterprise vulnerable if the provider is breached. Instead of having an immense amount of data to pore over and aggregate themselves, an attacker would already have the aggregate ready for them to take advantage of. This is why you should be cautious with how you let cloud providers handle your sensitive enterprise data.

Data Isolation

Data isolation is the technique of separating access and control of data from other users and services in the same system or environment. This is useful for making sure that only specific, authorized administrators can view and alter certain databases, whereas administrators of other databases have control only over their own. Some laws and regulations stipulate that data storage environments must isolate data on a per-user or per-customer basis. For example, a law might require that administrative access to a customer's financial information is only allowed for administrators in a particular jurisdiction. If administrators of the same institution but a different jurisdiction try to access this data, they will be denied.

Data isolation is a requirement for many organizations that sign up with cloud storage providers. Data might be kept in the same basic virtual space as data from other organizations, but it should still be isolated. This ensures that the client enterprise is the only one allowed access to its data storage space, and that other clients cannot take advantage of inadvertently shared sensitive data.

Resource Provisioning and De-provisioning

Because employees will be accessing crucial business data via the cloud, you must put in place security measures to protect the data from unauthorized access. It is up to you to make decisions about who should have access to the data and what level of access each employee will have. While the enterprise may be able to work with the cloud provider to streamline access, it is ultimately the responsibility of the enterprise to handle the provisioning, the assignment of privileges for data access, and de-provisioning, the removal of privileges for data access, for all users as they enter, move within, and exit the enterprise organization.

For in-house deployments, you will have greater control over provisioning and de-provisioning than just user access. The actual servers, virtual devices, and applications your enterprise operates with will need to change from time to time. Newer, more secure devices and software may replace legacy solutions to meet changing business needs. It is important that you have a plan to provision new resources and de-provision old ones, rather than just improvising as you go. Analyze how these resource changes will affect your existing deployment so that you can make an informed judgment that maintains your organization's security.

Virtual Machine Vulnerabilities

Some deployment models host virtual machines (VMs) for more than one enterprise on the same server or platform, which can present significant security vulnerabilities.

Hosting Scenario	Description and Vulnerabilities
Single physical server hosting multiple companies' VMs	In this virtualization hosting solution, multiple corporations are sharing the same singular physical server and singular host operating system for their virtualized environment. The biggest security concern for this hosting solution is the security of the host server. If an attack on the hosted VMs can somehow provide the attacker access to the host server, then the attacker could gain access to all of the VMs provided to many different organizations.
Single platform hosting multiple companies' VMs	In this virtualization hosting solution, multiple corporations are sharing a single platform for their virtualized environment, where the platform includes the operating environment and the delivery of services. This hosting solution is typically a cloud-based solution. The biggest security concern for this hosting solution is the security of the platform; specifically, if the proper security measures have been put in place to isolate the data and services for each of the companies on the host platform.

Virtual Environment Security

A virtual deployment introduces new components that you must secure: physical appliances and equipment with new services exposed, new virtual systems, networks, applications, storage devices, as well as VM migration traffic between hosts. Addressing the security of each of these components can be difficult because virtualization infrastructure is often a moving target; new systems added to the environment can create new or expanded threat vectors for attackers to target.

There are a number of measures you can take to secure the virtual environment:

- Ensure that any operating systems, applications, or software implemented within the virtualized infrastructure meet or exceed the existing security requirements established in the enterprise. The virtualized environment should always enforce stronger security controls whenever possible—never weaker controls.
- Limit physical access to the host systems within the virtualization infrastructure.
- Limit guest operating system resource usage—disk, central processing unit (CPU), memory, and network—so that no one VM can monopolize the host system's resources.
- Create and follow standardized guidelines for all guest operating systems deployed in the virtualization infrastructure, including operating system installation, patch management, and configuration management.
- Ensure any physical network switch ports connected to virtual switches are configured as static trunk links so no unintended connections are made between switches or network segments.
- Disable direct file sharing between host and guest systems.
- Separate roles for system administrators and network administrators within the virtualization infrastructure management framework, if possible.
- Establish and test a reliable backup and recovery process for VMs.
- Use separate VLANs for host-to-guest and guest-to-guest communications.
- Establish and follow a change management process that ensures no VMs are created without approval from the same stakeholders that approve deployment of physical systems.
- Enforce consistent risk classifications on physical host systems within the virtualization infrastructure to ensure a given physical system only hosts guest systems with the same data classification level.
- Enable audit logs for all virtualization infrastructure management tasks such as creation, deletion, starting, stopping, and migrating VMs.

- Enforce additional security controls through the use of purpose-built firewalls and intrusion prevention systems (IPSs) designed to protect virtualized environments.
- Keep the host updated, and apply all necessary security fixes.

 Note: It is important to remember that, rather than adding security after implementing virtualization, it is best to develop it as part of the virtualization architecture.

Network Segmentation

Network segmentation is the division of enterprise resources into distinct security domains or perimeters. To design a segmented network, you need to have a policy in place that describes which divisions, applications, services, and information should reside on a separate network. Network segmentation will assure that risks are contained and cause minimal impact on the organization. All compliance standards, from the National Institute of Standards and Technology (NIST) to the Federal Information Security Management Act (FISMA) to Payment Card Industry Data Security Standard (PCI DSS), recommend network segmentation. The basic principle behind network segmentation is to protect your most crucial data and information by ensuring that if one of the segments fails, the attacker still must deal with another layer.

To test your network segmentation, you should perform a risk assessment of the network to see how strong or segmented your network is. This risk assessment should give you a good idea of how well you are protecting the confidentiality, integrity, and availability of that critical information. Proper network segmentation will reduce network congestion, contain penetrated threats, and improve your overall network security.

Network Delegation

Network delegation is the transfer of administrative responsibilities to a security team within a newly acquired or segmented division of the parent company. As a CASP, you may be responsible for the security of the entire network for your organization, and for managing security policies and controls. Secure network delegation allows you to offload some of the responsibilities to others by providing some control back to other personnel within the organization. Delegation makes administrators less of a holdup when change needs to happen, and when it is done correctly, it does not jeopardize the integrity of the organization.

Delegation is a necessity for medium-size to large organizations where organizational unit or divisional lines are common. A good example of delegation would be allowing a corporate division to administer their own users and systems within a restricted area of your network.

Mergers and Acquisitions

Mergers and acquisitions may bring more than just new revenue—they'll often add systems and personnel to your already-functioning operations. New systems means new targets for attackers, and merely securing them on an individual level may not be enough. If new servers are added to your network during a merger, you need to make sure your network can support this new load from both an availability and breach-resistant standpoint. Likewise, more personnel means more human-centric risks. If these new employees aren't properly acclimated to your security environment, including familiarity with policy and procedures, then their integration could open up vulnerabilities in a number of different ways.

Demergers and divestitures may result in lost systems and personnel. Depending on the agreement, you may be required to retain sensitive data to transfer to another organization. In this situation, you need to make sure that the exchange is done securely and overseen by only qualified personnel. In some situations, you'll be keeping confidential data as part of a spin-off organization. You should evaluate any inter-operational processes you had in place prior to the demerger, and determine where your enterprise is still dependent on the other organization. Any remnant access rights or communication solutions could allow an attacker to use the other organization as a vector into your enterprise.

Guidelines for Selecting Technical Deployment Models

Use the following guidelines for selecting technical deployment models:

- Choose a cloud deployment or virtualization model that can adequately meet your business and security needs.
- Be aware of the security concerns of using an elastic cloud computing service.
- Consider that data deleted in the cloud might still remain.
- Choose a data wiping method like overwriting to remove data remnants.
- Be cautious of how your cloud provider handles sensitive data.
- Read cloud service agreements for any mention of data aggregation.
- Ensure that the cloud provider practices data isolation to keep data separate from its other clients.
- Consider how provisioning or deprovisioning a resource will affect your security.
- Be aware of the security issues with single servers and platforms hosting multiple VMs.
- Secure virtual environments to meet expanding threats.
- Practice network segmentation and delegation to maintain your network's integrity.
- Consider the added systems and personnel that you will need to secure in a merger or acquisition.
- Implement the careful exchange of sensitive data in a demerger or divestiture.

ACTIVITY 10-2
Selecting Technical Deployment Models

Scenario

Develetech has many different options for its technical deployment that go beyond standard physical infrastructure. Cloud and virtualization models are attractive to any business looking to streamline its operations, but before Develetech selects any such models, you need to be aware of the unique security strengths and weaknesses involved.

1. What type of virtualization hosting option provisions a single instance to multiple users?
   - ○ Public
   - ○ Hybrid
   - ○ Single tenancy
   - ○ Multi-tenancy

2. Before you select an elastic cloud computing service, what are some of the security issues that you need to account for?

3. As part of its security policy, Develetech takes snapshots of its databases that hold sensitive employee and customer information. After a certain period of time, those snapshots are deleted to make room for more current snapshots. You're concerned that, if you rely on the cloud for hosting these databases, the data in your snapshots will remain even after they should have been deleted. How can you ensure that there is no data remnants in the cloud?

4. Which of the following techniques are strong security measures to incorporate in a cloud deployment model? (Select two.)
   - ☐ Data aggregation
   - ☐ Data isolation
   - ☐ Provisioning and de-provisioning
   - ☐ Degaussing

5. Virtualizing key environments in Develetech's infrastructure may make those environments more efficient and reduce the clutter of physical systems. However, integrating a virtual deployment model in the enterprise will yield some new vulnerabilities. What security controls can you put in place to fix these vulnerabilities?

6. True or False? Network segmentation helps an organization avoid having a single point of failure in their network.

□ True

□ False

7. Develetech is moving to acquire a smaller business and integrate its operations into the rest of the enterprise. This acquisition will provide new computers and personnel to the enterprise. What concerns do you have from a security design standpoint?

TOPIC C

Secure the Design of the Enterprise Infrastructure

You've learned that incorporating security into the design of your systems is critical to the success of your enterprise. This is just as true from a holistic point of view. You'll secure your larger infrastructure design so that the combination of hosts, storage, networks, and applications is just as secure as each individual component.

Infrastructure Design Security

Secure infrastructure design requires that you place mission-critical resources within secure physical and virtual environments and protect all network resources from physical and virtual intrusion using detection and prevention technologies. Business requirements will dictate that a computer network and other components not only meet the current needs of the organization, but the projected needs as well. This is why infrastructure security includes not only the physical and logical diagramming and design of the network, it also includes the plans that the organization has in place to prevent and react to a data breach or other violations of the organization's network. Essentially, a secure infrastructure will be flexible with respect to future threats, risks, and vulnerabilities. This goes for all components of the enterprise infrastructure: the network itself, its hosts, storage solutions, and any applications developed or used.

There are several concerns involved in creating and maintaining a secure infrastructure design:

- How to design the logical mapping of the network.
- Where to place certain devices in a physical space.
- Where to integrate applications in the enterprise's day-to-day operations.
- Where to logically place defensive hardware and software (e.g., intrusion prevention system [IPS]/intrusion detection system [IDS]) on the network.
- Where to logically place networked storage systems.
- What components to virtualize versus what to keep actual.
- What systems to make redundant in the event of failure.
- What data to perform routine backups on.

Deployment Diagrams

Deployment diagrams map the physical or logical arrangement of all nodes in a system, typically a network (that is, its topology). Deployment diagrams are a critical troubleshooting resource when devices fail or the network comes under attack. When creating a map of the enterprise infrastructure, you can show the logical flow of data over a system and the corresponding physical location of its hosts. Common components of a logical deployment diagram include virtual local area networks (VLANs), information such as IP addresses, switching tables, and routing tables. Components of a physical diagram will specify the actual physical location of routers, switches, servers, workstations, firewalls, IPSs, storage systems, and other types of hardware. As a security professional, developing both types of diagrams will aid you in securing your overall infrastructure design.

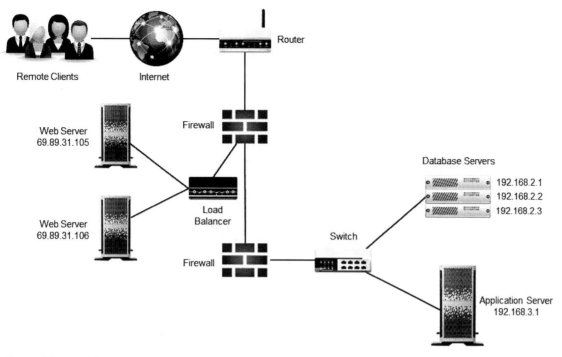

Figure 10-1: A deployment diagram.

Storage Integration

Storage integration is another important element of the enterprise security infrastructure. Safeguarding your organization's data stores while providing sufficient levels of access to that data are the primary drivers of storage integration with other resources on a network. Integration of network attached storage (NAS) and storage area networks (SANs) requires security precautions at the network perimeter, as well as inside the perimeter at the storage hosts to ensure data reliability, integrity, and secure access.

The design of the infrastructure should easily accommodate expanding storage media in order to ensure availability as the organization's data stores grow. Additionally, because storage media often interface with applications, they must both agree on the same security protocols and abide by similar policies. A database application that fails to meet the security standards of the SAN it works with, and vice versa, will put your company's sensitive information in jeopardy.

Guidelines for Securing the Design of the Enterprise Infrastructure

Use the following guidelines to secure the design of your enterprise infrastructure:

- Design your infrastructure to accommodate evolving business needs.
- Design your infrastructure to meet evolving threats, risks, and vulnerabilities.
- Decide where to place components both logically and physically to meet security needs.
- Draft both logical and physical deployment diagrams of systems in your enterprise, particularly your network topology.
- Ensure that storage media and protocols are secure both at the perimeter and inside the perimeter.
- Design the infrastructure to accommodate data storage growth.
- Ensure that storage media meet the security requirements of apps they interface with, and vice versa.

ACTIVITY 10-3
Securing the Design of the Enterprise Infrastructure

Scenario

The following image is a simple deployment diagram for a segment of Develetech's logical network. Using this diagram, you will consider the design of the network with security in mind. Being able to identify your network's security strengths and weaknesses from a topological perspective is essential in keeping your enterprise architecture secure by design.

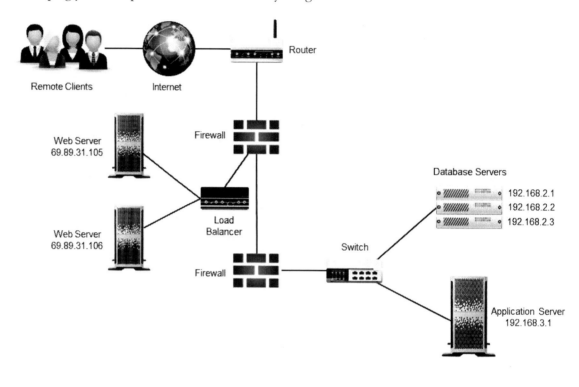

1. Using the deployment diagram, what security controls can you identify in this segment of the network?

2. Your IT team is thinking of adding a NAS server for employees to use as a general data storage solution. In this deployment diagram, where is the best place to put the NAS server?

  ○ In the existing DMZ with the web server.

  ○ In its own DMZ.

  ○ In the internal network, beyond the DMZ.

  ○ Before the perimeter firewall.

3. Your IT team is thinking of adding an SMTP gateway to handle any email traffic that is bound for the Internet or received from the Internet. In this deployment diagram, where is the best place to put the SMTP gateway?

  ○ In the existing DMZ with the web servers.

  ○ In its own DMZ.

  ○ In the internal network, beyond the DMZ.

  ○ Outside of the perimeter firewall.

4. What are some other infrastructure design security concerns that this deployment diagram doesn't address?

TOPIC D

Secure Enterprise Application Integration Enablers

Applications can be a powerful asset for any enterprise, whether or not they're developed in-house or purchased from an outside vendor. These applications cannot exist in a vacuum, however. You need to integrate them properly into your existing architecture that may already be complex as it is. These integration enablers are helpful in their own specific contexts, and what you choose will depend greatly on the application itself and how your enterprise is structured. It's important to recognize how these integration enablers can bolster your security, and how they can bring about a new set of risks.

Customer Relationship Management

A *customer relationship management (CRM)* system is a platform that enables a company to more easily work with customers and data about customers. CRM software can provide basic customer purchasing metrics, sales projections, and communication services to allow salespeople to interact with their clients. CRMs can also integrate with external programs like email clients to more easily manage contacts, calendar information, and meetings and appointments.

Because customer-related information is often very sensitive to an enterprise, a CRM should not expose this information in unsecured transmissions. In communication with databases that store the data, a CRM in your enterprise should implement transport encryption like Secure Sockets Layer/ Transport Layer Security (SSL/TLS) to prevent snooping. This will ensure that the constant flow of salespeople accessing customer data remains confidential to each session.

It's also important to understand that the personnel who will be using this CRM software every day might be unaware of its risks. Many CRM solutions will allow you to implement strict access control to keep certain personnel from accessing customer data that is beyond their authorization. Additionally, it may not be enough to secure only the CRM and assume salespeople will be protected. Because CRM systems often integrate with other apps, you need to make sure those apps are no less secure. For example, a salesperson might enter a new customer's information into a database through the CRM, but then use that CRM to send an email announcement out to interested parties. The CRM might use strong transport security during database sessions, but if the email client it uses doesn't implement encryption, then that will be a weak point you hadn't covered.

 Note: Salesforce.com and Zoho are examples of companies that provide CRM products.

Enterprise Resource Planning

An *enterprise resource planning (ERP)* solution contains software that monitors the day-to-day business operations of the enterprise and reports on the status of various resources and activities. ERP is very useful for giving an enterprise a view of how its systems and processes are integrated to maximize their efficiency and translate this into better business. ERPs can monitor customer orders, payroll information, revenue streams, spending activity, and more, all to make sure that these are working together to meet business goals.

Because ERPs enable the enterprise to get a crucial view of how its systems are integrated with one another, this might make it easier to track processes and information in real-time. This can help you monitor various operational functions for signs of anomalous behavior. Because an ERP solution centralizes business management, it will also be easier for you to apply enterprise-wide security policies.

ERPs typically incorporate databases in which to store resource analysis information. These databases need to be secure to prevent unauthorized users from gaining knowledge of core enterprise operations and the state of resources in the business. Additionally, centralizing management of enterprise resources means that access control should be a priority. Users should only have the rights they need to make changes in accordance with the principle of least privilege.

 Note: Sage ERP and Microsoft Dynamics® are examples of ERPs.

Governance, Risk, and Compliance

Governance, risk, and compliance (GRC) is a system for addressing these three information security needs within an enterprise. GRC solutions enable enterprises to collect information on how well these topics are integrated into business functions. Integrated forms of GRC are able to detect any deviation from governance policy, risk management approaches, or compliance with regulations and the law, and then alert security personnel to these changes. Highly risk-averse organizations, like financial institutions, are the most obvious candidates for GRC.

GRC solutions typically integrate and centralize sensors associated with existing security tools like IDSs, spam filters, change monitoring, data loss prevention, anti-malware scanning, event auditing, and more. Translating these tools into an overall GRC baseline enables the enterprise to maintain a high-level overview of how its systems should be running based on its security policy. An IPS can alert an administrator to an individual breach, but a GRC can aggregate alerts from many different systems to make sure the enterprise as a whole is operating within acceptable bounds.

 Note: SAP® is an example of a company that provides a GRC solution.

Enterprise Service Bus

An *enterprise service bus (ESB)* is middleware software that facilitates integration and communication between applications throughout the enterprise. The bus concept in ESB was developed based on practices commonly found in computer hardware architecture, where system messages from various hardware components are distributed and managed through a common channel, or bus. Based on the bus technology, ESBs can also be used to redirect messages and convert messages from one format to another. ESBs contain endpoints, which are the logical addresses of consumers and services.

To communicate with a service, the consumer sends a request message, along with the intended address of the service, to the bus. The bus, on its way to the service endpoint, also collects multiple messages from other consumers. When it reaches the specified logical address, it delivers the message there and starts its journey to deliver other messages. The message is delivered only to the logical address of the service and not the physical address, which means that, from the logical endpoint, the message travels farther to the designated location. Similarly, the service responds back to the endpoint via the bus. During the transaction, the message is monitored for any network policy violations.

ESBs can increase the flexibility of enterprise service communications and allow administrators to deploy changes more easily. However, ESBs typically increase overhead, which may impact service availability.

 Note: Mule ESB™ is an example of an open source ESB.

Service Oriented Architecture

Service-oriented architecture (SOA) is a method for designing and developing software applications in the form of interoperable services. These services are usually defined within the scope of functional business requirements that, when built as software components, can be reused for different purposes. From a business perspective, SOA provides an underlying flexibility and sustainability to network resources that promotes ongoing agility in the building and development process. It also provides an architectural method to integrate information across multiple business environments.

SOA provides a common method for consumers of services, such as web-based applications, to be aware of and access data from disparate sources. When installing an SOA, a company may develop and deploy services in different implementation languages and yet their respective clients will benefit from a common, well-defined interface to access them. Extensible Markup Language (XML) is often used for interfacing with SOA services, though this is not required. JavaScript Object Notation (JSON) is also becoming increasingly common.

Because SOA opens additional possibilities for information exchange and connectivity within and across organizations, you need to apply least privilege and default deny security frameworks, while at the same time providing needed levels of access to data and other network resources. In addition, you should enforce the integrity and confidentiality of messages routed within the environment by leveraging web services security (WS-security) extensions when implementing SOA.

Note: For more information on SOA as applied to business scenarios, visit **www.oracle.com/ technetwork/articles/javase/soa-142870.html** and **www.zdnet.com/blog/service-oriented/ten-examples-of-soa-at-work-circa-2008/1242**.

Note: Oracle® is an example of a company that provides an SOA solution.

SEA

While similar, a *service enabled architecture (SEA)* is different from an SOA. In an SOA, the architecture is designed around the services; in an SEA, the existing architecture is service-enabled through the implementation of various products, like an enterprise service bus (ESB). SEA focuses on reusing existing applications and making them both service-enabled and secure, rather than using new services to create a new architecture.

Directory Services

Directory services are centralized authentication systems used to provide a consistent and scalable mechanism to control access to applications, services, and systems. Directory services are often deployed by enterprises to more easily manage the entities in their network. From an application standpoint, a directory service provides an efficient way of facilitating information about these entities to various applications in a domain. The applications are thus more integrated with the overall network architecture, as they can directly access and share entity information.

Because directory services contain pertinent user and system information, it's necessary for them to exercise strong access control policies. Applications with too much control could pose a risk to the directory if they are compromised. An attacker could use the compromised application as a vector for stealing or altering entity data because of how closely the app is integrated with the directory service. In the opposite scenario, a user with more access than they need may be able to exploit functions of an application that put sensitive data or certain systems at risk. Maintaining frequent and robust auditing trails will also help you account for any security incidents that arise as a result of application integration with directory services.

Note: Microsoft® Active Directory® is a well-known example of a directory service.

Domain Name System

The Domain Name System (DNS) is a type of directory service that presents a hierarchal naming system for entities connected to a network, usually the Internet. DNS translates easy-to-remember names of domains into its corresponding host IP address to alleviate the burden of users remembering complex, unmemorable numbers. Applications may also rely on DNS servers for name resolution. While Internet service providers (ISPs) maintain common DNS servers, enterprises may integrate their own DNS servers to exercise much greater control over how domains are resolved in their environment. In certain environments, an in-house DNS server might perform better than users connecting to ISP-provided servers for every website they visit.

Enterprise DNS servers can be a target for attackers. Compromised data can poison the DNS cache, corrupting the source and misdirecting user traffic to another host. To mitigate the effects of DNS cache poisoning, the *Domain Name System Security Extension (DNSSEC)* was created. DNSSEC is a set of specifications to provide an added level of security to DNS, which was not originally designed with strong security features. DNSSEC provides origin authentication of DNS data, authenticated denial of existence, and data integrity. DNSSEC also supports zone signing, which uses digital signatures using public-key cryptography and a chain of trust to provide end-to-end protection to domain name data.

 Note: An example of a cloud-based DNS is Google Cloud DNS.

Zone Transfers and TSIG

Another potential weak point of DNS integration is zone transfer, a method used to replicate databases containing DNS data across DNS servers and to update DNS data for name servers. Zone transfers are particularly vulnerable to corruption or malicious interference, especially when the transfers occur over public networks like the Internet. *Transaction signatures (TSIG)* are used to secure these zone transfers by using shared secret keys and one-way hashing cryptography methods to securely identify each endpoint that is allowed to query or respond to a DNS update.

Configuration Management Database

A *configuration management database (CMDB)* is a database that contains information on each component within an enterprise's IT environment. CMDBs not only track and store information pertaining to components like software, hardware, policies, and personnel, but they also represent the relationships between these components. If the ways in which these components are integrated changes, then the CMDB can mark these changes. If, for example, you push an update to an app that causes hosts running the software to crash, then you can use the CMDB to compare the earlier app state to its new one. The CMDB does not contain snapshots of the app itself, but rather configuration metadata that helps you view the state of an app at a certain point in time.

For security, your applications and other systems can benefit from the CMDB verification process. Using CMDB audits and period reviews, you can verify that data is in an acceptable state and hasn't been misconfigured. You can also leverage the relationship and dependency mapping of CMDBs to conduct an impact analysis on any vulnerabilities that arise from integration. In integrated situations, a vulnerability in one application will likely have an effect elsewhere, so it's important to identify those dependencies to cover all surfaces. Like other application integration enablers, access control is an important element of CMDB security. Only authorized users should have access to sensitive metadata; a malicious user who knows all of your component dependencies can use this information to maximize the effectiveness of their attack.

 Note: ServiceNow® Configuration Management is an example of a CMDB.

Content Management System

A *content management system (CMS)* allows an enterprise to integrate documentation and other content into a centralized, easy-to-use solution. This solution gives administrators greater control over how these assets are organized and stored, while making it easier for users to analyze and update content. ECMs can be delivered through in-house software, but are often provided through cloud service platforms. Over time, CMSs have evolved to integrate different components in the management process, including communication and workflow software.

Attackers often use a CMS as a vector to attack the systems it is integrated with, including web servers that host the software. Improperly configured web-based CMSs are vulnerable to cross-site scripting (XSS), cross-site request forgery (XSRF), and other attacks that could compromise an entire website and not just the CMS itself. You should ensure that your CMS solution is up-to-date and patched. Input validation is also a necessity in identifying web-based input vulnerabilities. Additionally, you should harden the underlying operating system and any other components the CMS is integrated with. As always, your CMS should exhibit strong access control policies and auditing services.

 Note: WordPress and Drupal™ are examples of CMSs.

Guidelines for Securing Enterprise Application Integration Enablers

Use the following guidelines to secure enterprise application integration enablers:

- Exercise strong access control and auditing in any integration enabler.
- Harden any underlying components that integrate with software solutions.
- Implement transport encryption in CRMs to prevent attackers from snooping for sensitive customer information.
- Use ERPs to efficiently deploy policies.
- Secure databases that hold ERP information.
- Integrate a GRC solution with existing security tools like IPS and content filters to get a high-level view of risk in the enterprise.
- Consider the impact an ESB might have on your application and network availability.
- Enforce integrity and confidentiality of SOA messages using WS-security.
- Secure directory services to prevent oversharing of entity information.
- Implement DNSSEC to authenticate DNS queries.
- Implement TSIG to secure the integrity of DNS zone transfers.
- Use a CMDB to identify application states and dependencies with other components.
- Ensure that online CMSs are hardened against web-based attacks.

ACTIVITY 10-4
Securing Enterprise Application Integration Enablers

Scenario

Solutions that facilitate integration have been a big help in Develetech's day-to-day operations. Without these, the business would suffer losses to employee productivity and revenue. Therefore, it's important that you keep these integration enablers safe from threats. Although not every application may be relevant to the enterprise, it's important that you understand how each can be vulnerable so that you can then move to secure those vulnerabilities.

Additionally, Develetech would like to implement greater security in their DNS servers to mitigate the threat of cache poisoning. To do this, you'll enable DNSSEC on your server to authenticate DNS data sent over the network. You'll also validate DNS data by implementing zone signing, which will protect its integrity through digital signatures.

---

1. Develetech's sales staff works with a third-party CRM to manage their customers. The CRM also interfaces with your own in-house database. What security controls should this CRM implement to meet your standards?

2. How is a GRC solution's monitoring different than the monitoring of a control like an IDS?

3. What is an important security control that is common to many integration enablers, including ERP, CMDB, CMS, and directory services?
   - ○ Access control
   - ○ Load balancing
   - ○ Intrusion detection
   - ○ Anti-malware software

4. Which of the following protocols ensures the confidentiality and integrity of web services in a service oriented architecture (SOA)?
   - ○ SSL/TLS
   - ○ IPSec
   - ○ WS-security
   - ○ Kerberos

5. The DNSSEC extension provides which of the following security controls? (Select three.)
   - ☐ Zone signing
   - ☐ Data integrity
   - ☐ Data availability
   - ☐ Authenticated denial of existence

---

6. Enable DNSSEC on your server and sign the zone.
   a) From **Server Manager**, select **Tools→DNS**.
   b) In the navigation pane, expand your server object, then expand **Forward Lookup Zones**.
   c) Select **domain##.internal**, where **##** is your unique student number.

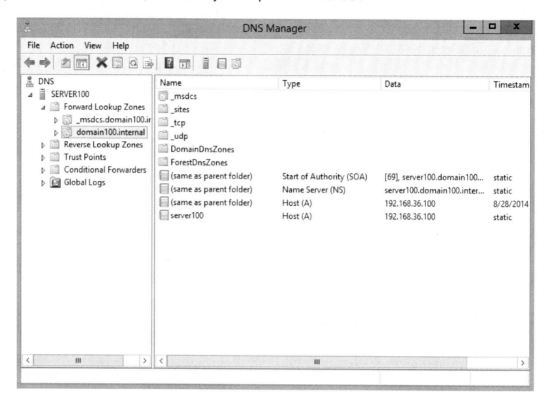

d) Right-click **domain##.internal** and select **DNSSEC→Sign the Zone**.

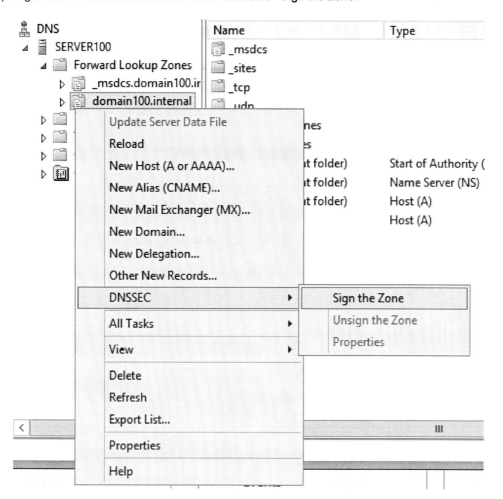

Note: Make sure you select the domain object before right-clicking it, otherwise the **DNSSEC** option might be grayed out.

e) In the **Zone Signing Wizard**, select **Next**.

f) On the **Signing Options** page, select **Use default settings to sign the zone**, then select **Next**.

g) On the **DNS Security Extensions (DNSSEC)** page, in the list of default parameters, scroll to verify the following information:

- The encryption algorithm used is RSA/SHA-256.
- The key length is 2,048 bits.
- The DNSKEY, which a DNS resolver uses to verify DNSSEC signatures, has a signature validity of 168 hours.
- NSEC3 is an extension that offers authenticated denial of existence.

h) Select **Next**.

i) After the zone is successfully signed, select **Finish** and close the **DNS Manager** window.

Summary

In this lesson, you implemented industry security standards in the enterprise; you assessed technical deployment models for their strengths and weaknesses, then you selected the ones that best fit your organization; you secured your enterprise by the design of its infrastructure; and you secured various technologies that enable application integration into your enterprise architecture. All of these tasks together fulfill a larger purpose for your enterprise duties: integrating hosts, storage, networks, and applications in a way that minimizes risk and maximizes business productivity.

What sort of standards do you adhere to in your organization?

What application integration enablers do you have in place in your enterprise, and what security concerns do you have about them?

 Note: Check your CHOICE Course screen for opportunities to interact with your classmates, peers, and the larger CHOICE online community about the topics covered in this course or other topics you are interested in. From the Course screen you can also access available resources for a more continuous learning experience.

11 | Conducting Vulnerability Assessments

Lesson Time: 4 hours, 30 minutes

Lesson Objectives

In this lesson, you will:

*   Select vulnerability assessment methods.

*   Select vulnerability assessment tools.

Lesson Introduction

Your enterprise architecture is established, and you designed it with security in mind. However, your job as a CASP isn't done. As thorough as you think you might have been, there is always room for error. These errors might be vulnerabilities that, if left untouched, could compromise your enterprise's assets and negatively impact your business operations. So, you'll survey the strength of your systems by conducting assessments and tests. These will help you identify any holes in your security that you may have missed, and then you'll be able to address them before an attacker or careless user has a chance to cause damage.

TOPIC A

Select Vulnerability Assessment Methods

There are many strategies and techniques you can use to assess and test your enterprise systems. Each one will provide a specific insight into the weaknesses and strengths of the target of your assessment, and some are more valuable than others depending on the context in which they are used. In this topic, you'll consider the different business scenarios that might benefit from a vulnerability assessment, then you'll select the appropriate technique in light of this information.

Vulnerability Assessments

A *vulnerability assessment* is an evaluation used to find security weaknesses within an organization. Vulnerability assessments are usually carried out using automated vulnerability scanning tools. These scanners examine an organization's systems, applications, and devices to determine their current state of operation and the effectiveness of any security controls. Typical results from a vulnerability scanner will identify misconfigurations and missing security patches or critical updates. This assessment method is normally carried out at regular intervals (for example, weekly, monthly, or quarterly) depending on the goals and requirements of the organization.

There are many ways to assess the weaknesses that exist within an organization; these methods usually differ based on the intensity or context of the assessment, or they target specific elements of the enterprise. Which assessment methods you choose to conduct will depend heavily on your organization's size, structure, and business needs.

Malware Sandboxing

Malware sandboxing is a technique in which virtual machines scan files and applications for the existence of malware. Like in an application sandbox, a malware sandbox is segregated from critical systems so that it may run in a restricted virtual environment. Organizations use malware sandboxes to not only detect and isolate malware from their systems, but to use the controlled environment to conduct assessments into the malware itself. This assessment may offer the organization a greater insight into the methods that malicious software uses to harm various systems.

Figure 11-1: Analyzing malware in a sandbox.

When you place malware in a malware sandbox, the sandbox will typically analyze the files and the virtual system, then generate reports that detail information about the malicious software and the system's state. This information can include: call traces the malware makes to operating system application programming interfaces (APIs); network dumps during the analysis; memory dumps of the virtual machine and relevant applications; copies of files created and deleted while the malware runs; snapshots of the system state; and so on.

The information you capture in a malware sandbox may expose vulnerabilities in your network and systems that you were otherwise unaware of. This is especially true of malware that is crafted specifically to attack your organization. An assessment of the vectors that the malware takes may point to a weakness that the attackers know of and you don't, or it might reveal a weakness you hadn't thought of.

Memory Dumping

A *memory dump* records the state of a system's or application's memory at a specific point in time. These reports are usually generated automatically when an application or system crashes. They can be used to debug the application or system by assessing what caused it to crash or otherwise malfunction. Because memory dumps can be very complex, they are often incomprehensible to human interpreters. Debugging tools attempt to aid the process of reading memory dumps by identifying variable addresses and structuring data output into a more manageable form.

Because buffer and integer overflows often cause an application or system to crash, it can be helpful to read memory dumps to scan for these vulnerabilities. Memory dumps can also expose data that existed in volatile memory when the application or system generated the dump; this can prove useful in the forensic analysis of attacks that only leave traces in Random Access Memory (RAM).

```
0000:  0E 04 80 00 01 00 00 00      . . . . . . . .
0008:  00 00 00 00 0B 00 04 C0      . . . . . . . À
0010:  03 01 00 00 00 00 00 00      . . . . . . . .
0018:  00 00 00 00 00 08 2D 00      . . . . . . -.
0020:  00 00 00 00 00 00 00 00      . . . . . . . .
0028:  2E B8 01 00 00 00 00 00      . . . . . . . .
0030:  FF FF FF FF 06 00 00 00      ÿÿÿÿ . . . .
0038:  58 00 00 00 00 00 00 00      X . . . . . . .
0040:  FF 00 06 12 0C 00 00 10      ÿ . . . . . . .
0048:  00 00 00 00 3C 00 00 00      . . . . < . . .
0050:  00 00 00 00 00 00 00 00      . . . . . . . .
0058:  40 F6 81 09 80 FA FF FF      @ö . úÿÿ
0060:  00 00 00 00 00 00 00 00      . . . . . . . .
```

Figure 11–2: A memory dump.

Runtime Debugging

Related to memory dumping is the concept of *runtime debugging*. While an application may dump its memory into an output file after a crash, a runtime debugger will actively monitor an application's memory usage at runtime for any errors or mishandling. This can greatly ease the burden of a programmer manually debugging their code by checking every way in which memory is handled. If the runtime debugger detects mismanagement memory, this could be evidence of an overflow vulnerability in an application that an attacker can exploit.

 Note: CorDbg is an example of a runtime debugger that comes with the Microsoft® .NET framework software development kit (SDK).

Penetration Testing

A *penetration test*, or pen test, uses active tools and security utilities to evaluate security by simulating an attack on a system. A penetration test will verify that a threat exists, then will actively test and bypass security controls, and will finally exploit vulnerabilities on the system. Such vulnerabilities may be the result of poorly or improperly configured systems, known or unknown hardware or software flaws, or operational weaknesses in processes or technical countermeasures. Any security issues that are found in the test and can be exploited are presented to the organization with an assessment of the impact and a mitigation proposal.

Penetration tests are less common and more intrusive than traditional vulnerability assessments. They tend to be driven by an organization's desire to determine the feasibility of an attack and the amount of business impact a successful exploitation of vulnerabilities will have on an organization. One of the major differences between penetration testing and typical vulnerability assessments is that the rating assigned to a vulnerability during a vulnerability assessment is subjective, whereas a penetration test will exploit a real vulnerability to test it. Penetration testing also tends to combine multiple vulnerabilities together to provide a more holistic understanding of an organization's vulnerability state.

It is important that penetration testing follows a method that is similar to what a real attacker would use, including phases in which the attacker makes preparations and learns what they can about the target. The difference between the execution of a real attack and a penetration test is that of intent, and you should have the explicit permission of the target organization before you begin the test. You should make sure that the organization is aware that the test should not stop until the attack has been fully carried out. Otherwise, the results of the test could be skewed, or the live systems themselves may be damaged.

 Caution: While the information gained from a penetration test is often more thorough, there is a risk that the system may suffer actual damage because of the security breach.

Reconnaissance

Reconnaissance, also known as *footprinting*, is the phase in an attack or penetration test in which the attacker or tester gathers information regarding the target organization before actually conducting the attack. The information they gather can center on the target's technology, personnel, and structuring. This information aids the attacker or tester by exposing vulnerabilities or easily-exploitable vectors with which to attack the organization.

Though this information can be extremely helpful, depending on the type of pen test you conduct, you may actually skip the reconnaissance phase and go straight to testing.

Whois & Quick Stats

Email	klukasik@comptia.org is associated with ~18 domains
	administrator@comptia.org is associated with ~191 domains
	customerservice@networksolutions.com is associated with ~506,048 domains
Registrant Org	CompTIA is associated with ~189 other domains
Dates	Created on 1995-08-15 - Expires on 2020-08-14 - Updated on 2011-07-28
IP Address	198.134.5.6 is hosted on a dedicated server
IP Location	- Illinois - Downers Grove - Comptia Inc.
ASN	AS393324 COMPTIA-1 - CompTIA, Inc.,US (registered Nov 26, 2013)
Domain Status	Registered And Active Website
Whois History	259 records have been archived since 2001-08-01
IP History	8 changes on 5 unique IP addresses over 9 years

Figure 11–3: Gathering domain information for www.comptia.org.

Examples

With a web browser and an Internet connection, an attacker can often determine the Internet protocol (IP) addresses of a company's Domain Name System (DNS) servers; the range of addresses assigned to the company; names, email addresses, and phone numbers of contacts within the company; and the company's physical address. DNS servers are common reconnaissance targets because, if not properly secured, they can provide a detailed map of an organization's entire network infrastructure.

Attackers also use dumpster diving, or searching through garbage, to find sensitive information in paper form. The names and titles of people within the organization enable the attacker to begin social engineering to gain even more private information.

The HTML code of a company's web page can provide information, such as IP addresses and names of web servers, operating system versions, file paths, and names of developers or administrators.

Black Box

In a *black box test*, the penetration tester is given little to no information regarding the systems or network being tested. This test simulates an outside attacker who knows little about the systems or the network they are attacking, other than what they can discover through basic reconnaissance techniques. This is also called a zero knowledge test, as the penetration tester must gather all types of information about the target before starting the testing phase of the penetration test. The penetration tester will need to verify the accuracy of the targets with the client organization before attempting to move into the testing phase. This verification ensures the test is being carried out in the correct scope and does not include targets that are out of scope or not controlled by the organization being tested.

Secrecy of Test

Another common, but not necessarily required, component of this type of test is that only a few key individuals within the targeted organization should be made aware of the testing. This provides additional insight into how effectively personnel within the target organization are following monitoring, detection, and incident response policies, along with the effectiveness of the technologies deployed to support these policies.

White Box

In a *white box test*, the penetration tester is provided knowledge concerning all aspects of the systems and networks being tested. The tester fully understands the function and design of the systems and networks before they carry out the test. The goal of this type of test is to simulate an inside attacker with high-level knowledge and understanding of the environment they are attacking. This type of test is the exact opposite of a black box test and is sometimes conducted as a follow-up to a black box test. A white box test typically starts with a testing phase, as reconnaissance is not needed. It is also known as a full-knowledge test, as the penetration tester does not have to gather any information manually before starting the testing phase.

Grey Box

In a *grey box test*, the penetration tester is provided with some knowledge and insight of internal architectures and systems or other preliminary information about the systems and networks they are testing. The goal of this type of test is to simulate an inside attacker who possesses an incomplete knowledge of the environment they are attacking. This type of test is also known as a partial knowledge test, as the penetration tester should still attempt to gather additional information about the network and systems they are testing by starting at the reconnaissance phase of the penetration test.

Fingerprinting

Fingerprinting is the technique of determining the type of operating system and services a target uses by studying the types of packets and the characteristics of these packets during a communication session. Fingerprinting typically relies on the Transmission Control Protocol/Internet protocol (TCP/IP) to provide this information. There are two types of fingerprinting: active fingerprinting and passive fingerprinting.

Active fingerprinting is performed with a scanning tool that sends specifically crafted packets and examines their responses to determine the operating system version and service-related information. For example, a penetration tester may simply establish a Telnet session or create a socket connection to an open port to observe the response. Web servers and mail servers are notorious for responding with operating system and application version information in the initial response header.

Passive fingerprinting attempts to learn more about a targeted service without the target knowing it. Passive fingerprinting is a form of packet sniffing in that the packets are captured during normal communications with the service and then are examined for specific characteristics and oddities. Every operating system's IP stack has its own idiosyncrasies, as it is up to the IP stack developer to determine how certain protocol communications are handled and set.

Code Review

An application *code review* is very different from a standard network or application-focused penetration test. Code reviews examine the actual source code of an application to identify potential vulnerabilities. If an organization develops its own applications or has specific applications developed for them, it is important that they perform code reviews alongside their standard penetration tests. This is a logical extension of standard penetration testing, as vulnerable applications could lead to the compromise of the organization's entire network or even a critical asset.

If your organization develops applications as a core part of its business, you should ensure that auditors carry out code reviews. Code auditors can carry out these reviews either manually or automatically using source code analysis tools. Both of these methods are useful in identifying potential weaknesses in an application, but the auditing team should understand the capabilities and limitations of the automated tools. Reviewing code is a highly technical skill that is not easily replaced by automation.

 Note: An extensive list of source code analysis tools is maintained by the National Institute of Standards and Technology (NIST) and can be found online at **http://samate.nist.gov/index.php/Source_Code_Security_Analyzers.html**.

Social Engineering

A *social engineering test* is another assessment that does not focus on the traditional systems and network infrastructure associated with standard penetration testing scenarios. Social engineering aims to exploit what is often the weakest link in security: the human. As it is commonly defined, social engineering is the process of deceiving people into giving away access or confidential information. When carrying out social engineering attacks, penetration testers are actively exploiting the human tendency to trust. This natural human willingness to accept someone at his or her word or appearance leaves many of us vulnerable to this style of attack.

It's relatively straightforward to implement security in software and hardware; you put a control in place to block unwanted access, or you implement a defense to stop a direct attack from breaching your system. However, because social engineering is indirect and deceptive, all it takes is one careless or technologically inexperienced user to compromise your entire operation. Because few organizations properly equip their employees with the knowledge to recognize social engineering attempts, attackers who prey upon human weaknesses are a danger to every information system. This is why it is extremely important to include social engineering penetration tests with the standard round of tests. The results from social engineering tests can produce great insight into the human vulnerabilities and risks associated with your organization.

Types of Social Engineering

The following table lists some of the most common types of social engineering attacks and tests.

Social Engineering Type	Description
Spoofing	This is a human-based or software-based attack where the goal is to pretend to be someone else for the purpose of identity concealment. Spoofing can occur in Internet Protocol (IP) addresses, network adapter hardware (Media Access Control or MAC) addresses, and email. If employed in email, various email message headers are changed to conceal the originator's identity.

Social Engineering Type	Description
Impersonation	This is a human-based attack where an attacker pretends to be someone they are not. A common scenario is when the attacker calls an employee and pretends to be calling from the help desk. The attacker tells the employee he is reprogramming the order-entry database, and he needs the employee's user name and password to make sure it gets entered into the new system.
	Impersonation is often successful in situations where an identity cannot be easily established. If the employee in the previous example doesn't know the real help desk worker or the help desk number, they may be less inclined to question the request.
Hoax	This is an email-based or web-based attack that is intended to trick the user into performing undesired actions, such as deleting important system files in an attempt to remove a virus. It could also be a scam to convince users to give up important information or money for an interesting offer.
	Like many social engineering techniques, hoaxes depend greatly on the amount of experience the target has with computer technology. An email that tells a user to delete a virus file on their computer will likely be ineffective if the user knows what the file does, or if they know that antivirus software is the preferred method for detecting and removing infected files.
Phishing, spear phishing, and *pharming*	These are common types of email-based social engineering attacks. In a phishing attack, the attacker sends an email that seems to come from a respected bank or other financial institution. The email claims that the recipient needs to provide an account number, Social Security number, or other private information to the sender to "verify an account." Ironically, the phishing attack often claims that the "account verification" is necessary for security reasons. Individuals should never provide personal financial information to someone who requests it, whether through email or over the phone. Legitimate financial institutions never solicit this information from their clients. When the attack targets a specific individual or institution, this social engineering technique is known as spear phishing. An attack similar to phishing, called pharming, can be done by redirecting a request for a website, typically an e-commerce site, to a similar-looking, but fake, website.
	Both phishing and pharming are some of the most prominent forms of social engineering, and even experienced computer users may be fooled by what appears to be an authority figure.
Vishing	This is a human-based attack where the goal is to extract personal, financial, or confidential information from the victim by using services such as a telephone system and IP-based voice messaging services (Voice over Internet Protocol or VoIP) as the communication medium. This is also called voice phishing.
	Vishing can be more effective than phishing because of the trust that people tend to place in others they can speak to in real time. In addition, users may be too used to traditional telecommunications to know that a VoIP identity can be much more easily spoofed due to the open nature of the Internet.

Social Engineering Type	Description
Baiting	Baiting exploits the human tendency toward curiosity by planting physical media in an area where someone will find it and then promptly use it. For example, a social engineer might install malware on a removable Universal Serial Bus (USB) drive, then place that drive on the ground in a parking lot outside of a corporate office. An employee who arrives for work may notice that drive, pick it up, then promptly insert it into their workstation. If their workstation has autorun enabled for removable media, the malware will immediately infect the host and may then spread to other hosts in the corporate network. A similar virtual attack occurs when a user is enticed to download free software, which an attacker has packaged with a Trojan horse.
Whaling	This is a form of spear phishing that targets individuals or organizations that are known to possess a good deal of wealth. Whaling targets individuals who work in Fortune 500 companies or financial institutions whose salaries are expected to be high.
	Whaling is a riskier method for social engineers, as security is bound to be more robust than it is with average users or small companies, and the consequences of being caught will likely be much more severe. However, exploiting the weakest link can result in a huge payoff for the attacker(s).
URL *hijacking*	Also called *typo squatting*, this is the tactic of exploiting typos that users sometimes make when entering a URL into a browser. For example, a malicious user might register a domain with the URL **www.comtpia.org**, which has a minor typo compared to the correct **www.comptia.org**. A user who makes this mistake when entering the URL into their browser will be directed to the attacker's site, which may mimic the real website or contain malicious software that will infect the victim's computer.
Spam and *spim*	Spam is an email-based threat where the user's inbox is flooded with emails which act as vehicles that carry advertising material for products or promotions for get-rich-quick schemes and can sometimes deliver viruses or malware. Spam can also be utilized within social networking sites such as Facebook and Twitter. Spim is an attack similar to spam that is propagated through instant messaging (IM) instead of through email.
	With the prevalence of spam filters in email clients and spim blockers in instant messaging services, these techniques are less effective than they used to be. However, the sheer volume of unsolicited messages sent in bulk every day keeps spam and spim as viable methods for deceiving inexperienced users.
Shoulder surfing	This is an attack where the goal is to look over the shoulder of an individual as they enter password information or a PIN. This is very easy to do today with camera-equipped mobile phones.
Dumpster diving	This is an attack where the goal is to reclaim important information by inspecting the contents of trash containers. This is especially effective in the first few weeks of the year as users discard old calendars with passwords written in them.
Tailgating	Also known as piggy backing, this is a human based attack where the attacker will slip in through a secure area following a legitimate employee. The only way to prevent this type of attack is by installing a good access control mechanism and educating users not to admit unauthorized personnel.

Note: To learn more about how to assess the vulnerabilities of the human element in your organization, check out the LearnTO **Conduct a Social Engineering Test** presentation from the **LearnTO** tile on the CHOICE Course screen.

Guidelines for Selecting Vulnerability Assessment Methods

Note: All Guidelines for this lesson are available as checklists from the **Checklist** tile on the CHOICE Course screen.

Use the following guidelines when selecting vulnerability assessment methods:

- Select vulnerability assessments based on your enterprise's risk management profile.
- Understand that typical vulnerability assessments are rated subjectively.
- Upload suspected or known malware to a sandbox for assessment.
- Review the malware sandbox assessment for weak points that the malware is targeting.
- Review memory dumps in systems and applications for mismanaged memory errors.
- Use a runtime debugger to automate mismanaged memory detection.
- Conduct a penetration test to simulate an attack on your systems.
- Make sure your organization is fully aware and consents to the pen test before it begins.
- Be aware that pen testing can cause real-world harm to a system.
- Conduct a black box test by footprinting a system for relevant information.
- Conduct a white box test to initiate a full-on attack against the target.
- Conduct a grey box test to simulate partial insider knowledge of the target.
- Mandate code reviews for development to catch vulnerabilities in an application.
- Conduct a social engineering test to evaluate your organization's human element.

ACTIVITY 11-1
Selecting Vulnerability Assessment Methods

Scenario

Your systems and personnel at Develetech have gone untested for quite some time. You can't afford to be ignorant of any vulnerabilities in your enterprise, so you'll begin to select the best methods for conducting assessments. These methods will reveal where your attention is most needed.

1. What is a major disadvantage of performing a penetration test as opposed to a traditional vulnerability assessment?

2. What is the function of a white box test?
   - ○ To gather information in preparation for an attack
   - ○ To simulate an attack by a threat who has some knowledge of the target.
   - ○ To simulate an attack by an outsider threat who has limited knowledge of the target.
   - ○ To simulate an attack by an insider threat who has complete knowledge of the target.

3. You suspect that an insidious form of malware has infected some of Develetech's hosts. You've isolated these hosts from the rest of the network, but instead of simply removing the malware and moving on, you'd like to see if you can learn more about the infection and possibly derive a point of origin or a method of operation. This information could help prepare you in case of future attacks. What technique can accomplish this, and how?

4. As you may recall, Develetech has a couple of applications undergoing development. An important step in assessing the vulnerabilities in these applications is a code review. Because your applications are so complex and your development team is under time constraints, your auditors will be using automated tools to help them in their code reviews. However, what do you need to remind your auditors of when it comes to these tools?

5. You'd like to test how susceptible your general staff is to social engineering attempts. You're concerned that these employees might leak sensitive information that could give competitors an edge and negatively impact Develetech's sales. Which type of attack(s) would you perform to test your general staff, and why?

TOPIC B

Select Vulnerability Assessment Tools

Now that you've selected the general methods involved in vulnerability assessment and penetration testing, you're ready to use the specific tools that will identify weaknesses within your enterprise systems. Whether you need to conduct an individual test or a battery of tests, using a tool from each category will give you the experience you need to successfully identify vulnerabilities in any dimension of your enterprise.

Vulnerability Scanners

A *vulnerability scanner* is designed to identify and report on known weaknesses found in devices, applications, and systems residing on a network. A vulnerability scan can use a number of different assessment techniques to detect flaws, and each scanner may target only specific technologies. Because they rely on prior knowledge of vulnerabilities, these scanners may be ill-equipped to assess new and emerging weaknesses.

There are a few key decisions that you need to make before implementing a vulnerability scanner on your network. The location in which the tool is executed is one of those key decisions, as devices such as firewalls or access control lists (ACLs) on routers can interfere with the vulnerability scanner's ability to accurately detect these weaknesses. Depending on what is being accessed, this may or may not be an issue. For example, if the goal of the test is to identify whether or not a security patch was implemented, firewalls or routers blocking access to these devices could cause inaccuracies in the vulnerability scanner's results. If the goal of the vulnerability scan is to assess the state of the entire network as seen from the Internet, then firewalls and routers blocking access to key systems and resources is expected and understood.

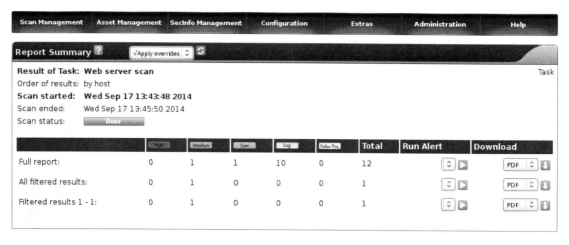

Figure 11–4: The results of a vulnerability scan of a web server.

Examples
Some common examples of vulnerability scanners include: Microsoft® Baseline Security Analyzer (MBSA), Nessus®, SAINTscanner®, GFI LanGuard®, OpenVAS, GoLismero, and Nmap.

ACTIVITY 11-2
Using a Vulnerability Scanner

Before You Begin

You have a Kali Linux virtual machine (VM) that you created earlier. You will use the GoLismero security tool on this VM to scan for vulnerabilities.

 Note: You will be using your Kali Linux VM throughout this topic and its activities.

Scenario

Now that you have your Kali Linux virtual machine ready to go, you'll use it to launch a series of tests that will assess the strength of your systems' security. To begin, you'll use a general vulnerability scanning tool to identify where your systems are the weakest. GoLismero is a tool that runs several other security tools like Nmap to generate a holistic vulnerability report. You'll use GoLismero to run a scan on your Windows host, which will prepare you for when you later decide to scan the other hosts in your network.

1. Load your Kali Linux virtual machine.
   a) From the desktop, open **Oracle VM VirtualBox**.
   b) With **Server##-Kali** selected, select the **Start** button.
   c) If necessary, close any VM warnings at the top of the window.

2. Run a vulnerability scan on your Windows host using GoLismero.
   a) In your Kali Linux VM, select the **Terminal** icon to open a command terminal.

   b) At the command prompt, enter *golismero scan HOST_IP -o /root/Desktop/vuln-report.html* where *HOST_IP* is the IP address of your Windows host computer.

```
root@kali:~# golismero scan 192.168.36.100 -o /root/Desktop/vuln-report.html
```

   After GoLismero scans the host, it will output its results in a visual web page format.

c) Verify that GoLismero is running its various plugins to scan the host.

3. Verify the results of the scan.

   a) After GoLismero finishes its scan, close the command terminal.

    Caution: Make sure not to close the terminal until the command prompt returns, indicating that the scan is finished.

   b) From the desktop, double-click the **vuln-report.html** file to open it in the Iceweasel web browser.

   c) Maximize the browser window.

d) Verify that the report lists information about the scan, which detected no vulnerabilities.

The information in the report includes:

- The target of the scan.
- The start time, end time, and total elapsed time of the scan.
- The number of vulnerabilities detected in the scan.
- Each detected vulnerability categorized in terms of its type and criticality.
- More information about individual vulnerabilities that were detected in the scan.

4. Close Iceweasel.

Port Scanners

A *port scanner* is a device or application that scans a network to identify what devices are reachable (alive), what ports on these devices are active, and what protocols these active ports use to communicate. A port scanner typically relies on the most common network protocols (for example, Transmission Control Protocol [TCP], User Datagram Protocol [UDP], and Internet Control Message Protocol [ICMP]) to retrieve this information. The port information revealed in a scan can help you pinpoint vulnerabilities in your network, as attackers will often use open ports as an intrusion vector.

ICMP is typically used by a port scanner to perform the preliminary check, determining what devices on the network are alive and responding before a real port scan is carried out. This is done for optimization reasons, as a full port scan of all 65,535 ports for both the UDP and TCP protocols can be time consuming. By checking if the device is alive and responding using ICMP discovery, you can reduce the overall length of time it takes to port scan a large network. Take caution when using this default setting, as devices can be configured to not respond to ICMP echo requests and will be skipped by the port scanner.

```
Starting Nmap 6.46 ( http://nmap.org ) at 2014-09-17 13:51 UTC
Nmap scan report for 192.168.36.100
Host is up (0.0026s latency).
Not shown: 85 filtered ports
PORT        STATE  SERVICE
53/tcp      open   domain
80/tcp      open   http
88/tcp      open   kerberos-sec
135/tcp     open   msrpc
139/tcp     open   netbios-ssn
389/tcp     open   ldap
443/tcp     open   https
445/tcp     open   microsoft-ds
1723/tcp    open   pptp
3389/tcp    open   ms-wbt-server
49152/tcp   open   unknown
49153/tcp   open   unknown
49154/tcp   open   unknown
49155/tcp   open   unknown
49157/tcp   open   unknown

Nmap done: 1 IP address (1 host up) scanned in 9.76 seconds
```

Figure 11–5: The results of a port scan.

Examples

The most popular port scanning tool is Nmap, which runs on a wide variety of operating systems including Windows®, Linux®, and OS X®. Other common port scanners include Snort®, Netcat, SuperScan, ShieldsUP, and hping.

 Note: Keep in mind that many of these tools can perform several different types of vulnerability assessments.

Port Scanning Techniques

The following table describes various port scanning techniques.

Technique	Description
TCP full connection	This scan completes the standard TCP three-way handshake process to identify open ports.
TCP SYN	This scan is often referred to as a half-open scan, as the port scanner sends a SYN packet, but the full three-way handshake is never completed. If the port scanner receives a SYN-ACK from a targeted device, the port is marked as listening; if it receives a RST-ACK, the port is marked as closed.
TCP FIN	With a TCP FIN scan, the FIN flag is set in the TCP packet by the port scanner. According to RFC 793, an RST should be sent back for all closed ports, so if the port scanner receives an RST packet from the targeted device, the port is marked as closed. If nothing is received, the port is marked as open.

Technique	Description
TCP Xmas	This scan is often referred to as a Christmas tree scan, as all TCP flags are set and the TCP packet is said to be lit up like a Christmas tree. According to RFC 793, an RST should be sent back for all closed ports, so if the port scanner receives a RST packet from the targeted device, the port is marked as closed. If nothing is received, the port is marked as open.
TCP NULL	This scan is the opposite of a TCP Xmas scan in that all flags are unset or turned off. According to RFC 793, an RST should be sent back for all closed ports, so if the port scanner receives a RST packet from the targeted device, the port is marked as closed. If nothing is received, the port is marked as open.
UDP	This type of scan works by sending a UDP packet to every targeted port from the port scanner. If an ICMP port unreachable error is returned, the port is closed. If other ICMP unreachable errors are returned, the port is marked as filtered. If no response is received, the port is classified as opened; however, this doesn't mean the port is really open and further scanning is required to verify if the port is actually open.

ACTIVITY 11-3
Using a Port Scanner

Before You Begin

You will be working with a partner in this activity. You will be scanning for open ports on your partner's server.

Scenario

You need to make sure your new Windows Server® 2012 R2 servers are secure by scanning them for open ports. Develetech's IT department has had problems in the past with attackers gaining access to applications on servers by getting through the firewall and accessing open ports on the servers. You have already hardened your servers and now want to check your work.

Before connecting the new Windows Server 2012 R2 servers to your network, you need to make sure not only that the base operating system is hardened, but also that no unnecessary ports are open on the servers to minimize the likelihood of attacks. You are responsible for scanning your Windows Server 2012 R2 computer. You will initiate the scan with Nmap, a port scanning utility. Nmap will identify the common ports that are open on your server, and with this knowledge, you can better account for some of the vulnerabilities in your network.

---

1. Use Nmap to scan for open ports on your partner's server.

   a) From the Kali Linux desktop, select **Applications→Kali Linux→Information Gathering→Network Scanners→zenmap**.

    Note: Zenmap is the graphical user interface (GUI) version of Nmap.

   b) Maximize the **Zenmap** window.
   c) In the **Target** text box, type your host server's IP address.
   d) From the **Profile** drop-down list and select **Regular scan**.
   e) In the top-right of the **Zenmap** window, select the **Scan** button to start the scan.

2. Examine the scan results.

a) When the scan is complete, verify that several TCP ports were detected as open, indicating vulnerable areas on your host server.

```
Not shown: 981 filtered ports
PORT        STATE   SERVICE
22/tcp      open    ssh
53/tcp      open    domain
88/tcp      open    kerberos-sec
135/tcp     open    msrpc
139/tcp     open    netbios-ssn
389/tcp     open    ldap
445/tcp     open    microsoft-ds
464/tcp     open    kpasswd5
593/tcp     open    http-rpc-epmap
636/tcp     closed  ldapssl
3268/tcp    open    globalcatLDAP
3269/tcp    closed  globalcatLDAPssl
49152/tcp   open    unknown
49153/tcp   open    unknown
49154/tcp   open    unknown
49155/tcp   open    unknown
49157/tcp   open    unknown
49158/tcp   open    unknown
49159/tcp   open    unknown
```

b) Select the **Host Details** tab.

c) Verify the number of ports on the host that are open, filtered, and closed.

Closed ports are accessible, but no applications are responding to any requests on these ports.
Filtered ports are unreachable by the scan, usually because they are being blocked by a firewall.

3. Save the report.

a) From the top-left of the **Zenmap** window, select **Scan→Save Scan**.

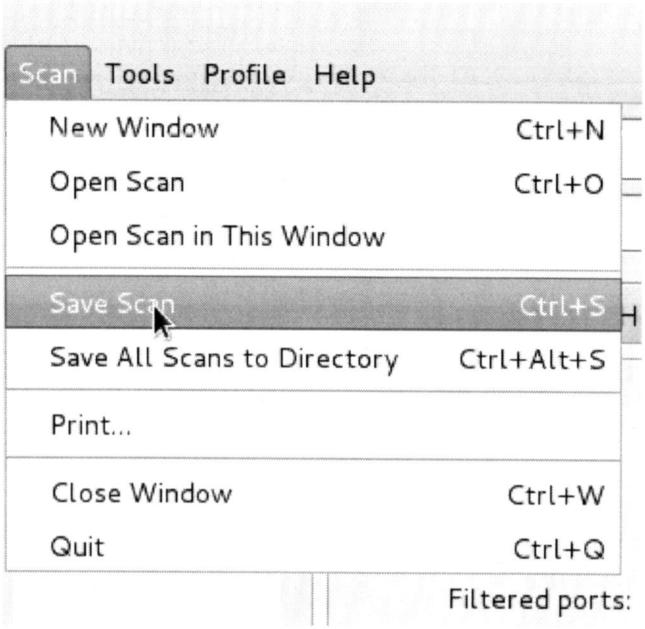

b) In the **Name** text box, type **server##_portscan** where **##** is your unique student number.
c) In the navigation pane, select **Desktop**.
d) Select **Save**, then close **Zenmap**.

Protocol Analyzers

A *protocol analyzer* can decode and analyze the traffic sent over a network communication session. By presenting the conversation to the end user in an easily understood manner, this decode process simplifies the interpretation of the protocols used in the traffic. Protocol analyzers are useful for diagnosing network connectivity issues, detecting anomalous network behavior, and gathering traffic statistics that can be used to assess which protocols are most vulnerable in a network.

Similar to a protocol analyzer, a *packet analyzer* captures and decodes the actual content of particular network packets sent using various network protocols. This can be useful for filtering certain packets from communicating across the network, as well as verifying that security controls, like firewalls, are working as intended.

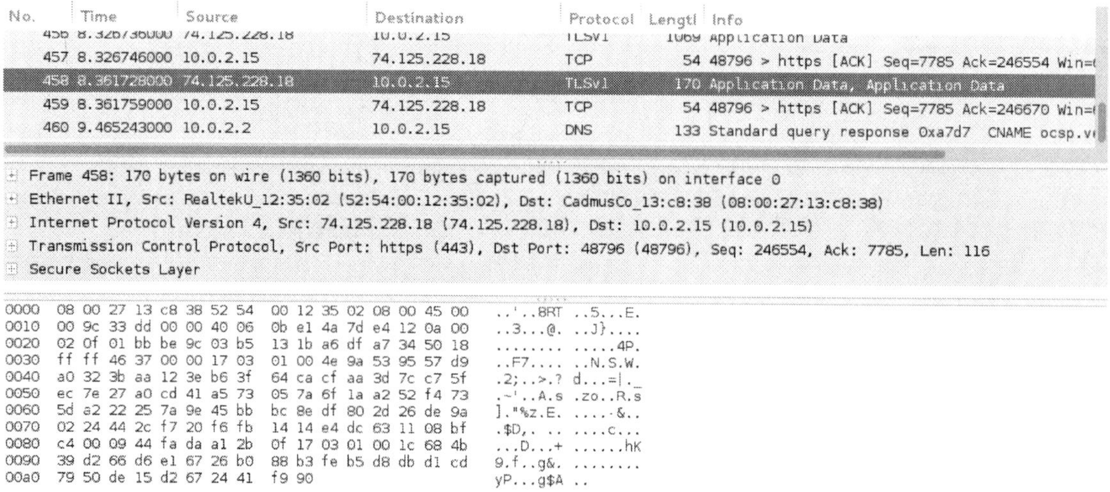

Figure 11–6: The results of a packet analysis.

Examples

The most popular protocol/packet analyzer is Wireshark®, which has an easy-to-use GUI and many built-in analysis features. Other protocol/packet analyzers include NetStumbler, dsniff, OmniPeek®, Ettercap, Microsoft Message Analyzer, tcpdump, WinDump, and Cain & Abel.

ACTIVITY 11-4
Using a Protocol Analyzer

Before You Begin

Your Windows Server 2012 computer is hosting an insecure File Transfer Protocol (FTP) server. You will use the protocol/packet analyzer Wireshark to capture packets sent to this FTP server.

Scenario

One of the most powerful tools in any security professional's arsenal is one that can analyze protocols used in network transmissions and decode the contents of network packets sent over the wire. Using the popular network analysis program Wireshark, you'll identify and assess how particular protocols and communications are vulnerable to attack. Using your recently created FTP server as an example, you'll discover what kinds of information an attacker can capture by simply sniffing packets that get sent over the network. Transmissions that are easily decodable can put your network and its sensitive data in jeopardy, and analysis tools like Wireshark will help you uncover the weaknesses inherent in your network communications.

1. Start Wireshark and begin listening for network transmissions.
    a) From the Kali Linux desktop, select **Applications→Kali Linux→Top 10 Security Tools→wireshark**.
    b) Select **OK** twice to close both warning messages.
    c) In **The Wireshark Network Analyzer** window, under the **Capture** column, select the **eth0** network adapter.

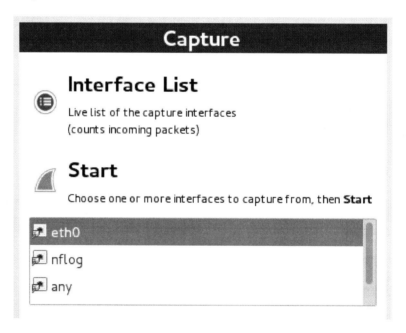

    d) Select **Start**.
       Wireshark will begin listening to network traffic on your VM's primary network adapter.

2. Generate FTP traffic over the network.
    a) Open the **Terminal**.
    b) At the prompt, enter *ftp HOST_IP* where *HOST_IP* is your host server's IP address.

c) Verify that you successfully connected to the FTP server.

```
root@kali:~# ftp 192.168.36.100
Connected to 192.168.36.100.
220 Microsoft FTP Service
Name (192.168.36.100:root):
```

d) At the **Name** prompt, enter *Administrator*

e) At the **Password** prompt, enter *!Pass1234*

 Caution: Be careful when inputting the password, as the characters will not appear for you to check.

f) Verify that you are logged in.

```
root@kali:~# ftp 192.168.36.100
Connected to 192.168.36.100.
220 Microsoft FTP Service
Name (192.168.36.100:root): Administrator
331 Password required
Password:
230 User logged in.
Remote system type is Windows_NT.
ftp>
```

3. Analyze the packets captured by Wireshark.

a) Close the terminal window and return to Wireshark.

b) From the toolbar, select the **Stop the running live capture** button.

c) If necessary, drag the middle pane down so that you can see the individual packets more easily.

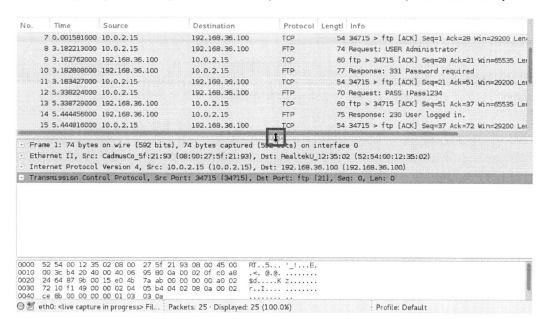

d) Verify that Wireshark captured several packets, and that each packet is classified in the following ways:
- The time it was captured.
- Its source IP address.
- Its destination IP address.
- The protocol it used to communicate.
- Its payload length in bits.
- Information about its content.

e) Find the FTP packet that reveals the Administrator user name and select it.

```
 6 0.001556000 192.168.36.100    10.0.2.15        FTP    81 Response: 220 Microsoft FTP Service
 7 0.001581000 10.0.2.15         192.168.36.100   TCP    54 34715 > ftp [ACK] Seq=1 Ack=28 Win=29200
 8 3.182213000 10.0.2.15         192.168.36.100   FTP    74 Request: USER Administrator
 9 3.182762000 192.168.36.100    10.0.2.15        TCP    60 ftp > 34715 [ACK] Seq=28 Ack=21 Win=6553
10 3.182808000 192.168.36.100    10.0.2.15        FTP    77 Response: 331 Password required
```

f) In the bottom pane, verify that the packet contents include the Administrator user name in plaintext.

```
0010   00 3c b4 24 40 00 40 06   95 6c 0a 00 02 0f c0 a8   .<.$@.@. .l......
0020   24 64 87 9b 00 15 e0 4b   7a ac 03 55 84 1d 50 18   $d.....K z..U..P.
0030   72 10 f1 49 00 00 55 53   45 52 20 41 64 6d 69 6e   r..I..US ER Admin
0040   69 73 74 72 61 74 6f 72   0d 0a                     istrator ..
```

g) Analyze the FTP packet that reveals the Administrator password, and verify that the password was also sent in plaintext.

```
0010   00 38 b4 26 40 00 40 06   95 6e 0a 00 02 0f c0 a8   .8.&@.@. .n......
0020   24 64 87 9b 00 15 e0 4b   7a c0 03 55 84 34 50 18   $d.....K z..U.4P.
0030   72 10 f1 45 00 00 50 41   53 53 20 21 50 61 73 73   r..E..PA SS !Pass
0040   31 32 33 34 0d 0a                                    1234..
```

4. Save the capture.
   a) Select **File→Save As**.
   b) Navigate to the desktop and save the file as *ftp_packetcap*

    Note: The default file format is .pcapng, which improves on the traditional .pcap format.

   c) Close Wireshark.

Network Enumerators

A *network enumerator* gathers information on users, groups, and services on a network without authenticating to the device. Network enumerators often use protocols like ICMP and SNMP to discover network hosts and retrieve the information. Networks vulnerable to enumeration can assist an intruder in the preparatory phase by providing them with information that can shape their attack. For instance, an attacker who uses a network enumerator may be able to find a seldom-used or poorly secured administrator account that they can focus their password cracking attempts on. Enumerators can reveal many other directory-related vulnerabilities in your network that you need to address.

```
Host script results:
|_nbstat: NetBIOS name: JSMITH-PC, NetBIOS user: <unknown>, NetBIOS MAC: c4:60:00:3f:c4:a7
(Asustek Computer)
| smb-os-discovery:
|   OS: Windows 7 Professional 7601 Service Pack 1 (Windows 7 Professional 6.1)
|   OS CPE: cpe:/o:microsoft:windows_7::sp1:professional
|   Computer name: JSmith-PC
|   NetBIOS computer name: JSmith-PC
|   Domain name: int.develetech.com
|   Forest name: int.develetech.com
|   FQDN: JSmith-PC.int.develetech.com
|_  System time: 2014-09-17T10:22:19-04:00
| smb-security-mode:
|   Account that was used for smb scripts: guest
|   User-level authentication
|   SMB Security: Challenge/response passwords supported
|_  Message signing disabled (dangerous, but default)
|_smbv2-enabled: Server supports SMBv2 protocol
```

Figure 11-7: The results of a network enumeration.

Examples

Examples of network enumerators include Nmap, Nessus®, snmpwalk, and Cain & Abel.

ACTIVITY 11-5
Using a Network Enumerator

Before You Begin

You and your fellow students have your hosts on the same subnet, and the last octet of each host's IP address is #, where # is unique to each student.

Your host firewall has been pre-configured to allow outbound network discovery traffic.

Scenario

A crucial part of any tester's reconnaissance will be the enumeration of the enterprise's network. You can learn more about the high-level topology or the individual nodes in your network, and what an enumeration reveals can point to vulnerabilities within these components. So, you will begin by attempting to discover the hosts on one of your network's subnets using Nmap. After you've found active hosts in this subnet, you'll begin to fingerprint each one to learn more about what operating systems they are running and how each host is uniquely identified. This information may indicate vulnerabilities in legitimate hosts, like an unpatched operating system or obsolete network protocol, or it may even reveal rogue devices attached to your network if the device's characteristics aren't consistent with your policy.

---

1. Enumerate the student hosts on your subnet.

   a) Open Zenmap.

   b) In the **Command** text box, type *nmap -sn 192.168.y.#-#* where *y* is your subnet and *#-#* is the range your classroom setup is using. For example, if the instructor's host is 192.168.1.100, and there are 20 students in the class, then you would type *nmap -sn 192.168.1.100-120*
   The **sn** flag turns off port scanning and Nmap will simply scan for hosts in the range you specified.

   c) Select **Scan** and verify that Nmap displays a list of all student hosts.

```
Nmap scan report for 192.168.36.108
Host is up (2.2s latency).
Nmap scan report for 192.168.36.109
Host is up (2.0s latency).
Nmap scan report for 192.168.36.110
Host is up (2.0s latency).
Nmap scan report for 192.168.36.111
Host is up (2.0s latency).
Nmap scan report for 192.168.36.112
Host is up (2.0s latency).
Nmap scan report for 192.168.36.113
Host is up (3.2s latency).
Nmap scan report for 192.168.36.114
Host is up (3.2s latency).
```

 Note: Depending on the range, it may take a moment for the scan to complete.

2. Use the enumerated hosts to scan thoroughly once more.

---

a) Choose any active student host in the list of hosts you just enumerated and remember its IP address.

b) In the **Command** text box, type *nmap -T4 -A -F TARGET_IP* where *TARGET_IP* is the IP address of the student host you chose.

   The **T4** flag performs a fast, aggressive scan. The **A** flag detects operating system and version information, and performs a script scan. The **F** flag scans fewer ports than the default scan would.

c) Select **Scan** and verify that Nmap outputs scan results similar to a port scan, but with more information about the operating system and protocol versions under the **VERSION** column.

 Note: It may take a moment for the scan to complete.

d) Scroll down to the **Host script results** section and verify that Nmap ran a script that outputs more information about the target host, including:

   - The NetBIOS name.
   - The NetBIOS MAC address.
   - The operating system and version.
   - The computer name.
   - The domain and forest names.
   - Server Message Block (SMB) security configurations.

```
Host script results:
|_nbstat: NetBIOS name: SERVER100, NetBIOS user: <unknown>, NetBIOS MAC: c8:60:00:33:c4:a9
(Asustek Computer)
| smb-os-discovery:
|   OS: Windows Server 2012 R2 Standard 9600 (Windows Server 2012 R2 Standard 6.3)
|   OS CPE: cpe:/o:microsoft:windows_server_2012::-
|   Computer name: Server100
|   NetBIOS computer name: SERVER100
|   Domain name: domain100.internal
|   Forest name: domain100.internal
|   FQDN: Server100.domain100.internal
|_  System time: 2014-07-10T12:53:53-07:00
| smb-security-mode:
|   Account that was used for smb scripts: guest
|   User-level authentication
|   SMB Security: Challenge/response passwords supported
|_  Message signing required
|_smbv2-enabled: Server supports SMBv2 protocol
```

3. Save the report.

   a) Select **Scan→Save Scan**.

   b) In the **Choose a scan to save** dialog box, select the drop-down arrow and select the scan you just performed on the specific host.

   c) Select **Save**.

   d) In the **Name** text box, type *server##_enumeration* where *server##* is the computer name of the host you scanned.

   e) In the navigation pane, select **Desktop**.

   f) Select **Save**, then close **Zenmap** without saving the other scan.

Password Crackers

A *password cracker* is used to recover secret passwords from data stored or transmitted by a computer. Password crackers typically crack passwords in one of the following three methods: brute-force, dictionary, or hybrid.

Brute-force password cracking uses random characters and numbers to crack a password. Brute-force password cracking is extremely resource intensive and can take a long time to be successful, as password crackers generate every possible permutation for a given set of characters and numbers defined by a minimum and maximum length. This process can take anywhere from seconds to thousands of years depending on the strength and complexity of the password being cracked.

Dictionary password cracking uses a targeted technique of successively trying all the words in a pre-written, exhaustive list. This type of password cracking is typically faster than brute-force attacks, as it only tries possible passwords that are likely to be found or used. The main reason dictionary password cracking tends to be successful is because many people have a tendency to choose passwords that are short, single words found in standard dictionaries, and easily predicted variations on words such as appending a digit or special character to a simple word.

Hybrid password cracking uses a combination of both brute-force and dictionary password cracking techniques. A hybrid password cracking application will modify a wordlist or dictionary by making common substitutions to letters, such as replacing the letter "a" with the "@" sign. These tools also typically append characters and numbers to the end of dictionary words; for example, the password "password" may be guessed as: p@ssword, p@ssw0rd, password1, password01, pa$$word, and so on. This technique tends to be faster than standard brute-force attacks, but slower than standard dictionary attacks.

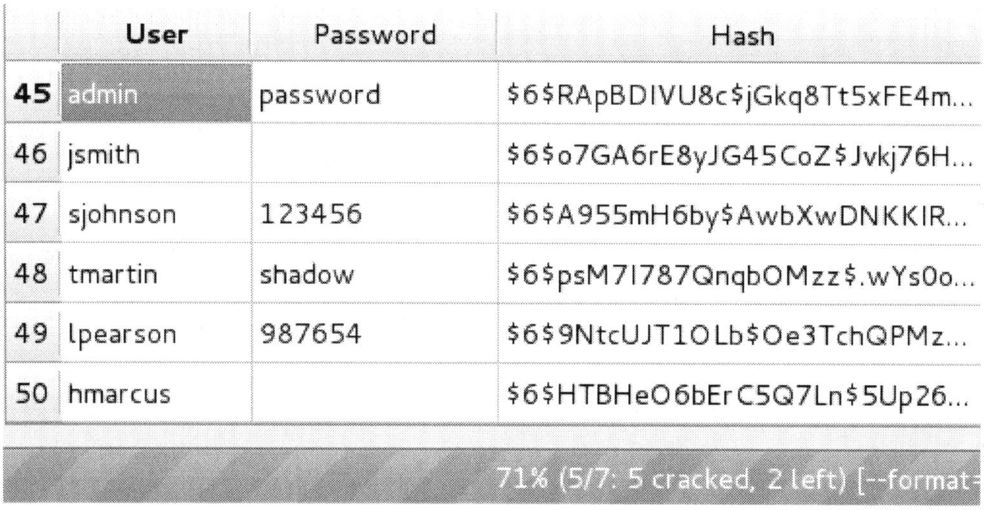

	User	Password	Hash
45	admin	password	6RApBDIVU8c$jGkq8Tt5xFE4m...
46	jsmith		6o7GA6rE8yJG45CoZ$Jvkj76H...
47	sjohnson	123456	6A955mH6by$AwbXwDNKKIR...
48	tmartin	shadow	6psM71787QnqbOMzz$.wYsOo...
49	lpearson	987654	$6$9NtcUJT1OLb$Oe3TchQPMz...
50	hmarcus		6HTBHeO6bErC5Q7Ln$5Up26...

71% (5/7: 5 cracked, 2 left) [--format=

Figure 11-8: The results of a password crack.

Examples

Examples of password crackers include John the Ripper, Cain & Abel, THC-Hydra, pwdump, Ophcrack, and Medusa.

ACTIVITY 11-6
Using a Password Cracker

Before You Begin

You will be using John the Ripper, a password cracking utility. Kali Linux user account passwords are stored using the SHA-512 hash function.

Scenario

Because passwords are so ubiquitous in the everyday function of any organization, you realize how important it is to ensure that the passwords Develetech uses are suitably strong. Short and simplistic passwords are easy prey for password cracking tools, which often use a combination of dictionary and brute force attacks to reveal the plaintext source of a hashed value.

Lately, you've been concerned that your IT team is not properly following your password policy. You'll demonstrate to them using John the Ripper how easy it is to crack short passwords or passwords based on common dictionary words. An attacker who gains access to a host's password hash database will make short work of such weak credentials, seriously threatening the security of the enterprise's systems.

---

1. Create a test account with a weak password.
   a) From the Kali Linux desktop, select **Applications→System Tools→Preferences→System Settings**.
   b) In the **System Settings** window, in the **System** section, double-click **User Accounts**.
   c) In the **User Accounts** window, select the plus sign to add an account.

   d) In the **Create new account** dialog box, in the **Full name** text box, type *testaccount*
   e) Select **Create**.

f) With **testaccount** selected, select **Account disabled**.

g) In the **Changing password for testaccount** dialog box, in the **New password** text box, type *security*
h) In the **Confirm password** text box, type the same password.
i) Verify that the dialog box indicates that the password is weak.

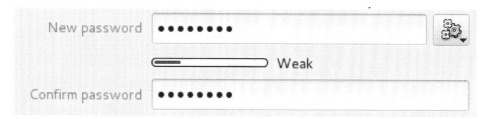

j) Select **Change**.
k) Close the **User Accounts** window.

2. Crack the password hash using John the Ripper.
   a) Select **Applications→Kali Linux→Password Attacks→Offline Attacks→johnny**.

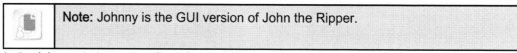
   Note: Johnny is the GUI version of John the Ripper.

   b) In the **Johnny** window, select **Open Passwd File**.
   c) Navigate to **/etc** and open the **shadow** file.
   The Kali Linux user account hashes are stored in this **shadow.txt** file.
   d) Verify that the root user is listed, and scroll down to the end and verify that the testaccount user is also listed.

e) From the navigation pane on the left, select **Options**.

f) From the **Format** drop-down list, select **crypt**.
This indicates that John the Ripper will use different hash functions (including SHA-512) at the same time to crack passwords.

g) Verify that the **Mode selection and settings** is set to **Default behavior**.
John the Ripper will start with a fast "single crack" mode, which uses plaintext account and system information like full names and home directory names to use as password guesses. It then moves on to a dictionary attack using a basic wordlist, and ends with a thorough brute force attack.

h) From the navigation pane, return to **Passwords** and select **Start Attack**.

i) Verify that John the Ripper cracks both the root password (**toor**) and the testaccount password (**security**).

	User	Password	Hash
1	root	toor	X014elvznJq7E
45	testaccount	security	6Mn7qhhniOP...

j) Close the **Johnny** window.

Fuzzers

A *fuzzer* sends an application random input data to see if it will crash or expose a vulnerability. These tools can be useful in detecting any faults in an application, especially web apps, that will expose sensitive information.

A good fuzzer should be protocol aware and capable of scripting so that it can provide a thorough test of known problems with the protocol being tested. Advanced fuzzers can process and decode responses within applications or the protocol being tested. These responses can be used to craft or build further requests to target potential vulnerabilities found in different states of the protocol or application being fuzzed.

Figure 11-9: An application that has crashed due to fuzzing.

Examples

Examples of fuzzers include Peach Fuzzer™, w3af, Simple Fuzzer, skipfish, and SPIKE.

ACTIVITY 11-7
Using a Fuzzer

Data Files

C:\093023Data\Conducting Vulnerability Assessments\vulnerable-echo-server.c

C:\093023Data\Conducting Vulnerability Assessments\buff-fuzz.cfg

Before You Begin

You will be fuzzing a TCP echo server written in C to detect a buffer overflow vulnerability. You will need a removable USB drive to transfer the source code and configuration file to your guest VM. You may also exchange the files from host to guest using email.

Scenario

Develetech has plans to develop new applications to extend their market presence and fulfill customer needs. As a security professional, you understand that any application is vulnerable to attacks that exploit input variables. The effects of such an attack will vary depending on the attack's payload and the app it targets, but certain malicious or even accidental inputs may compromise your app's confidentiality, integrity, or availability.

To demonstrate the risk that poor or non-existent input validation brings to an app, you'll use a fuzzer called Simple Fuzzer to send a TCP echo server app an input that exceeds its assigned buffer space. When you see for yourself how certain fuzzing techniques can harm an app, you'll be better prepared to communicate to your development team the importance of proper input and memory handling.

---

1. Transfer the data files to the guest VM.

   a) Put the data files **vulnerable-echo-server.c** and **buff-fuzz.cfg** on a removable USB drive and make sure the drive is inserted into a port on your host computer.

   b) From the **VirtualBox VM** window, select **Devices→USB Devices→USB Driver** to activate your USB drive on the guest.

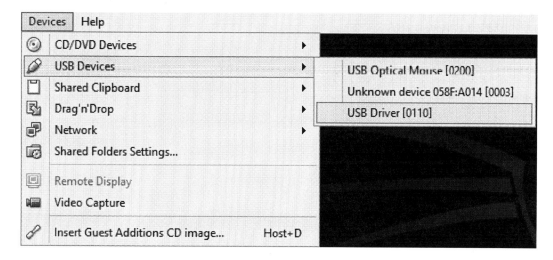

Note: Your USB device driver may appear differently in the VirtualBox menu.

c) If your USB device did not open automatically, from the Kali Linux desktop, double-click **Computer** and select your USB drive.

d) Copy the **vulnerable-echo-server.c** and **buff-fuzz.cfg** files from your USB drive to the **/root** directory.

e) Right-click your USB drive and select **Safely Remove Drive**, then remove your USB drive from your computer.

2. Inspect the vulnerability in the echo server's source code.

a) Double-click **vulnerable-echo-server.c** to open the source code in VIM, a text editor.

This application creates a TCP server that a client connects to. The client can send a string input to the server, and the server then echoes this string back to the client.

b) If necessary, scroll down to view the **void copy_data** function.

```
void copy_data(char *buffer, int buffer_len)
{
        char vulnerable_buffer[100];

        memcpy(vulnerable_buffer, buffer, buffer_len);

}
```

This function creates a buffer of size 100 bytes, and allows the application to copy memory into this buffer. However, this code does not check to see if the length of the memory exceeds the buffer. Any input that exceeds 100 bytes will overflow the buffer.

c) Close the VIM window.

3. Compile the source code to create the server executable, then run the server.

a) Open a terminal.

b) At the command prompt, enter `gcc ./vulnerable-echo-server.c -o echoserv`
This command compiles the source code and outputs an executable named **echoserv** at the root folder.

c) At the command prompt, enter `./echoserv 9999`
This runs the server on localhost (127.0.0.1) and has it listen on port 9999.

d) Keep the server terminal running.

4. Verify that the server is operational.

a) Open a new terminal and enter `telnet 127.0.0.1 9999`

b) Verify that you are connected to the server, then enter `hello` at the prompt.

```
root@kali:~# ./echoserv 9999
New Client connected from port no 50280 and IP 127.0.0.1
Sent message: hello

                                                        root@kali: ~

    File  Edit  View  Search  Terminal  Help
    root@kali:~# telnet 127.0.0.1 9999
    Trying 127.0.0.1...
    Connected to 127.0.0.1.
    Escape character is '^]'.
    hello
    hello
```

The server echoes the message back to you, and the terminal running the server also displays the message sent to it.

c) Close the Telnet client terminal and return to the file manager.

5. Inspect the configuration file and run Simple Fuzzer with it loaded.
   a) Double-click **buff-fuzz.cfg** to open it in VIM.
   b) Verify that the `sequence` is "X" and the `maxseqlen` is "500".

```
sequence=X

maxseqlen=500

endcfg
FUZZ
--
~
~
~
~
```

   Simple Fuzzer will use this configuration file to send 500 bytes of the letter "X" to the echo server.
   c) Close VIM.

6. Run the fuzzer.
   a) Open a new terminal and enter `sfuzz -TO -f buff-fuzz.cfg -S 127.0.0.1 -p 9999`
   This runs Simple Fuzzer on the TCP echo server listening on port 9999 of localhost. The configuration file defines what fuzzing actions Simple Fuzzer will take.
   b) Switch to the terminal running the server and verify that your message was sent and received by the server, which suffered a segmentation fault.

   Because your fuzzing input of 500 bytes exceeded the 100 byte buffer, the echo server crashed.
   c) Using a terminal, attempt to connect to the echo server again using Telnet. Verify that you are unable to connect.

```
root@kali:~# telnet 127.0.0.1 9999
Trying 127.0.0.1...
telnet: Unable to connect to remote host: Connection refused
root@kali:~#
```

7. Close all open windows in Kali Linux.

HTTP Interceptors

An *HTTP interceptor* is an application or device used to read HTTP communications or web traffic. In most cases, HTTP interceptors work just like standard HTTP proxies by forwarding traffic from the tester's web browser to the web server. This proxy tends to be an application running on the tester's local system, but it can reside on the network if it is configured to operate in that manner. The HTTP interceptor will monitor or capture every request and response made to or from the web application. This type of tool is extremely useful for a penetration tester, as it can make data normally not visible to the tester, like POST data values and HTTP headers, easily accessible.

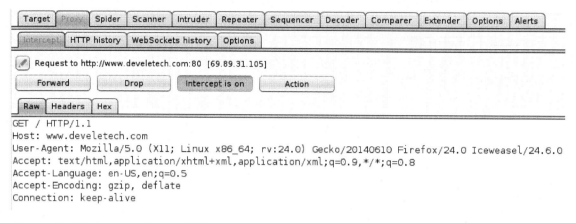

Figure 11-10: Intercepting an HTTP request.

Examples

Some examples of HTTP interceptors include Burp Suite, Paros, WebScarab, and Fiddler.

ACTIVITY 11-8
Using an HTTP Interceptor

Before You Begin

You will be using Burp Suite, a web application testing platform with an integrated HTTP interceptor. You'll also configure the Iceweasel web browser to use this interceptor proxy.

Scenario

Like most organizations, Develetech sees enormous amounts of HTTP traffic pass through the network throughout the workday. Because the web is such a popular target for attackers, you want to make sure that this traffic is not opening the enterprise up to any excessive risk. The types of web-based data sent to and received from the Internet are of particular concern. For example, an HTTP request or response with certain HTML parameters may open up a cross-site scripting (XSS) vulnerability to the client, compromising their host.

To ensure that your employees use the web in compliance with policy and that they don't introduce vulnerabilities into the organization, you'll use a proxy to intercept HTTP traffic from both the client and server and review its details. For now, you'll test your intercepting capabilities on your virtual machine to glean more information about simple requests and responses. With this experience, you'll be more prepared to define complex HTTP interception rules to later apply to your network as a whole.

---

1. Open Burp Suite to its HTTP interceptor function.
   a) From the Kali Linux desktop, select **Applications→Kali Linux→Web Applications→Web Vulnerability Scanners→burpsuite**.
   b) In the **Burp Suite Free Edition** window, select **I Accept** to confirm the licensing agreement.
   c) In the **Burp Suite Free Edition v1.6** window, select the **Proxy** tab.

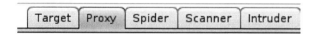

   d) Select the **Options** subtab.

2. Verify and configure interceptor settings.

---

a) In the **Proxy Listeners** section, verify that your localhost (127.0.0.1) is using a proxy to listen in on HTTP traffic that passes through it.

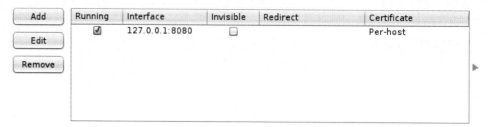

The proxy is listening on port 8080.

b) In the **Intercept Client Requests** section, verify that the proxy will intercept client requests based on certain rules.

By default, the interceptor will not display request information that is in a format like .jpg or .png.

c) In the **Intercept Server Responses** section, check the **Intercept responses based on the following rules** check box.

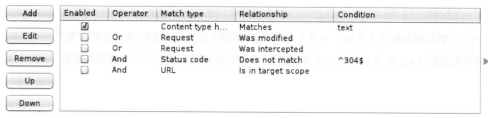

By default, the interceptor will capture responses to requests and display information that matches a text format.

3. Configure Iceweasel to use the proxy.

a) Open the Iceweasel web browser.

b) Select **Edit→Preferences**.

c) In the **Iceweasel Preferences** window, select the **Advanced** tab.

General   Tabs   Content   Applications   Privacy   Security   Sync   Advanced

d) Select the **Network** subtab.

e) In the **Connection** section, select **Settings**.
f) In the **Connection Settings** dialog box, select **Manual proxy configuration**.
g) In the **HTTP Proxy** text box, type *127.0.0.1*
h) In the corresponding **Port** text box, type *8080*

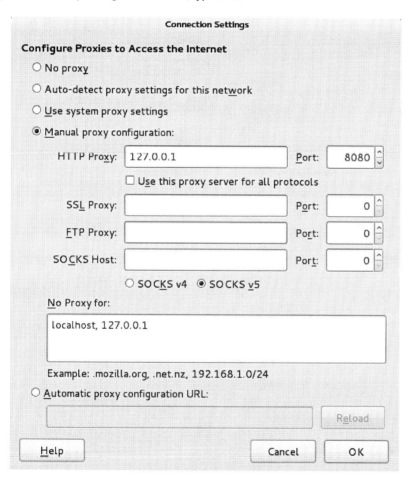

i) Select **OK**, then select **Close**.

4. Attempt to connect to **www.google.com** and intercept the request.
   a) Navigate to **www.google.com**.
   b) Verify that your connection to Google stalls.
   c) Open up Burp Suite and select the **Intercept** subtab.

d) Verify that your interceptor proxy has captured the HTTP GET request that you just initiated.

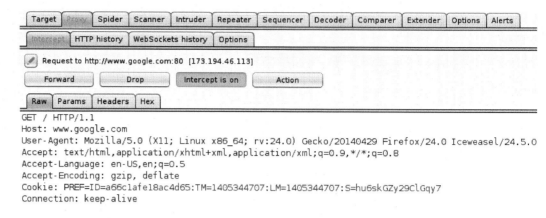

The interceptor collects information about the request, including:

- The host site it was sent to.
- The browser used.
- The data, language, and encoding types it is using.
- Cookie information.
- Connection status.

5. Forward the request and intercept the response.
   a) Select **Forward** to allow the connection to proceed.
   b) Verify that your interceptor proxy captured Google's response to the request.

```
HTTP/1.1 302 Found
Location: https://www.google.com/?gws_rd=ssl
Cache-Control: private
Content-Type: text/html; charset=UTF-8
Set-Cookie:
NID=67=LALF(3Cq5juculp6G4RNLR4etMeYh7htOR2KMvL8JsBYxlPpr2hlwklwYiSheUZHHX9luCJZaVZOBCrWwQq-DidwQdRPDAIQhD3N5rgDgGcSSPSWZ
wcekw6cmIq51D8o; expires=Tue, 13-Jan-2015 14:10:28 GMT; path=/; domain=.google.com; HttpOnly
P3P: CP="This is not a P3P policy! See http://www.google.com/support/accounts/bin/answer.py?hl=en&answer=151657 for
more info."
Date: Mon, 14 Jul 2014 14:10:28 GMT
Server: gws
Content-Length: 231
X-XSS-Protection: 1; mode=block
X-Frame-Options: SAMEORIGIN
Alternate-Protocol: 80:quic
```

The interceptor collects information about the response, including:

- The time and location it originates from.
- The type of content it uses.
- Cookie information.
- Scripting protection information.

   c) Forward the response, and, if necessary, forward any subsequent requests and responses.

   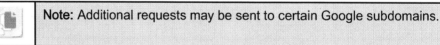

   Note: Additional requests may be sent to certain Google subdomains.

   d) Return to Iceweasel and verify that you have successfully connected to Google's home page.

6. Stop Iceweasel from using the proxy.
   a) Select **Edit→Preferences**.
   b) From the **Advanced** tab, select the **Network** subtab and select **Settings**.
   c) Select **No proxy** and select **OK**.
   d) Select **Close**, then close Iceweasel and Burp Suite.

Exploitation Tools and Frameworks

An *exploitation framework* provides a consistent and reliable environment to create and execute exploit code against a target. Exploit frameworks have drastically changed the exploitation process: in the past, an attacker would have to code custom one-off exploits for each and every vulnerability being targeted. Now attackers can customize scripts and variable settings found within the exploit frameworks to modify exploits for hundreds of different targets and systems.

There are many benefits provided by exploit frameworks, but one of the most valuable is the modularization of exploit code that has encouraged code reuse. Before these frameworks existed, exploits and payloads were heavily tied to a given exploit and would normally only do one thing or carry out a single action. This one thing or single action could be something like creating a new user on the compromised system or executing a command shell. Now, with exploit frameworks, a single exploit can be used to deliver virtually any payload within the framework.

```
[---]           The Social-Engineer Toolkit (SET)          [---]
[---]            Created by: David Kennedy (ReL1K)          [---]
[---]                    Version: 6.0                       [---]
[---]                 Codename: 'Rebellion'                 [---]
[---]          Follow us on Twitter: @TrustedSec            [---]
[---]          Follow me on Twitter: @HackingDave            [---]
[---]        Homepage: https://www.trustedsec.com           [---]

        Welcome to the Social-Engineer Toolkit (SET).
         The one stop shop for all of your SE needs.

      Join us on irc.freenode.net in channel #setoolkit

   The Social-Engineer Toolkit is a product of TrustedSec.

             Visit: https://www.trustedsec.com

Select from the menu:

   1) Social-Engineering Attacks
   2) Fast-Track Penetration Testing
   3) Third Party Modules
   4) Update the Metasploit Framework
   5) Update the Social-Engineer Toolkit
   6) Update SET configuration
   7) Help, Credits, and About
```

Figure 11–11: An exploitation framework.

Examples

Currently there are three frameworks that are widely used: Metasploit®, CANVAS, and Core Impact. Other exploitation tools include Social-Engineer Toolkit, w3af, and sqlmap.

ACTIVITY 11-9
Using an Exploitation Framework

Before You Begin

You will be working with a partner in this activity. You will be attacking your partner's Remote Desktop Protocol (RDP) with the Social-Engineer Toolkit, an exploitation framework that interfaces with Metasploit and other tools.

Scenario

Exploitation frameworks provide a great way to custom-tailor a penetration test to attack a system, and you can see the benefit of trying the many different test scenarios that these frameworks offer. What you choose will depend heavily on your security needs, but for now, you want to test out one of the attack scenarios on your systems to see how effective they really can be.

You've noticed that some of your network administrators have been using the Windows built-in RDP to remote into their servers, and have experienced some crashes and outright loss of functionality at times. You've discovered that the Social-Engineer Toolkit has a custom scenario for initiating a Denial of Service (DoS) attack on an RDP, so you run this scenario to assess how vulnerable your RDP version is and how easily its security can be compromised.

 Note: This exploit targets an RDP vulnerability that fails to correctly process packets in memory. The exploit creates specialized RDP packets that attempt to access an object that is not correctly initialized in memory or has been deleted, causing RDP to crash.

1. Enable Windows Remote Desktop on your host computer.
   a) Switch to your Windows Server 2012 R2 host, right-click the **Start** button and select **System**.
   b) From the navigation pane on the left, select **Remote settings**.

   Control Panel Home

   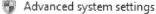

   c) In the **Systems Properties** dialog box, in the **Remote Desktop** section, select the **Allow remote connections to this computer** radio button.
   d) Select **OK** twice to accept the warning and close the dialog box.
   e) Close the **System** window.

2. Verify that you can connect to your partner's host over Remote Desktop.
   a) Open a command prompt on your Windows host.
   b) At the prompt, enter **mstsc** to open the **Remote Desktop Connection** window.
   c) In the **Computer** text box, enter the IP address of your partner's host and select **Connect**.

d) Verify that a **Windows Security** window opens and asks for credentials, verifying that you can connect to your partner's host.

e) Close the **Windows Security** window.

3. Use the SE Toolkit to initiate a DoS condition on your partner's RDP service.
    a) Switch to your Kali Linux VM and open a terminal.
    b) At the command prompt, enter `setoolkit`
    c) Enter **y** to accept the repository updates, then enter **y** again to accept the terms of service.

d) At the prompt, enter **2** to select **Fast-Track Penetration Testing**.
    e) Enter **2** to select **Custom Exploits**.
    f) Enter **4** to select **RDP | Use after Free - Denial of Service**.
    g) At the **Enter the IP address to crash (remote desktop)** prompt, enter your partner's host IP address.

4. Verify that your DoS attack successfully took down your partner's RDP service.
    a) Return to your Windows Server host and the **Remote Desktop Connection** window.
    b) With your partner's IP address in the **Computer** text box, select **Connect**.

c) Verify that you are unable to connect, indicating that your DoS condition was successful.

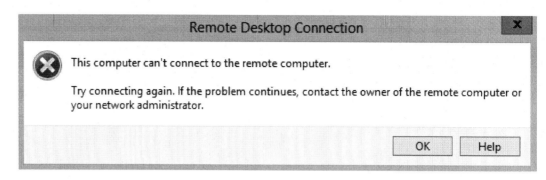

5. Close the terminal on the Kali Linux VM and close any open command prompts and Remote Desktop windows on the Windows Server host.

Passive Reconnaissance and Intelligence Gathering Tools

A *passive reconnaissance tool*, also known as an *intelligence gathering tool*, aids in the process of footprinting a system to discover key information without being detected. There are several methods of discretely gathering system and network intelligence, such as:

- Taking advantage of people's tendency to reveal too much information on social media sites like Facebook, LinkedIn, and Twitter.
- Using whois to retrieve Internet registration information like domain names, IP addresses, company names, geographic region, and contact information.
- Mapping a network's topology through exposed routing tables, thereby streamlining intrusion efforts.

Nodes	Type	Value	△ Wei...	Incom...	Outgo...
www.microsoft.com	Website	www.microsoft.com	0	0	21
65.55.57.27	IPv4 Addr..	65.55.57.27	100	1	0
IIS 8	Builtwith ..	IIS 8	100	1	0
ASP.NET	Builtwith ..	ASP.NET	100	1	0
Application Request Routing	Builtwith ..	Application Request..	100	1	0
IIS	Builtwith ..	IIS	100	1	0
WebTrends Optimize	Builtwith ..	WebTrends Optimize	100	1	0
jQuery Mobile	Builtwith ..	jQuery Mobile	100	1	0
jQuery 1.7.2	Builtwith ..	jQuery 1 7.2	100	1	0
jQuery	Builtwith ..	jQuery	100	1	0
newsletters@wideworldimporters.com	Email Ad...	newsletters@wide..	100	1	0
msccatus@microsoft.com	Email Ad..	msccatus@micros..	100	1	0
mslowend@msmexico.com.mx	Email Ad...	mslowend@msme..	100	1	0
support@hotmail.com	Email Ad ..	support@hotmail.c..	100	1	0
hotmailprivacy@hotmail.com	Email Ad...	hotmailprivacy@ho..	100	1	0

Figure 11-12: Gathering intelligence on a website.

Examples

Examples of passive reconnaissance tools include Netcraft, FOCA, and Maltego.

ACTIVITY 11-10
Using an Intelligence Gathering Tool

Before You Begin

You will be using Maltego, an open source intelligence gathering tool, to scan **www.comptia.org**. An email address is required to sign up with Maltego Community to use its intelligence gathering transforms.

Scenario

A crucial phase in any attack involves gathering information on the target. This gives the attacker unique and effective ways to compromise your security. For example, an external user might gather information on email addresses attached to your domain to identify potential targets for a social engineering attack. To mitigate such risks, you need to first identify what information your enterprise exposes to the wider world and how this information can be a vulnerability.

Once Develetech's new website is operational, you plan to use an intelligence gathering tool to see how much useful information you can glean from the perspective of an outside user. For now, you'll use Maltego to scan a website and visually represent the various pieces of information that it can discover about that site. With this knowledge, you can empower yourself to harden security where it's needed most—in the most public and exposed areas.

 Note: In this activity, you will try out the Maltego tool by scanning CompTIA's website, **www.comptia.org**.

---

1. Register an account with Maltego Community.
   a) From the Kali Linux desktop, select **Applications→Kali Linux→Information Gathering→OSINT Analysis→maltego**.
   b) In the **Welcome to Maltego!** wizard, select **Next**.
   c) On the **Login** page, select the **register here** link.

   The registration web page opens in Iceweasel.
   d) On the web page, in the **Register** section, fill out the forms with your information.
   e) When finished, select the **Register!** button.

f) Open your email and look for a message sent by **maltego@paterva.com**. Open the message and follow the activation link.

g) Select the **Activate Account** button and confirm that your account was activated.

> **Account successfully activated! You may now login into your Maltego community edition!**

h) Close any open browser windows and return to Maltego.

2. Log in to Maltego and update the transforms.
a) At the **Login** page of the wizard, type in your credentials and select **Next**.
b) On the **Login result** page, verify that you have successfully logged in and select **Next**.
c) On the **Select transform seeds** page, verify that **Maltego public servers** is checked and select **Next**. Maltego's transforms will start updating. Transforms are code that links information with other information or entities.
d) On the **Update transforms** page, select **Open a blank graph and let me play around**, then select **Finish**.

3. Run intelligence gathering transforms on CompTIA's website.
a) In the **Maltego Kali Linux Edition 3.4.0** window, from the **Palette** panel, select **Infrastructure**.

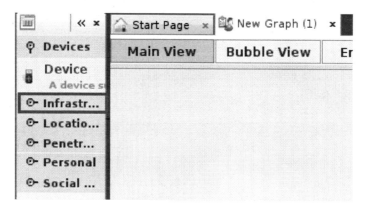

 Note: You may wish to drag the navigation panel to the right to make it easier to read.

b) Under **Infrastructure**, click and drag **Website** to the graph pane in the middle.

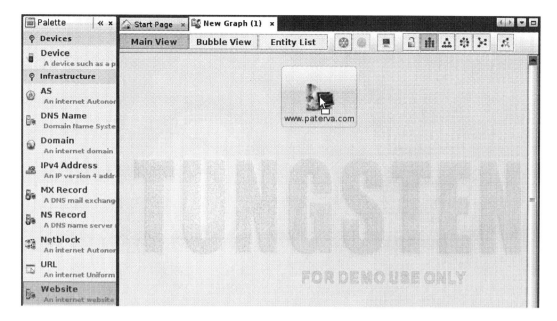

An icon appears to represent the website entity.

c) Double-click the **www.paterva.com** text under the Icon and enter *www.comptia.org*

d) Right-click the entity icon and select **Run Transform→Other transforms→Mirror: Email addresses found**.

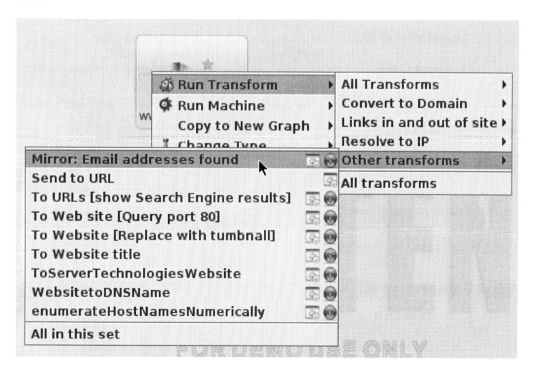

e) Right-click the entity icon and select **Run Transforms→Resolve to IP→To IP Address [DNS]**.

f) Right-click the entity icon and select **Run Transform→Other transforms→ToServerTechnologiesWebsite**.

g) In the **Required inputs** dialog box, check the **I accept the above disclaimer** check box and select **Run!**.

4. View the results of the transforms.

a) Verify that Maltego has created a graph with several different information types branching off of the main website entity.

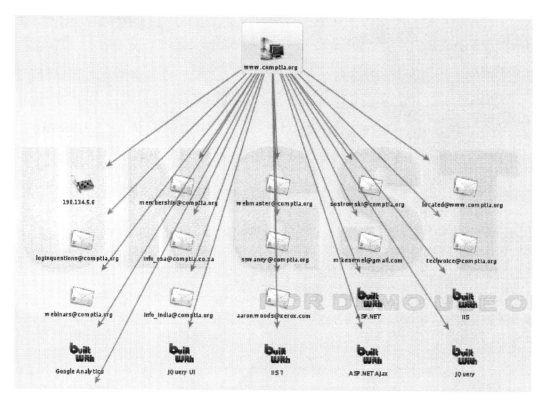

 Note: There are several ways you get can a better view of the main graph: use the **Zoom** controls on the ribbon, resize some of the surrounding panels, select the **Maximize Window** button at the top-right of the graph panel, or select within the **Overview** panel to focus on a specific area.

b) In the graph panel, select the **Entity List** button.

c) Verify that each information entity is listed.

✉ info_rsa@comptia.co.za	Email Add..	info_rsa@comptia.co.za	100	1	0	⭐
✉ loginquestions@comptia.org	Email Add..	loginquestions@comp..	100	1	0	⭐
✉ located@www.comptia.org	Email Add..	located@www.compti..	100	1	0	⭐
🖧 198.134.5.6	IPv4 Addr..	198.134.5.6	100	1	0	⭐
Telerik Sitefinity	BuiltWith ...	Telerik Sitefinity	100	1	0	⭐
jQuery	BuiltWith ...	jQuery	100	1	0	⭐
ASP.NET Ajax	BuiltWith ..	ASP.NET Ajax	100	1	0	⭐
IIS 7	BuiltWith ...	IIS 7	100	1	0	⭐
jQuery UI	BuiltWith ..	jQuery UI	100	1	0	⭐
Google Analytics	BuiltWith ...	Google Analytics	100	1	0	⭐
IIS	BuiltWith ..	IIS	100	1	0	⭐
ASP.NET	BuiltWith ...	ASP.NET	100	1	0	⭐

Using the transforms you chose, Maltego has gathered certain information about CompTIA's website, including email addresses associated with the site, the IP address of the site, and the types of technology with which the website was built.

5. Save your work.
   a) Select the **Application Menu** button.

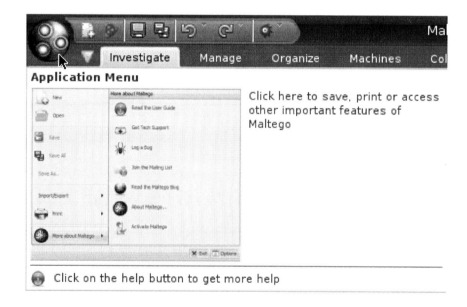

   b) Select **Save As**.
   c) Save the graph to the desktop as *comptia_recon.mtgx*
   d) Close Maltego.

6. Shut down the virtual machine.
   a) In the virtual machine toolbar, select **Machine→Close**.
   b) In the **Close Virtual Machine** dialog box, if necessary, select **Save the machine state**.
   c) Select **OK**.
      VirtualBox saves the current state of the virtual machine and then closes it.
   d) Close the **Oracle VM VirtualBox Manager** window.

Summary

In this lesson, you identified the general assessment methods that can test your enterprise systems for security weaknesses. Based on your enterprise needs, you selected the appropriate method. Then, you selected the actual tools used in these tests and used each one to discover flaws in your systems. With experience in both the methods and tools used to conduct vulnerability assessments, you will be able to survey and test your enterprise environment for any related situation that presents a risk of a security incident.

What types of vulnerabilities do you test for or would like to test for in your enterprise?

What security tools do you use in your enterprise? What are their strengths and weaknesses?

Note: Check your CHOICE Course screen for opportunities to interact with your classmates, peers, and the larger CHOICE online community about the topics covered in this course or other topics you are interested in. From the Course screen you can also access available resources for a more continuous learning experience.

12 | Responding to and Recovering from Incidents

Lesson Time: 3 hours

Lesson Objectives

In this lesson, you will:

- Design systems to facilitate incident response.
- Conduct incident and emergency responses.

Lesson Introduction

You've spent this entire course bolstering your enterprise security through a variety of ways. But no matter how strong your enterprise security is, no matter how thorough you are in protecting your assets, unforeseeable or unavoidable incidents may still occur. You simply can't afford to assume that this won't happen to your enterprise. Instead, you need to prepare for breaches and accidents so that, if they do happen, you won't be caught off guard. Security is therefore a cyclical process that never ends. In this lesson, you'll focus on how best to respond when risks to your enterprise become reality.

TOPIC A

Design Systems to Facilitate Incident Response

Because security incidents are often unavoidable, your systems need to be able to respond quickly and in useful ways. This will make your recovery efforts easier, as well as aid you in any investigations you choose to conduct after the fact. In this topic, you'll design your enterprise systems so that your incident response procedures are more efficient and effective.

Internal and External Violations

Security violations result from two different vectors. *Internal violations* emanate from within the enterprise perimeter, often by an employee, contractor, or someone who impersonates either. *External violations* emanate from outside the enterprise perimeter where security administrators have less control. Both internal and external threat vectors can be damaging to a company, and neither one is less serious than the other. However, the approaches you take to resolve them may differ.

Some specific examples of internal violations include:

- An employee abuses their permissions to view or copy data that they are not meant to have access to.
- A contractor violates a security policy by divulging company secrets to unauthorized personnel.
- An imposter tailgates at a secure building entrance, making his way inside and stealing sensitive documents that have been left on employees' desks.

Some specific examples of external violations include:

- A hacker breaks into the network and poisons the Address Resolution Protocol (ARP) cache, redirecting some traffic back to him.
- An attacker launches a Distributed Denial of Service (DDoS) against the company's network and takes out several web servers.
- A social engineer coaxes an employee's password out of him, then logs in to the employee's workstation remotely and deletes important data.

Security Violations and System Design

Beyond the general categories of internal and external, there are several types of security violations that you should be aware of. The following table describes these violations and offers ways in which you should design your enterprise systems to respond to them in case they occur.

Security Violation	Description	Design Considerations
Insider threat	An insider threat comes from someone that directly works in or with an organization, including employees, contractors, and subcontractors. These threats are usually difficult to defend against, since employees and contractors need access to certain data to perform their duties.	<ul><li>Follow the principle of least privilege in all systems.</li><li>Implement job rotation, mandatory vacations, and other administrative security practices.</li><li>Streamline access control policies so that access can be taken away easily should an employee abuse their power.</li></ul>

Security Violation	Description	Design Considerations
Privacy policy	A privacy policy violation includes breaches of information that is either private to employees or private to customers and clients. Organizations that work heavily with personal data, including financial and healthcare companies, must be particularly vigilant.	• Define a privacy policy that conforms to all laws and regulations and ensure that your customers agree to its terms. • Stipulate how data will be collected, stored, accessed, and retrieved. • Encrypt all personal data that must remain confidential.
Criminal actions	The more severe security violations may prompt you to take legal action against attackers. This is especially true of larger enterprises that are public-facing. In some cases, you may actually be required to report criminal behavior, even if you don't end up pressing charges against the attackers.	• Know your country's and industry's laws and regulations regarding cybercrime. • Enact a response plan for gathering evidence involved in a breach. • Enact a response plan for reporting criminal activity, including who to contact.
Non-malicious threats/ misconfigurations	Not all security violations are intentional. Some may result from absent-mindedness, like someone forgetting to log out of a session on a public computer. Some may simply result from errors in implementation, like a network administrator pushing a firmware update to a live environment, causing it to crash and lose data.	• Make sure that all employees read through and understand your end-user security policy. • Ensure that your incident response plan accounts for mistakes in judgment, and whether repeated instances warrant consequences. • Always trial run new updates, patches, hotfixes, configurations, and any other major alteration to your system on a test environment.

System, Audit, and Security Logs

The most crucial action an enterprise can take when responding to incidents is to ensure appropriate controls and tools are in place to provide forensic evidence during an investigation. These actions must take place prior to systems being compromised, and are integral to developing a well-rounded security incident response process. As part of any investigation, your team will need access to the event and audit logs found on systems and network devices. However, unless those logs are sent in real-time to a remote system, it is probable they can be either destroyed or altered as part of the attack. Therefore, it is crucial for effective incident response that all devices are set up to send their logging data to a security information event management system (SIEM).

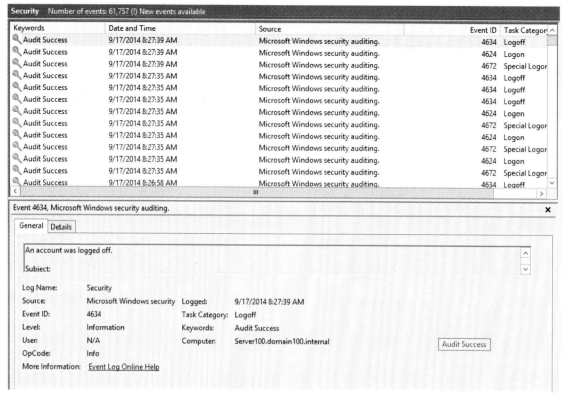

*Figure 12-1: The security log of a Windows® operating system.

As you design your logging activity around a SIEM to facilitate effective incident response, you need to document the approach you take to integrating with the SIEM. Likewise, all devices that report to the SIEM should be audited regularly to ensure compliance. You should also carefully consider the different types of logs that may be relevant to your setup. Beyond operating system (OS) logging, you may want to configure application logs to record a certain level of information. This includes applications such as Simple Mail Transfer Protocol (SMTP) gateways, web servers, Domain Name System (DNS) servers, Dynamic Host Configuration Protocol (DHCP) servers, databases, financial applications, and other applications critical to the enterprise or that contain sensitive information. In the event of a security incident, the information in these logs will be invaluable to your investigation.

Guidelines for Designing Systems to Facilitate Incident Response

 Note: All Guidelines for this lesson are available as checklists from the **Checklist** tile on the CHOICE Course screen.

Use the following guidelines to design your system to facilitate incident response:

- Account for both internal and external violations, and recognize that your system is vulnerable to both.
- Follow security principles like least privilege, job rotation, and mandatory vacations to mitigate insider threats.
- Define privacy policies that conform to all applicable laws and regulations.
- Encrypt confidential information so that it doesn't fall into the wrong hands.
- Enact a plan for gathering evidence in the event of a criminal breach.
- Ensure that all employees understand the best practices of security through end-user policies and training.
- Account for mistakes and don't assume that all incidents have malicious intent.

- Always trial run changes to your system on a test environment.
- Establish a SIEM for securing logs and event records.
- Audit devices to ensure interoperability with the SIEM.
- Keep logs of important activity in your organization's system, especially when sensitive data is handled.
- Know the hierarchy and interdependencies of all systems in your enterprise.
- After an incident, learn from what did and did not go right to craft a better response for the future.
- Always be up-to-date on the latest threats to your enterprise.

ACTIVITY 12-1

Designing Systems to Facilitate Incident Response

Before You Begin

You will be using the SSHclient account for some of the activity.

Scenario

Auditing and logging will help keep you prepared in the event of a security incident, but these methods are only useful when your systems are designed around them. At Develetech, you want to guarantee that your new servers will start recording key events the moment they are put into production. This will make it much easier for you and your team to both detect an incident and follow the trail back to the culprit, and it may even assist you in recovering functionality and key configurations.

On your domain controller, you'll enable auditing of logon events, changes to individual account values, and changes to policies. An attacker may be able to use changes to accounts and policies to create a vector through which they can attack the server. Likewise, keeping a record of logon events will give you better idea of who may have been responsible for an incident, or at the very least, what credentials were used to carry it out. To test your auditing configurations, you'll log in under a different account and change some values that could compromise security. You'll then become more acquainted with security logging by reviewing how Windows recorded the changes that you made. This is how you and your team can stay informed about what was changed and how.

---

1. Enable auditing of certain events on the domain.
   a) Open a command prompt and enter `gpedit`

b) In the **Local Group Policy Editor** window, expand **Computer Configuration→Windows Settings→Security Settings→Local Policies** and select **Audit Policy**.

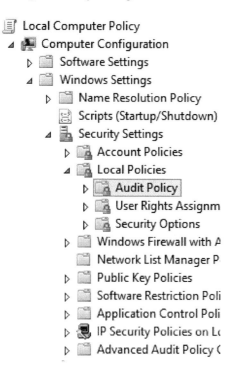

c) In the details pane, under the **Policy** column, double-click **Audit account logon events**.
d) In the **Audit account logon events Properties** dialog box, check the **Success** and **Failure** check boxes.
   Any time a user attempts to log in to the domain with any account, even if they fail, the attempt will be logged.
e) Select **OK**.
f) Double-click **Audit account management** and check the **Success** and **Failure** check boxes, then select **OK**.
   Attempted changes to existing accounts on the domain, or creating and deleting accounts, will be logged.
g) Enable **Success** and **Failure** for **Audit policy change**.
   Any attempt to alter user rights assignment policy, audit policy, account policy, or trust policy will be logged.
h) Verify the **Security Settings** column shows **Success, Failure** for the three audit policies.

Policy	Security Setting
Audit account logon events	Success, Failure
Audit account management	Success, Failure
Audit directory service access	No auditing
Audit logon events	No auditing
Audit object access	No auditing
Audit policy change	Success, Failure
Audit privilege use	No auditing
Audit process tracking	No auditing
Audit system events	No auditing

i) Close the **Local Group Policy Editor** window and the command prompt.

2. Sign out of the Administrator account and sign in under SSHclient.

    a) Right-click the **Start** button and select **Shut down or sign out→Sign out**.

    b) Press **Ctrl+Alt+Delete**, then select the **Other user** icon.

    c) At the **Other user** login screen, type *SSHclient* as the user name and type any incorrect value for the password.

    d) Attempt to sign in, then select **OK** when prompted to try again.

    e) Sign in with the correct password of *!Pass1234*

    f) Select the **Desktop** tile.

3. Change a property for an individual account.

    a) In **Server Manager**, select **Tools→Active Directory Users and Computers**.

    b) If necessary, in the navigation pane, expand your domain object and select **Users**.

    c) In the details pane, right-click the **SSHclient** user and select **Properties**.

    d) In the **SSHclient Properties** dialog box, select the **Account** tab.

    e) In the **Account options** list, check the **Password never expires** check box and select **OK**.

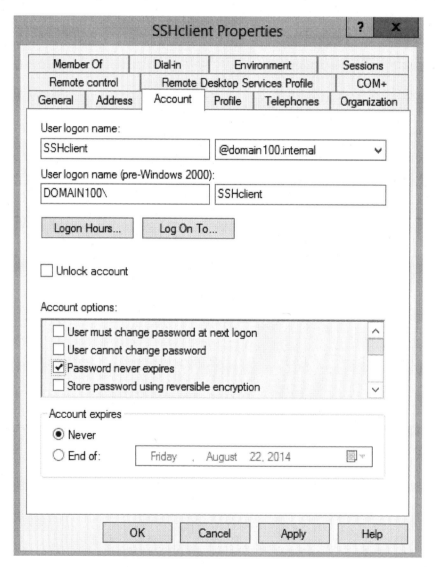

    f) Close **Active Directory Users and Computers**.

4. Change the state of an audit policy to disabled.

    a) Open a command prompt and enter `gpedit`

    b) Expand **Computer Configuration→Windows Settings→Security Settings→Local Policies** and select **Audit Policy**.

c) In the details pane, double-click **Audit account logon events**.

d) In the **Audit account logon events Properties** dialog box, uncheck **Success** and **Failure**, then select **OK**.

e) Close **Local Group Policy Editor** and the command prompt.

5. Review the security logs of the events that were audited.

a) Sign out of SSHclient, then sign back in as Administrator.

b) In **Server Manager**, select **Tools→Event Viewer**.

c) In the navigation pane, expand **Windows Logs** and select **Security**.

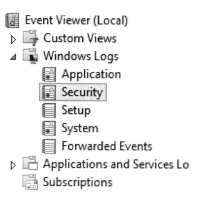

d) Verify that the details pane has several audit entries, each with the following attributes:

- Whether Windows audited a success or a failure.
- The date and time of the audit.
- The source type of the audit.
- The event ID of the entry.
- The audit type category.

e) From the **Actions** pane on the right, select **Find**.

f) In the **Find** dialog box, in the **Find what** text box, type *Kerberos Authentication Service*

g) Select **Find Next** until it highlights an **Audit Failure** entry with a **Task Category** of **Kerberos Authentication Service**.

Audit Success	7/23/2014 9:59:42 AM	Microsoft Windows securi...	4662	Directory Service Access
Audit Success	7/23/2014 9:58:36 AM	Microsoft Windows securi...	4670	Authorization Policy Chan...
Audit Success	7/23/2014 9:55:15 AM	Microsoft Windows securi...	4670	Authorization Policy Chan...
Audit Success	7/23/2014 9:55:15 AM	Microsoft Windows securi...	4670	Authorization Policy Chan...
Audit Success	7/23/2014 9:55:12 AM	Microsoft Windows securi...	4769	Kerberos Service Ticket O...
Audit Success	7/23/2014 9:55:12 AM	Microsoft Windows securi...	4768	Kerberos Authentication S...
Audit Failure	7/23/2014 9:55:06 AM	Microsoft Windows securi...	4771	Kerberos Authentication S...
Audit Success	7/23/2014 9:54:48 AM	Microsoft Windows securi...	4719	Audit Policy Change
Audit Success	7/23/2014 9:54:48 AM	Microsoft Windows securi...	4719	Audit Policy Change
Audit Success	7/23/2014 9:54:48 AM	Microsoft Windows securi...	4719	Audit Policy Change
Audit Success	7/23/2014 9:54:48 AM	Microsoft Windows securi	4719	Audit Policy Change

h) Select **Cancel** to close the **Find** dialog box.

i) In the **General** tab at the bottom, scroll down and verify the failed login attempt with a failure code of 0x18.

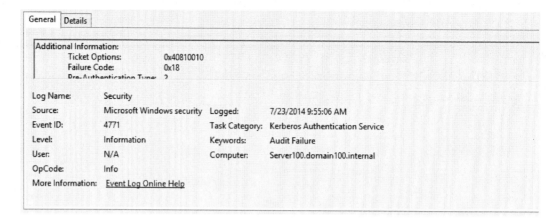

This indicates a bad password was used in an attempt to log in to the SSHclient account.

j) Using the **Find** dialog box, search for *don't expire password*

k) Verify that an entry with a **Task Category** of **User Account Management** is highlighted.

l) Scroll down in the **General** tab, and under the **Changed Attributes** section, verify that the **User Account Control** property shows the **Don't Expire Password** value as enabled.

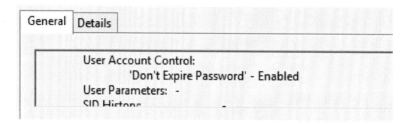

m) Search for the following phrase: *success removed, failure removed*

n) Verify that an entry with a **Task Category** of **Audit Policy Change** is highlighted.

o) Scroll down in the **General** tab, and verify that the entry logs SSHclient as removing the auditing success and failure conditions from the account logon policy.

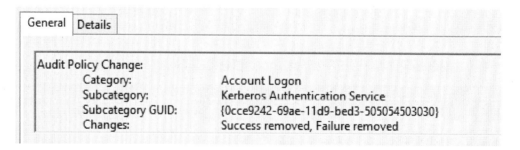

6. Close **Event Viewer**.

TOPIC B

Conduct Incident and Emergency Responses

Now that your systems are designed to facilitate incident response, you'll conduct various analysis and investigative procedures in the event of a security breach. These procedures can support legal action your enterprise may take, or they can simply help support your recovery and reinforcement efforts.

E-Discovery

Electronic discovery (e-discovery) is the process of identification, collection, analysis, and retention of electronic data for the discovery phase of litigation. The process of e-discovery was defined by the United States Supreme Court in 2006 as part of amendments to the Federal Rules of Civil Procedure. An enterprise must define its procedures and policies to meet the standards set forth by the Supreme Court, and these requirements vary by industry. Failure to comply can result in fines during the litigation process, exposing the organization to significant financial risk.

 Note: A 26(f) conference—based on Rule 26(f) of the Federal Rules of Civil Procedure (FRCP)—is a meeting that takes place before litigation between attorneys and technical specialists and/or forensic analysts to lay out a discovery plan in preparation for litigation.

E-Discovery Policy

A well-rounded e-discovery policy contains information on the following topics.

E-Discovery Topic	Description
Electronic inventory and asset control	Every organization is expected to maintain asset lists for devices under their control. This includes all workstations, servers, network devices, mobile devices, and data storage devices such as CDs, DVDs, and flash drives. For each of these assets, your organization should define procedures for collecting evidence that may be relevant to potential litigation.
Data retention policies	For each type of data (e.g., firewall logs, intrusion detection logs, system logs, and application logs), your organization should define a retention period. What is meant by "retention" varies by industry, and there are many organizations such as the SANS Institute and the National Institute of Standards and Technology (NIST) that provide guides to help organizations define appropriate retention periods, and there are also industry-specific groups like EDRM that provide a more specialized service. It is important to include legal counsel in your organization's data retention policies, as not meeting requirements can bring about unwanted liability.

E-Discovery Topic	Description
Data recovery and storage	For data to be used within a court of law, you must prove that the evidence was not tampered with. To accomplish this, you should consider implementing hashing and encryption techniques to secure the integrity of evidence prior to trial. Once the evidence is needed, you can hash the data and then compare the hashes with the pre-trial hashes. If the hashes do not match, it is evident that the data has been modified and may no longer be allowed during litigation. When using encryption, you can ensure that the data is unreadable until trial, guaranteeing that sensitive information remains confidential and out of the hands of malicious parties.
Data ownership	Every enterprise should have a component of their overall security policy that stipulates who maintains ownership of data entrusted to the organization's care. This is especially true for service providers who receive data from their clients on behalf of the client's customers, or for organizations responsible for sensitive information, like personally identifiable information (PII), card holder data, or protected health information (PHI). Your policy should also define how data is to be returned or destroyed when the data is no longer needed or the data owner no longer employs the services of the organization.
Data handling	Handling e-discovery information is very similar to handling forensic evidence during a security incident. You must preserve a careful trail of how the evidence was gathered, who has touched it, and who is responsible for it in a chain of custody. Failure to follow chain of custody rules could make the evidence inadmissible, which could bring financial risk to the organization.
Legal holds	An attorney or other legal counsel will issue a legal hold on evidence so that the organization will discontinue disposing of data in the way it normally does. This is intended to make absolutely certain that any relevant data that could be used as evidence is not destroyed or otherwise lost. You should ensure that anyone who stores and maintains data that is subject to the hold knows that they should not dispose of it until the trial is concluded. Identifying what data is affected by the hold is best facilitated by tagging data based on how it is defined in the e-discovery policy.

Data Breach

A *data breach* is a security incident that involves the unauthorized access of data stored in a secure location. The data is then viewed, copied, transmitted, or sold to illegitimate recipients who might use the data for personal gain, corporate espionage, or simply to embarrass the legitimate owner of the data. The attacker might even destroy the original data at the source as part of the breach. Because a large enterprise network often has a sizable attack surface with multiple points of access, a data breach can have serious implications for both the legitimate owner and the unauthorized person or entity that accessed the data. Financial losses resulting from a data breach can easily be in the millions of dollars, and the business or personal impact might be extensive enough to make this loss unrecoverable. The unauthorized person or entities that breached the data source can face prison time, sanctions by governments, or other legal consequences.

Data Breach Response

As a CASP, you must be constantly vigilant and follow security policies and procedures to detect and defend against data breaches so that losses can be mitigated quickly. Should the worst occur, you must be prepared. The steps outlined in the following table make up a strong response to data breaches.

Response	Description
Detection and collection	Before you can address a data breach, you must, of course, detect it. There are various tools that you can put in place to help aid you in this, like software that performs data analytics. But know that it may take more than just relying on a software utility to detect a breach. Oftentimes, a CASP will need to investigate many different areas of a system to piece together the evidence and eventually arrive at a conclusion.
	If you determine that a breach has occurred, you then must collect evidence of that breach. This will include everything that influenced your conclusion that a data breach occurred, but there will likely be more evidence to collect than what you've already gone through. Examples of potential evidence are network traffic patterns, host authentication logs, and physical hard drives that store the data in question. However, not all data will be affected. If you fail to define a correct scope in your investigation, the organization risks increased financial costs, even if you over-report evidence.
Mitigation	Some breaches are one-time occurrences, and others will continue on even well after you've detected them. For example, you may immediately restrict access for specific users to halt an internal breach in progress or keep an internal breach from reoccurring. A more drastic approach would be to take all access offline, but you may want to consider this a last resort as it could critically impact your enterprise's operations. Other mitigate techniques include: locating and verifying backups, identifying the cause(s) of the breach, hardening your defenses once vulnerabilities are identified, and reviewing system event and security logs.
	One other important mitigation technique is called *minimization*. To minimize a data breach is to reduce the potential for harm before it affects the enterprise. There are several ways to accomplish an acceptable level of minimization. You may outsource your organization's data storage to a cloud provider who can provide better security, and you could isolate data so that breached data stores are moved outside of normal use and hardened. Doing this prevents the affected devices from altering other elements of a system, or vice versa. These methods will not prevent a breach, but they are designed to lessen the impact that a breach has.
Recovery/ reconstitution	Recovery from a data breach can be a long and expensive process. Many times, an enterprise will outsource recovery to third-party vendors who specialize in supporting organizations affected by a breach. As you are responsible for the security of your enterprise, you should identify some of these vendors prior to a breach and get an understanding of their capabilities and the scope of their services.
	Whether you choose to initiate recovery in-house or externally, you should be aware of the techniques involved: restoring data to its pre-breach state (reconstitution), validating data with users and applications, and returning required access to authorized users. Testing these recovery methods regularly is also crucial.

Response	Description
Disclosure	Disclosure is an optional step, and it may not necessarily come last. In larger enterprises, especially those that service a great deal of customers, a data breach will affect more than just the owners or executives. It becomes incumbent upon the business to either disclose to the public that a breach has occurred, disclose to certain affected parties that a breach has occurred, or not disclose the breach at all. A breach that affects the operations of the business and leads to financial loss will almost always need to be disclosed to stakeholders. Different categories of stakeholders are notified at different times, and the level of detail you disclose may also vary between certain individuals or depend on the category of information. If a breach affects your customers' personal information, you should also publicly disclose the breach, and may be required to by law.

In some cases, you may not need to or even be required to disclose a data breach to the public. For example, if the breach is relatively minor and you have determined that no sensitive information was lost or stolen, and all necessary steps have been taken to mitigate the breach, then there may not be a reason to announce the breach to the outside. Even more significant breaches that only affect the business itself and do not tread on its customers or its partners may go undisclosed to anyone but authorized internal personnel. |

Chain of Custody

The *chain of custody* is the record of evidence handling from collection through presentation in court. The evidence can be hardware components, electronic data, or telephone systems. The chain of evidence reinforces the integrity and proper custody of evidence from collection, to analysis, to storage, and finally to presentation. Every person in the chain who handles evidence must log the methods and tools they used.

Figure 12-2: The chain of custody from evidence collection to presentation in court.

When security breaches go to trial, the chain of custody protects an organization against accusations that evidence has either been tampered with or is wholly different than it was when it was collected.

Example

Consider the following scenario:

1. Adam, the security administrator, detects an abnormal amount of outgoing traffic from a database that stores password hashes. No one besides the security team is authorized to access this database. The destination IP of the outgoing traffic is attached to the workstation of an IT employee who is currently on vacation.

2. Adam notifies his boss, Barry, of the abnormal traffic. Barry tasks security engineer Emily with taking snapshots of the database as it is in its current state, and cautions her to make sure backups from at least a week prior are retained.

3. Emily uses her workstation to remotely log in to the server with the affected database and takes a snapshot. She then extends the retention period of all backups saved in the past week.

4. Meanwhile, Barry commandeers the IT workstation and locks it in a security closet to which only he, the building manager, and the CEO have keys to.

5. After Emily is finished, Barry takes her workstation and the server with the affected database and locks them in the same closet.

6. Barry asks the building manager for the security camera footage of the past 24 hours, and places a copy of this footage in the closet.

7. Barry writes up an incident report and details every step of the process, mentioning every individual involved in the evidence collection.

Analysis

Assuming the camera footage shows someone accessing the absent employee's workstation, this incident may go to trial and charges may be levied against the person identified on camera. However, if Barry had never documented the chain of custody of each piece of evidence as it passed from his coworkers' hands to his own, the suspect could bring reasonable doubt to the legitimacy of this evidence. What if the database logs that record the outgoing traffic were tampered with to point to an erroneous IP address? What if the camera footage was not from that day, but previous footage of the suspect using the employee workstation with permission? These are questions that a defense team will raise to cast doubt on the investigation. Since Barry wisely kept the chain of custody on record, it will be much more difficult for the defense to convince the judge that the evidence should be inadmissible in court.

Forensic Analysis of Compromised Systems

Computer forensics is the skill that deals with collecting and analyzing data from storage devices, computer systems, networks, and wireless communications and presenting this information as a form of evidence in a court of law. There are various procedures you can follow to help you analyze compromised systems in the event of a breach.

Forensic Procedure	Description
Capture system image	One of the most important steps in computer forensic evidence procedures is to capture exact duplicates of the evidence, also known as forensic images. This is accomplished by making a bit-for-bit copy of a piece of media as an image file with high accuracy.
Examine network traffic and logs	Attackers always leave behind traces; you just need to know how and where to look. Logs record everything that happens in an intrusion prevention system (IPS) or intrusion detection system (IDS), and in routers, firewalls, servers, desktops, mainframes, applications, databases, antivirus software, and virtual private networks (VPNs). With these logs, it is possible to extract the identity of hackers and provide the evidence needed.
Capture video	Video forensics is the method by which video is scrutinized for clues. Tools for computer forensics are used in reassembling video to be used as evidence in a court of law.

Forensic Procedure	Description
Record time offset	The format in which time is recorded against a file activity, such as file creation, deletion, last modified, and last accessed, has developed to incorporate a local time zone offset against Greenwich Mean Time (GMT). This makes it easier for forensic investigators to determine the exact time the activity took place even if the computer is moved from one time zone to another or if the time zone has deliberately been changed on a system.
Take hashes	Federal law enforcement agencies and federal governments maintain a list of files, such as files relating to components of Microsoft® Windows® and other application software. The hash codes generated by a file or software can be compared to the list of known file hashes and hacker tools if any are flagged or marked as unknown.
Take screenshots	You should capture screenshots of each and every step of a forensic procedure, especially when you are retrieving evidence using a forensic tool. This will ensure that data present on a compromised system is not tampered with and also provides the court with proof of your use of valid computer forensic methods while extracting the evidence.
Identify witnesses	Courts generally accept evidence if it is seconded by the testimony of a witness who observed the procedure by which the evidence was acquired. A computer forensics expert witness is someone who has experience in handling computer forensics tools and is able to establish the validity of the evidence.
Track man hours and expense	When the first incidents of computer crimes occurred, it would usually take less than 40 man hours to complete a forensic investigation because incidents usually involved a single computer. Now, with the advances in technology and the advent of new digital media (such as voice recorders, cameras, laptop computers, and mobile devices), computer forensics procedures can take up an exponentially greater amount of man hours and expenses. Also, the increase in storage device capacities and encryption affect the amount of man hours that it can take to assess any damage, and consequently increase expenses incurred in any computer forensics investigation. Capturing this expense is part of the overall damage assessment for the incident.

 Note: To learn more about the forensic analysis of systems, access the LearnTO **Follow the Forensic Process** presentation from the **LearnTO** tile on the CHOICE Course screen.

COOP

A *continuity of operations plan (COOP)* outlines how an organization will maintain operations if a major adverse event were to occur. This is similar to a business continuity plan (BCP), but a COOP typically encompasses a large-scale recovery plan in the event of a significant disaster, whereas a BCP will be more focused on individual security risks. In many organizations, a COOP would therefore account for the safety of people in a catastrophe. For example, a COOP may help a business establish a secondary office or shelter should the primary work site be destroyed in a natural disaster.

COOP documents typically identify the following:

- The various phases of a response.
- Mission-critical functions.
- Key personnel and other points of contact.

- The property and physical assets needed to resume operations elsewhere.
- The logistics of an immediate response to a disaster.
- The logistics of an eventual recovery.

COOPs are most often useful for large, public organizations, like governments, universities, and hospitals. Despite their difference in scope, BCPs can occasionally support COOPs, and vice versa.

U.S. Government COOP

COOP may also specifically refer to a U.S. government initiative that requires all federal branches to have a continuity of operations plan in place to respond to a disaster. For example, the Department of Homeland Security uses the Mount Weather Emergency Operations Center in Virginia as a relocation center for key civilian and military personnel in case of a national emergency.

Order of Volatility

Data is volatile, and the ability to retrieve or validate data after a security incident depends on where it is stored in a location or in a memory layer of a computer or external device. For example, data on backup CDs or thumb drives can last for years, while data in Random Access Memory (RAM) may last for only nanoseconds.

The order in which you need to recover data after an incident before the data deteriorates, is erased, or is overwritten is known as the *order of volatility*. From most volatile to least volatile, the general order of volatility for storage media is:

- Processor registers, processor caches, and RAM.
- Network caches and virtual memory.
- Hard drives, flash drives, and solid state drives (SSDs).
- CD-ROMs, DVD-ROMs, magnetic tape, and printouts.

 Note: Volatility may also refer to the memory's impermanence when disconnected from a power source. RAM loses its memory when it loses power, and is therefore volatile. A hard disk will retain its memory even when it loses power, and is therefore non-volatile.

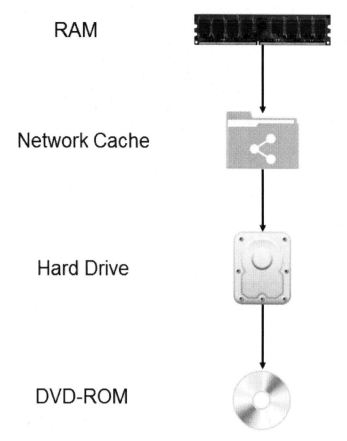

RAM

Network Cache

Hard Drive

DVD-ROM

Figure 12–3: Order of volatility.

The order of volatility is another factor that will influence your response to incidents. Highly volatile memory like RAM may not be worth your time to present it as evidence, as any trace of an intrusion might be gone from the cache before you can possibly capture it. Still, some experiments have shown that cryogenically frozen memory may be able to retain its non-degraded state for several days. For most organizations, this will not be a feasible option, but could be a viable means of forensic preservation in the future.

Guidelines for Conducting Incident and Emergency Responses

Use the following guidelines for conducting incident and emergency responses:

- Draft an e-discovery policy to prepare for any potential litigation.
- Include asset control, data retention, recovery and storage, ownership, handling, and legal hold information in your e-discovery policy.
- Respond to data breaches by retaining and collecting data, mitigating damage, recovering and reconstituting systems, and disclosing the breach.
- Maintain a chain of custody in evidence handling to uphold accountability.
- Implement forensic procedures like capturing system images, taking hashes, and reviewing network traffic logs to analyze evidence after a breach.
- Draft a COOP if your organization is susceptible to major disasters that will affect the safety of many people.
- Prioritize data recovery by following the order of volatility.

ACTIVITY 12-2
Conducting E-Discovery and Forensic Analysis

Data Files

C:\093023Data\Responding to and Recovering from Incidents\autopsy-3.0.10-64bit.msi

C:\093023Data\Responding to and Recovering from Incidents\DDoS Attack.zip

Before You Begin

You will be using Autopsy, a forensic analysis tool. A forensic scan has already been performed on a target system.

Scenario

Yesterday around noon your security team discovered that its web servers were under a DDoS attack. This attack took the servers down for several hours and left customers without access to Develetech's storefront during that time. Your incident response team (IRT) took the necessary actions to perform e-discovery and other evidence gathering techniques on computers they suspected to be involved in the attack. One such computer is a workstation used by an employee in the IT department. Your team used a forensic analysis tool called Autopsy to scan this computer, and they've followed the chain of custody and have given the scan results to you for analysis.

Using these scan results, you'll load Autopsy and review the target computer's web browsing usage for any suspicious activity. User browser habits can often give a forensic investigator valuable insight into a suspect's intentions. After reviewing the browser cookie information, you'll see if you can follow the browsing pattern to a Denial of Service (DoS) tool that could have been used to carry out the attack. Once you've gathered the relevant information about the target computer's hard drive, you'll generate a report of your findings and review it for any incriminating evidence that could be used in court.

---

1. Install Autopsy.
   a) In File Explorer, navigate to **C:\093023Data\Responding to and Recovering from Incidents**.
   b) Double-click **autopsy-3.0.10-64bit**.
   c) In the **Autopsy Setup** wizard, select **Next**.
   d) On the **Select Installation Folder** page, select **Next** to accept the default location.
   e) On the **Ready to Install** page, select **Install**.
   f) After installation completes, select **Finish**.

2. Extract the DDoS case file to your **Documents** folder.
   a) In File Explorer, right-click **DDoS Attack** and select **Extract All**.

b) On the **Select a Destination and Extract Files** page, in the **Files will be extracted to this folder** text box, type the path to your **Documents** folder.

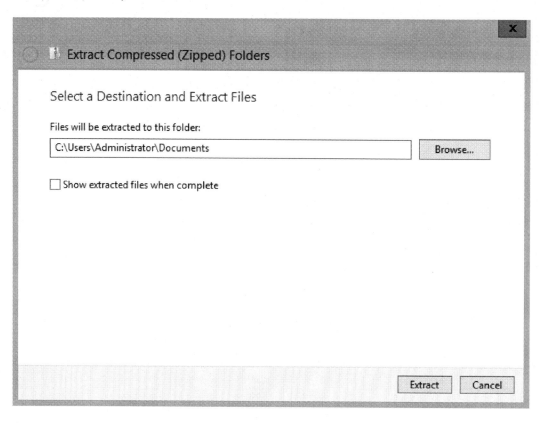

c) If necessary, uncheck the **Show extracted files when complete** check box.
d) Select **Extract**.
e) After extraction completes, close File Explorer.

3. Import the DDoS attack case into Autopsy.
   a) From the desktop, double-click the **Autopsy** icon to open the application.

   b) In the **Welcome** dialog box, select the page icon next to **Open Existing Case**.
   c) In the **Open** dialog box, navigate to the **DDoS Attack** directory that you extracted and open the **DDoS Attack.aut** file.

4. Search the captured web cookies for a website of interest.

a) From the navigation pane on the left, under **Results→Extracted Content**, select **Web Cookies**.

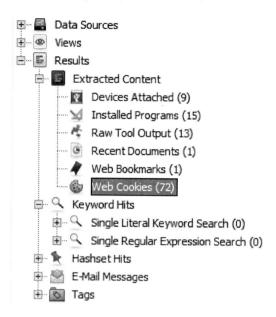

b) In the details pane, verify that text files tied to various websites are listed, and that there are columns with additional information about each entry.

The specific details for each cookie source file include:

- The URL it is tied to.
- The date and time it was created.
- Its name.
- Its value.
- The browser that accessed it.
- The domain name of the site it is tied to.
- The volume it was found in.

c) Scroll down until you see an entry with a URL of **resources.infosecinstitute.com/**.

The InfoSec Institute offers training in and various information about cybersecurity. Like many security resources, it can be used for legitimate purposes, or it can be a way for malicious users to glean information about exploits, attack tools, and vulnerabilities.

d) Right-click the **AZOF4PEO.txt** entry and select **Tag Result→Tag and Comment**.

e) In the **Tag and Comment** dialog box, in the **Comment** text box, type *Possibly used as a resource for attack* and select **OK**.

This marks the result as an item of interest so that it can be used later in a report.

5. Search the web for DoS-related resources on the InfoSec Institute's website.

a) Open Internet Explorer® and navigate to **www.google.com**.

b) In the search box, enter *resources.infosecinstitute.com dos*

c) Verify that a search returns a web page from InfoSec Institute's domain about free DoS attack tools.

DOS Attacks and Free DOS Attacking Tools - InfoSec Institute
resources.infosecinstitute.com/dos-attacks-free-dos-attacking-tools/ ▾
Oct 29, 2013 - The **denial of service** (DOS) attack is one of the most powerful
attacks ... bypass caching engines, thus it directly hits the server's **resource** pool.

DOS Deflate: Layer 7 DOS Protection Tool - InfoSec Institute
resources.infosecinstitute.com/dos-deflate-layer-7-dos-protection-tool/ ▾
May 27, 2014 - DOS or DDOS is a type of attack in which a machine or a network
resource is unavailable to its intended users. This is one of the most ...

Dangerous DDoS (Distributed **Denial of Service**) on the rise ...
resources.infosecinstitute.com/dangerous-ddos-distributed-denial-of-serv... ▾
by Pierluigi Paganini - May 28, 2013 - If the attack succeeds, it consumes the
resources of the target, usually causing ... It must be clear that **Denial-of-Service**
attacks are considered violations of .... The **InfoSec Institute** Ethical Hacking course
goes in-depth into the ...

LOIC (Low Orbit Ion Cannon) - **DOS** attacking tool - InfoSec ...
resources.infosecinstitute.com/loic-dos-attacking-tool/ ▾
by Deepanker Verma - Dec 20, 2011 - The DOS (**Denial of service**) attack is one of

d) Follow the link to the page. Verify that it describes the basics of DoS and DDoS attacks, then lists some free tools that can be used in an attack.

e) Scroll down to the end of the first entry, which is about Low Orbit Ion Cannon (LOIC), a popular DoS attack tool. Copy the download link **http://sourceforge.net/projects/loic/** and navigate to it in your browser.

f) At the tool's SourceForge page, take note of the download file link.

6. Review the cookie entries for any mention of SourceForge or LOIC.

a) Return to Autopsy and look for a cookie entry with the URL of **downloads.sourceforge.net/**.

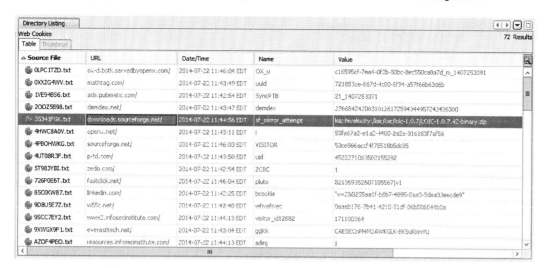

b) Verify that the cookie's value indicates the computer attempted to download the **LOIC-1.0.7.42-binary.zip** file, which is hosted on SourceForge and contains the binary of the LOIC DoS attack tool.

 Note: The version number of the download file may have changed since the target system accessed it.

c) Right-click the **35341FGK.txt** entry and select **Tag Results→Tag and Comment**.

d) In the **Tag and Comment** dialog box, in the **Comment** text box, type *Indicates that user attempted to download a DoS attack tool* and select **OK**.

7. Search for more evidence of the LOIC tool on the scanned system.

a) From the Autopsy toolbar, select **Tools→File Search by Attributes**.

b) In the **File Search by Attributes** dialog box, in the **Name** text box, type *loic* and select **Search**.

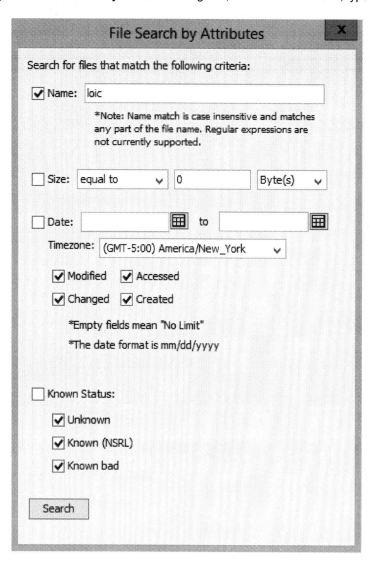

c) Verify that the search results returned two web pages and a .lnk file with the LOIC binary name you identified.

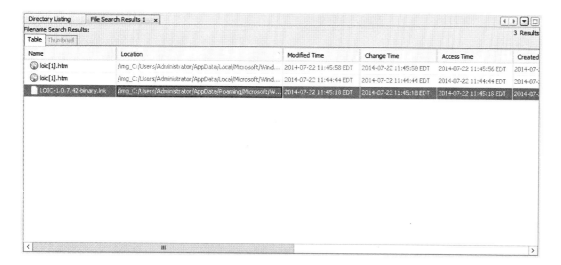

A .lnk file is a Windows shortcut that points to another file. File shortcuts like this one may remain in a temporary or hidden folder like **AppData** even after the file it points to has been deleted. This implies that the LOIC binary ZIP file was on the scanned volume at some point.

d) Select the **Directory Listing** tab to return to the cookie entry and review its date and time.

e) Select the **File Search Results 1** tab to return to the .lnk file entry and verify that it was created at the same time as the cookie.

This implies that the file shortcut's creation is consistent with the cookie entry for the download link, and that the computer did indeed download the file from that source.

f) Right-click the .lnk file and select **Tag File→Tag and Comment**.

g) In the **Tag and Comment** dialog box, in the **Comment** text box, type *Indicates that user downloaded the tool from aforementioned source* and select **OK**.

8. Generate a report of your findings.

a) Below the toolbar, select the **Generate Report** button.

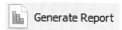

b) In the **Generate Report** wizard, in the **Report Modules** section, select the **Results - HTML** radio button.

c) Select **Next**.

d) On the **Configure Artifact Reports** page, select **Tagged Results**, check the **Bookmark** check box, then select **Finish**.

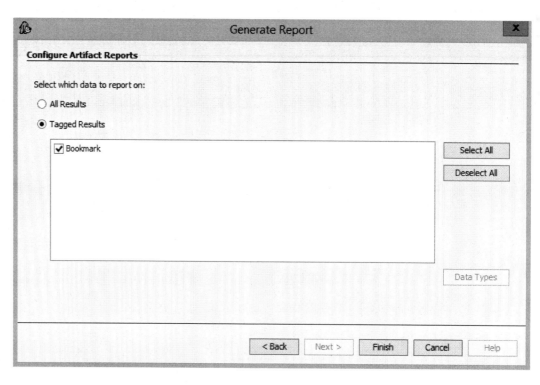

e) On the **Report Generation Progress** page, select the link to the HTML file that was created. The report page opens in Internet Explorer.

9. Review the report.
   a) In the **Report Navigation** pane on the left, select **Result Tags (2)**.
   b) Verify that the cookie entries that you tagged are listed, and each entry is commented.

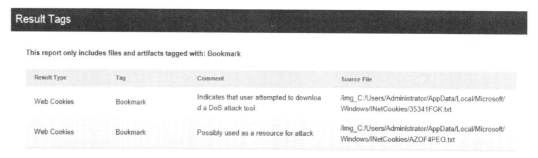

c) In the **Report Navigation** pane on the left, select **Web Cookies (2)**.

d) Verify that specific details about the cookie entries that you tagged are listed.

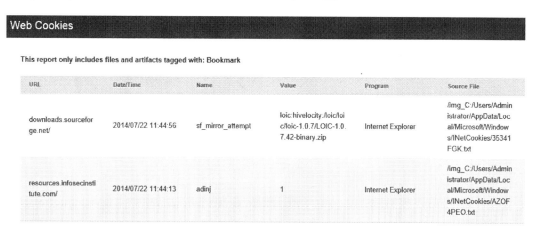

e) In the **Report Navigation** pane on the left, select **File Tags (1)**.

f) Verify that the .lnk file that you tagged is listed, along with your comment.

 Note: There is also a link to view the file, but because you are not working from the target system, it will not work.

10. Assuming the times identified in this report occurred shortly before your team detected the DDoS condition, what conclusions can you draw from this forensic evidence?

11. Close Internet Explorer and Autopsy.

Summary

In this lesson, you designed your enterprise systems to facilitate incident response, and you then conducted the procedures that are commonly part of an incident response. Being able to both prepare for and efficiently address potential complications in your enterprise's security is a useful skill for a CASP.

What systems and other operational elements do you audit in your organization?

What forensic analysis procedures have you performed or would you perform in the event of a breach?

Note: Check your CHOICE Course screen for opportunities to interact with your classmates, peers, and the larger CHOICE online community about the topics covered in this course or other topics you are interested in. From the Course screen you can also access available resources for a more continuous learning experience.

Course Follow-Up

Congratulations! You have completed the *CompTIA® Advanced Security Practitioner (CASP) (Exam CAS-002)* course. You have gained the skills and information you will need to successfully implement and maintain security in complex enterprise environments.

You also covered the objectives that you will need to prepare for the CompTIA Advanced Security Practitioner (Exam CAS-002) certification examination. If you combine this class experience with review, private study, and hands-on experience, you will be well prepared to demonstrate your advanced security expertise both through professional certification and solid technical competence on the job.

What's Next?

Your next step after completing this course will probably be to prepare for and obtain your CASP certification. In addition, there are a number of specialized security courses and certifications that you might want to pursue following the *CompTIA® Advanced Security Practitioner (CASP) (Exam CAS-002)* course, including CompTIA® Mobility+® certification and CompTIA® Mobile App Security+® certification for Android™ or iOS® development. You might also wish to pursue further technology-specific training in operating system or network design, implementation and support, or in application development and implementation.

You are encouraged to explore computer and network security further by actively participating in any of the social media forums set up by your instructor or training administrator through the **Social Media** tile on the CHOICE Course screen.

Mapping Course Content to CompTIA Advanced Security Practitioner (CASP) Exam CAS-002

Obtaining CompTIA Advanced Security Practitioner (CASP) certification requires candidates to pass exam CAS-002. This table describes where the objectives for exam CAS-002 are covered in this course.

Domain and Objective	Covered In
Domain 1.0 Enterprise Security	
1.1 Given a scenario, select appropriate cryptographic concepts and techniques	
• Firewalls	Lesson 5, Topic B
• Key stretching	
• Hashing	
• Code signing	
• Pseudorandom number generation	
• Perfect forward secrecy	
• Transport encryption	
• Data at rest encryption	
• Digital signature	

Domain and Objective	Covered In
• Concepts	Lesson 5, Topic A

- • Entropy
- • Diffusion
- • Confusion
- • Non-repudiation
- • Confidentiality
- • Integrity
- • Chain of trust/Root of trust
- • Cryptographic applications and proper/improper implementations
- • Advanced PKI concepts
  - • Wild card
  - • OCSP vs. CRL
  - • Issuance to entities
  - • Users
  - • Systems
  - • Applications
  - • Key escrow
- • Steganography
- • Implications of cryptographic methods and design
  - • Stream
  - • Block
  - • Modes
    - • ECB
    - • CBC
    - • CFB
    - • OFB
  - • Known flaws/weaknesses
  - • Strength vs. performance vs. feasibility to implement vs. interoperability

• Implementations	Lesson 5, Topic C

- • DRM
- • Watermarking
- • GPG
- • SSL
- • SSH
- • S/MIME

1.2 Explain the security implications associated with enterprise storage

Domain and Objective	Covered In
• Storage types	Lesson 7, Topic A
• Virtual storage	
• Cloud storage	
• Data warehousing	
• Data archiving	
• NAS	
• SAN	
• vSAN	
• Storage protocols	Lesson 7, Topic A
• iSCSI	
• FCoE	
• NFS, CIFS	
• Secure storage management	Lesson 7, Topic B
• Multipath	
• Snapshots	
• Deduplication	
• Dynamic disk pools	
• LUN masking/mapping	
• HBA allocation	
• Offsite or multisite replication	
• Encryption	
• Disk	
• Block	
• File	
• Record	
• Port	

1.3 Given a scenario, analyze network and security components, concepts, and architectures

• Advanced network design	Lesson 8, Topic C
• Remote access	
• VPN	
• SSH	
• RDP	
• VNC	
• SSL	
• IPv6 and associated transitional technologies	
• Transport encryption	
• Network authentication methods	
• 802.1X	
• Mesh networks	

Domain and Objective	Covered In
• Security devices	Lesson 8, Topic A
• UTM	
• NIPS	
• NIDS	
• INE	
• SIEM	
• HSM	
• Placement of devices	
• Application and protocol aware technologies	
• WAF	
• NextGen firewalls	
• IPS	
• Passive vulnerability scanners	
• DAM	
• Virtual networking and security components	Lesson 8, Topic A
• Switches	
• Firewalls	
• Wireless controllers	
• Routers	
• Proxies	
• Complex network security solutions for data flow	Lesson 8, Topic D
• SSL inspection	
• Network flow data	
• Secure configuration and baselining of networking and security components	Lesson 8, Topic D
• ACLs	
• Change monitoring	
• Configuration lockdown	
• Availability controls	
• Software-defined networking	Lesson 8, Topic C
• Cloud-managed networks	Lesson 8, Topic C
• Network management and monitoring tools	Lesson 8, Topic D
• Advanced configuration of routers, switches, and other network devices	Lesson 8, Topic D
• Transport security	
• Trunking security	
• Route protection	
• Security zones	Lesson 8, Topic D
• Data flow enforcement	
• DMZ	
• Separation of critical assets	

Domain and Objective	Covered In
• Network access control	Lesson 8, Topic D
• Quarantine/remediation	
• Operational and consumer network-enabled devices	Lesson 8, Topic C
• Building automation systems	
• IP video	
• HVAC controllers	
• Sensors	
• Physical access control systems	
• A/V systems	
• Scientific/industrial equipment	
• Critical infrastructure/Supervisor Control and Data Acquisition (SCADA)/Industrial Control Systems (ICS)	Lesson 8, Topic D

1.4 Given a scenario, select and troubleshoot security controls for hosts

Domain and Objective	Covered In
• Trusted OS (e.g., how and when to use it)	Lesson 6, Topic A
• Endpoint security software	Lesson 6, Topic A
• Anti-malware	
• Antivirus	
• Anti-spyware	
• Spam filters	
• Patch management	
• HIPS/HIDS	
• Data loss prevention	
• Host-based firewalls	
• Log monitoring	
• Host hardening	Lesson 6, Topic B
• Standard operating environment/configuration baselining	
• Application whitelisting and blacklisting	
• Security/group policy implementation	
• Command shell restrictions	
• Patch management	
• Configuring dedicated interfaces	
• Out-of-band NICs	
• ACLs	
• Management interface	
• Data interface	
• Peripheral restrictions	
• USB	
• Bluetooth	
• Firewire	
• Full disk encryption	

Domain and Objective	Covered In

• Security advantages and disadvantages of virtualizing servers
  • Type I
  • Type II
  • Container-based
	Lesson 6, Topic C

• Cloud-augmented security services
  • Hash matching
    • Antivirus
    • Anti-spam
    • Vulnerability scanning
  • Sandboxing
  • Content filtering
	Lesson 6, Topic D

• Boot loader protections
  • Secure boot
  • Measured launch
  • IMA - Integrity Measurement Architecture
  • BIOS/UEFI
	Lesson 6, Topic E

• Vulnerabilities associated with co-mingling of hosts with different security requirements
  • VM escape
  • Privilege elevation
  • Live VM migration
  • Data remnants
	Lesson 6, Topic C

• Virtual Desktop Infrastructure (VDI)	Lesson 6, Topic C
• Terminal services/application delivery services	Lesson 6, Topic C
• TPM	Lesson 6, Topic A
• vTPM	Lesson 6, Topic C
• HSM	Lesson 6, Topic A

1.5 Differentiate application vulnerabilities and select appropriate security controls

Domain and Objective	Covered In
• Web application security design considerations • Secure: by design, by default, by deployment	Lesson 9, Topic C

Domain and Objective	Covered In
• Specific application issues	Lesson 9, Topic A; Lesson 9, Topic B; Lesson 9, Topic C
• Insecure direct object references	
• XSS	
• Cross-site request forgery (CSRF)	
• Clickjacking	
• Session management	
• Input validation	
• SQL injection	
• Improper error and exception handling	
• Privilege escalation	
• Improper storage of sensitive data	
• Fuzzing/fault injection	
• Secure cookie storage and transmission	
• Buffer overflows	
• Memory leaks	
• Integer overflows	
• Race conditions	
• Time of check	
• Time of use	
• Resource exhaustion	
• Geo-tagging	
• Data remnants	
• Application sandboxing	Lesson 9, Topic C
• Application security frameworks	Lesson 9, Topic C
• Standard libraries	
• Industry accepted approaches	
• Web services security (WS-security)	
• Secure coding standards	Lesson 9, Topic C
• Database activity monitor (DAM)	Lesson 9, Topic C
• Web application firewalls (WAF)	Lesson 9, Topic C
• Client-side processing vs. server-side processing	Lesson 9, Topic C
• JSON/REST	
• Browser extensions	
• ActiveX	
• Java Applets	
• Flash	
• HTML5	
• AJAX	
• SOAP	
• State management	
• JavaScript	

Domain 2.0 Risk Management and Incident Response

Domain and Objective	Covered In
2.1 Interpret business and industry influences and explain associated security risks	
• Risk management of new products, new technologies, and user behaviors	Lesson 1, Topic B

• New or changing business models/strategies
  • Partnerships
  • Outsourcing
  • Cloud
  • Merger and demerger/divestiture
	Lesson 1, Topic B

• Security concerns of integrating diverse industries
  • Rules
  • Policies
  • Regulations
  • Geography
	Lesson 1, Topic B

• Assuring third party providers have requisite levels of information security	Lesson 1, Topic B

• Internal and external influences
  • Competitors
  • Auditors/audit findings
  • Regulatory entities
  • Internal and external client requirements
  • Top-level management
	Lesson 1, Topic B

• Impact of de-perimeterization (e.g., constantly changing network boundary)
  • Telecommuting
  • Cloud
  • BYOD
  • Outsourcing
	Lesson 1, Topic B

2.2 Given a scenario, execute risk mitigation planning, strategies, and controls	
• Classify information types into levels of CIA based on organization/industry	Lesson 1, Topic C
• Incorporate stakeholder input into CIA decisions	Lesson 1, Topic C
• Implement technical controls based on CIA requirements and policies of the organization	Lesson 1, Topic C
• Determine aggregate score of CIA	Lesson 1, Topic C
• Extreme scenario planning/worst case scenario	Lesson 1, Topic C
• Determine minimum required security controls based on aggregate score	Lesson 1, Topic C
• Conduct system-specific risk analysis	Lesson 1, Topic C

Domain and Objective	Covered In
• Make risk determination	Lesson 1, Topic B
• Magnitude of impact	
• ALE	
• SLE	
• Likelihood of threat	
• Motivation	
• Source	
• ARO	
• Trend analysis	
• Return on investment (ROI)	
• Total cost of ownership	
• Recommend which strategy should be applied based on risk appetite	Lesson 1, Topic C
• Avoid	
• Transfer	
• Mitigate	
• Accept	
• Risk management process	Lesson 1, Topic C
• Exemptions	
• Deterrence	
• Inherent	
• Residual	
• Enterprise Security Architecture frameworks	Lesson 1, Topic B
• Continuous improvement/monitoring	Lesson 1, Topic C
• Business continuity planning	Lesson 1, Topic D
• IT governance	Lesson 1, Topic C

2.3 Compare and contrast security, privacy policies, and procedures based on organizational requirements

• Policy development and updates in light of new business, technology, risks, and environment changes	Lesson 1, Topic D
• Process/procedure development and updates in light of policy, environment, and business changes	Lesson 1, Topic D
• Support legal compliance and advocacy by partnering with HR, legal, management, and other entities	Lesson 1, Topic D

Domain and Objective	Covered In
• Use common business documents to support security	Lesson 1, Topic D
• Risk assessment (RA)/Statement of applicability (SOA)	
• Business impact analysis (BIA)	
• Interoperability agreement (IA)	
• Interconnection security agreement (ISA)	
• Memorandum of understanding (MOU)	
• Service-level agreement (SLA)	
• Operating-level agreement (OLA)	
• Non-disclosure agreement (NDA)	
• Business partnership agreement (BPA)	
• Use general privacy principles for sensitive information (PII)	Lesson 1, Topic D
• Support the development of policies that contain	Lesson 1, Topic D
• Separation of duties	
• Job rotation	
• Mandatory vacation	
• Least privilege	
• Incident response	
• Forensic tasks	
• Employment and termination procedures	
• Continuous monitoring	
• Training and awareness for users	
• Auditing requirements and frequency	

2.4 Given a scenario, conduct incident response and recovery procedures

• E-discovery	Lesson 12, Topic B
• Electronic inventory and asset control	
• Data retention policies	
• Data recovery and storage	
• Data ownership	
• Data handling	
• Legal holds	
• Data breach	Lesson 12, Topic B
• Detection and collection	
• Data analytics	
• Mitigation	
• Minimize	
• Isolate	
• Recovery/reconstitution	
• Response	
• Disclosure	

Domain and Objective	Covered In
• Design systems to facilitate incident response	Lesson 12, Topic A
• Internal and external violations	
• Privacy policy violations	
• Criminal actions	
• Insider threat	
• Non-malicious threats/misconfigurations	
• Establish and review system, audit, and security logs	
• Incident and emergency response	Lesson 12, Topic B
• Chain of custody	
• Forensic analysis of compromised system	
• Continuity of operations plan (COOP)	
• Order of volatility	

Domain 3.0 Research, Analysis, and Assessment

3.1 Apply research methods to determine industry trends and impact to the enterprise

• Perform ongoing research	Lesson 3, Topic A
• Best practices	
• New technologies	
• New security systems and services	
• Technology evolution (e.g., RFCs, ISO)	
• Situational awareness	Lesson 3, Topic A
• Latest client-side attacks	
• Knowledge of current vulnerabilities and threats	
• Zero day mitigating controls and remediation	
• Emergent threats and issues	
• Research security implications of new business tools	Lesson 3, Topic A
• Social media/networking	
• End-user cloud storage	
• Integration within the business	
• Global IA industry/community	Lesson 3, Topic A
• Computer emergency response team (CERT)	
• Conventions/conferences	
• Threat actors	
• Emerging threat sources/threat intelligence	
• Research security requirements for contracts	Lesson 3, Topic A
• Request for Proposal (RFP)	
• Request for Quote (RFQ)	
• Request for Information (RFI)	
• Agreements	

3.2 Analyze scenarios to secure the enterprise

• Create benchmarks and compare to baselines	Lesson 3, Topic B

Domain and Objective	Covered In
• Prototype and test multiple solutions	Lesson 3, Topic B
• Cost benefit analysis	Lesson 3, Topic B
• ROI	
• TCO	
• Metrics collection and analysis	Lesson 3, Topic B
• Analyze and interpret trend data to anticipate cyber-defense needs	Lesson 3, Topic B
• Review effectiveness of existing security controls	Lesson 3, Topic B
• Reverse engineer/deconstruct existing solutions	Lesson 3, Topic B
• Analyze security solution attributes to ensure they meet business needs	Lesson 3, Topic B
• Performance	
• Latency	
• Scalability	
• Capability	
• Usability	
• Maintainability	
• Availability	
• Recoverability	
• Conduct a lessons learned/after-action report	Lesson 3, Topic B
• Use judgment to solve difficult problems that do not have a best solution	Lesson 3, Topic B

3.3 Given a scenario, select methods or tools appropriate to conduct an assessment and analyze results

• Tool type	Lesson 11, Topic B
• Port scanners	
• Vulnerability scanners	
• Protocol analyzer	
• Network enumerator	
• Password cracker	
• Fuzzer	
• HTTP interceptor	
• Exploitation tools/frameworks	
• Passive reconnaissance and intelligence gathering tools	
• Social media	
• Whois	
• Routing tables	

Domain and Objective	Covered In
• Methods	Lesson 11, Topic A
• Vulnerability assessment	
• Malware sandboxing	
• Memory dumping, runtime debugging	
• Penetration testing	
• Black box	
• White box	
• Grey box	
• Reconnaissance	
• Fingerprinting	
• Code review	
• Social engineering	

Domain 4.0 Integration of Computing, Communications, and Business Disciplines

4.1 Given a scenario, facilitate collaboration across diverse business units to achieve security goals

• Interpreting security requirements and goals to communicate with stakeholders from other disciplines	Lesson 2, Topic A
• Sales staff	
• Programmer	
• Database administrator	
• Network administrator	
• Management/executive management	
• Financial	
• Human resources	
• Emergency response team	
• Facilities manager	
• Physical security manager	
• Provide objective guidance and impartial recommendations to staff and senior management on security processes and controls	Lesson 2, Topic A
• Establish effective collaboration within teams to implement secure solutions	Lesson 2, Topic A
• IT governance	Lesson 2, Topic A

4.2 Given a scenario, select the appropriate control to secure communications and collaboration solutions

Domain and Objective	Covered In
• Security of unified collaboration tools	Lesson 2, Topic B
• Web conferencing	
• Video conferencing	
• Instant messaging	
• Desktop sharing	
• Remote assistance	
• Presence	
• Email	
• Telephony	
• VoIP	
• Collaboration sites	
• Social media	
• Cloud-based	
• Remote access	Lesson 2, Topic B
• Mobile device management	Lesson 2, Topic B
• BYOD	
• Over-the-air technologies concerns	Lesson 2, Topic B

4.3 Implement security activities across the technology life cycle

Domain and Objective	Covered In
• End-to-end solution ownership	Lesson 2, Topic C
• Operational activities	
• Maintenance	
• Commissioning/decommissioning	
• Asset disposal	
• Asset/object reuse	
• General change management	
• Systems development life cycle	Lesson 2, Topic C
• Security System Development Life Cycle (SSDLC)/ Security Development Lifecycle (SDL)	
• Security Requirements Traceability Matrix (SRTM)	
• Validation and acceptance testing	
• Security implications of agile, waterfall, and spiral software development methodologies	
• Adapt solutions to address emerging threats and security trends	Lesson 2, Topic C
• Asset management (inventory control)	Lesson 2, Topic C
• Device tracking technologies	
• Geo-location/GPS location	
• Object tracking and containment technologies	
• Geo-tagging/geo-fencing	
• RFID	

Domain 5.0 Enterprise Security

Domain and Objective	Covered In
5.1 Given a scenario, integrate hosts, storage, networks, and applications into a secure enterprise architecture	
• Secure data flows to meet changing business needs	Lesson 10, Topic A
• Standards	Lesson 10, Topic A
• Open standards	
• Adherence to standards	
• Competing standards	
• Lack of standards	
• Defacto standards	
• Interoperability issues	Lesson 10, Topic A
• Legacy systems/current systems	
• Application requirements	
• In-house developed vs. commercial vs. commercial customized	
• Technical deployment models (Outsourcing/insourcing/managed services/partnership)	Lesson 10, Topic B
• Cloud and virtualization considerations and hosting options	
• Public	
• Private	
• Hybrid	
• Community	
• Multi-tenancy	
• Single tenancy	
• Vulnerabilities associated with a single physical server hosting multiple companies' virtual machines	
• Vulnerabilities associated with a single platform hosting multiple companies' virtual machines	
• Secure use of on-demand/elastic cloud computing	
• Data remnants	
• Data aggregation	
• Data isolation	
• Resource provisioning and de-provisioning	
• Users	
• Servers	
• Virtual devices	
• Applications	
• Securing virtual environments, services, applications, appliances, and equipment	
• Design considerations during mergers, acquisitions, and demergers/divestitures	
• Network secure segmentation and delegation	
• Logical deployment diagram and corresponding physical deployment diagram of all relevant devices	Lesson 10, Topic C

Domain and Objective	Covered In
• Secure infrastructure design (e.g., decide where to place certain devices/applications)	Lesson 10, Topic C
• Storage integration (security considerations)	Lesson 10, Topic C

• Enterprise application integration enablers
   • CRM
   • ERP
   • GRC
   • ESB
   • SOA
   • Directory Services
   • DNS
   • CMDB
   • CMS
	Lesson 10, Topic D

5.2 Given a scenario, integrate advanced authentication and authorization technologies to support enterprise objectives

• Authentication
   • Certificate-based authentication
   • Single sign-on
	Lesson 4, Topic A

• Authorization
   • OAuth
   • XACML
   • SPML
	Lesson 4, Topic A

• Attestation	Lesson 4, Topic B
• Identity propagation	Lesson 4, Topic B

• Federation
   • SAML
   • OpenID
   • Shibboleth
   • WAYF
	Lesson 4, Topic B

• Advanced trust models
   • RADIUS configurations
   • LDAP
   • AD
	Lesson 4, Topic A

Lesson Labs

Lesson labs are provided for certain lessons as additional learning resources for this course. Lesson labs are developed for selected lessons within a course in cases when they seem most instructionally useful as well as technically feasible. In general, labs are supplemental, optional unguided practice and may or may not be performed as part of the classroom activities. Your instructor will consider setup requirements, classroom timing, and instructional needs to determine which labs are appropriate for you to perform, and at what point during the class. If you do not perform the labs in class, your instructor can tell you if you can perform them independently as self-study, and if there are any special setup requirements.

Lesson Lab 1–1
Managing Risk with a Security Policy

Activity Time: 30 minutes

Before You Begin

To complete this activity, you will need a computer with a web browser and a connection to the Internet. You will also need a word processing application like Microsoft Word.

Scenario

You have recently been hired to oversee information security at Richland State College at Greene City, a mid-size college. In the past, the college administration hasn't employed any formal risk management strategy. You've convinced them that this is a major security issue, and they task you with creating that ERM strategy. To make it easier for you and your team to manage risk, you'll use templates from the SANS Institute to create security policies for your fellow employees and students to follow.

---

1. Open your web browser and navigate to **www.sans.org/security-resources/policies**.

2. Select the policy template that you believe is the most relevant to the college's security needs.

3. Download the policy template document and open it in a word processor.

4. Read the template document and identify its scope and purpose.

5. Edit the policy document based on the college's security needs. Add items that define and address the risks associated with that particular area of concern, and change or add response techniques based on what you think is the best course of action.

6. Add your name and today's date to the document's revision history, or create one, if necessary.

7. Save the document and close your word processing application.

Lesson Lab 2-1
Researching Communications Technologies

Activity Time: 30 minutes

Before You Begin

To complete this activity, you will need a computer with a web browser and a connection to the Internet.

Scenario

As part of your duties at the Richland State College, you'll need to make sure that your employees are communicating and collaborating safely and effectively. To meet their own needs and concerns, you'll research the types of tools out there that they may currently use or want to use in the future, and you'll consider the security concerns associated with these tools. You'll also research how the BYOD phenomenon may impact your enterprise security.

---

1. Open your web browser and connect to the Internet search site of your choice.

2. Search for articles and information related to the security concerns of individual communication/ collaboration tools that you're familiar with or have heard of. Explore the content on some of the sites you find.

3. Search for articles and information about what communication tools specific business disciplines tend to use and how they use those tools. Explore the content on some of the sites you find.

4. Search for articles and information related to BYOD vulnerabilities and any experiences that other security professionals share. Explore the content on some of the sites you find.

5. Search for articles and information related to the security concerns associated with specific mobile devices or operating systems. Explore the content on some of the sites you find.

6. Search for articles and information related to how other security professionals dispose of or decommission obsolete communication technology. Explore the content on some of the sites you find.

Lesson Lab 3-1

Exercising Careful Judgment in Research and Analysis

Activity Time: 15 minutes

Scenario

In your job at Richland State College, you need to be constantly aware of your own security environment, as well as the industry trends that may affect it. However, passively accepting research and analysis is not enough. You must be able to approach both objectively, so that you won't be misled or misinformed. So, you'll need to exercise discretion when consulting other sources and performing analyses on your systems.

1. You come across a blog that mentions statistics about trending attacks on security. The blog's author indicates that, based on these numbers, attackers are increasingly targeting web apps while abandoning attacks on other fronts. The author concludes that security professionals should refocus their efforts on securing their enterprise web apps rather than areas like cloud hosting and social media. What do you need to be mindful of before you trust this report and its conclusion?

2. You decide to research new business tools like social media sites and end user cloud storage. Each solution's website advertises its product/service as secure and reliable, and that user privacy is their number-one concern. What should you be mindful of before making a decision on which solution to choose?

3. Your employer wants you to conduct a cost-benefit analysis (CBA) on your security solutions. Depending on the results of this analysis, the college will eliminate any solutions that do not meet a certain threshold. You will conduct this analysis based on a return on investment (ROI) calculation. To give your employer the most accurate CBA you can, what additional factor do you need to account for in your ROI, and why?

Lesson Lab 4-1
Implementing Advanced Authentication Techniques

Activity Time: 15 minutes

Scenario

Richland State College has had trouble in the past with unauthorized users accessing sensitive resources on its network. Part of your duties as the college's security lead will be to establish authentication techniques that will keep unwanted users out, while allowing legitimate users in. This will help keep the college's data from falling into malicious hands.

1. Your security team has performed an audit of passwords in use in the enterprise and discovered that many employees are choosing poor passwords. Because of this, you decide to investigate certificate-based authentication and to determine if its use will mitigate the risk posed by the bad passwords. What benefits would a certificate-based approach to authentication bring?

2. A vendor has approached the college about integrating their SSO solution into your existing network. You must ensure that the SSO solution will provide at least the same level of authentication and access security as what currently exists on the network. What precautions and considerations will you take?

3. Because the college has many employees and students, it needs to use a robust directory service to keep track of individual users and devices. What are the benefits of implementing a secure directory service?

Lesson Lab 5-1
Examining an SSL Certificate

Activity Time: 15 minutes

Before You Begin

To complete this activity, you will need a computer with a web browser and a connection to the Internet.

Scenario

Due to its new learning management system (LMS), Richland State College at Greene City will need to update its website to accommodate secure transmissions. Before you go ahead and purchase a public certificate from a certificate authority, you'll want to learn more about how your website will present its certificate to clients that connect. It's important that your digital certificate use strong cryptography so that your SSL implementation will guarantee that students' and teachers' credentials remain confidential when sent over the Internet.

1. Open a browser and navigate to a website that uses SSL, like **www.google.com**.

2. Select the lock icon next to the URL and open the site's digital certificate.

3. Observe the tabs in the dialog box. Select the tab that displays the certificate's details.

4. Verify the following information about the certificate:
   - The issuer.
   - The signature algorithm used.
   - The period of time it is valid.
   - The public key encryption algorithm used.

    Note: If you're using Mozilla® Firefox®, you may need to select each item to display its information.

5. Verify the certification path and the root CA of the certificate.

Lesson Lab 6-1
Researching Cloud Augmented Security Services

Activity Time: 20 minutes

Before You Begin

To complete this activity, you will need a computer with a web browser and a connection to the Internet.

Scenario

Because of financial and time restraints, Richland State College at Greene City may be unable to provide the necessary level of security in-house. You've convinced the administration that dropping these security processes entirely is extremely dangerous, and that instead the college should look for a cloud company that will take on the burden. So, it's up to you to research the various cloud companies that provide security services and determine which is the best fit for your organization. Entrusting a third party with your information's welfare is a huge risk, so you need to be as informed as possible before making a decision.

1. Open your web browser and connect to the Internet search site of your choice.

2. Search for *cloud-based security* and identify and explore articles that mention specific cloud-based security services.

3. Navigate to the websites of any cloud-based security providers that interest you. Identify what security services they provide and how they purport to help enterprises or individuals protect their information.

4. Search for third-party articles or discussion posts about each cloud-based security provider that you examined. Identify any reviews or shared experiences about each service.

Lesson Lab 7–1
Researching Cloud Storage Solutions

Activity Time: 20 minutes

Before You Begin

To complete this activity, you will need a computer with a web browser and a connection to the Internet.

Scenario

Instead of storing student and employee data on its own servers, Richland State College is considering using a cloud provider. As you're concerned about the data's security in the cloud, you want to research some of the availability solutions and learn more about what security they do or do not offer.

---

1. Open your web browser and connect to the Internet search site of your choice.

2. Search for *cloud storage*. Identify and explore articles that mention specific cloud storage providers, or navigate directly to a provider's website.

3. From the article or provider website, look for information about what kind of security the provider offers, including authentication schemes, encryption, availability controls, and more.

4. If available, search for additional third-party reviews of that particular cloud provider and pay attention to any security concerns others may have.

5. Repeat this process with other cloud storage providers.

Lesson Lab 8-1
Enforce Network Access Control Policies

Activity Time: 30 minutes

Before You Begin

To complete this activity, you will need a Windows Server® 2012 R2 domain controller with Network Policy Server installed. If you have a VPN configured, you may be able to test some of these policies, depending on what those policies are.

Scenario

Richland State College has set up a VPN for personnel that work outside of its private network. To make sure that this VPN conforms to your security requirements, you'll enforce Network Access Control (NAC) policies. One such policy should stipulate that clients running obsolete and unsupported operating systems like Windows XP will be denied access to the VPN. After configuring this policy, you'll create new ones that will help keep the VPN in line with your best security practices.

---

1. From **Server Manager**, open **Network Policy Server**.

2. Open your **Network Policies**, and create a new one.

3. Name the policy *VPN Client OS Policy*.

4. Set an **Operating System** condition that denies any clients running a Windows OS version less than 6.0.

 Note: Version 6.0 refers to Windows Vista® and Windows Server® 2008. Higher version numbers indicate a later generation operating system, like Windows® 8 or Windows Server® 2012. Immediately preceding 6.0 is 5.2, which refers to Windows® XP 64-bit, Windows Server® 2003, and Windows Server® 2003 R2.

5. Configure any other relevant parameters and select **Finish** in the wizard to save the policy.

6. Create additional network policies with different conditions. Some suggested conditions: **User Groups**, **Health Policies**, and **Access Client IPv4 Address**.

7. If you're able to, test any of these policies on your VPN server.

Lesson Lab 9-1
Testing Web App Vulnerabilities

Activity Time: 30 minutes

Data File

C:\093023Data\Implementing Security Controls for Applications\script_exploit.html

Before You Begin

To complete this activity, you will need a computer with a web browser and a connection to the Internet. You will be using Gruyere, a sandbox web app that teaches web developers about the various exploits that their apps are vulnerable to. You will be exploiting a scripting vulnerability in Gruyere that allows you to execute a script in HTML, exposing cookie information on the domain.

Scenario

There are many potential vulnerabilities that could compromise Richland State College's web app, and you need to make sure that your developers are accounting for as many of them that they can. To do this, you'll demonstrate the various ways in which someone could launch an attack on the app, starting with one of the most common vectors: scripting.

---

1. Navigate to **https://google-gruyere.appspot.com/start** and start the web app.

2. Use the **Sign up** link to create a test account.

3. Sign in under that test account.

4. Use the **Upload** link to upload **script_exploit.html**.

5. Navigate to the file link that you are given.

6. Verify that the web page loads with a message box that contains cookie information about the Gruyere domain.

    Note: If you wish, open the HTML file in a text editor to see the source of the script.

7. Navigate to **https://google-gruyere.appspot.com/part1** and use the table of contents to find more information about the many different web app vulnerabilities you can exploit in this sandbox environment. Try some of the ones that interest you.

Lesson Lab 10-1
Designing a Secure Network Infrastructure

Activity Time: 45 minutes

Data File

C:\093023Data\Integrating Hosts, Storage, Networks, and Applications in a Secure Enterprise Architecture\Solution\Designing a Secure Network Infrastructure.pptx.

 Note: This file contains the unsolved diagram, as well as the solution. To open and/or modify the file, you must have PowerPoint 2013 or an equivalent application.

Scenario

Richland State College has called on you to help deploy various security features in their network. They have provided you with a deployment diagram of their current network infrastructure so that you may identify where best to place these features.

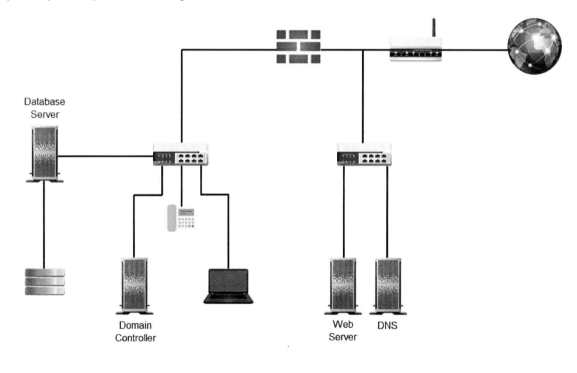

1. On the diagram, where would you label the implementation of secure directory services?

2. What are the security benefits of implementing any of the types of secure directory services?

3. On the diagram, where would you label the integration of a VLAN?

4. Why would you place the VLAN where you did? What security measures does it help implement?

5. On the diagram, where would you label the implementation of a database activity monitor (DAM)?

6. Why is DAM an important part of network security?

7. On the diagram, where would you label the implementation of IPv6?

8. Why would you implement IPv6 where you suggested?

9. On the diagram, where would you label the implementation of an NIDS/NIPS?

10. What are some of the possible ramifications of integrating NIDS/NIPS in this location regarding data that your employees may be accessing?

11. On the diagram, where would you label the implementation of the DNSSEC?

12. Why is implementing DNSSEC an important network security measure?

13. Compare your completed diagram to the sample solution.

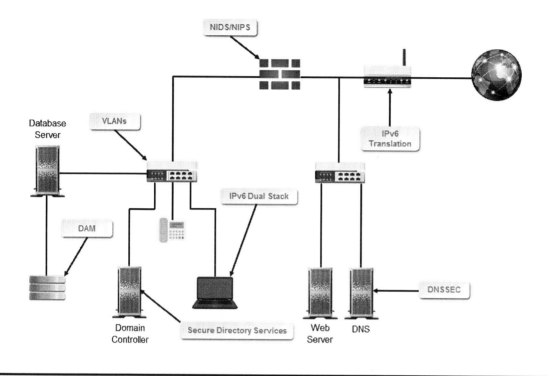

Lesson Lab 11-1
Researching Security Tools

Activity Time: 30 minutes

Before You Begin

To complete this activity, you will need a computer with a web browser and a connection to the Internet.

Scenario

You've established a great deal of security measures in Richland State College at Greene City, and now you want to test that security. To do so, you'll first have to select which tools will best help you conduct your assessment. So, you'll research the many tools available and select the ones that are relevant to your needs.

---

1. Using the Internet search site of your choice, look for specific tools in each of the following categories:

    *   General vulnerability scanners
    *   Port scanners
    *   Protocol/packet analyzers
    *   Network enumerators
    *   Password crackers
    *   Fuzzers
    *   HTTP interceptors
    *   Exploitation frameworks
    *   Passive reconnaissance/intelligence gathering tools

     Note: One good resource for these tools is **www.sectools.org**.

2. Read more about each tool to learn its functionality. If available, read any reviews of the tool.

3. **Which of these tools do you use or might want to use to secure your own enterprise? Why?**

Lesson Lab 12–1
Responding to a Security Incident

Activity Time: 20 minutes

Scenario

You received an alert from a member of your security team at Richland State College that the student records database is unavailable and employees are unable to access it. Suspecting a data breach, you move to respond.

---

1. What immediate precautions might you take to mitigate the damage?

2. What types of evidence should you collect?

3. Assuming you identify a suspect and engage in legal action, why would you specify that the data you collected from the database be hashed?

4. What knowledge from dealing with this incident could you apply to future incidents?

Solutions

ACTIVITY 1–1: Identifying the Importance of Risk Management

1. Develetech, a relatively large electronics manufacturer, is looking to expand its business over the next couple of years. This may include everything from taking on new staff to establishing additional offices and warehouses. Why would these changes necessitate the development of an ERM strategy?

   A: Answers will vary, but significant changes can bring about risk in many different ways. It may become more challenging to secure sensitive information and keep it out of unauthorized hands, or it may simply require more resources to secure more at-risk areas. Managing risk to information and systems will help your enterprise avoid legal and financial disaster. Additionally, there will be pressure from stakeholders, customers, and regulatory entities to conform to their expectations and meet standardization requirements. There is also the chance that an increase in the amount of communications in the enterprise will exponentially increase the amount of risk that these communication channels take on. You need to make sure that changes to your enterprise can uphold risk management expectations.

2. What are the specific types of risk that could affect Develetech as it expands its business?

   A: Answers will vary, as there are many potential risks. Additional offices and warehouses will require an infrastructure overhaul, which will require a reevaluation of its integrity. Certain physical assets, including computers and networking equipment, may not be able to sustain an increase in operational capacity. More personnel may increase the risk of a safety incident. Failing to ascertain laws and regulations, especially when moving operations into a foreign country, may place the organization in legal trouble. Financially, a security breach could cost the organization a great deal, and its reputation may suffer as a result.

3. **You've identified a risk to the availability of your file servers at peak traffic hours. How would you prefer to calculate Develetech's risk exposure in this area? What are the strengths and weaknesses of the analysis you chose, and why do you think it's more beneficial than the others?**

   A: Answers will vary, but some may prefer a quantitative analysis because it can be used more objectively to manage risk. Such an analysis is heavily based in historical precedent and current trend data, and upholds well to experimentation. However, some will point out that a quantitative analysis is unsuitable because of how difficult it is to accurately measure a concept like risk. Statistics may provide a predictive model of risk to the file servers, but it will not necessarily be of any practical value to the organization itself. A qualitative analysis will allow you to more easily tailor the analysis based on your enterprise's subjective beliefs, but it still falls short of providing concrete, testable results. Others may attempt to find a middle ground by incorporating a semi-quantitative analysis, but this can convolute the process and make it more challenging to apply practically. When it comes to risk, there is not necessarily an objectively right answer. Students may need more information about a situation before the best approach becomes obvious.

ACTIVITY 1-2: Assessing Risk

1. **One of the possibilities involved in expanding Develetech is the adoption of new technology. Your CEO may decide to drop legacy products, or even drop certain vendors altogether and replace them. What are the important things to remember about assessing new products and technologies, along with threats that inevitably come with them?**

   A: Answers may vary. If a new product or technology is introduced, you need to determine how large of an impact this will have on your operations. Small changes may not deserve as much attention to your ERM strategy as large ones. You also must take into account what these products interact with, especially if that happens to be sensitive company data. Each product and technology may have its own set of vulnerabilities that you need to test for, even if that product or technology fulfills the same basic role. Consulting with other departments and legal counsel may also aid you in your assessment. Like products and technology, threats are evolving and you must understand how they target your systems not just now, but on a recurring basis.

2. **Besides its in-house technology, Develetech may decide to change its core business strategy. Recently, the other officers at the company have been discussing the viability of moving to a cloud provider for most of the company's web hosting infrastructure. How would a move to the cloud impact your risk assessment?**

   A: Answers may vary. Because the software and hardware would be out of your immediate reach, the entire infrastructure of your web hosting services may need to be reassessed. Depending on the cloud provider's transparency, you may not be able to conduct as full of an assessment as you'd like, relying instead on the cloud company to provide you with risk information. You may not necessarily have all of the facts to truly assess how a compromise of these cloud services could compromise the enterprise. You must also be prepared for the possibility that your security requirements and standards won't necessarily apply to the cloud provider; depending on the nature of your relationship with them, they may adhere to their own standards which you find inadequate.

3. **You've identified compliance to be one of the biggest concerns for the expansion. How will both internal and external compliance factors influence your risk assessment?**

   A: Answers may vary. Your internal staff needs to comply with your ERM plan once it has been put in place. This may mean that training certain staff is required; otherwise, they might not be properly equipped to meet compliance. Because internal users access your systems constantly, they can bring a great deal of risk. Externally, your organization must comply with all applicable laws and regulations. Even failure to comply with non-legally binding industry-accepted standards may place your organization's finances or reputation in jeopardy. However, external compliance will not guarantee security. You may find that your risk is still too high even though you adhere to security requirements.

ACTIVITY 1-3: Mitigating Risk

1. Which classification denotes information that only certain personnel in an enterprise are authorized to access?

   ○ Private

   ○ Confidential

   ◉ Restricted

   ○ Public

2. Develetech is interested in implementing routine backups of all customer databases. This will help uphold availability because you will be able to quickly and easily restore the backed up copy, and it will also help uphold integrity in case someone tampers with the database. What controls can you implement to round out your risk mitigation strategy and uphold the components of the CIA triad?

   A: Answers will vary, but a strong way to secure confidentiality is through encryption. Encrypting the database will prevent unauthorized users from making sense of the stored data. You could also implement access control to prevent an intrusion before it even begins. This will keep your databases out of the hands of an attacker.

3. In choosing which risks to prioritize in your mitigation efforts, you use an aggregate CIA score to make a determination. How will you calculate this score, and how will you determine which risk to prioritize?

   A: Each risk is divided into the three components of the CIA triad (confidentiality, integrity, availability), and each component is scored based on how valuable it is to the organization. This value is multiplied by how harmful the risk is to produce a total amount of risk. The totals for each of the three components are added together to form the aggregate score. The risk with the highest aggregate score should be first priority.

4. During their risk assessment, your team has identified a security flaw in an application your organization developed. To conduct a proper analysis of how this could bring risk to your enterprise, what are some of the questions you need to ask?

   A: Answers will vary, but you should ask how easily exploitable the flaw is, and what the scope of an exploit could be. Can an exploit expose confidential information? Can it crash the app or otherwise render other systems unavailable? What attack vectors exist that could allow an attacker to carry out this exploit? What mitigation plans, if any, are in place to address this flaw? How easily and quickly can you patch the flaw, and how will you deploy it so that all of the app's users are covered?

5. You've analyzed the application flaw and discovered that it could allow an unauthorized user to access the customer database that the app integrates with if the app uses poor input validation. If an attacker were to access the database this way, they could glean confidential customer information, making the impact to your business relatively high. However, you determine that your app's current input validation techniques account for all known exploits of this kind. How will you respond to this risk?

   A: The answer is debatable and may require more careful analysis. However, some may argue that the strong input validation controls already in place imply that you should just accept the risk and save yourself the time, effort, and cost of an active response. Others will say that this is inadequate because it only accounts for known values, and that an attacker could find a way around the validation. This would necessitate a response like mitigation, in which more application security controls are implemented to harden the app against attack. Some might suggest transferring the risk to another organization that can provide more reliable security. Some might even argue that the risk to your customers' confidentiality is too great, and that you should avoid the risk entirely by dropping the internally developed app and using a different solution.

ACTIVITY 1-4: Integrating Documentation into Risk Management

7. **What are some of the other best security practices you can incorporate in a social engineering policy like this one?**

   A: Answers will vary, but you could mandate job rotation and separation of duties to ensure that individual employees are not repeated and frequent targets of social engineering attempts while working the help desk. You can also outline incident response and forensic procedures in case social engineering attempts do succeed, and supplement those procedures with strong auditing requirements. This will help you mitigate the damage these attacks can do.

8. **Why is it important to maintain a revision history in policies like this one?**

   A: Answers may vary, but security policies, procedures, and processes are living documents. This means that, in the event of newly identified threats or vulnerabilities, you can adjust the document accordingly. Documents that cannot keep up with ever-shifting enterprise risk factors are unhelpful to their intended audience. Recording revision history will ensure that there is a trail of changes and that each change is known in the context of when it was made, and that the person(s) who made the changes are held accountable.

ACTIVITY 2-1: Facilitating Collaboration Across Business Units

1. **Which of the following are key elements for successful collaboration within teams? (Select three.)**

   ☑ Communicate goals to the team.

   ☐ Withhold progress reports unless asked.

   ☑ Play to each individual's strengths.

   ☑ Include all relevant team members in the decision making process.

2. **You've already communicated your security expectations to the teams in the IT department. Now you must do the same for sales, finance, and human resources. How will you communicate the importance of security to these personnel that may not have the technical experience that your IT department has?**

   A: Answers may vary. Because sales staff generate revenue for the company, they need to know that being lax about security could compromise their ability to make a sale and the enterprise's ability to turn a profit. Sales staff have access to a large amount of possibly sensitive data, so they need to be careful about who they share that data with. For finance team members, you should speak in terms of risk; without the proper budget for security controls, the organization will take on a great deal of risk. You should clearly outline the cost of this risk. HR personnel should be charged with disseminating employee security policies across the organization. Without their help in making personnel aware of these policies, the organization could suffer a breach of security.

3. You plan on installing a demilitarized zone (DMZ) along Develetech's network perimeter to isolate a large chunk of the network from external traffic. This external traffic will only be able to access the servers you place inside the DMZ and not any outside it. How should you communicate the need for this security control to your CEO?

   A: Answers may vary, but you should pitch your DMZ idea by qualifying it as part of a security control group and specific category. You could explain that the DMZ is part of your organization's technical controls, and specifically, that it acts as a firewall(s) to block unwanted connections from outside the network. You can also explain the DMZ in terms of it being a preventative control, as it is able to prevent an attacker from intruding on the larger network. Additionally, you may wish to explain the DMZ in less technical terms, like comparing it to the company's lobby. Your security personnel only allow certain people to enter the lobby, and they also only allow certain people to continue on into the rest of the office. This creates a buffer similar to a DMZ.

ACTIVITY 2-3: Implementing Security Activities Throughout the Technology Life Cycle

1. Which of the following are phases or principles of most SDLCs? (Select three.)
   - ☑ Validation and acceptance testing.
   - ☑ Post-deployment maintenance.
   - ☑ Deployment and implementation.
   - ☐ Risk mitigation.

2. How will creating a Security Requirements Traceability Matrix (SRTM) help the requirements building phase of your SDLC model?

   A: Answers may vary, but an SRTM will allow you to compare your requirements with the policy they originate from, as well as the control that is intended to bring about or guarantee these requirements. You can use SRTMs to trace requirements back to their implementations, or vice versa. This makes it easier to evaluate whether or not the requirement is being upheld and is still viable.

3. Your IT colleagues have determined that your server hardware is out of date, so they've begun the process of replacing it with more current systems. They've also determined that the old hardware is not salvageable or otherwise of any use, so they move to throw it out. Before they go through with this, what security activity do you need to remind them to take to ensure proper end-to-end solution handling?

   A: Answers will vary, but throwing out hardware with the trash will not necessarily completely erase information from its memory. The IT team should exercise proper asset disposal by either using data erasure tools to ensure that no sensitive information remains, or they should physically destroy the disk and memory components to the point where it is impossible to recover any data.

4. In asset management, what is the process of creating geographic boundaries to prevent devices from working within or outside of certain areas?
   - ○ Geo-location
   - ○ Geo-tagging
   - ◉ Geo-fencing
   - ○ Radio-frequency identification (RFID)

5. In software development, whether your team uses a waterfall, agile, or spiral method, what are the best security principles to follow? (Select two.)
   - ☐ Implement security measures as issues arise.
   - ☑ Incorporate security at the beginning of the development life cycle.
   - ☑ Incorporate security at every phase of the development life cycle.
   - ☐ Incorporate security after development ends.

ACTIVITY 3-1: Determining Industry Trends and Effects on the Enterprise

5. While Develetech's operations are growing, the marketing team would like to have a greater social media footprint. They plan on sharing information with customers via Twitter, Facebook, and YouTube. What measures should you take to ensure your organization's security when using these business tools? Can you think of any enterprise security incidents that resulted from these tools being used improperly?

   A: Answers will vary, but students will likely raise concerns about employees in the organizations divulging sensitive information on social media sites. They may offer security training or supply new security policies to employees who will be using the social media sites. They might also be concerned about less obvious risks, like social media sites that have poor security and privacy features. In this case, they'll want to research each site and determine if the security it offers is adequate. Students may also wish to mandate that employees keep their personal accounts separate from their work accounts. Some might discourage social media use in the enterprise altogether if they determine that the risk is too great.

6. Develetech is looking to expand its data storage infrastructure by implementing a Fibre Channel solution. This will give the organization greater speed and scalability in accessing and backing up its ever-growing pool of databases. The CEO has already sent out a Request for Information (RFI) to contractors who can provide Fibre Channel equipment and installation. Before he finalizes an agreement with any of the responding contractors, you convince the CEO to let you take time to consider security issues first. What will your focus be during the other contract phases?

   A: Answers will vary, but a CASP should be heavily involved in the Request for Proposal (RFP) phase. This will give them time to evaluate the equipment the contractor will be installing, as well as determine any ways that this new infrastructure could leave their existing network vulnerable. The CASP might not be involved in the Request for Quote (RFQ), but this is sometimes when testing is done, so they'll want to learn as much as they can from the results. Lastly, the CASP will want to select the appropriate agreement type and incorporate any legal or regulatory requirements.

ACTIVITY 3-2: Analyzing Scenarios to Secure the Enterprise

5. What are some of the vulnerable areas of your domain controller that fail to meet the baseline? How could these discrepancies lead to a security issue?

   A: The Windows Update service does not automatically check for updates, so an administrator might miss a key security fix that Microsoft publishes. The Guest account's password does not expire, so if the account were enabled and its password set, an attacker will have more time to crack it. Auditing of logon events is disabled, so there is no trail of accountability with regard to who accessed the server at certain times. Finally, the World Wide Web Publishing Service is installed, which is typically unnecessary for a domain controller and may increase its attack surface.

LAB 3-1: Exercising Careful Judgment in Research and Analysis

1. You come across a blog that mentions statistics about trending attacks on security. The blog's author indicates that, based on these numbers, attackers are increasingly targeting web apps while abandoning attacks on other fronts. The author concludes that security professionals should refocus their efforts on securing their enterprise web apps rather than areas like cloud hosting and social media. What do you need to be mindful of before you trust this report and its conclusion?

   A: Answers may vary, but you should verify that the statistics the author mentions are properly cited, and that the cited sources are reputable. If possible, you may also consult the sources themselves to identify the methods used to conduct their analysis and data gathering.

2. You decide to research new business tools like social media sites and end user cloud storage. Each solution's website advertises its product/service as secure and reliable, and that user privacy is their number-one concern. What should you be mindful of before making a decision on which solution to choose?

   A: Answers will vary, but the solution's own website will undoubtedly be biased with respect to what claims it is making. The site may advertise an attractive security feature, but will not necessarily go into depth with how it is implemented. That's why it's important to consult unbiased third parties who have first-hand experience with a solution. They'll be able to evaluate how effective or comprehensive the security control is so that you may make a more informed decision.

3. Your employer wants you to conduct a cost-benefit analysis (CBA) on your security solutions. Depending on the results of this analysis, the college will eliminate any solutions that do not meet a certain threshold. You will conduct this analysis based on a return on investment (ROI) calculation. To give your employer the most accurate CBA you can, what additional factor do you need to account for in your ROI, and why?

   A: You should account for each solution's total cost of ownership (TCO). Without this, your ROI will simply account for the cost of acquisition, and not for the cost of continual maintenance. Accounting for TCO will allow you to make a more informed decision with regard to your CBA.

ACTIVITY 4-2: Implementing Advanced Identity Management

1. What is the process called that would involve verifying the privileges that specific employees possess?
   - ○ Identity federation
   - ○ Identity propagation
   - ○ Resource-focused attestation
   - ◉ User-focused attestation

2. Develetech has a shared SQL database that stores customer records. There are three different departments that need some sort of access to this database: accounts receivable to generate billing information, sales to update customer records, and the database administrators to perform routine maintenance and oversight. You want to design the SQL database so that identities can propagate through its different functions, streamlining authentication and authorization. What are some of the security concerns involved in this?

   A: Answers may vary, but you should also take care to restrict how identity propagates; a member of accounts receivable will likely only need read-only access to generate billing information; a salesperson will need both read and write access to alter the database's records; and administrators will need full access to perform any of the necessary functions. Essentially, identity propagation should respect access control and authorization policies.

3. Which of the following identity federation systems asks a user what institution they are from before it grants the user access?

- ⦿ WAYF
- ○ SAML
- ○ OpenID
- ○ Shibboleth

4. Shibboleth uses which XML-based framework to send authentication information?

- ○ XACML
- ⦿ SAML
- ○ DITA
- ○ SPML

LAB 4-1: Implementing Advanced Authentication Techniques

1. Your security team has performed an audit of passwords in use in the enterprise and discovered that many employees are choosing poor passwords. Because of this, you decide to investigate certificate-based authentication and to determine if its use will mitigate the risk posed by the bad passwords. What benefits would a certificate-based approach to authentication bring?

   A: Answers may vary, but one benefit is that certificates remove the need for passwords, which fixes the weak password issue. Second, when dealing with compromised accounts using passwords, administrators must change the password and then wait for it to propagate to all the services across the network. With certificates, the stolen certificate can simply be revoked and then it will no longer be valid across the network.

2. A vendor has approached the college about integrating their SSO solution into your existing network. You must ensure that the SSO solution will provide at least the same level of authentication and access security as what currently exists on the network. What precautions and considerations will you take?

   A: Answers may vary, but you should consider the issues with compromised SSO credentials leading to attackers having access to multiple resources. There is also added complexity when dealing with multi-factor authentication, such as provisioning access cards to supplement passwords.

3. Because the college has many employees and students, it needs to use a robust directory service to keep track of individual users and devices. What are the benefits of implementing a secure directory service?

   A: Answers may vary, but secure directory services help protect confidentiality by preventing unauthorized users from accessing public data that they should not have access to. This could be as simple as making sure that internal employees and students do not have access to data beyond what they need, also known as the principle of least privilege. Using Active Directory or any secure LDAP service can make that security much easier to manage and maintain by allowing network administrators to create and modify ACLs.

ACTIVITY 5-1: Discussing Cryptographic Concepts

1. **In cryptography, what is the purpose of entropy?**
   ○ To generate a great deal of change in ciphertext even, if the plaintext input is altered only slightly.
   ○ To obscure the relationship between an encryption key and its corresponding ciphertext.
   ◉ To generate a certain amount of randomness with which to strongly encrypt data.
   ○ To hide information within media like video and audio files.

2. **Which of the following concepts guarantees that the sender of a transmission cannot deny having sent it?**
   ○ Integrity
   ○ Confidentiality
   ◉ Non-repudiation
   ○ Chain of trust

3. **Which statement accurately describes stream ciphers?**
   ◉ Faster and less secure than block ciphers.
   ○ Slower and more secure than block ciphers.
   ○ Faster and more secure than block ciphers.
   ○ Slower and less secure than block ciphers.

4. **What are some of the key design principles when considering encryption schemes?**
   A: Answers will vary. Encryption should be strong; that is, the key should be of a certain length that makes breaking the encryption unfeasible. Still, encryption keys can't be too long, otherwise performance will suffer. You should also take into account how certain equipment or software may not support certain encryption protocols. This could be due to the equipment or software being outdated, or it might be that vendors will create their product to target only specific encryption schemes. In this case, you need to make sure that the cryptography used by systems of different vendors are interoperable.

5. **You're interested in implementing a Public Key Infrastructure (PKI) within Develetech so entities within your domain can exchange cryptographic keys securely. What are some of your concerns about how certificates are issued in this infrastructure?**
   A: Answers will vary, but certificate issuances can be automated, which makes certificates easier to acquire but removes some degree of administrative control; whether or not to use wild card certificates for certain entities; how long certificates should last before they expire; whether or not to purchase public certificates for externally-facing applications; and how to disseminate certificate revocation information.

ACTIVITY 6-1: Selecting Host Hardware and Software

1. **What is endpoint security software that detects and actively stops anomalous behavior on a host?**
   ○ DLP
   ○ Host-based firewall
   ○ HIDS
   ◉ HIPS

2. Which of the following are functions of patch management software? (Select three.)

   ☑ Obtaining updates from a repository.

   ☑ Deploying updates to multiple hosts in a network.

   ☐ Monitoring host health after updates have been applied.

   ☑ Rolling back updates to a previous version.

3. Develetech has a huge amount of host security and event logs that analysts must comb through to perform auditing duties. The current process of viewing logs is inefficient and unproductive. What kind of software solution would you suggest the company implement to streamline auditing? Why?

   A: The best choice would be log monitoring software, as it can help ease the burden of too many hosts producing too many logs with too much detail. Instead of a human reviewing each log, an automated process will search the logs for anomalies or other unwanted behavior. This will increase productivity and bring security issues to the attention of analysts faster.

4. How does an HSM typically ensure the integrity of data? What other security functions can an HSM provide?

   A: HSMs typically use message authentication codes (MACs) to establish a baseline value for valid data. If that data is tampered with, the HSM will detect that the MAC is different than the expected value. HSMs can also be used to generate strong cryptographic keys, such as for a PKI or an application that communicates using SSL/TLS. HSMs may also provide clustering and load balancing capabilities.

5. What are some of the common security characteristics of trusted operating systems?

   A: A trusted OS will usually isolate resources and services from any applications that run on the OS. A trusted OS will also categorize access levels based on roles, and may provide the option to disable root access. When assigning rights and privileges, a trusted OS should help administrators exercise the principle of least privilege.

ACTIVITY 6–4: Implementing Cloud Augmented Security Services

1. One of Develetech's options is to offload anti-malware and anti-spam scanning to a cloud provider. What are the advantages and disadvantages to relying on cloud hash matching for these services?

   A: Answers will vary, but cloud-provided hash matching will likely reduce overhead on hosts in the network because an external service is handling the scanning process. Another advantage of hash matching is that the company doesn't have to devote time and focus to keeping its signatures current; the cloud provider will always be up-to-date on the latest vulnerabilities. However, if the cloud provider does not implement proper security on their end, then an attacker could glean information about your systems and their vulnerabilities. It is especially vital to use transport encryption when opening a connection channel to the cloud service.

2. How can a cloud-based sandbox help Develetech test its internally developed applications?

   A: Answers will vary, but a cloud sandbox can allow developers to test the application using many different environment configurations without risking serious damage to a host or the rest of the network. Sandboxes can also assist developers in identifying and addressing bugs or vulnerabilities that appear in certain contexts that the enterprise cannot necessarily provide.

3. What situations can you think of that could warrant cloud content filtering for Develetech?

   A: Answers will vary. A company like Develetech that works with a lot of sensitive electronics might want to filter out hosts using vulnerable software like Java to avoid the risks it presents. You can also streamline filtering by using the cloud to block websites deemed inappropriate or irrelevant to the enterprise and apply these configurations on a per-host basis. Develetech may also want to implement cloud filtering if its hosts are especially susceptible to malware infection.

ACTIVITY 7-1: Discussing Enterprise Storage Types and Protocols

1. What are some of the security implications of cloud storage that you need to consider before choosing that solution?

   A: Answers will vary. Outsourcing storage to the cloud will leave the organization with less control over it. This could be magnified if any business changes affect the provider, like a merger or divestiture, or if you stop doing business with the provider. This is especially true when it comes time to audit; the cloud provider needs to work with you and abide by your policies in order for you to be comfortable with its level of security. Cloud storage may also fail to segregate data from other client companies appropriately, which could enable an intruder to steal more of your data than they otherwise would have. You also need to consider that the forensic process may be difficult to carry out in a cloud storage environment.

2. Which of the following typically describes a NAS? (Select two.)
   - ☑ Ideal for smaller organizations.
   - ☐ Uses the iSCSI protocol.
   - ☐ Uses the Fibre Channel protocol.
   - ☑ Uses the CIFS protocol.

3. Develetech manages thousands of online transactions a day on its store and needs a storage solution that will manage its accounts data, purchasing transactions, and payroll information. This storage solution is mission critical, needs to be readily available, and needs to allow for extremely minimal downtime. Cost is not an issue and the solution must be very fast. What type of storage solution would you recommend, and why?

   A: Answers may vary, but the ideal solution would be a SAN on a private network. The storage solution is mission critical, and redundancy and availability are a primary concern. Because the SAN will be on its own private network, it will be isolated from the rest of your systems. SANs are also fast, and if cost is no object, then they will provide a great benefit to Develetech and its many transactions.

4. True or False? By default, iSCSI encrypts network traffic.
   - ☐ True
   - ☑ False

5. What are some of the pitfalls of enabling Fibre Channel to run over Ethernet?

   A: Answers may vary, but since TCP/IP traffic is running over Ethernet, there is only one wire to monitor for intruders. The intruders could more easily rebuild unencrypted data passed through Ethernet. FCoE is also susceptible to a DoS attack, as it is no longer completely isolated from the network like a typical Fibre Channel SAN configuration. Rather, Fibre Channel and TCP/IP are sharing one network, potentially making it easier for an attacker to cripple all network bandwidth.

ACTIVITY 8-1: Analyzing Network Security Components and Devices

1. Develetech might implement a UTM to centralize various utilities that secure the network. However, what are the drawbacks of using a UTM? (Select two.)

   ☐ It is difficult to manage.

   ☑ It creates a single point of failure.

   ☑ It can have latency issues.

   ☐ It is difficult to update.

2. Develetech wants some way to prevent a breach compromising the network. What solution, NIDS or NIPS, would you suggest, and why?

   A: Answers will vary. Some will suggest using an NIDS, as there are several free, open source tools available. While both NIDS and NIPS are susceptible to false positives, an NIDS will not actively block legitimate traffic; instead, it will alert an administrator, who will then determine that the tool is in error and adjust accordingly. Others may suggest using an NIPS, as they offer much more powerful and efficient means of stopping an attack before it does too much damage. This is especially useful in large networks that process great volumes of traffic throughout their day-to-day operations.

3. Which of the following security devices provides a real-time analysis of alerts generated by network components?

   ○ HSM

   ◉ SIEM

   ○ INE

   ○ WAF

4. What does it mean for a security device to be application aware? How does an NGFW benefit from being application aware?

   A: An application aware device can recognize the applications that are connected to it, and can analyze the state of those applications. An NGFW can perform deeper packet inspection on packets that target the application layer of the OSI model, allowing it to detect unwanted transmissions. Attacks targeting the application layer are becoming more and more common.

5. What are the advantages of virtualizing a network? (Select three.)

   ☑ You can more easily control the flow of specific data.

   ☑ You can consolidate physical devices to increase performance.

   ☑ You can more easily restrict resources used by each port.

   ☐ You can more easily manage the network's topology in a large, complex environment.

6. Your team has established firewalls, an NIDS, and other security devices around your network perimeter. This topology is very secure against virtual threats from external—and even internal—attacks. However, their task of securing the network is not yet done. What else do you need to remind them of with regard to the security of these devices?

   A: Answers may vary, but a network is not truly safe through its virtual topology alone. You need to make sure they keep the devices physically safe from theft or harm by placing them in access controlled rooms. Additionally, they should consider installing monitoring devices in these rooms to detect any intruders. For example, keeping these devices in a card-locked server room under a surveillance camera will make it much more difficult for an attacker to compromise the security of the network.

ACTIVITY 8-2: Analyzing Network-Enabled Devices

1. If Develetech chooses to implement a BAS, specifically with HVAC controllers and sensors, what are some of the security concerns you should raise?

    A: Answers will vary. An attacker who is able to compromise networked HVAC systems can cause serious damage to equipment, including equipment that the HVAC system regulates, like servers. The attacker can also use temperature and ventilation controls to turn the work environment into an uncomfortable or even unsafe one. Even if the attacker doesn't directly control the HVAC systems, they can still manipulate monitoring results by remotely tampering with sensors. The simplified software that sensors often use may make them vulnerable to such attacks.

2. You're worried that some guests or unauthorized employees might use an administrators' smart card to gain access to the locked server room. How can you ensure that your security team has the tools necessary to deny access to the server room on-the-fly, or quickly revoke an administrators' authorization after their smart card has been stolen?

    A: Answers may vary, but physical access control systems like card locks can be networked over TCP/IP communications to allow security personnel to quickly manage access. A security team member could send a signal to the card lock reader telling it to deny access to anyone using the stolen smart card, all without having to physically program the device.

3. What control is vital in securing an IP camera from eavesdropping?

    ○ Logging

    ○ Configuration lockdown

    ○ Storage encryption

    ◉ Transport encryption

ACTIVITY 8-3: Analyzing Advanced Network Design

1. What are some of the advantages that IPv6 has over IPv4? (Select three.)

    ☑ A much larger address space.

    ☐ Backward compatibility.

    ☑ Built-in encryption support.

    ☑ Greater network management efficiency.

2. Develetech is planning on setting up a VPN that will allow employees to access the network from home. Which type of tunneling protocol should the VPN employ for optimum security?

    ○ PPTP

    ○ L2TP

    ◉ L2TP/IPSec

    ○ PPP

3. How can the 802.1X protocol help Develetech uphold network authentication?

    A: Answers may vary, but 802.1X can integrate with a RADIUS server to provide authentication information. If a device connects to an access point, the 802.1X service would encapsulate any requests for authentication in the EAP framework to send to the RADIUS server. If authentication is successful, 802.1X would enable network traffic on that particular access point. If authentication fails, the device will be blocked from receiving traffic over any protocol other than 802.1X. This helps keep unauthorized users from attaching to your network.

4. Develetech's network engineers have raised concerns that the company's current configuration is putting the network at risk of unacceptable downtime. They suggest converting to a mesh configuration to solve this problem. What are your thoughts and concerns?

   A: Answers will vary. Mesh networks are certainly advantageous to a company that is averse to the risk of unavailability, and they can also guarantee more accurate routing of information. However, you should remind the network engineers that mesh networks can be very costly to construct and maintain. You should remind them that this fact might outweigh the need for a more reliable topology. Additionally, networks that are difficult to manage may lead to difficulties in applying and maintaining network security policies.

5. What are some of the security implications of using SDN and cloud-managed networking?

   A: Answers will vary, but one of the most vulnerable entities in these kinds of networks is the controller. An attacker who can compromise the network controller can cause a great deal of damage to the network, especially by initiating a DoS condition. Any communications between the controller and the forwarding device in an SDN or controller and cloud service should be encrypted in a protocol like SSL/TLS.

ACTIVITY 9-1: Identifying General Application Vulnerabilities

1. Develetech purchased an app that its employees use on a daily basis, and most employees have non-administrator access to its features. However, an attacker is able to use their normal employee credentials to acquire administrator permissions. What vulnerability is present in the application?

   ○ Buffer overflow

   ○ Integer overflow

   ○ Horizontal privilege escalation

   ◉ Vertical privilege escalation

2. As your development team begins designing the new app for the company, there are a few security concerns you'd like them to be conscious of so that the app doesn't present any unreasonable risk. One of those concerns is error and exception handling. What do your developers need to keep in mind when incorporating this technique?

   A: Answers may vary, but exceptions should not be overly verbose and give away too much about what has caused a fault in the app. An exception that reveals too much may give an attacker the information they need to execute an attack and exploit bugs in code. Another way to keep error and exception handling secure is to use `try...catch` statements. These will protect code that may throw an exception so that it can recover gracefully without compromising the app.

3. Which of the following describes a vulnerability in which an attacker exploits the time between when an application checks a resource and when it actually uses the resource?

   ◉ TOCTTOU

   ○ Memory leak

   ○ Resource exhaustion

   ○ Data remnants

4. As expected, Develetech's app development team is planning on designing the app with storage encryption functionality to protect any sensitive information that it handles. To make sure that this security initiative is successful, what are some of the pitfalls that the development team should avoid when incorporating storage encryption?

   A: Answers will vary. The team should make sure that the app properly stores encryption keys, certificates, and passwords so that they are not easily retrievable. The team should also ensure that sensitive data is not mishandled in volatile memory like Random Access Memory (RAM), exposing it in plaintext to an attacker. If the app generates keys, it should do so using a strong source of randomness and not predictable sources like timestamps. The encryption algorithms themselves should be industry-accepted, not custom built. The actual key exchange process needs to be secure as well.

5. Your employees will primarily use your app on mobile devices like smartphones and tablets. Using the app, you want them to be able to upload photos they take to public galleries on Develetech's website, but you're concerned that the metadata in these photos will give away too much information to competitors, especially the whereabouts of management and sales staff. What security precautions would you suggest either the app's developers or the app's users take?

   A: Answers will vary. Some will want to caution users about the geo-tagging feature on the app, explaining to them that they should be careful about what types of photos they publish online. Others will suggest adding a function that allows users to turn off geo-tagging when they want to take a picture without metadata. Still, some will simply conclude that the risk is too high, and that the developers should remove geo-tagging from the app altogether.

ACTIVITY 9-2: Identifying Web Application Vulnerabilities

---

1. The web app includes support for several different social features, including forums that customers can use to discuss Develetech's products and any technical issues they may be having. You've received reports that several forum users have had their accounts hijacked. These hijacked accounts started spamming the forums, which led to them being banned. In your investigation, you noticed that all of the users that were impersonated had either commented on or simply visited a specific forum thread. In this thread, a user invoked an HTML script in their comment. This could be a(n):

   ○ XSRF attack

   ◉ Stored XSS attack

   ○ Reflected XSS attack

   ○ DOM-based attack

2. Develetech's web app integrates with an SQL database that holds customer records; what are the possible consequences of a successful SQL injection attack?

   A: The database entries could be exposed to unauthorized users. They could also be changed, corrupted, or deleted. This could compromise customer PII, and subsequently, the confidence that customers have in your business. Theft and damage of sensitive customer information could also bring legal trouble to the enterprise.

3. True or False? Session prediction is an attack in which an attacker forces an already known session onto a target user's browser.

   ☐ True

   ☑ False

4. Which one of the following HTML elements is abused in a clickjacking attack?

   ○ Comments

   ○ Tables

   ○ Forms

   ◉ iframes

---

5. You want to communicate to your web app development team that insecure cookie handling can be a security issue for your users. What can you tell them about both session and persistent cookies?

    A: Answers may vary, but failing to encrypt cookie transmissions or properly dispose of them after a time can give an attacker the opportunity to hijack the cookies and thus hijack the session. This can be a major threat if the session is meant to handle personal, financial, or other sensitive customer and employee information. Cookies that are not properly secured in transmission and storage can also be poisoned, allowing an attacker to use the cookie to execute malicious code within the app.

ACTIVITY 10-1: Implementing Security Standards in the Enterprise

1. What are some of the important factors to consider when choosing security standards to implement in the enterprise?

    A: Answers will vary. You should be aware that some standards contradict others, or may offer a different solution to the same problem. It's important to research and analyze these standards in the current information security climate. Other factors of note include how much support the standard is given, how scalable it is, and how interoperable with other standards it is.

2. Since taking on the role of CISO of Develetech, you've updated the company's security standards to meet enterprise risk management (ERM) requirements. With these standards in mind, what sort of interoperability issues might there be in legacy systems?

    A: Answers may vary, but legacy systems may be so outdated that they don't even support the more current standards and protocols. This presents a security risk, and may require you to either adjust your standards or adjust your systems to meet your standards. Even legacy systems that are interoperable may not provide the optimal level of security that you require.

3. How can data flow security methods help a company like Develetech uphold enterprise standards for network availability?

    A: Answers will vary. The enterprise can employ traffic shaping to prioritize the flow of data packets across the network, optimizing speed and streamlining bandwidth. This can ensure better performance and more uptime for users. Virtual circuits can provide error correction and automatic re-transmission of signals to make the network more reliable as a whole. Both of these techniques can put quality of service (QoS) standards into practice.

ACTIVITY 10-2: Selecting Technical Deployment Models

1. What type of virtualization hosting option provisions a single instance to multiple users?
    - ○ Public
    - ○ Hybrid
    - ○ Single tenancy
    - ◉ Multi-tenancy

2. **Before you select an elastic cloud computing service, what are some of the security issues that you need to account for?**

   A: Answers will vary. Integrating a third-party identity-management solution with the cloud provider might add complexity to the organization. Cloud providers may not necessarily offer sufficient service-level or availability agreements. You also need to be convinced that the cloud provider is offering adequate physical security for their premises, as this may be overlooked. There are also laws and regulations that providers may need to follow, so you should verify that they are doing so.

3. **As part of its security policy, Develetech takes snapshots of its databases that hold sensitive employee and customer information. After a certain period of time, those snapshots are deleted to make room for more current snapshots. You're concerned that, if you rely on the cloud for hosting these databases, the data in your snapshots will remain even after they should have been deleted. How can you ensure that there is no data remnants in the cloud?**

   A: The most effective choice is to encrypt the data prior to storing it with the cloud, so that any remnants will be indecipherable without the proper key.

4. **Which of the following techniques are strong security measures to incorporate in a cloud deployment model? (Select two.)**

   ☐ Data aggregation

   ☑ Data isolation

   ☑ Provisioning and de-provisioning

   ☐ Degaussing

5. **Virtualizing key environments in Develetech's infrastructure may make those environments more efficient and reduce the clutter of physical systems. However, integrating a virtual deployment model in the enterprise will yield some new vulnerabilities. What security controls can you put in place to fix these vulnerabilities?**

   A: There are many different ways to secure virtual environments, and answers will vary. Some of the more prominent ways include: using trusted OSs and software inside the VM; limiting physical access to hosts; disabling direct sharing between the host and guest; creating backup procedures for the VM; using separate VLANs for host-to-guest and guest-to-guest communications; and enabling logging for all VM-related actions.

6. **True or False? Network segmentation helps an organization avoid having a single point of failure in their network.**

   ☑ True

   ☐ False

7. **Develetech is moving to acquire a smaller business and integrate its operations into the rest of the enterprise. This acquisition will provide new computers and personnel to the enterprise. What concerns do you have from a security design standpoint?**

   A: Answers may vary, but new equipment like servers and workstations should be checked to see if they currently meet your security standards, especially from a host-hardening perspective. You should also consider what effect this new equipment will have on your network, as additional hosts may place a strain on your available bandwidth. As for the new personnel, you need to ensure that they are trained properly on your security policies and procedures so that they can integrate into the enterprise environment without bringing unwanted risks.

ACTIVITY 10-3: Securing the Design of the Enterprise Infrastructure

1. Using the deployment diagram, what security controls can you identify in this segment of the network?

   A: External Internet traffic is routed directly to a perimeter firewall, which is connected to an internal firewall. In between these two firewalls are two web servers, which creates a demilitarized zone (DMZ). This DMZ confines Internet traffic bound for the web servers into its own isolated segment, while preventing that traffic from reaching the rest of Develetech's private network. Also in the DMZ is a load balancer, which helps maintain the web servers' availability by optimizing their throughput and preventing individual components like processors or storage media from overloading. Beyond the DMZ is a switch that broadcasts traffic to either the database servers or the application server. This constitutes Develetech's internal network, which is protected from web server traffic by the internal firewall.

2. Your IT team is thinking of adding a NAS server for employees to use as a general data storage solution. In this deployment diagram, where is the best place to put the NAS server?
   - ○ In the existing DMZ with the web server.
   - ○ In its own DMZ.
   - ◉ In the internal network, beyond the DMZ.
   - ○ Before the perimeter firewall.

3. Your IT team is thinking of adding an SMTP gateway to handle any email traffic that is bound for the Internet or received from the Internet. In this deployment diagram, where is the best place to put the SMTP gateway?
   - ◉ In the existing DMZ with the web servers.
   - ○ In its own DMZ.
   - ○ In the internal network, beyond the DMZ.
   - ○ Outside of the perimeter firewall.

4. What are some other infrastructure design security concerns that this deployment diagram doesn't address?

   A: Answers will vary. The current diagram represents a logical topology of the network, which doesn't account for the physical placement of devices within the enterprise. The diagram also doesn't differentiate between virtualized and actual systems. Additionally, there are no apparent redundancies or storage backups to ensure availability.

ACTIVITY 10-4: Securing Enterprise Application Integration Enablers

1. Develetech's sales staff works with a third-party CRM to manage their customers. The CRM also interfaces with your own in-house database. What security controls should this CRM implement to meet your standards?

   A: Answers may vary, but the CRM should use transport encryption when communicating with the database to ensure the confidentiality of customer information. The CRM should also have strict access controls to keep unauthorized personnel from retrieving this information.

2. How is a GRC solution's monitoring different than the monitoring of a control like an IDS?

   A: An IDS will monitor for individual events, whereas a GRC will aggregate individual events to get a high-level view of a network or other systems. This helps analysts see how the business as a whole is performing with respect to governance, risk, and compliance.

3. What is an important security control that is common to many integration enablers, including ERP, CMDB, CMS, and directory services?
   - ⦿ Access control
   - ○ Load balancing
   - ○ Intrusion detection
   - ○ Anti-malware software

4. Which of the following protocols ensures the confidentiality and integrity of web services in a service oriented architecture (SOA)?
   - ○ SSL/TLS
   - ○ IPSec
   - ⦿ WS-security
   - ○ Kerberos

5. The DNSSEC extension provides which of the following security controls? (Select three.)
   - ☑ Zone signing
   - ☑ Data integrity
   - ☐ Data availability
   - ☑ Authenticated denial of existence

LAB 10-1: Designing a Secure Network Infrastructure

1. On the diagram, where would you label the implementation of secure directory services?

   A: Secure directory services should be implemented at the domain controller. (See the finished diagram provided in the solution.)

2. What are the security benefits of implementing any of the types of secure directory services?

   A: Answers may vary. Secure directory services help protect confidentiality by preventing unauthorized users from accessing data they should not have access to. This could be as simple as making sure that internal employees do not have access to data beyond what they need, following the principle of least privilege. Using services like LDAP or Active Directory can make that security much easier to manage and maintain by allowing network administrators to create and manipulate ACLs.

3. On the diagram, where would you label the integration of a VLAN?

   A: A VLAN should be integrated at the switch behind the firewall. (See the finished diagram provided in the solution.)

4. Why would you place the VLAN where you did? What security measures does it help implement?

   A: In the internal network, the VLAN should be placed on the switch behind the firewall because it allows the security administrator to monitor traffic in each network segment.

5. On the diagram, where would you label the implementation of a database activity monitor (DAM)?

   A: DAM should be implemented at the database. (See the finished diagram provided in the solution.)

6. **Why is DAM an important part of network security?**

A: Answers may vary. DAM is used for monitoring database activities. It alerts or creates a log of the activities. Monitoring the activity on the database protects the confidentiality and integrity of your data. Since crucial information is stored in the database, and it is often unencrypted, it is important to protect the data in other ways from potential attacks.

7. **On the diagram, where would you label the implementation of IPv6?**

A: IPv6 could be implemented through translation at the router or through dual stack at the end workstation. (See the finished diagram provided in the solution.)

8. **Why would you implement IPv6 where you suggested?**

A: Answers may vary. IPv6 will be a cumbersome process regardless, but organizations can choose where they want to deal with that process, either by using a dual stack method on the client, or by using a translation method at the router. Either location is technically correct, and either location has its own advantages and disadvantages. The placement of the NIDS/NIPS may be a source of discussion or debate between students.

9. **On the diagram, where would you label the implementation of an NIDS/NIPS?**

A: NIDS/NIPS should be implemented at the firewall. (See the finished diagram provided in the solution.)

10. **What are some of the possible ramifications of integrating NIDS/NIPS in this location regarding data that your employees may be accessing?**

A: Answers may vary. By implementing NIDS/NIPS at the firewall, there is the potential to block legitimate traffic that your employees may still need to access. During design, it is important to take into consideration the kinds of information you work with when deciding where and how you will implement IDPS systems. Do you want detection? Prevention? Active responses or passive responses?

11. **On the diagram, where would you label the implementation of the DNSSEC?**

A: DNSSEC should be implemented at the DNS server. (See the finished diagram provided in the solution.)

12. **Why is implementing DNSSEC an important network security measure?**

A: DNSSEC is important because it provides the authentication and integrity of data from the DNS server with digital signatures. It also protects against DNS cache poisoning.

13. Compare your completed diagram to the sample solution.

A:

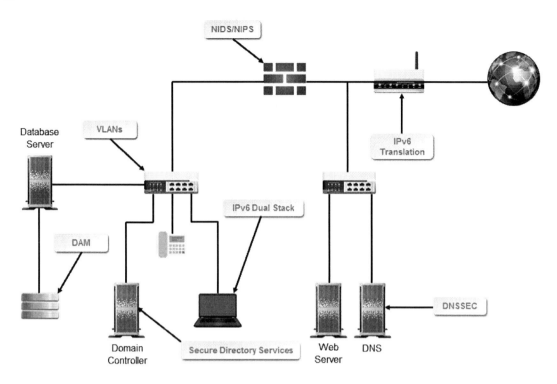

ACTIVITY 11-1: Selecting Vulnerability Assessment Methods

1. What is a major disadvantage of performing a penetration test as opposed to a traditional vulnerability assessment?

A: Penetration tests can be so intrusive that they take down systems either temporarily or permanently. This could cause damage to an enterprise's resources and impact its business operations.

2. What is the function of a white box test?

○ To gather information in preparation for an attack.

○ To simulate an attack by a threat who has some knowledge of the target.

○ To simulate an attack by an outsider threat who has limited knowledge of the target.

◉ To simulate an attack by an insider threat who has complete knowledge of the target.

3. You suspect that an insidious form of malware has infected some of Develetech's hosts. You've isolated these hosts from the rest of the network, but instead of simply removing the malware and moving on, you'd like to see if you can learn more about the infection and possibly derive a point of origin or a method of operation. This information could help prepare you in case of future attacks. What technique can accomplish this, and how?

A: Malware sandboxing can provide a safe environment in which a security expert can investigate the nature of malicious software. Some of the information you can glean from a malware sandbox analysis includes any call traces the malware makes to operating system APIs; network and memory dumps; copies of files that the malware creates or deletes; and snapshots of the system state as it is infected.

4. As you may recall, Develetech has a couple of applications undergoing development. An important step in assessing the vulnerabilities in these applications is a code review. Because your applications are so complex and your development team is under time constraints, your auditors will be using automated tools to help them in their code reviews. However, what do you need to remind your auditors of when it comes to these tools?

A: Answers may vary, but code review is a highly technical task and even the more advanced automated tools may be inadequate. The auditors need to know where these tools are weak, and how the tools may produce false positives or false negatives, or even fail to detect vulnerabilities. The automated tools should be an aid to, not a replacement for, human judgment.

5. You'd like to test how susceptible your general staff is to social engineering attempts. You're concerned that these employees might leak sensitive information that could give competitors an edge and negatively impact Develetech's sales. Which type of attack(s) would you perform to test your general staff, and why?

A: Answers will vary. You can use spoofing or impersonate an authority figure through email, phone, or voice chat to solicit sensitive information from employees. Phishing and pharming might be used to lure employees into giving away their credentials on what they believe to be a legitimate website linked from an email message. You can also try physical social engineering tactics like shoulder surfing and dumpster diving to test how well employees conceal and dispose of sensitive information.

LAB 11-1: Researching Security Tools

3. Which of these tools do you use or might want to use to secure your own enterprise? Why?

A: Answers will vary depending on the needs of the enterprise and its architecture. Many organizations will find packet analyzers like Wireshark and tcpdump helpful in monitoring their network traffic. More application-oriented organizations will want to use fuzzers, like Simple Fuzzer and Peach Fuzzer, to test the integrity of their software. If you plan to take a more offensive role in security through penetration testing, you will likely consider exploitation frameworks like Metasploit and w3af. The specific tools that you choose may also be influenced by the cost and licensing status of each. Free, open-source tools like Snort are attractive to many organizations large and small, but some may gravitate toward proprietary software like Core Impact Pro to receive consistent professional support.

ACTIVITY 12-2: Conducting E-Discovery and Forensic Analysis

10. Assuming the times identified in this report occurred shortly before your team detected the DDoS condition, what conclusions can you draw from this forensic evidence?

A: Answers will vary, but the forensic scan indicates that whomever used the computer at the times listed visited a security information website, as well as a repository for a popular DoS attack tool. Further evidence shows that a shortcut file points to the same attack tool file on the local disk, and that the actual file itself was not present on the system at the time of scanning. This implies that the file was deleted. However, this evidence does not demonstrate that the tool was actually used. It also suggests, but does not prove, that the computer's primary user is the one who downloaded the file.

LAB 12-1: Responding to a Security Incident

1. **What immediate precautions might you take to mitigate the damage?**

   A: Answers may vary. Some will want to make sure the database is physically unplugged from the network to ensure that it can't be breached again. Others will want to keep it operational so that they may monitor any additional malicious activity to help identify the attacker. As far as recovery, if the college has any backup or replicated student records databases, it may be beneficial to bring them online to decrease downtime.

2. **What types of evidence should you collect?**

   A: Answers may vary, but you should seek to collect any relevant evidence, including the physical database servers, authentication logs, network traffic logs, and employee testimony. It's also important that this process follow a chain of custody if the evidence changes hands.

3. **Assuming you identify a suspect and engage in legal action, why would you specify that the data you collected from the database be hashed?**

   A: Hashing collected data will verify in court that the source data is precisely the same. Hashing provides a safeguard against data tampering between collection and presentation in a legal proceeding.

4. **What knowledge from dealing with this incident could you apply to future incidents?**

   A: Answers will vary, but recording incident response activities, results, and lessons learned can provide a basis for responding to subsequent incidents.

Glossary

802.1X
An IEEE standard used to provide a port-based authentication mechanism over a LAN or wireless LAN.

AAR
(after-action report) A post-incident report that includes lessons learned to improve security for the future.

accountability
In security terms, the process of determining who to hold responsible for a particular activity or event.

ACL
(access control list) A list that specifies which objects in a system have which permissions.

AD
(Active Directory) Microsoft's LDAP-compatible directory service.

AES
(Advanced Encryption Standard) The most common type of block cipher, available in 128, 192, and 256-bit key sizes and used in symmetric encryption.

agile method
A software development method in which development occurs in short, iterative time periods with a focus on adapting to change.

ALE
(annual loss expectancy) The total cost of a risk to an organization on an annual basis.

application blacklist
A list of specific undesirable programs prevented from running on a host or computer network.

application sandboxing
The technique of isolating an application running on a system.

application security framework
A framework that can be embedded in standard application development processes to facilitate a secure approach.

application streaming
The technique in which a server offers efficient on-demand streaming of applications to thin clients.

application whitelist
A list of approved programs that may run on a host or computer network.

ARO
(annual rate of occurrence) How many times per year a particular loss is expected to occur.

asset management
The process of taking inventory of an enterprise's technology assets and tracking their usage.

attestation
The technique of verifying that only the individuals who need certain access privileges have those privileges.

authentication
The process of validating a particular individual or entity's unique credentials.

authorization
The process of determining what rights and privileges a particular entity has.

baiting
A form of social engineering in which an attacker leaves infected physical media in an area where a victim finds it and then inserts it into a computer.

bandwidth shaping
See traffic shaping.

bare metal
A computer without an operating system installed.

BAS
(building automation system) A system that centralizes the monitoring and control of networked building resources like lighting, heating, ventilation, power, and physical security.

BCP
(business continuity planning) The process of defining how normal day-to-day business will be maintained in the event of a business disruption or crisis.

bcrypt
A key-derivation function based on the Blowfish cipher algorithm.

BIA
(business impact analysis) A document that identifies present organizational risks and determines the impact to ongoing, business-critical operations if such risks actualize.

BIOS
(Basic Input/Output System) A standard motherboard firmware interface and boot loader that the vast majority of computers have used for decades.

black box test
A penetration test in which the tester is given no information about the system being tested.

block cipher
A type of symmetric encryption that encrypts data one block at a time, often in 64-bit blocks. It is usually more secure, but is also slower, than stream ciphers.

bluejacking
A method used by attackers to send out unwanted Bluetooth signals from smartphones, mobile phones, tablets, and laptops to other Bluetooth-enabled devices.

bluesnarfing
A method in which attackers gain unauthorized access to information on a wireless device using a Bluetooth connection.

Bluetooth
A short-range wireless radio network transmission medium usually used between two personal devices, such as between a mobile phone and wireless headset.

BPA
(business partnership agreement) An agreement that defines how a business partnership will be conducted.

brand damage
The devaluation of a company's image after the company fails to meet customer expectations, especially if it mishandles personal information.

buffer overflow
When data assigned to a buffer is too large for its boundaries, causing the buffer to overflow and data to be corrupted.

BYOD
(bring your own device) The practice in which employees bring their own personal

devices (usually mobile) into the office and use them for work-related purposes.

CA

(Certificate Authority) A server that can issue digital certificates and the associated public/private key pairs.

canary

A known value used to alert an application to a buffer overflow.

CBA

(cost-benefit analysis) The process of weighing the benefit of using a solution against the cost to implement, use, and maintain it.

CBC

(Cipher Block Chaining) A block encryption mode where before a block is encrypted, information from the preceding block is added to the block.

CC

(Common Criteria) A government-funded set of security standards that are used to evaluate and rate technologies and services.

CERT

(computer emergency response team) A team of security professionals that responds to computer-related incidents that threaten an organization.

certificate-based authentication

An authentication scheme in which an entity verifies the authenticity of another entity by its digital certificate.

CFB

(Cipher Feedback) A block encryption mode that allows encryption of partial blocks rather than requiring full blocks for encryption.

chain of custody

The record of evidence history from collection, to presentation in court, to disposal.

chain of trust

The concept in which entities in a hierarchal relationship are valid at each level of the hierarchy.

change monitoring

The process of scanning a system for any alterations that deviate from the accepted baseline.

CHAP

(Challenge Handshake Authentication Protocol) An encrypted remote access protocol that uses a challenge-response mechanism and MD5 hashing for passwords.

CIA triad

(confidentiality, integrity, availability) The three principles of security control and management. Also known as the information security triad.

CIFS

(Common Internet File System) The modern implementation of SMB.

clickjacking

An attack that forces a user to unintentionally click a link. An attacker uses opaque layers or multiple transparent layers to trick a user.

client-side processing

The set of activities performed within a user's web browser when they interact with a web page or web app.

CMDB

(configuration management database) A database that tracks configuration metadata of various IT components, including software, hardware, policies, and personnel.

CMS

(content management system) A centralized solution that allows users to easily manage documentation and other content.

COBIT

(Control Objectives for Information and Related Technology) An IT governance framework that incorporates elements of risk management and mitigation.

code review

An evaluation of source code used to identify potential weaknesses in an application.

code signing
The method of applying a digital signature to a piece of programming code to ensure its integrity and authenticity.

cold boot attack
An attack in which an attacker retrieves encryption keys from RAM after booting a computer from an off state.

collision resistance
A characteristic of a strong hash function in which it is infeasible to produce two different plaintext values that have the same hash.

computer forensics
A skill that deals with collecting and analyzing data from storage devices, computer systems, networks, and wireless communications and presenting this information as a form of evidence in a court of law.

confidentiality
The fundamental security goal of keeping information and communications private and protecting them from unauthorized access.

configuration lockdown
The technique of preventing users from altering the configurations on a device or network.

confusion
In cryptography, the technique of making the relationship between the key and the ciphertext as complex as possible.

container-based virtualization
The method of virtualization in which a single host operating system provisions resources to several individual guest containers.

content filtering
A technique that restricts what types of content a user is allowed to access.

continuous monitoring and improvement
The technique of constantly evaluating an environment for changes so that new risks may be more quickly detected and business operations improved upon.

cookie hijacking
An attack where an attacker takes over a session cookie by injecting malicious code into it.

cookie poisoning
An attack where an attacker modifies the contents of a cookie to exploit web app vulnerabilities.

COOP
(continuity of operations plan) A document that outlines how an organization will maintain operations in the event of a major disaster affecting mission-critical components.

COSO
(Committee of Sponsoring Organizations of the Treadway Commission) An industry standard that provides guidance on a variety of governance-related topics including fraud, controls, finance, and ethics.

critical infrastructure
Assets that, if damaged or destroyed, would have a significant negative impact on the economy, public health and safety, or security of a society.

CRL
(Certificate Revocation List) A list of certificates that are no longer valid.

CRM
(customer relationship management) A software solution that allows enterprise employees to more easily work with customers and data about customers.

CTR
(Counter) A block encryption mode that is similar to OFB and uses a counter as input.

CVE
(Common Vulnerabilities and Exposure) A government-funded database that keeps track of publicly known information security vulnerabilities.

CVSS
(Common Vulnerability Scoring System) An open standard for assessing the impact of computer vulnerabilities in an organization.

DAM

(database activity monitor) Technology that tracks user, administrator, and third-party activities and enforces policies to limit access to databases either partially or completely.

data aggregation

The process of collating data from many sources for high-level trend analysis.

data archiving

The process of moving older, less-frequently accessed data to separate data stores.

data at rest encryption

The technique of encrypting data that is not transmitted across a network.

data breach

The unauthorized access of data stored in a secure location.

data isolation

The practice of separating access and control of data from other users or services in an environment.

data remnants

Data that remains on a physical storage medium despite basic attempts to delete it.

data sanitization

The method used to repeatedly delete and overwrite any traces or bits of sensitive data that may remain on a device after data wiping has been done.

data warehousing

The process of analyzing and reporting on data in storage.

data wiping

A method used to remove any sensitive data from a mobile device and permanently delete it.   .

database encryption

An encryption method that targets databases and the data they contain, rather than individual files or whole disks.

DDP

(Dynamic Disk Pools) A data redundancy technique that uses an algorithm to dynamically distribute resources across a pool of storage drives.

de facto standard

A standard that has yet to be formalized, but still achieves dominance in the marketplace.

de jure standard

A standard that has been formalized by a standards organization.

de-perimeterzation

The process of shifting, reducing, or removing an enterprise's boundaries to facilitate interaction with the outside world.

deduplication

Data compression technology that eliminates redundant data in storage.

deployment diagram

A mapping of the logical or physical arrangement of all nodes in a computer system, typically a network.

deployment model

A framework that defines how a system will be put into practice in an organization.

Diameter

An authentication protocol that allows for a variety of connection types, such as wireless.

diffusion

In cryptography, the technique of ensuring that even minor changes to plaintext input will result in drastic changes to the ciphertext.

digital signature

An encrypted hash value that is appended to a message to identify the sender and the message.

digital watermarking

The steganographic process of embedding source data within copyrighted media for DRM purposes.

direct object reference
A programming element that refers to the actual name of a system object that the application uses.

DLP
(data loss prevention) Software that stops data in a system from being stolen.

DMZ
(demilitarized zone) A small section of a private network that is located between two routers and made available for secure public access.

DNSSEC
(Domain Name System Security Extension) A set of specifications that provide authentication and other security mechanisms to DNS data.

DOM-based attack
(Direct Object Model-based attack) An attack where an attacker executes malicious scripts solely on the client of a web app that uses JavaScript.

DRM
(digital rights management) Technology that controls how digital content can and cannot be accessed after it has been sold.

dumpster diving
A human-based attack where the goal is to reclaim important information by inspecting the contents of trash containers.

e-discovery
The process of identification, collection, analysis, and retention of electronic data to prepare for litigation.

EAL
(Evaluation Assurance Level) A numerical system that rates the security level of technologies and services with respect to the Common Criteria standards.

EAP
(Extensible Authentication Protocol) A protocol that allows clients and servers to authenticate with each other using one of a variety of plugins.

ECB
(Electronic Code Book) A block encryption mode where each block is encrypted by itself. Each occurrence of a particular word is encrypted exactly the same.

EFS
(Encrypting File System) Microsoft's file-level encryption feature available for use on NTFS file systems.

end-to-end solution
An integrated set of computing products that is supported by a single provider and that meets the business and security needs of an organization.

endpoint
Any host that is exposed to another host in a communication channel.

entropy
The amount of randomness in a system.

ERM
(enterprise risk management) The comprehensive process of evaluating, measuring, and mitigating risk in an organization to achieve pre-defined business objectives.

ERP
(enterprise resource planning) A solution that centralizes the monitoring and administration of various business assets and processes.

error handling
See exception handling.

ESA
(enterprise security architecture) A framework for defining the baseline, goals, and methods used to secure a business.

ESB
(enterprise service bus) Software that enables integration and communication between applications in an enterprise.

exception handling
The programming technique of responding to errors in execution.

exploitation framework
A tool that provides a consistent and modular environment for exploiting vulnerabilities in various systems.

external violation
A security violation that emanates from outside the enterprise perimeter.

fault injection
See fuzzing.

FCoE
(Fibre Channel over Ethernet) Fibre Channel implementations that use high-speed Ethernet networks to transmit and store data.

file encryption
A method of encrypting individual files or folders on a disk.

fingerprinting
The technique of determining a computer's operating system and service information by studying TCP/IP packets used in network communication.

FireWire
Apple's name for IEEE 1394, a peripheral communications interface with data transfer and power functionality.

FISMA
(Federal Information Security Management Act) A law enacted in 2002 that includes several provisions that require federal organizations to more clearly document and assess information systems security.

footprinting
Also known as reconnaissance. The phase in an attack or penetration test in which the attacker or tester gathers information about the target before attacking it.

full disk encryption
A method of encrypting an entire physical storage medium to secure its contents.

fuzzer
Sends an application random input data to see if it will crash or expose a vulnerability.

fuzzing
A testing method used to identify vulnerabilities and weaknesses in an application, by sending the application a range of random or unusual input data and noting failures and crashes. Also known as fault injection

geo-fencing
The technique of setting a virtual boundary for wireless device usage in a real-world geographic area.

geo-location
The process of identifying the real-world geographic location of an object, often by associating a location such as a street address with an IP address, hardware address, Wi-Fi positioning system, GPS coordinates, or some other form of information.

geo-tagging
Adding metadata to media that identifies the geographic location of a device and its user when the media was created or modified.

GLBA
(Gramm-Leach-Bliley Act) A law enacted in 1999 that deregulated banks, but also instituted requirements that help protect the privacy of an individual's financial information that is held by financial institutions.

GPG
(GNU Privacy Guard) A free, open-source version of PGP that provides equivalent encryption and authentication services.

GRC
(governance, risk, and compliance) A solution for monitoring these three security concepts as they are implemented in an enterprise.

grey box test
A test in which the tester may have knowledge of internal architectures and systems, or other preliminary information about the system being tested.

hash
The value that results from hashing encryption. Also known as hash value or message digest.

hash matching

The technique of comparing a cryptographic hash value to known hash values to identify a match.

hashing

One-way encryption that transforms cleartext into a coded form that is never decrypted.

HBA

(host bus adapter) A component that connects a host to other devices in a storage network.

HBA allocation

The technique of configuring HBAs in an iSCSI network to handle certain types of traffic.

Heartbleed

A major bug in OpenSSL that allowed attackers to send malformed heartbeat requests to a server, which could respond by disclosing sensitive information like plaintext user names, passwords, and cryptographic keys.

HIDS

(host-based intrusion detection system) A security control that can detect an intrusion by monitoring a host for suspicious behavior.

HIPAA

(Health Insurance Portability and Accountability Act) A law enacted in 1996 to establish several rules and regulations regarding healthcare in the United States.

HIPS

(host-based intrusion prevention system) A security control that can both detect and stop an intrusion by monitoring a host for suspicious behavior.

hoax

An email-based or web-based attack that tricks the user into performing undesired actions, such as deleting important system files in an attempt to remove a virus, or sending money or important information via email or online forms.

horizontal privilege escalation

A type of privilege escalation in which an attacker accesses or modifies specific resources that they are not entitled to.

HSM

(hardware security module) A physical device that can generate cryptographic keys for authentication.

HTTP interceptor

A tool that can capture HTTP communications using a web proxy.

HVAC controller

(heating, ventilation, and air conditioning controller) A mechanism that can manually or automatically regulate comfort levels in a physical environment.

hypervisor

Software that separates and manages virtual machines from the physical hardware they run on.

IA

(information assurance) The concept of protecting information's confidentiality, integrity, availability, authenticity, and non-repudiation.

IaaS

(Infrastructure as a Service) A cloud computing method that provides any or all infrastructure needs to users.

ICS

(industrial control system) Any system that allows users to control industrial and critical infrastructure assets.

identity federation

The practice of linking a single identity and its characteristics across many different management systems.

identity propagation

The technique of replicating identity authentication through several different processes in a system.

IETF

(Internet Engineering Task Force) An organization that develops Internet standards and publishes the Request for Comments (RFC).

IMA

(Integrity Measurement Architecture) An open source Linux-based component that verifies the integrity of files before they are loaded.

impersonation

A type of spoofing in which an attacker pretends to be someone they are not, typically an average user in distress or a help desk representative.

incident response

The principle that states how an organization will react to and report security breaches within an acceptable time period.

INE

(inline network encryptor) A device that encrypts communications between two or more secured networks that pass through an intermediary unsecured network.

input validation

Any technique used to ensure that the data entered into a field or variable in an application is within acceptable bounds for the object that will receive the data.

insider threat

A threat to an organization that comes from employees, contractors, and anyone else that may have willingly been given insider knowledge.

integer overflow

An attack in which a computed result is too large to fit in its assigned storage space, leading to crashing, corruption, or triggering a buffer overflow.

integrity

The fundamental security goal of ensuring that electronic data is not altered or tampered with.

intelligence gathering tool

See passive reconnaissance tool.

internal violation

A security violation that emanates from inside the enterprise perimeter.

interoperability agreement

The general term for any document that outlines a business partnership or collaboration in which all entities exchange some resources while working together.

inventory control

See asset management.

IP camera

(Internet Protocol video camera) A camera used in surveillance that is connected to a network like the Internet.

IPSec

(Internet Protocol Security) A set of open, non-proprietary standards used to secure data through authentication and encryption as the data travels across a network like the Internet.

IPv6

(Internet Protocol version 6) An Internet standard that increases the available pool of IP addresses by implementing a 128-bit binary address space.

iQN

(iSCSI Qualified Name) A unique identifier assigned to clients in an iSCSI architecture.

ISA

(interconnection security agreement) A agreement that focuses on securing technology in a business relationship.

iSCSI

(Internet Small Computer System Interface) A protocol that implements links between data storage networks using IP.

ISO

(International Organization for Standardization) An organization with global reach that promotes standards for many different industries.

IT governance

(information technology governance) A concept in which stakeholders ensure that those who govern IT resources are fulfilling objectives and strategies and creating value for the business.

job rotation

The principle that establishes that no one person stays in a vital job role for too long a time period.

Kerberos

An authentication system in which authentication is based on a time-sensitive ticket-granting system. It uses an SSO method where the user enters access credentials that are then passed to the authentication server, which contains the allowed access credentials.

key escrow

A method for backing up private keys to protect them while allowing trusted third parties to access the keys under certain conditions.

key stretching

A technique that strengthens potentially weak cryptographic keys, such as passwords or passphrases created by people, against brute force attacks.

LDAP

(Lightweight Directory Access Protocol) A simple network protocol used to access network directory databases, which store information about authorized users and their privileges, as well as other organizational information.

LDAPS

(Lightweight Directory Access Protocol Secure or Secure LDAP) A method of implementing LDAP using SSL/TLS encryption.

LEAP

(Lightweight Extensible Authentication Protocol) A protocol that establishes mutual authentication and generates WEP keys for wireless communication.

least privilege

The principle that states that users and software should only have the minimal level of access that is necessary for them to perform the duties required of them.

live VM migration

The technique of moving a virtual machine from one physical host to another without compromising its availability.

LLR

(lessons learned report) See AAR.

lockout

A method of restricting access to data on a device without deleting that data.

LUN

(logical unit number) A number used to uniquely identify each logical partition in a storage device, often associated with a storage area network (SAN).

LUN mapping

The process of assigning hosts in a SAN their own unique LUN.

LUN masking

The process of concealing LUNs to hosts in a SAN that are not associated with each other.

malware sandboxing

The technique of isolating malware in a virtual environment to safely test and assess the malware.

man–in–the–middle attack

A form of eavesdropping where the attacker makes an independent connection between two victims and steals information to use fraudulently.

mandatory vacation

The principle that states when and how long an employee must take time off from work so that their activities may be subjected to a security review.

measured launch

The process of validating system resources against a list of expected measurements at boot time.

memory dump

The outputted state of an application's or system's memory during a period of time.

memory leak
The result of failing to release memory that is allocated by an application.

mesh network
A network topology in which all nodes are directly connected to all other nodes in the network.

message authentication code
A short code that can be used to verify the integrity and authenticity of a message.

message digest
The value that results from hashing encryption. Also known as hash or hash value.

MIME
(Multipurpose Internet Mail Extensions) A standard that defines advanced capabilities of email messages.

minimization
A technique that reduces the potential for harm before it can affect an organization.

MOU
(memorandum of understanding) An informal business agreement that is not legally binding and does not involve the exchange of money.

multi-tenancy
A type of virtual environment in which all users share the same software instance.

multipath
A method of routing data through several different paths to increase network availability.

multisite replication
The process of saving data backups and distributing them to many different physical locations.

NAC
(Network Access Control) The collection of protocols, policies, and hardware that govern access on devices to and from a network.

NAP
(Network Access Protection) Microsoft Windows Server technology that uses RADIUS to evaluate the health state of a host in a network.

NAS
(network-attached storage) A category of devices connected to a network that are optimized to provide data file storage and sharing functionality in a LAN.

NDA
(non-disclosure agreement) An agreement that stipulates that entities will not share confidential information, knowledge, or materials with unauthorized third parties.

network delegation
The technique of transferring administrative responsibilities to a team within a specific network segment.

network enumerator
A tool that can reveal information about a network's users, groups, services, and shares.

network segmentation
The practice of dividing enterprise resources into distinct security domains or perimeters.

NFS
(Network File System) An older network protocol that is predominantly used in Linux/UNIX environments.

NGFW
(next-generation firewall) A firewall that can operate at the application layer and protocol stack to block threats that target these levels.

NIDS
(network intrusion detection system) A system that uses passive hardware sensors to monitor traffic on a specific segment of the network.

NIPS
(network intrusion prevention system) An active, inline security device that monitors suspicious network traffic and reacts in real time to block it.

non-repudiation
The security goal of ensuring that the party that sent a transmission or created data

remains associated with that data and cannot deny sending or creating that data.

NPS
(Network Policy Server) Microsoft's implementation of a RADIUS server that aids in administrating VPNs and wireless networks.

OAuth
An open authorization standard that uses tokens to access services without needing to share credentials.

OCSP
(Online Certificate Status Protocol) An HTTP-based alternative to a certificate revocation list that checks the status of certificates.

OFB
(Output Feedback) A block encryption mode that converts a block cipher into a stream cipher, which is fed back as input of a block cipher.

offsite replication
The process of saving data backups and moving them outside of the organization.

OLA
(operating-level agreement) A business agreement that outlines the relationship between divisions or departments in an organization.

open standard
A standard that is publicly available and imposes limited licensing restrictions.

OpenID
A method of authenticating users with a federated identity management system.

OpenSSL
A widely used open-source implementation of the SSL/TLS protocol that was affected by the Heartbleed bug.

operating system–level virtualization
See container-based virtualization.

order of volatility
The order in which volatile data should be recovered from various storage locations and devices following a security incident.

OTAP
(over-the-air programming/provisioning) A method of wirelessly pushing software updates and configurations to mobile devices in a centralized, on-demand fashion.

out-of-band
Communication that occurs outside of standard channels.

PaaS
(Platform as a Service) A cloud computing method that provides any platform-type services to users.

packet analyzer
A tool that can decode the content of packets used in network communications.

padding
In block encryption, this is the process of filling a block with excess data if the plaintext does not fill the block exactly.

PAP
(Password Authentication Protocol) A remote access authentication service that sends user IDs and passwords as plaintext.

parameterized statement
See prepared statement.

passive reconnaissance tool
A tool that provides key information about a system without being detected. Also known as intelligence gathering tool.

password cracker
A tool that can recover the passwords for an account.

patch management
The practice of monitoring for, evaluating, testing, and installing software patches and updates.

PBKDF2

(Password-Based Key Derivation Function 2) A key derivation function used in key stretching to make potentially weak cryptographic keys, such as passwords, less susceptible to brute force attacks.

PCBC

(Propagating or Plaintext Cipher Block Chaining) A block encryption mode that propagates a single bit change in the ciphertext.

PEAP

(Protected Extensible Authentication Protocol) A protocol that encapsulates EAP in an encrypted SSL tunnel.

penetration test

A method of evaluating security by simulating an attack on a system.

peripheral

Any device that connects to a host computer that isn't considered a fundamental part of it.

persistent cookie

A cookie that is stored in non-volatile memory so that it may be used even after its original session has been terminated.

PFS

(perfect forward secrecy) A characteristic of session encryption that ensures that if a key used during a certain session is compromised, it should not affect previously encrypted data.

PGP

(Pretty Good Privacy) A method of securing emails created to prevent attackers from intercepting and manipulating email and attachments by encrypting and digitally signing the contents of the email using public key cryptography.

pharming

An attack in which a request for a website, typically an e-commerce site, is redirected to a similar-looking, but fake, website.

phishing

A type of email-based social engineering attack in which the attacker sends email from a spoofed source, such as a bank, to try to elicit private information from the victim.

PII

(personally identifiable information) The pieces of information that can be used to identify an individual.

PKI

(Public Key Infrastructure) A system that is composed of a CA, certificates, software, services, and other cryptographic components, for the purpose of enabling authenticity and validation of data and/or entities.

port scanner

A tool that scans a network for open ports and active services.

pre-image resistance

A characteristic of a strong hash function in which it is infeasible to generate a plaintext value based on its hash.

prepared statement

A template for SQL querying where certain constants are substituted when the command is run. Also known as parameterized statement.

privilege elevation

See vertical privilege escalation.

privilege escalation

An attack where an attacker is able to access resources or functionality that they are not normally allowed access to.

PRNG

(pseudorandom number generator) An algorithm that approximates true randomness in creating numbers while being more practical and efficient.

protocol analyzer

A tool that can decode network traffic and reveal protocol information used in communications.

qualitative analysis

The technique of using descriptive words to calculate risk exposure.

quantitative analysis
The technique of using numeric values to calculate risk exposure.

race condition
When the output of execution processes is dependent upon a certain order of events.

RADIUS
(Remote Authentication Dial-In User Service) A standard protocol for providing centralized authentication and authorization services for remote users.

RC4
The most common type of stream cipher, available for use in many different protocols.

reconnaissance
Also known as footprinting. The phase in an attack or penetration test in which the attacker or tester gathers information about the target before attacking it.

reflected attack
An attack where the attacker poses as a legitimate user and sends information to a web server in the form of a page request or form submission.

resource exhaustion
When resources requested are greater than resources available, causing a denial of service.

reverse engineering
The process of deconstructing a system to find out how it functions from its basest level.

RFC
(Request for Comments) A collection of documents that detail standards and protocols for Internet-related technologies.

RFI
(Request for Information) The first phase in the contract requirement process, in which a company sends out notices to prospective vendors or contractors asking them for their experience and qualification in filling the business's need for services or equipment.

RFID
(radio-frequency identification) A method of wirelessly identifying and tracking objects.

RFP
(Request for Proposal) The second phase in the contract requirement process, in which a company asks prospective vendors or contractors for their proposed solutions to the business's needs.

RFQ
(Request for Quote) The third phase in the contract requirement process, in which a company negotiates the financial details of their relationship with prospective vendors or contractors.

risk acceptance
The response of determining that a risk is within the organization's appetite and no additional action is needed.

risk avoidance
The response of eliminating the source of a risk so that the risk is removed entirely.

risk exposure
The property that measures how susceptible an organization is to risk, usually calculated as the product of the probability that a risk will occur and the expected impact or loss if it does.

risk management
The cyclical process of identifying, assessing, analyzing, and responding to risks.

risk mitigation
The response of reducing risk to fit within an organization's risk appetite.

risk transference
The response of moving the responsibility of risk to another entity.

rogue machine
An unknown or unrecognized device that is connected to a network, often for nefarious purposes.

ROI
(return on investment) A calculation that determines the overall monetary benefit of a

solution, usually expressed as the quotient of the solution's monetary gains and its monetary cost.

root of trust
Technology that provides several cryptographic functions to ensure integrity in a hardware platform, as well as forming the basis of a chain of trust.

runtime debugging
The technique of monitoring for mishandled memory in an application while it is running.

S/MIME
(Secure/Multipurpose Internet Mail Extensions) An extension to the MIME standard that adds digital signatures and public key cryptography to email communications.

SaaS
(Software as a Service) A cloud computing method that provides application services to users.

salt
Random data added to a hash value to strengthen it against password cracking attempts.

SAML
(Security Assertion Markup Language) An XML-based data format used to exchange authentication information between a client and a service.

SAN
(storage area network) A specialized private network comprised of multiple storage devices that implement block-level storage operations.

sandboxing
The technique of isolating data in a closed virtual environment to run tests and analysis on the data.

SCADA
(supervisory control and data acquisition) A type of industrial control system that typically monitors water, gas, and electrical assets, and can issue remote commands to those assets.

SDL
(Security Development Lifecycle) Microsoft's security framework for application development that supports dynamic development processes.

SDLC
(systems development life cycle) The practice of designing and deploying technology systems from initial planning all the way to end-of-life.

SDN
(software-defined networking) An approach to networking architecture that simplifies management by centralizing control over a network.

SEA
(service enabled architecture) A method of creating service-enabled applications in an existing architecture.

second pre-image resistance
A characteristic of a strong hash function in which it is infeasible to modify a plaintext value without also modifying its hash.

secure boot
A feature of UEFI that prevents unwanted processes from executing during boot time.

security baseline
A collection of security configurations applied to a system to be used as a point of comparison or reference.

security benchmark
The current state of a system after it has run through security-related tests, to be compared to a baseline or other benchmarks.

security by default
The philosophy that an app or system should be, in its default use state, as hardened as is feasible.

security by deployment
The philosophy that an app or system should incorporate external elements of security wherever possible, and that it should be released to consumers with security in mind.

security by design
The philosophy that an app or system should be secured from the very beginning, instead of reacting to vulnerabilities when they are found.

security through obscurity
The philosophy that an app or system should attempt to hide its vulnerabilities instead of fix them.

semi-quantitative analysis
The technique of using both descriptive words and numeric values to calculate risk exposure.

separation of duties
The principle that establishes that no one person should have too much power or responsibility.

server-side processing
The set of activities performed on a web server before it sends data to the client.

service-oriented architecture
Also known as SOA. A method of designing and developing applications in the form of interoperable services.

session cookie
A cookie that exists in temporary memory and lasts only for as long as an established session is active.

session fixation
An attack that forces a user to engage in a session that the attacker can later hijack.

session management
The practice of securing active sessions between clients and web apps.

session prediction
An attack in which an attacker can correctly guess a poorly generated session ID and hijack the session.

Shibboleth
A SAML-based federated identity management system used by universities and public service organizations.

shoulder surfing
A human-based attack where the goal is to look over the shoulder of an individual as they enter password information or a PIN.

SIEM
(security information and event management) A solution that provides real-time or near real-time analysis of security alerts generated by network systems.

single tenancy
A type of virtual environment in which users have access to their own individual software instances.

situational awareness
The technique of staying appraised of your enterprise environment so that you can more adequately combat threats and vulnerabilities.

SLA
(service-level agreement) A business agreement that outlines what services and support will be provided to a client.

SLE
(single loss expectancy) The financial loss expected from a single adverse event.

SMB
(Server Message Block) A networking protocol used primarily for file sharing with Windows environments. It is currently known as Common Internet File System (CIFS).

snapshot
A static view of data as it existed at a certain point in time.

SOA
(statement of applicability) A document that identifies present organizational risks and determines the impact to ongoing, business-critical operations if such risks actualize.

social engineering test
A test in which a tester evaluates how susceptible an organization's personnel are to deception and manipulation.

SOX
(Sarbanes-Oxley Act) A law enacted in 2002 that dictates requirements for the storage and retention of documents relating to an organization's financial and business operations.

spam
An email-based threat that floods the user's inbox with emails that typically carry unsolicited advertising material for products or other spurious content, and which sometimes deliver viruses. It can also be utilized within social networking sites such as Facebook and Twitter.

spear phishing
An email-based or web-based form of phishing which targets specific individuals.

spim
An IM-based attack just like spam, but which is propagated through instant messaging instead of through email.

spiral method
A software development method the combines iterative and waterfall approaches while introducing risk analysis into every phase of the life cycle.

SPML
(Service Provisioning Markup Language) An XML-based authorization standard used to automate the provisioning of resources across networks and organizations.

spoofing
A human-based or software-based attack where the goal is to pretend to be someone else for the purpose of identity concealment.

SQL
(Structured Query Language) A programming and query language common to many large-scale database systems.

SQL injection
An attack that injects an SQL query into the input data directed at a server by accessing the client side of the application.

SRTM
(Security Requirements Traceability Matrix) A method of tracking security requirements and how effectively they are implemented in a system.

SSDLC
(Security System Development Life Cycle) A method of system development that incorporates security controls in every phase of system's life cycle.

SSH
(Secure Shell) A protocol for secure remote logon and secure transfer of data.

SSL
(Secure Sockets Layer) A security protocol that uses certificates for authentication and encryption to protect web communication. Superseded by TLS.

SSL inspection
The technique of scanning the contents of SSL/TLS packets for threats.

SSO
(single sign-on) A technique that provides users with one-time authentication to multiple resources, servers, or sites.

stack overflow
When the return address of a function is overwritten on the system stack, allowing the execution of an application to change.

steganography
The practice of attempting to obscure the fact that information is present.

storage segmentation
The process of dividing data storage along certain predefined lines.

stored attack
An attack where an attacker injects malicious code or links into a website's forums, databases, or other data.

stream cipher
A relatively fast type of encryption that encrypts data one bit at a time.

tailgating
A human-based attack where the attacker will slip in through a secure area following a legitimate employee.

TCG
(Trusted Computing Group) An implementation of TPM that is used to verify trusted operating systems.

TCO
(total cost of ownership) The total cost of a solution beyond its acquisition cost, when all additional costs are factored in.

technology evolution
The process by which outdated technology is replaced by newer, more effective technology.

terminal emulator
Software that emulates a terminal a client can interface with, usually from a remote machine.

thin client
A computer client that depends on a server to handle the majority of the processing workload.

threat intelligence
The process of investigating and collecting information about emerging threats and threat sources.

TLS
(Transport Layer Security) A security protocol that uses certificates for authentication and encryption to protect web communication. See SSL.

TOCTTOU
(time of check to time of use) A race condition vulnerability in which a resource is changed between the time it is checked and the time it is used.

TPM
(Trusted Platform Module) A hardware-based encryption specification that can perform a number of cryptographic functions.

traffic shaping
Also called bandwidth shaping. The technique of prioritizing the flow of certain packets over others in a network.

transport encryption
The technique of encrypting data that is in transit, usually over a network like the Internet.

TrueCrypt
A popular open source file and disk encryption program that was abruptly abandoned in May of 2014.

trust model
A method of defining the ways in which resources establish and maintain trust.

trusted OS
(trusted operating system) An operating system that meets certain standards of security and that typically isolates OS resources and services from applications.

TSIG
(transaction signature) A method of authenticating updates used in DNS zone transfers.

TXT
(Trusted Execution Technology) Intel's implementation of TPM that is used to verify trusted operating systems.

typo squatting
Also called URL hijacking. An attack that exploits user errors in typing by registering malicious websites with common misspellings of legitimate words and websites.

UC
(unified communications or unified collaboration) The integration of many communication and collaboration platforms that traverse different networking technologies.

UEFI
(Unified Extensible Firmware Interface) A new standard firmware interface and boot loader that will likely replace BIOS in the future.

URL hijacking

Also called typo squatting. An attack that exploits user errors in typing by registering malicious websites with common misspellings of legitimate words and websites.

USB

(Universal Serial Bus) A popular communications protocol used to connect a wide range of devices and computers.

UTM

(unified threat management) The process of centralizing various security techniques into a single device.

VDI

(virtual desktop infrastructure) The technique of separating a personal desktop computing environment from a user's physical machine.

vertical privilege escalation

A type of privilege escalation in which an attacker obtains privileges of a higher level than what they have been assigned.

virtual circuit

A component that connects logical endpoints in a network by identity rather than physical location.

virtualization

The process of creating a simulated environment of computing technology that already exists in its actual form.

vishing

A human-based attack where the attacker extracts information while speaking over the phone or leveraging IP-based voice messaging services (VoIP).

VLAN

(virtual local area network) A point-to-point physical network that is created by grouping selected hosts together, regardless of their physical location.

VM

(virtual machine) Software that can virtualize computer hardware, operating systems, applications, and other computing environments.

VM escape

(virtual machine escape) An attack in which an attacker is able to force an application running in a virtual machine to interact directly with the hypervisor.

vSAN

(virtual storage area network) A virtual implementation of a storage area network (SAN) that uses Fibre Channel switches to segment SAN communication over certain ports.

vTPM

(Virtual Trusted Platform Module) A method of running virtual machines with TPM functionality on a physical host.

vulnerability assessment

An evaluation of an organization's systems to check for security weaknesses.

vulnerability scanner

A security utility that identifies and quantifies weaknesses within a system.

WAF

(web application firewall) A solution that filters incoming traffic to and outgoing traffic from a specific application.

waterfall method

A software development method in which each phase of development cannot proceed until its preceding phase is complete.

WAYF

(Where Are You From) A single sign-on system which verifies the institution a user is from before they can access a service.

whaling

An email-based or web-based form of phishing which targets particularly wealthy individuals.

white box test

A test in which the tester knows about all aspects of the systems and understands the function and design of the system before the test is conducted.

wild card

A special character used in public key certificates that can be used to extend the certificates' coverage to multiple subdomains.

WPA

(Wi-Fi Protected Access) A wireless encryption protocol that generates a 128-bit key for each packet sent. Superseded by WPA2.

WS-security

(web services security) An extension to the Simple Object Access Protocol that provides end-to-end message integrity and confidentiality in Internet communications.

XACML

(Extensible Access Control Markup Language) An XML-based standard for authorization and access control that centralizes management.

XSRF

(cross-site request forgery) A type of application attack where an attacker takes advantage of the trust established between an authorized user of a website and the website itself.

XSS attack

(cross-site scripting attack) A type of application attack where the attacker takes advantage of scripting and input validation vulnerabilities in an interactive website to attack legitimate users.

zero day attack

An attack that targets a previously unknown vulnerability before the vendor has had time to patch it.

Index

R

race conditions *273*

radio-frequency identification, *See* RFID

RADIUS *105, 246*

RC4 *129*

reflected attack *279*

Remote Authentication Dial-In User Service, *See* RADIUS

Request for Comments, *See* RFC

resistance *134*

resource exhaustion *273*

return on investment, *See* ROI

reverse engineering *91*

RFC *78*

RFID *68*

risk analysis

    qualitative *3*

    quantitative *3*

    risk exposure *3*

    risk types *4*

    semi-quantitative *3*

    system-specific *22*

risk assessment

    changing business models *9*

    cloud model *10*

    demergers and divestitures *11*

    de-perimeterization *14*

    integration of diverse industries *11*

    internal and external influences *12*

    mergers *10*

    new products and technologies *7*

    outsourcing model *10*

    partnership model *9*

    third-party providers *12*

risk determination

    annual loss expectancy *15*

    annual rate of occurrence *15*

    single loss expectancy *15*

risk management

    BCP *35*

    best practices *31*

    business documentation *36*

    continuous monitoring and improvement *25*

    extreme events *22*

    policy development *29, 33*

    process and procedure development *30*

    processes *24*

    strategies for new risk *7*

risk mitigation

    aggregate CIA scores *21*

    worst case scenarios *22*

risk response techniques

    risk acceptance *23*

    risk avoidance *23*

    risk mitigation *23*

    risk transference *23*

rogue machine *229*

ROI *89*

root of trust *125*

S

S/MIME *150*

SaaS *193*

salting *134*

SAML *117*

SAN *207*

sandboxing *195, 286*

SCADA *259*

SDL *65, 287*

SDLC

    phases and frameworks *65*

SDN *249*

SEA *316*

second pre-image resistance *134*

Secure/Multipurpose Internet Mail Extensions, *See* S/MIME

secure boot *199*

secure coding standards *288*

Secure LDAP, *See* LDAPS

Secure Shell, *See* SSH

Secure Sockets Layer, *See* SSL

security

    and sensitive data *270, 274*

    baselines and benchmarks *87*

    control groups and categories *49*

    interoperability issues *298*

    ongoing research *76*

    processes and controls *48*

    requirements for contracts *82*

    review methods *91*

    solution attributes *92*

    standards *298*

    technologies *78*

Security Assertion Markup Language, *See* SAML

security best practices

    incident response *31*

    job rotation *31*

    least privilege *31*

    mandatory vacation *31*

    separation of duties *31*

093023S rev 1.1
ISBN-13 978-1-4246-2288-7
ISBN-10 1-4246-2288-3